"This book will change the way you read the Old and the New Testaments. Beyond this, if you are a pastor or teacher, this book will change the way you preach and teach from the Old and the New Testaments. Thankfully, while Jason DeRouchie's ideas are big, the words and the chapters are not. I will joyfully wear out my copy."

Tom Kelby, President, Hands to the Plow Ministries; President, Table Fellowship Churches

"Jason DeRouchie's love of the Old Testament is contagious. He loves the Old Testament because it leads him to his Savior. Neglecting the Old Testament results in an impoverished understanding of the words and works of Christ. Even though the Old Testament's language, culture, and worldview can strike modern readers as foreign or arcane, DeRouchie demonstrates how the Old Testament can be both accessible and awe-inspiring. He does more than merely inform his readers; he seeks to inflame their hearts, beginning with the Law and all the Prophets. DeRouchie serves the global church by opening the treasures of the Old Testament, allowing them to illuminate the New Testament, exalt Jesus, and lead readers to greater faithfulness and deeper worship."

Joe M. Allen III, Assistant Professor of Missions, Midwestern Baptist Theological Seminary and Spurgeon College

"We love to tell the stories of the Old Testament to children but, sadly, often fail to rejoice in it for ourselves. In *Delighting in the Old Testament*, Jason DeRouchie helps us see Christ in this part of God's word, resulting in a joy-filled faith. I highly recommend this book to you, whether you are a Christian in the pew or a leader in the church. Don't rush through it. You will see the Old Testament Scriptures as you have never seen them before!"

Conrad Mbewe, Pastor, Kabwata Baptist Church, Lusaka, Zambia; Founding Chancellor, African Christian University

"While Christians may confess that the first three-quarters of the Bible is 'breathed out by God' (2 Tim. 3:16) and bears witness about Jesus (John 5:39), and although they may affirm that it is 'profitable for teaching, for reproof, for correction, and for training in righteousness' (2 Tim. 3:16), they often find it difficult to discover in it the kinds of life-transforming riches that would lead them to be 'complete, equipped for every good work' (2 Tim. 3:17). Put another way, it is one thing to believe that the Old Testament is a bottomless mine of life-transforming gospel gold, and it is quite another to experience its riches as one mines deeply. With *Delighting in the Old Testament*, Jason DeRouchie has handed us a tool for mining, helped us get started, and given us instructions so that we can dig deeply for the rest of our lives. This book provides a model for Christ-saturated and biblically grounded reading of the Old Testament as Christian Scripture. Church groups and classrooms will be blessed as they learn how to read, see, hope, and live in light of the Christ-centered message of the first three-quarters of the Bible."

Ian J. Vaillancourt, Professor of Old Testament and Hebrew, Heritage Theological Seminary; author, *The Dawning of Redemption* and *Treasuring the Psalms*

"When it comes to Old Testament studies, Jason DeRouchie is one of this generation's most trusted authors. In *Delighting in the Old Testament*, he brings his considerable gifts to bear as he walks the reader through how to read the Old Testament in light of the person and work of Christ. This accessible, reader-friendly volume will biblically inform and spiritually inspire all who read it. Whether you're a new believer or an established scholar, I highly recommend this book."

Jason K. Allen, President, Midwestern Baptist Theological Seminary and Spurgeon College

Delighting in the Old Testament

Delighting in the Old Testament

Through Christ and for Christ

Jason S. DeRouchie

Foreword by Steven J. Wellum

:: CROSSWAY®

WHEATON, ILLINOIS

Published by Crossway
    1300 Crescent Street
    Wheaton, Illinois 60187

Cover design: Jordan Singer

First printing 2024

Printed in the United States of America

Trade paperback ISBN: 978-1-4335-9122-8
ePub ISBN: 978-1-4335-9124-2
PDF ISBN: 978-1-4335-9123-5

Library of Congress Cataloging-in-Publication Data

Names: DeRouchie, Jason Shane, 1973– author.
Title: Delighting in the Old Testament : through Christ and for Christ / Jason S. DeRouchie ; foreword by Steven J. Wellum.
Description: Wheaton, Illinois : Crossway, 2024. | Includes bibliographical references and indexes.
Identifiers: LCCN 2023005477 (print) | LCCN 2023005478 (ebook) | ISBN 9781433591228 (trade paperback) | ISBN 9781433591235 (pdf) | ISBN 9781433591242 (epub)
Subjects: LCSH: Jesus Christ—Biblical teaching. | Bible. Old Testament—Criticism, interpretation, etc.
Classification: LCC BT225 .D476 2024 (print) | LCC BT225 (ebook) | DDC 221.606—dc23/eng/20230726
LC record available at https://lccn.loc.gov/2023005477
LC ebook record available at https://lccn.loc.gov/2023005478

Crossway is a publishing ministry of Good News Publishers.

LB		33	32	31	30	29	28	27	26	25	24
15	14	13	12	11	10	9	8	7	6	5	4	3	2	1

To Tom Kelby and Andy Naselli,
brothers who have seen, savored, served, supported, and stimulated

Contents

Illustrations

Figures

Tables

Foreword

THE BIBLE IS A BIG BOOK that spans centuries and consists of many topics and diverse literature. Yet, the Bible, despite being written by multiple
authors and addressing various subjects, is one grand metanarrative whose
central message is about what our triune Creator-covenant God planned in
eternity and executed in time to glorify himself by redeeming his people,
judging sin, and making all things new in Christ Jesus (Rom. 11:33–36;
Eph. 1:9–10; Col. 1:15–20). Indeed, from Genesis to Revelation, the Bible's
main message is first about the triune God before it's about us and how
he—although perfectly complete and satisfied in himself—has graciously
chosen to share himself with us, which results to the praise of his glorious
name, his sovereign grace, and our eternal good (Eph. 2:1–10).

However, if we are to grasp and comprehend the Bible's central message,
Scripture cannot be read in a piecemeal way, as if we could isolate one text from
another. Instead, we must approach and interpret Scripture according to what
Scripture *is*, or better, we must read it *on its own terms*. What, then, is Scripture, and what are its own terms? We can answer this by noting three truths.

First, Scripture *is* God's word written through the agency of human authors unfolding God's eternal plan (2 Tim. 3:15–17; 2 Pet. 1:20–21). Given
this truth, despite Scripture's diversity of content, there is an overall unity
and coherence to it precisely because it *is God's* word written. Furthermore,
since Scripture is God's word given through human authors, we cannot
know what God is saying to us apart from the writing(s) and intention(s)
of the human authors. What Scripture says, God says. And given that God
has spoken through multiple authors over time, this requires a careful *inter-
textual* and *canonical* reading to understand God's full revelation of himself.
Scripture does not come to us all at once. Instead, as God's plan unfolds,

more revelation is given, and later revelation, building on the earlier, results in more clarity and understanding from the perspective of the later authors. As more revelation is given, God's unfolding "mystery" is unveiled (see Rom. 16:25–26; Eph. 1:9; 3:3–6; Col. 1:25–27), and we discover how the individual parts fit with the whole. Even more significantly, we discover *who* is central to that plan, namely our Lord Jesus Christ.

Second, Scripture is God's word written *over time*, hence the idea of the *progress* of revelation and the unfolding nature of revelation in redemptive history. Revelation, alongside redemption, occurs *progressively*, largely demarcated by the biblical covenants located within the larger categories of creation, fall, redemption, and the dawning of the new creation in Christ. Thus, to understand the "whole counsel of God" (Acts 20:27), we must carefully trace God's unfolding plan as unveiled through the biblical covenants. This is why our exegesis of specific texts and entire books must result in a "biblical theology" that is concerned to read Scripture and put together the entire canon in terms of its redemptive-historical unfolding. Scripture consists of many literary forms that require careful interpretation, but what unites the biblical books is God's unfolding plan, starting in Genesis with creation, accounting for the fall, unpacking God's redemptive promises through the covenants, and culminating with Christ's coming and inauguration of the new creation by the ratification of a new covenant.

Third, Scripture is God's word *centered* in our Lord Jesus Christ. Although some think this statement is controversial, it is simply true to what Scripture teaches. As the New Testament opens, Jesus is presented as the fulfillment of God's saving promises from the Old Testament (Matt. 1:1–17; Luke 1–3). All that has preceded Christ—promises, types, and covenantal unfolding—has anticipated his coming. In fact, our Lord himself unambiguously teaches us this truth. In a staggering statement, Jesus claims that he is the *fulfillment* of the Law and the Prophets, meaning not only that the entire Old Testament pointed to him but also that its continuing and abiding authority must be understood in light of his person and work (Matt. 5:17–20). By this statement, Jesus views himself as the eschatological goal of the Old Testament; he is the one to whom the Old Testament pointed forward and in whom all God's plans and promises are realized.

But Jesus's statement in Matthew 5 is not merely a one-off. In Matthew 11, as he teaches us about his relationship to John the Baptist, the last of the old covenant prophets, Jesus views himself as the focal point and center of all of history, the one who fulfills all of God's plans and purposes in himself. The same truth is taught in Luke 24. As Jesus comes alongside to comfort two downcast disciples, he does so by going back to the Old Testament and rehearsing how the Law, Prophets, and Psalms properly spoke of him and anticipated the events occurring in his life, death, and resurrection (Luke 24:13–35, 44). A crucified Messiah isn't something strange but precisely what the Old Testament taught and anticipated. As Jesus unpacks Scripture, he magnificently explains how the Old Testament, properly interpreted and despite its diversity, is about him.

These truths are also taught by the opening thesis statement of the book of Hebrews. "Long ago," the author reminds his readers, "God spoke to our fathers by the prophets," and he did so "at many times and in many ways" (Heb. 1:1). God's word is given over time, and it points forward to something more to come. In fact, the phrase, "at many times and in many ways," underscores this point. God gave the Old Testament revelation, and it is, therefore, fully true and authoritative. Yet it is purposely incomplete as it points beyond itself to Christ's coming. But what the prophets looked forward to—namely, "the last days" and the coming of Messiah Jesus, now, "in Son" (*en huiō*, Heb. 1:2)—is here. In other words, in Christ's coming and work, the entirety of God's previous revelation and redemptive purposes have now reached their fulfillment. All of this reminds us that there was no reduction of the Old Testament's authority, but God intended the Old Testament to point beyond itself to his full self-disclosure in Christ Jesus our Lord.

Although these truths are plainly taught in Scripture, unfortunately today's evangelical church has a difficult time making sense of them. We struggle over how Scripture, especially the Old Testament, is to be applied to our lives and how it is rightly about our Lord Jesus Christ. The Old Testament has become almost a foreign book to many in our churches. Even some prominent pastors advocate a Marcion-like "unhitching" of the Old Testament from the New, since, after all, the church is the people of the new covenant, not the old. But the problem with this kind of teaching is that it denies what Scripture teaches in a whole host of ways.

For starters, it denies what Paul teaches in 2 Timothy 3:15–17. In this important statement, we often forget that Paul's reference to "Scripture" is first referring to the Old Testament as God's breathed-out word and, thus, as fully authoritative for Christians. What he assumes is that the church is grounding its doctrine and life on the Old Testament, since the New Testament is still being written. As a result, it is not only wrong but also dangerous to ignore the Old Testament since it, along with the New Testament, functions for us as the basis for how we are rightly to think about God and live before him as his redeemed people in Christ. No doubt it is true that as Christians we are not "under the law" *as a covenant* now that Christ has come. However, this does not mean that the entire Old Testament, including the Mosaic covenant, does not continue to function for us *as Scripture* and, thus, to demand our complete devotion, study, and obedience.

Furthermore, this kind of teaching undercuts the biblical and theological foundation for the New Testament and thus seriously risks misunderstanding who Jesus is, along with the entire message of the gospel. Our Lord Jesus Christ does not appear *de novo* in the New Testament, that is, out of thin air. Instead, who Jesus is and what he has done in his redemptive work is entirely dependent on the biblical-theological framework, content, and structures of the Old Testament. Unless we ground the gospel first in the Old Testament, we will quickly lose the central truths of Christian theology. This is why ignorance of the Old Testament is no small matter. In truth, it's a matter of life and death, and as such, given our lack of knowing the Old Testament, it is not surprising that the theological life and health of today's evangelical church is in trouble.

Given this sober truth and stark reality, I am thrilled to recommend Jason DeRouchie's excellent and timely work, *Delighting in the Old Testament: Through Christ and for Christ*. For the time in which we live, this book helps the church properly recover the breadth, depth, and beauty of the Old Testament. In a succinct way, DeRouchie teaches the church how to read the Old Testament properly and apply it to our lives in light of Christ's incarnation and new covenant work. What the church is desperately lacking about how to understand and apply the Old Testament *as Christian Scripture* to our lives, DeRouchie remedies by providing sound instruction. In so doing, he teaches us how the Bible's covenantal storyline, types, and glorious promises are centered in Christ, fulfilled in him, and applied to the church. Probably the most helpful feature of the book is the various case studies. For example, by applying specific texts, DeRouchie illustrates how to read and apply the Mosaic law to our lives as new covenant believers. By avoiding the extremes of a strict continuity or total discontinuity of the application of the law-covenant to us today, he moves beyond mere theory to practice and masterfully demonstrates how to apply correctly God's word to our lives.

Generally speaking, the evangelical church is deficient in basic biblical and theological knowledge and literacy. If this serious problem is not remedied, the church will continue to drift as she is tossed back and forth by every wind of doctrine (Eph. 4:14). The remedy to our present situation is sound and faithful biblical and theological exposition, which DeRouchie wonderfully provides. My prayer is that this book will be widely read, digested, and applied. If it is, then the church will be strengthened, fortified, and better equipped to know and glorify our triune God as we learn to proclaim anew the unsearchable riches of Christ (Col. 1:27–28) from the whole counsel of God (Acts 20:27).

Stephen J. Wellum
PROFESSOR OF CHRISTIAN THEOLOGY
THE SOUTHERN BAPTIST THEOLOGICAL SEMINARY
LOUISVILLE, KY

Preface

What's the Point of This Book?

Is the Old Testament still significant for believers today? Can Christians faithfully see anticipations of Christ there and celebrate him? How should believers engage Old Testament texts that address ancient covenants and kingdoms and that are filled with promises and laws from a different age in salvation history? This book guides readers into delighting in the Old Testament through Christ and for Christ.

Through my parenting, pastoral ministry, biblical counseling, international missions, and leadership training both in the academy and in rural and urban churches, the Lord has continued to show me how vitally important his Old Testament word is for Christians today. So many doctrinal and ethical challenges arise from unhealthy approaches to the Old Testament.[1] Furthermore, the Old Testament clarifies most doctrinal and ethical answers when Christians read it properly through Christ and for Christ.

This book seeks to be immensely practical, for it addresses:

- *reading* the Old Testament how God intends (part 1),
- *seeing* Jesus where Scripture discloses him (part 2),
- *hoping* in all God's promises for us (part 3), and
- *living* faithfully in relation to God's law (part 4).

Three-fourths of our Christian Bible is *Old* Testament, which was written "for our instruction" and to serve us (Rom. 15:4; 1 Cor. 10:11; 1 Pet. 1:12). Indeed, "all Scripture is breathed out by God and profitable for teaching,

---

1 Some of those challenges this book addresses include health and wealth prosperity teaching and the Christian's relationship to old covenant promises and laws.

for reproof, for correction, and for training in righteousness" (2 Tim. 3:16). This volume seeks to equip Christian laypeople and leaders to delight in the reality that the Old Testament is Christian Scripture.

Jesus stands at the center of God's purposes in creation and salvation. All the Old Testament's laws, history, prophecy, and wisdom point to Jesus in various ways, and through him God fulfills all that the Old Testament anticipates (Matt. 5:17–18; Mark 1:15; Acts 3:18; 1 Cor. 1:23–24). "Christ is the end of the law for righteousness to everyone who believes" (Rom. 10:4), and "all the promises of God find their Yes in him" (2 Cor. 1:20). The old covenant regulations regarding "food and drink . . . festival or a new moon or a Sabbath" were all "a shadow of the things to come, but the substance belongs to Christ" (Col. 2:16–17). "He is before all things, and in him all things hold together" (Col. 1:17).

Paul told Timothy, "What you have heard from me in the presence of many witnesses entrust to faithful men, who will be able to teach others also" (2 Tim. 2:2). The apostle envisioned four generations of multiplication, and I write this book with a similar intent. I hope Christian laypeople and leaders will learn from this tool and then guide others through family devotions, Bible studies, classroom instruction, and sermons, all so that more and more Christians can receive from and relish the Old Testament as God intended.

One great way to profit from this book is to approach it in a small group, one chapter per week, under the care of a coach who has already worked through the material. Once complete, the group members could each become coaches in new groups.

An Overview of the Book

After an introduction that supplies ten reasons why the Old Testament is important for believers, the book has four parts:

1. "Reading Well—How Jesus Helps Christians Interpret the Old Testament" (chaps. 1–3): Both Old and New Testament authors recognized that God gave the Old Testament for those connected to the messianic era and that only through Jesus does God enable people to read the Old Testament as God intends. Christians alone bear the spiritual ability to interpret the full meaning of the Old

Testament, and Christ's life, death, and resurrection provide a necessary lens for understanding rightly all God means.

2. "Seeing Well—How Jesus's Bible Testifies about Him" (chaps. 4–6):
   Along with reading through Christ, Christians must see that Christ's
   glory is the end to which God gave the Old Testament. This section
   offers seven ways the biblical authors model reading the Old Testament *for Christ*. It concludes with a case study in reading Genesis
   this way.

3. "Hoping Well—How Jesus Secures Every Divine Promise"
   (chaps. 7–9): In Jesus, *Old* Testament promises remain a vital
   means for Christians to grow in holiness and persevere through
   suffering. This section highlights weaknesses in the way prosperity
   preachers approach biblical promises. It then offers key principles
   that guided the New Testament authors when they appropriated
   Old Testament promises and shows how Jesus fulfills promises by
   maintaining them (with or without extension), transforming them,
   or completing them.

4. "Living Well—How Jesus Makes Moses's Law Matter" (chaps. 10–
   13): None of Moses's law-covenant is directly binding on believers
   today, but *all* of Moses's law still guides us when read in view of how
   Christ fulfills the law. Specifically, Moses's law still matters in the way
   it reveals God's character, anticipates the saving work of Christ, and
   models what justice and love looked like in the age before Christ.
   This section evaluates alternative approaches to old covenant law,
   including several defective and dangerous perspectives. It then supplies four case studies to show how Jesus maintains the law (with or
   without extension), transforms the law, or annuls the law.

The conclusion provides seven tips for delighting in the Old Testament.
Every chapter (as well as the introduction and conclusion) closes with
"Review and Reflection" questions, and the book ends with a glossary of
key terms for easy reference.

A Word about Footnotes and the Term "Law"

This book has many footnotes, some of which are lengthy. Sometimes these
notes show my homework, but other times they simply direct the reader to

other resources that handle the topic at hand. I encourage all lay readers to skip the footnotes since they sometimes include academic material that is only pertinent to advanced readers. Nothing substantial will be lost from the book's message if you skip them all, so please don't let their presence overwhelm or distract you!

Within both the ESV and this book's body, the capitalized term "Law" usually refers to the first canonical division of Jesus's Hebrew Scriptures. These five books of Moses (Genesis–Deuteronomy) are also known as the Pentateuch, and some refer to the corpus by the Hebrew term "Torah." In contrast, the lower-case term "law" refers to instruction or a legal prescription, which elsewhere some render as "torah." Thus, "Moses's law" or "the law" commonly refers to the body of guiding precepts that shape the stipulations of the old Mosaic covenant and that are found within the Law/Torah/Pentateuch, most specifically in Exodus–Deuteronomy.

Some Words of Thanks

This book captures my maturing reflections on the central role Christ plays in biblical interpretation. They are now decades in the making and saturated with Yahweh's grace. After equipping me through formal education, God used a single lunch conversation eighteen years ago with John Piper and Justin Taylor to right the trajectory of my life and ministry and to set me on a path of gospel hope and of seeing and savoring Jesus in all of Scripture. After listening to me speak of my desire to make much of God's glory as an Old Testament professor, Taylor kindly asserted, "I hear a lot about God's glory and very little about Jesus."

As a Christian, did my hermeneutical approach and ministry practice align with the truth that God created all things (including the Old Testament) by the Son, through the Son, and for the Son (Col. 1:16) and that "all the promises of God find their Yes in [the Son of God, Jesus Christ]" (2 Cor. 1:20)? Could I, who like Paul was a teacher of Jesus's Bible, say with the apostle, "I decided to know nothing among you except Jesus Christ and him crucified" (1 Cor. 2:2; cf. 1:23)? Did I approach Abraham as one who saw and rejoiced in Jesus's day (John 8:56), even if from afar (Heb. 11:13; cf. Matt. 13:17), and did I affirm that Moses, in his writings, wrote of the divine Son (John 5:46–47; cf. 5:39)? Did I grasp that to "understand the [Old Testament] Scriptures" means that in them I should find a unified message declaring the saving work of the Messiah and the mission he would spark (Luke 24:45–46; cf. Acts 26:22–23)? Did I truly believe that "God foretold by the mouth of all the prophets, that his Christ would suffer" (Acts 3:18; cf. 3:24), and did I recognize that they were all carefully searching and inquiring about the person and time of Christ's sufferings and subsequent glories and yet "were serving not themselves" but us (1 Pet. 1:10–12; cf. Acts 10:43; Rom. 15:4; 1 Cor. 10:11)? Did I affirm that Paul and Timothy's sacred writings could only make others wise for salvation—past, present, and future—when linked to faith in Christ (2 Tim. 3:15)? Did the principles guiding my interpretation of the Old Testament affirm that there were "mysteries" kept secret there that only the lens of Christ's coming could disclose (Rom. 16:25–26; cf. Isa 29:18; Jer. 30:24; Dan. 12:8–9) and that, because of this, the apostolic teaching provides a necessary grid for properly grasping all that God wants us to gain from the Old Testament (Acts 2:42; Eph. 2:20)? In short, did I interpret and preach old covenant materials in a way that embraces that "only through Christ" does God lift the veil, allowing us to fully understand and appropriate their significance (2 Cor. 3:14–15)?[2]

With such questions shaping my soul, the years that followed sitting under Piper's faithful preaching at Bethlehem Baptist Church sharpened the sword I had been taught to wield and awakened a commitment within me and my family to spread a passion for the supremacy of God in all things for the joy of all peoples through Jesus Christ. I am especially grateful to Pastor John for his investment in my life through the years and for his modeling what it means to study, practice, and teach God's word in a way that seeks the obedience of faith among all the nations for the sake of Christ's name (Rom. 1:5). Much of what this book teaches I shaped during our years of partnership at Bethlehem College & Seminary. Piper has faithfully committed to cherish the majesty of the triune God through careful study, the treasuring of truth, humble holiness, and pastoral and joyful proclamation shaped in a context of divine sovereignty and driven by love for the nations. I have received all of these from him, and I thank him for leading me and so many others to love Jesus and to treasure the gospel more.

2 This paragraph came from Jason S. DeRouchie, "Lifting the Veil: Reading and Preaching Jesus' Bible through Christ and for Christ," *SBJT* 22, no. 3 (2018): 158. Used with permission.

I thank Midwestern Baptist Theological Seminary's trustees, President Jason Allen, Provost Jason Duesing, and other administrators for granting me a research sabbatical in spring 2022 to complete this book. To be *for the church* around the globe means that we must remain *for Christ* in all things. I am grateful to be part of an institution that is committed to this vision.

I also thank the Crossway team for their commitment to biblical faithfulness and for accepting and supporting this project. Chris Cowan served as my editor, and he provided Christ-honoring oversight, careful copyediting, and wise counsel that have made the whole book better.

Many other notes of thanks are in order. I thank my doctoral fellow Brian Verrett for aiding my initial ponderings in how best to shape this book. I thank former students Joel Dougherty, Ryan Eagy, and Joey Karrigan for helping me design the book's images. I also thank those who read through the manuscript and offered useful feedback: Joey Allen, Brandon Benziger, Teresa DeRouchie, Tyler Hall, Scott Jamison, Tom Kelby, Joey Reichhoff, Ian Vaillancourt, and Nate Weller. I rejoice in my wife Teresa and all my children who encouraged me and celebrated with me in seeing this volume completed.

I dedicate this study to two of my dear friends—Tom Kelby and Andy Naselli. Their companionship, brotherhood, and gospel collaboration have been sweet gifts to my soul through many years, trials, and joys. My work with Tom began in 2008 with the training of rural pastors in Wisconsin. His joy in the Lord, his faithfulness, and his biblical wisdom and practice have been a rich blessing to me and my family. I celebrate our relationship and partnership that now continue through the global service of Hands to the Plow Ministries. Andy and I were colleagues for many years at Bethlehem College & Seminary, and at that time we co-taught an advanced biblical theology course during which I solidified many of this book's elements. I praise the Lord for our years of friendship and the deep commitments to Scripture, Christ, and his church that I have witnessed in his life. May the Lord keep us faithful and use us to see all the nations he has made worship before him and glorify his name (Ps. 86:9).

Jason S. DeRouchie
SAVORING THE SWEETNESS OF THE LIGHT (ECCL. 11:7–8)
CHRISTMAS 2022

Abbreviations

AB	Anchor Bible
ABD	*Anchor Bible Dictionary.* Edited by David Noel Freedman. 6 vols. New York: Doublday, 1992
ApOTC	Apollos Old Testament Commentary
BBR	*Bulletin for Biblical Research*
BECNT	Baker Exegetical Commentary on the New Testament
Bib	*Biblica*
BSac	*Bibliotheca Sacra*
BZNW	Beihefte zur Zeitschrift für die alttestamentliche Wissenschaft
DBSJ	*Detroit Baptist Seminary Journal*
DJG	*Dictionary of Jesus and the Gospels.* Edited by Joel B. Green and Scott McKnight. Downers Grove, IL: InterVarsity Press, 1992
DLNT	*Dictionary of the Later New Testament and Its Development.* Edited by R. P. Martin and P. H. Davids. Downers Grove, IL: InterVasity Press, 1997
DNTUOT	*Dictionary of the New Testament Use of the Old Testament.* Edited by G. K. Beale, D. A. Carson, Benjamin A. Gladd, and Andrew David Naselli. Grand Rapids: Baker Academic, 2023
DOTP	*Dictionary of the Old Testament: Pentateuch.* Edited by T. Desmond Alexander and David W. Baker. Downers Grove, IL: InterVarsity Press, 2003
EBC	Expositor's Bible Commentary
ExpTim	*Expository Times*
GTJ	*Grace Theological Journal*
HALOT	*The Hebrew and Aramaic Lexicon of the Old Testament.* Ludwig Koehler, Walter Baumgertner, and Johann J. Stamm. Translated

	and edited under the supervision of Mervyn E. J. Richardson. 4 vols. Leiden: Brill, 1994–1999
JBL	*Journal of Biblical Literature*
JBMW	*Journal of Biblical Manhood and Womanhood*
JBTS	*Journal of Biblical and Theological Studies*
JETS	*Journal of the Evangelical Theological Society*
JSNT	*Journal for the Study of the New Testament*
JSOT	*Journal for the Study of the Old Testament*
JSOTSup	Journal for the Study of the Old Testament Supplement Series
JSPHS	*Journal for the Study of Paul and His Letters*
LHBOTS	The Library of Hebrew Bible/Old Testament Studies
LNTS	The Library of New Testament Studies
LQ	*Lutheran Quarterly*
LXX	Septuagint
MJT	*Midwestern Journal of Theology*
NAC	New American Commentary
NDBT	*New Dictionary of Biblical Theology*. Edited by T. Desmond Alexander and Brian S. Rosner. Downers Grove, IL: InterVarsity Press, 2000
NICNT	New International Commentary on the New Testament
NICOT	New International Commentary on the Old Testament
NIDB	*The New Interpreter's Dictionary of the Bible*. Edited by Katherine Doob Sakenfeld. 5 vols. Nashville: Abingdon, 2007
NIDOTTE	*New International Dictionary of Old Testament Theology and Exegesis*. Edited Willem A. VanGemeren. 5 vols. Grand Rapids: Zondervan, 1997
NIVAC	NIV Application Commentary
NovT	*Novum Testamentum*
NSBT	New Studies in Biblical Theology
NTS	*New Testament Studies*
PNTC	Pillar New Testament Commentary
RB	*Revue biblique*
RTR	*Reformed Theological Review*
SBJT	*The Southern Baptist Journal of Theology*
SOTBT	Studies in Old Testament Biblical Theology
StBibLit	Studies in Biblical Literature (Lang)

STR   *Southeastern Theological Review*

TDOT   *Theological Dictionary of the Old Testament.* Edited by G. Jo-
hannes Botterweck, Helmer Ringgren, and Heinz-Joseph Fabry.
Translated by John T. Willis et al. 8 vols. Grand Rapids: Eerdmans, 1974–2018

Them   *Themelios*

TJ   *Trinity Journal*

TLOT   *Theological Lexicon of the Old Testament.* Edited by Ernst Jenni,
with assistance from Claus Westermann. Translated by Mark E.
Biddle. 3 vols. Peabody, MA: Hendrickson, 1997

TMSJ   *The Master's Seminary Journal*

TNTC   Tyndale New Testament Commentary

TynBul   *Tyndale Bulletin*

WBC   Word Biblical Commentary

WTJ   *Westminster Theological Journal*

WUNT   Wissenschaftliche Veröffentlichungen der deutschen
Orient-Gesellschaft

ZECNT   Zondervan Exegetical Commentary on the New Testament

Introduction

Ten Reasons the Old Testament
Matters for Christians

For our instruction.

ROMANS 15:4

IS CHRIST REALLY PART OF the Old Testament message? Should I as a believer in the twenty-first century claim Old Testament promises as mine? Do the laws of the Mosaic covenant still matter today for followers of Jesus? In short, is the Old Testament *Christian* Scripture, and if so, how should we approach it?

Delighting in the Old Testament: Through Christ and for Christ seeks to help Christians make connections to Christ and practical application to the Christian life from every page of the Old Testament. As we will see, this goal is *not* to turn "all Old Testament texts into predictions of or, more precisely, pictures foreshadowing the coming of Jesus,"[1] though this is true of some texts. Instead, it seeks to clarify what the apostle Paul, as an Old Testament preacher, meant when he told the Corinthians, "I decided to know nothing among you except Jesus Christ and him crucified" (1 Cor. 2:2). In D. A. Carson's words,

> This does not mean that this was a new departure for Paul, still less that Paul was devoted to blissful ignorance of anything and everything other than the

---

1 Richard L. Schultz, *Out of Context: How to Avoid Misinterpreting the Bible* (Grand Rapids, MI: Baker Books, 2012), 33. Schultz's caution is merited but misses the heart of what I mean by Christocentric interpretation.

1

cross. No, what he means is that all he does and teaches is tied to the cross. He cannot long talk about Christian joy, or Christian ethics, or Christian fellowship, or the Christian doctrine of God, or anything else, without finally tying it to the cross. Paul is gospel-centered; he is cross-centered.[2]

Therefore, this book is a study in biblical and practical theology. It supplies a rationale for thinking about the Old Testament like Jesus and Paul did. It also guides Christians in faithfully reading the Old Testament and in properly responding to its claims. For all who are looking to Jesus as Savior, sovereign, and satisfier, this book seeks to help you:

- by *faith* see and celebrate Christ as we read the Old Testament in faithful ways,
- rightly *hope* in Old Testament promises through Jesus, and
- genuinely *love* others with the help of the old covenant law when appropriating it in view of how Jesus fulfills it.

To understand the Old Testament fully, we must start reading it as believers in the resurrected Jesus, with God having awakened our spiritual senses to perceive and hear rightly. As Paul notes, Scripture's truths are "spiritually discerned" (1 Cor. 2:14) and only *through Christ* does God enable us to read the old covenant materials as God intended (2 Cor. 3:14). This, in turn, allows our biblical interpretation as Christians to reach its rightful end of "beholding the glory of the Lord" and "being transformed into the same image from one degree of glory to another" (2 Cor. 3:14–18). Thus, we read *for Christ*.

Some Christians may query, if we are part of the new covenant, why should we seek to understand and apply the Old Testament? While I will develop my response throughout the remainder of this book, I will give ten reasons here why the first word in the phrase "*Old* Testament" must not mean "unimportant or insignificant to Christians."[3]

---

2 D. A. Carson, *The Cross and Christian Ministry: Leadership Lessons from 1 Corinthians* (Grand Rapids, MI: Baker Books, 2004), 41.

3 The following ten reasons are adapted from Jason S. DeRouchie, *How to Understand and Apply the Old Testament: Twelve Steps from Exegesis to Theology* (Phillipsburg, NJ: P&R, 2017), 6–11. Used with permission.

1. The Old Testament Was Jesus's Only Bible and Makes Up 75 Percent of Our Christian Scripture

If word count says anything, the Old Testament matters to God, who gave us his word in a book. In fact, it was his first special revelation, and it set a foundation for the fulfillment we find in Jesus in the New Testament. The Old Testament was the only Bible of Jesus and the earliest church (e.g., Luke 24:44; Acts 24:14; 2 Tim. 3:15), and it is a major part of our Scriptures. Jesus said, "Do not think that I have come to abolish the Law or the Prophets; I have not come to abolish them but to fulfill them" (Matt. 5:17). "The Law and the Prophets" to which he refers is the Old Testament.

2. The Old Testament Influences Our Understanding of Key Biblical Teachings

By the end of the Law (Genesis–Deuteronomy), the Bible has already described or alluded to all five of the major covenants that guide Scripture's plot structure (Adamic/Noahic, Abrahamic, Mosaic, Davidic, and new). The rest of the Old Testament then builds on this portrait in detail. Accordingly, the Old Testament story heightens hope for a better king, a blessed people, and a broader land, all of which the New Testament then realizes. Specifically, as I note elsewhere:

> The *Adamic-Noahic covenant* with creation establishes the crisis and context of global curse and common grace out of which the other covenants clarify God's solution and saving grace. The *Abrahamic covenant* forecasts the hope of Christ and new creation through its conditional yet certain kingdom promises of land(s), seed, blessing, and divine presence. The remaining covenants clarify how God fulfilled these promises in two progressive phases. In the *Mosaic covenant* (phase 1) Abraham's offspring as a single nation experience blessing and curse, which results in their exile from the promised land. The *Davidic covenant* recalls the promises of a royal Deliverer and declares the specific line through whom he will rise. Then the *new covenant* (phase 2) realizes these hopes in an already-but-not yet way through the person and perfect obedience of Christ Jesus, whose kingdom work overcomes the curse with universal blessing, makes Abraham the father of many

nations to the ends of the earth, and reconciles all things to God through the new creation.[4]

Without the Old Testament, we wouldn't understand the problem for which Jesus and the New Testament supply the solution. "As one trespass led to condemnation for all men, so one act of righteousness leads to justification and life for all men" (Rom. 5:18). Similarly, we would miss so many features of God's salvation story without the Old Testament. Just consider how Paul speaks regarding the Israelites: "To them belong the adoption, the glory, the covenants, the giving of the law, the worship, and the promises. To them belong the patriarchs, and from their race, according to the flesh, is the Christ, who is God over all, blessed forever. Amen" (Rom. 9:4–5). Finally, without the Old Testament, we wouldn't grasp the various types and shadows that point to Jesus. The Old Testament alone clarifies what John meant when he said of Jesus, "Behold, the Lamb of God, who takes away the sin of the world!" (John 1:29). And the Old Testament indicates what Jesus meant when he said of his body, "Destroy this temple, and in three days I will raise it up" (John 2:19, 21).

Furthermore, there are some doctrines of Scripture that are best understood only from the Old Testament. For example, where is there a clearer description of how God created the world than Genesis 1:1–2:3? Where else can we go other than the Old Testament to rightly understand sacred space and the temple? Where other than the Psalter should we go to know what Paul means by "psalms and hymns and spiritual songs" (Eph. 5:19; Col. 3:16)?[5] Where better than Isaiah 40 does the Bible declare the incomparability of God, whose revealed name is "Yahweh" (usually rendered in English translations as "the LORD"), which means, "he causes to be."[6] Where other than Isaiah 53 can we get a more succinct expression of penal

---

4   Jason S. DeRouchie, "An Arc of the Covenant: Tracing How the Bible's Storyline Climaxes in Christ," *SBJT* 26, no.1 (2022): 37 (emphasis added). Cf. Jason S. DeRouchie, "Question 22: What Is a Biblical Theology of the Covenant?," in Jason S. Derouchie, Oren R. Martin, and Andrew David Naselli, *40 Questions about Biblical Theology* (Grand Rapids, MI: Kregel, 2020), 215–26.

5   The Greek translation of the headings in Pss. 67 and 76 includes the same terms for "psalms . . . hymns . . . and spiritual songs" that we find in Eph. 5:19 and Col. 3:16.

6   "Yahweh" is the personal name by which the one true God identified himself and that the seers, sages, and songwriters employed in worship and preaching. Yahweh is both the Creator of all things and Israel's covenant Lord. As his name declares, Yahweh alone is the only uncaused being from whom, through whom, and to whom are all things.

substitutionary atonement—when God poured out his wrath for our sin on his Son?[7] All of these are principally derived from our understanding of the Old Testament.

Finally, the New Testament worldview and teachings are built on the framework supplied in the Old Testament. In the New Testament we find literally hundreds of Old Testament quotations, allusions, and echoes, none of which we will fully grasp apart from saturating ourselves in Jesus's Bible.[8]

3. We Meet the Same God in Both Testaments

Note how the book of Hebrews begins: "Long ago, at many times and in many ways, God spoke to our fathers by the prophets, but in these last days he has spoken to us by his Son" (Heb. 1:1–2). The very God who spoke through Old Testament prophets like Moses, Isaiah, and Malachi speaks through Jesus!

Now you may ask, "But isn't the Old Testament's God one of wrath and burden, whereas the God of the New Testament is about grace and freedom?" Let's consider some texts, first from the Old Testament and then from the New.

Perhaps the clearest and most significant Old Testament statement of Yahweh's character and action is Exodus 34:6: "The LORD, the LORD, a God merciful and gracious, slow to anger, and abounding in steadfast love and faithfulness." The Old Testament then reasserts this truth numerous times to clarify why it is that God continued to pardon and preserve a wayward people: "But the LORD was gracious to them and had compassion on them, and he turned toward them, because of his covenant with Abraham, Isaac,

---

7   This very important biblical teaching declares that Christ Jesus died on the cross as a substitute for sinners who believe. God imputed or counted the sins of the elect to Christ and counted his perfect righteousness to us. God punished Christ in our place and by this satisfied the demands of justice so that God would justly forgive sinners without compromising his holy standard. For more on this concept, see Rom. 5:18–19; 2 Cor. 5:21; Phil. 3:9. For its specific relationship to Isa. 52:13–53:12, see Thomas D. Petter, "The Meaning of Substitutionary Righteousness in Isa 53:11: A Summary of the Evidence," *TJ* 32, no. 2 (2011): 165–89; J. V. Fesko, "Imputed Righteousness: The Apostle Paul and Isaiah 53," *TMSJ* 32, no. 1 (2021): 5–19.
8   See, e.g., G. K. Beale and D. A. Carson, eds., *Commentary on the New Testament Use of the Old Testament* (Grand Rapids, MI: Baker Academic, 2007); G. K. Beale et al., eds., *Dictionary of the New Testament Use of the Old Testament* (Grand Rapids, MI: Baker Academic, 2023); cf. Gary Edward Schnittjer, *Old Testament Use of Old Testament: A Book-by-Book Guide* (Grand Rapids, MI: Zondervan Academic, 2021).

and Jacob, and would not destroy them, nor has he cast them from his presence until now" (2 Kings 13:23). "For if you return to the Lord, your brothers and your children will find compassion with their captors and return to this land. For the Lord your God is gracious and merciful and will not turn away his face from you, if you return to him" (2 Chron. 30:9). "Many years you bore with them and warned them by your Spirit through your prophets. Yet they would not give ear. Therefore you gave them into the hand of the peoples of the lands. Nevertheless, in your great mercies you did not make an end of them or forsake them, for you are a gracious and merciful God" (Neh. 9:30–31). Thus, God's grace fills the Old Testament.

Furthermore, in the New Testament, Jesus speaks about hell more than anyone else. He declares, "Do not fear those who kill the body but cannot kill the soul. Rather fear him who can destroy both soul and body in hell" (Matt. 10:28). Similarly, "Whoever causes one of these little ones who believe in me to sin, it would be better for him to have a great millstone fastened around his neck and to be drowned in the depth of the sea" (Matt. 18:6). Paul, citing Deuteronomy 32:35, asserts, "Beloved, never avenge yourselves, but leave it to the wrath of God, for it is written, 'Vengeance is mine, I will repay, says the Lord'" (Rom. 12:19). Also, the author of Hebrews says, "For if we go on sinning deliberately after receiving the knowledge of the truth, there no longer remains a sacrifice for sins, but a fearful expectation of judgment, and a fury of fire that will consume the adversaries" (Heb. 10:26–27). Peter spoke of his own role as a messenger of judgment and then contrasted this with how the Old Testament prophets like Samuel, Jeremiah, and Zechariah pointed to Jesus as the one through whom people would receive forgiveness: "He commanded us to preach to the people and to testify that he is the one appointed by God to be judge of the living and the dead. To him all the prophets bear witness that everyone who believes in him receives forgiveness of sins through his name" (Acts 10:42–43).

God is as wrathful in the New Testament as he is in the Old, and the Old Testament is filled with manifestations of God's saving grace. Certainly, there are numerous expressions of Yahweh's righteous anger in the Old Testament, just as there are massive manifestations of blood-bought mercy in the New Testament. Indeed, in Jesus all saving grace reaches its climax. Nevertheless, what is important is to recognize that *we meet the same God in the Old Testament as we do in the New*. In the whole Bible we meet a God who is faithful to his promises both to bless and to curse. He takes both sin and repentance seriously, and so should we!

4. The Old Testament Announces the Very "Good News" We Enjoy

Gospel means "good news" and refers to the truth that, through Jesus's life, death, and resurrection, God reigns over all and saves and satisfies sinners who believe. Paul states that "the Scripture, foreseeing that God would justify the Gentiles by faith, preached *the gospel* beforehand to Abraham, saying, 'In you shall all the nations be blessed'" (Gal. 3:8). Abraham was already aware of the message of global salvation we now enjoy. Similarly, in the opening of Romans, Paul stresses that the Lord "promised beforehand through his prophets in the holy Scriptures" (i.e., the Old Testament prophets) the very powerful "gospel of God . . . concerning his Son" that he preached and in which we now rest (Rom. 1:1–3, 16). Foremost among these prophets was Isaiah, who anticipated the day when Yahweh's royal servant (the Messiah) and the many servants identified with him would herald comforting "good news" to the poor and broken—news that the saving God reigns through his anointed royal deliverer (Isa. 61:1; cf. 40:9–11; 52:7–10; Luke 4:16–21). Reading the Old Testament, therefore, is one of God's given ways for us to better grasp and delight in the gospel (see also Heb. 4:2).

5. Both the Old and New Covenants Call Us to
Love and Clarify What Love Looks Like

Within the old covenant, love was *what* Yahweh called Israel to do (Deut. 6:5; 10:19); all the other commandments clarified *how* to do it. This was part of Jesus's point when he stressed that all the Old Testament hangs on the call to love God and neighbor: "You shall love the Lord your God with all your heart and with all your soul and with all your mind. This is the great and first commandment. And a second is like it: You shall love your neighbor as yourself. On these two commandments depend all the Law and the Prophets" (Matt. 22:37–40). Christ emphasized, "Whatever you wish that others would do to you, do also to them, for this is the Law and the Prophets" (Matt. 7:12). Similarly, Paul notes, "The whole law is fulfilled in one word: 'You shall love your neighbor as yourself'" (Gal. 5:14; cf. Rom. 13:8, 10). As with Israel, the Lord calls Christians to lives characterized by love. However, he now gives all members of the new covenant the ability to do what he commands. As Moses himself asserts, the very reason God promised to circumcise hearts in the new covenant age was "so that you will love the Lord your God with all your heart and with all your soul" (Deut. 30:6). Moses's old covenant law called for life-encompassing love, and Christians today can gain clarity from the Old Testament on the wide-ranging impact of love in all of life. As we will see, this happens rightly only when we account for how Jesus fulfills every particular law.

6. Jesus Came Not to Set Aside the Old Testament but to Fulfill It

Moses said that those enjoying circumcised hearts in the new covenant age would "obey the voice of the Lord and keep all his commandments that I command you today" (Deut. 30:8). Moses knew that the laws he was proclaiming in Deuteronomy would matter for those living in the days of restoration.

Similarly, far from setting aside the Old Testament, Jesus stressed that he came to fulfill it, and he highlighted how the Old Testament's instruction was lastingly relevant for his followers.

> Do not think that I have come to abolish the Law or the Prophets; I have not come to abolish them but to fulfill them. For truly, I say to you, until heaven and earth pass away, not an iota, not a dot, will pass from the Law until all is accomplished. Therefore whoever relaxes one of the least of these commandments and teaches others to do the same will be called least in the kingdom of heaven, but whoever does them and teaches them will be called great in the kingdom of heaven. (Matt. 5:17–19)

In chapters 10–13 we'll consider further the significance of this text, but what is important to note here is that, while the age of the old covenant has come to an end (Rom. 6:14–15; 1 Cor. 9:20–21; Gal. 5:18; cf. Luke 16:16), the Old Testament itself maintains lasting relevance for us in the way it displays the character of God (e.g., Rom. 7:12), points to the excellencies of Christ, and portrays for us the scope of love in all its facets (Matt. 22:37–40).

7. Jesus Said That All the Old Testament Points to Him

After his first encounter with Jesus, Philip announced to Nathanael, "We have found him of whom Moses in the Law and also the prophets wrote"

(John 1:45). Do you want to see and celebrate Jesus as much as you can? The Old Testament authors wrote about him! As Jesus himself said, "You search the Scriptures because you think that in them you have eternal life; and it is they that bear witness about me" (John 5:39; cf. 5:46–47). Then, following his resurrection, "beginning with Moses and all the Prophets, he interpreted to them in all the Scriptures the things concerning himself" (Luke 24:27). Abner Chou notes, "The text does not say Jesus read all the Scriptures as about himself. It states he expounded the things concerning himself that are throughout the Scriptures."[9] This distinction is important, for the Old Testament addresses many things other than Christ—an array of experiences, persons, powers, and perspectives. Nevertheless, we must not limit Jesus's meaning to a handful of "specific messianic prophecies" or to his affirmation that he is "the embodiment of YHWH" and "embodies the fulfillment of the whole promise of the Hebrew Bible" as the biblical story climaxes in Jesus.[10]

Indeed, as the use of Scripture in Luke and Acts illustrates, the phrase "all the Scriptures" in Luke 24:27 points not only to these elements but also "to patterns and prefigurements that anticipate the arrival of David's greater Son."[11] When Jesus "opened . . . the Scriptures" and his disciples' "minds to understand" them (Luke 24:32, 45), he shows that his entire Bible—the Law, the Prophets, and the Writings—declares a unified message of the Messiah's suffering and triumph and the mission his life would generate: "that the Christ should suffer and on the third day rise from the dead, and that repentance and forgiveness of sins should be proclaimed in his name to all nations, beginning from Jerusalem. You are witnesses of these things" (24:46–48; cf. 24:44). As Brian Tabb articulates, "Luke 24:47 establishes the Christological focus of his disciples' preaching (in Jesus's name), their central message (repentance for the forgiveness of sins), and the universal scope of their mission (to all

9 Abner Chou, *The Hermeneutics of the Biblical Writers: Learning to Interpret Scripture from the Prophets and Apostles* (Grand Rapids, MI: Kregel, 2018), 133; see also I. Howard Marshall, *The Gospel of Luke: A Commentary on the Greek Text*, NIGTC (Grand Rapids, MI: Eerdmans, 1978), 897; Daniel I. Block, "Christotelic Preaching: A Plea for Hermeneutical Integrity and Missional Passion," *SBJT* 22, no. 3 (2018): 12.
10 Against Block, "Christotelic Preaching," 13.
11 Brian J. Tabb, *After Emmaus: How the Church Fulfills the Mission of Christ* (Wheaton, IL: Crossway, 2021), 24. Tabb's entire book shows how "Luke 24:44–47 summarizes the essential message of the Scriptures and offers disciples a hermeneutical model or lens for reading the Bible with the proper focus" (36–37).

nations).["12] Similarly, Paul taught "nothing but what the prophets and Moses said would come to pass: that the Christ must suffer and that, by being the first to rise from the dead, he would proclaim light both to our people and to the Gentiles" (Acts 26:22–23).[13] As an Old Testament preacher, he could declare, "I decided to know nothing among you except Jesus Christ and him crucified" (1 Cor. 2:2). As we will see in chapters 4–6, if you want to know Jesus more, read the Old Testament through believing eyes!

8. New Testament Authors Expect Us to Read the Old Testament

The New Testament often cites the Old Testament in ways that call us to look back at the original context. For example, Matthew 27–28 portray Christ's tribulation and triumph at the cross by recalling Psalm 22 many times. Jesus quotes Psalm 22:1 when he declares, "My God, my God, why have you forsaken me?" (Matt. 27:46). In stating, "And when they had crucified him, they divided his garments among them by casting lots" (Matt. 27:35), Matthew alludes to Psalm 22:16, 18, which reads,

> They have pierced my hands and feet—
> . . . .
> They divide my garments among them,
>   and for my clothing they cast lots.[14]

The apostle notes how those passing by "derided him, wagging their heads" (Matt. 27:39) and how the Jewish leaders mocked Jesus, asserting, "He trusts in God; let God deliver him now, if he desires him" (27:43). Both statements come from Psalm 22:7–8:

> All who seek me mock me;
>   they make mouths at me; they wag their heads;
> "He trusts in the Lord; let him deliver him;
>   let him rescue him, for he delights in him!"

---

12 Tabb, *After Emmaus*, 32. For a fuller exposition of this text, see 21–30.

13 For an exposition of this text, see Tabb, *After Emmaus*, 30–33.

14 "They have pierced my hands and feet" is the preferred reading in all the major English versions except the NET Bible. For justification of this majority reading, see DeRouchie, *How to Understand and Apply the Old Testament*, 129–31; cf. Conrad R. Gren, "Piercing the Ambiguities of Psalm 22:16 and the Messiah's Mission," *JETS* 48, no. 2 (2005): 283–99.

And after Jesus's resurrection he directs the women, "Go and tell my brothers to go to Galilee, and there they will see me" (Matt. 28:10). Envisioning that Yahweh would rescue him, the suffering king in Psalm 22 declares,

> I will tell of your name to my brothers;
>> in the midst of the congregation I will praise you. (Ps. 22:22)

We then learn,

> All the ends of the earth shall remember
>> and turn to the LORD,
> and all the families of the nations
>> shall worship before you.
> For kingship belongs to the LORD,
>> and he rules over the nations.
> . . . .
> they will come and proclaim his righteousness to a people yet unborn,
>> that he has done it. (Ps. 22:27–28, 31)

And it is from this context that Jesus, then, declares to his brothers, "All authority in heaven and on earth has been given to me. Go therefore and make disciples of all nations, baptizing them in the name of the Father and of the Son and of the Holy Spirit, teaching them to observe all that I have commanded you. And behold, I am with you always, to the end of the age" (Matt. 28:18–20). To fully understand their words, the New Testament authors call us back to the Old Testament through their quotations and allusions.

9. New Testament Authors Recognized That God Gave the Old Testament for Christians

Regarding the Old Testament prophets, Peter explains, "It was revealed to them that they were serving not themselves but you" (1 Pet. 1:12).[15] Similarly, Paul was convinced that the Old Testament authors wrote *for* new covenant believers—those following Jesus on this side of his death and resurrection.

---

15 In chap. 2 we'll see evidence from the Old Testament that the prophets knew they were writing for those associated with the Messiah at the end of the age.

"For whatever was written in former days was written *for our instruction,* that through endurance and through the encouragement of the Scriptures we might have hope" (Rom. 15:4; cf. 4:23–24). "Now these things happened to [the Israelites] as an example, but they were written down *for our instruction,* on whom the end of the ages has come" (1 Cor. 10:11).

In the Old Testament we find many "profitable" things that call for "repentance toward God" and "faith in our Lord Jesus Christ" (Acts 20:20–21). Indeed, in the Old Testament we find the very "gospel of the grace of God" (Acts 20:24). Based on this fact, New Testament authors regularly used the Old Testament in their Christian teaching (e.g., 1 Cor. 9:8–12; Eph. 6:2–3; 1 Tim. 5:18; 1 Pet. 1:14–16). Later in the book we will consider how Christians should relate to Old Testament promises (chaps. 7–9) and laws (chaps. 10–13). Nevertheless, the point stands that the prophets of old wrote what we call the Old Testament for Christians. Part 1 of this book will delve further into this fact and its implications for interpreting the Old Testament as God intends.

10. Paul Demands That Church Leaders Preach the Old Testament

Paul was a herald of the good news of God's kingdom in Christ (e.g., Acts 19:8; 20:25; 28:30–31), which he preached from the Law of Moses and the Prophets—the Old Testament (Acts 28:23; cf. 26:22–23). He testified to the Ephesian elders, "I am innocent of the blood of all, for I did not shrink from declaring to you the whole counsel of God" (Acts 20:26–27). The *whole counsel of God* refers to the entirety of God's purposes in salvation history as revealed in Scripture. Luke wants us to know that, had the apostle failed to make known the Lord's redemptive plan of blessing overcoming curse through the person of Jesus, he would have stood accountable before God for any future doctrinal or moral error that the Ephesian church carried out (cf. Ezek. 33:1–6; Acts 18:6). With the New Testament, Scripture is complete, and we now have "the faith that was once for all delivered to the saints" (Jude 3). This "faith," however, is only understood rightly within the framework of "the whole counsel of God." So may we be people who guard ourselves from blood guilt by making much of the Old Testament in relation to Christ.

Significantly, Paul was referring to the Old Testament when he spoke of the "sacred writings" that are able to make a person "wise for salvation" and of the "Scripture" that is "breathed out by God and profitable" (2 Tim. 3:15–16). Knowing this fact colors our understanding of his following charge:

> Preach the word; be ready in season and out of season; reprove, rebuke, and exhort, with complete patience and teaching. For the time is coming when people will not endure sound teaching, but having itching ears they will accumulate for themselves teachers to suit their own passion, and will turn away from listening to the truth and wander off into myths. (2 Tim. 4:2–4)

Paul believed Christians like Timothy needed to preach the Old Testament to guard the church from apostasy. While we now have the New Testament, we still must study, practice, and teach the Old Testament like Jesus and his apostles did for the good of God's church.

Conclusion

Paul urged Timothy, "Do your best to present yourself to God as one approved, a worker who has no need to be ashamed, rightly handling the word of truth" (2 Tim. 2:15). This study seeks to supply believers with an interpretive framework and guide for rightly handling the Old Testament as God's word for us. Part 1 calls for *reading well* the Old Testament by interpreting it through and for Christ. Part 2 then develops this call by indicating how Christians can *see well* Christ's person and work within the Old Testament. Part 3 considers how to *hope well* in Old Testament promises, which through Christ become certain for all who are in the church. Finally, part 4 overviews how to *live well* by applying Old Testament laws in view of how Christ fulfills them. May this book result in faith, hope, and love abounding more and more as Jesus's followers increasingly embrace the Old Testament for the Christian Scripture it is.

Review and Reflection

1. What place has the Old Testament had in your own walk with Christ?
2. Give an example of how God has used the *Old* Testament in your own life "for teaching, for reproof, for correction, and for training in righteousness" (1 Tim. 3:16). How have you used the Old Testament in someone else's life?

3. What does the author mean by interpreting the Old Testament *through* Christ and *for* Christ?

4. What are some key biblical teachings for which the Old Testament provides foundational understanding?

5. How would you respond to someone who claimed the Old Testament God is one of wrath, but the New Testament God is one of grace?

6. How would you define the "gospel"? Can you give an example of where the Old Testament promises it?

7. Give an example of how the Old Testament points to Jesus.

8. Which of the ten reasons why the Old Testament still matters for Christians was most compelling? Why?

9. What was the greatest insight you gained in reading this chapter? What is your greatest takeaway?

10. What are you most eager to learn in studying this book?

PART 1

READING WELL

How Jesus Helps Christians Interpret the Old Testament[1]

To you has been given the secret of the kingdom of God,
but for those outside everything is in parables, so that

"'they may indeed see but not perceive,
and may indeed hear but not understand,
lest they should turn and be forgiven.'"

MARK 4:11–12

Now to him who is able to strengthen you according to
my gospel and the preaching of Jesus Christ, according
to the revelation of the mystery that was kept secret for
long ages but has now been disclosed and through the
prophetic writings has been made known to all nations.

ROMANS 16:25–26

---

1 Much of part 1 updates material first published in Jason S. DeRouchie, "The Mystery Revealed: A Biblical Case for Christ-Centered Old Testament Interpretation," *Them* 44, no. 2 (2019): 226–48. Used by permission. Cf. Jason S. DeRouchie, "Question 21: What Role Does 'Mystery' Play in Biblical Theology?," in Jason S. DeRouchie, Oren R. Martin, and Andrew David Naselli, *40 Questions about Biblical Theology* (Grand Rapids, MI: Kregel, 2020), 205–14.

> *Their minds were hardened. For to this day, when they*
> *read the old covenant, that same veil remains unlifted,*
> *because only through Christ is it taken away. Yes, to this*
> *day whenever Moses is read a veil lies over their hearts.*
> *But when one turns to the Lord, the veil is removed.*
>
> 2 CORINTHIANS 3:14–16

One of the reasons Jesus spoke in parables was to extend the mission of judgment that Yahweh first gave to the prophet Isaiah:

Keep on hearing, but do not understand;
keep on seeing, but do not perceive. (Isa. 6:9)

Yet Jesus explained the parables to his disciples, disclosing what he called the "secret/mystery" of God's kingdom (Mark 4:11–12). Paul notes how God through the gospel and the preaching of Jesus was revealing the same "mystery" that for so long was unknown to the multitudes but that now all nations were grasping through the Old Testament's prophetic writings (Rom. 16:25–26). The apostle stresses how turning to the Lord Christ becomes the means for reading the old covenant materials as God intended (2 Cor. 3:14–16). Indeed, he later notes how "the god of this world has blinded the minds of the unbelievers, to keep them from seeing the light of the gospel of the glory of Christ" (2 Cor. 4:4). Nevertheless, Paul proclaims this glorious message because the "God, who said, 'Let light shine out of darkness,' has shone in our hearts to give the light of the knowledge of the glory of God in the face of Jesus Christ" (2 Cor. 4:6).

Part 1 of this book supplies a biblical-theological foundation for Christ-centered interpretation of the Old Testament. Using more technical language, it supplies an initial framework for a biblical theology of hermeneutics. Biblical theology is the study of how the whole Bible progresses, integrates, and climaxes in Christ. Hermeneutics is the branch of knowledge that deals with interpreting literary texts, especially the Bible.

My thesis is twofold. *First*, I will argue (1) that the Old Testament is Christian Scripture, (2) that God originally gave it with Christians in mind, and (3) that the Old Testament authors had a sense that most of their words would be more meaningful for those living in the messianic age of restoration than for those living before it, whether believer or nonbeliever. Thus, the Old Testament message is in many ways clearer and more relevant for Christians today than it ever was for those before Christ. *Second*, I will argue (1) that faith in Christ alone supplies the necessary light for seeing and savoring God's revelation in the Old Testament and (2) that Jesus's appearing in salvation history supplies the necessary lens for most fully understanding and appropriating the divine author's intended meaning in the Old Testament.

I will sustain this twofold thesis over the next three chapters. Chapters 1 and 2 parallel each other. Both chapters argue that the Old Testament authors wrote their texts to instruct Christians and that Christians today can understand the Old Testament's message better than the old covenant unbelieving majority or believing remnant because of the coming of Christ. Chapter 1 does this from a New Testament perspective, while chapter 2 does it from an Old Testament perspective. Chapter 3 concludes the argument by demonstrating that Christ must be both our light and lens for properly interpreting the Old Testament. My hope is that, at the end of part 1, you will believe that Jesus alone enables us to understand and appropriate the meaning of the Old Testament as God intended.

1

The Old Testament's Audience and Comprehension

New Testament Perspective

Serving not themselves.

1 PETER 1:12

ACCORDING TO THE NEW TESTAMENT AUTHORS, the Old Testament authors knew that they were speaking and writing for new covenant believers, and they also had some level of conscious awareness about who the Christ would be and when he would rise. With Christ's coming, anticipation gave rise to fulfillment, and types found their antitype, which means that new covenant members can comprehend the fullness of the Old Testament's meaning better than the old covenant rebel or remnant.

The Old Testament's Audience

Paul believed that God gave the Old Testament for *new* covenant believers. Referring to the statement in Genesis 15:6 that Abram's faith was "counted to him as righteousness," Paul asserts that "the words 'it was counted to him' were not written for his sake alone, but for ours also" (Rom. 4:23–24). Similarly, just after identifying Christ as the subject in Psalm 69, the apostle emphasizes, "For whatever was written in former days was written for our instruction, that through endurance and through the encouragement of the

19

Scriptures we might have hope" (Rom. 15:4).[1] Furthermore, upon recalling Israel's history in the wilderness, Paul says, "Now these things happened to them as an example, but they were written down for our instruction, on whom the end of the ages has come" (1 Cor. 10:11). In each of these three texts, Paul stresses that the Old Testament author wrote his text for the benefit of believers living this side of the cross. The apostle does not clarify whether this was only God's intent as the ultimate author, or whether this was also the Old Testament human authors' intent. What is clear, however, is that for Paul, the Old Testament was *Christian* Scripture and fully applicable to believers when read through Christ.

The apostle says this much to Timothy, who was raised on the Old Testament by his Jewish mother and grandmother (Acts 16:1; 2 Tim. 1:5). Paul writes that the "sacred writings" of Timothy's upbringing—what we call the Old Testament Scriptures—"are able to make you wise for salvation through faith in Christ Jesus" (2 Tim. 3:15). People today can get saved from God's wrath and from the enslavement of sin by reading the Old Testament through faith in Christ! Thus, Paul then asserts, "All Scripture is . . . profitable for teaching, for reproof, for correction, and for training in righteousness, that the man of God may be competent, equipped for every good work" (2 Tim. 3:16–17). New covenant believers can correct and reprove straying brothers and sisters from the Old Testament when it is read in relation to Jesus. Because of this, Paul calls his young protégé to "preach the word" (2 Tim. 4:2). God gave the Old Testament for Christians. It's part of our Christian Scriptures, and we must use it to know God and savor Christ.

Based on this fact, New Testament authors frequently cite Old Testament instructions in their exhortations, assuming their relevance for believers today. For example, Paul, as a new covenant preacher, draws from a series of execution texts in Deuteronomy when arguing for the excommunication of the sexually immoral man in 1 Corinthians 5:13 (cf. Deut. 13:5; 17:7, 12; 21:21; 22:21, 22, 24; 24:7).[2] The apostle also has no problem using the Ten Commandments when he charges children, " 'Honor your father and mother'

---

1   For a careful supporting analysis of Paul's claim in Rom. 15:4, see George W. Knight III, "The Scriptures Were Written for Our Instruction," *JETS* 39, no. 1 (1996): 3–13.

2   Knight rightly notes, "Here the apostle takes account of the difference that fulfillment [through Jesus] has brought about and at the same time maintains the principle continuity for the instruction as it relates to the Church, and in doing so he also has 'written for our instruction.'" Knight, "The Scriptures Were Written for Our Instruction," 10.

(this is the first commandment with a promise), that it may go well with you and that you may live long in the land" (Eph. 6:2–3; cf. Ex. 20:12; Deut. 5:16). Similarly, Paul tells the young pastor, "Let the elders who rule well be considered worthy of double honor, especially those who labor in preaching and teaching. For the Scripture says, 'You shall not muzzle an ox when it treads out the grain'" (1 Tim. 5:17–18; cf. Deut. 25:4; 1 Cor. 9:8–12). Likewise, Peter recalls the refrain in Leviticus when he writes, "Be holy in all your conduct, since it is written, 'You shall be holy, for I am holy'" (1 Pet. 1:15–16; cf. Lev. 11:44–45; 19:2; 20:26). Because we are now part of the new covenant and not the old, there are natural questions that rise regarding how exactly the Christian should relate to specific old covenant laws or promises.[3] Nevertheless, the point stands that God gave the Old Testament to instruct Christians.

Now, as noted, when Paul states that the Old Testament "was written" for our instruction, he was not explicit as to whether the Old Testament human authors understood this. Peter, however, makes this clear when he writes that the Old Testament prophets knew that they *"were serving not themselves but you,* in the things that have now been announced to you through those who preached the good news to you by the Holy Spirit sent from heaven, things into which angels long to look" (1 Pet. 1:12). The apostle emphasizes that God revealed to the inspired human authors themselves that their words in the Old Testament were principally *not for themselves* but for those living after the arrival of the Christ. Therefore, far from being not applicable for believers, the Old Testament is *more relevant* for Christians today than it was for the majority in the old covenant era.

The Old Testament Prophets' Understanding of Christ's Person and Time

Jesus declared, "Your father Abraham rejoiced that he would see my day. He saw it and was glad" (John 8:56). The patriarch eagerly expected the Messiah and his coming. Similarly, reflecting on Psalm 16:8–11, Peter calls King David a "prophet" and asserts, "Knowing that God had sworn with an oath to him that he would set one of his descendants on his throne, he foresaw and spoke about the resurrection of the Christ" (Acts 2:30–31; cf. Luke 18:31–33; Acts

---

3   For an explanation of how old covenant promises relate to Christians, see chaps. 7–9; for old covenant laws, see chaps. 10–13.

3:18, 24; 10:43). Peter believed that David himself anticipated Christ's coming in Psalm 16,[4] and David's last words before death affirm that this author of many psalms was hoping in a just ruler who would overcome the curse and initiate a new creation (2 Sam. 23:3–7).[5] Similarly, the writer of Hebrews stresses, "These all died in faith, not having received the things promised, but having seen them and greeted them from afar" (Heb. 11:13). The Old Testament remnant enjoyed some level of light, by which they could see clearly and understand rightly many of the things God used them to declare; they themselves wrote of the Christ and hoped in him.

On the other hand, we also read, "I tell you that many prophets and kings desired to see what you see, and did not see it, and to hear what you hear, and did not hear it" (Luke 10:24; cf. Matt. 13:17). It seems that we should understand Yahweh's prophets of old as truly seeing God's beauty and purposes, as well as the hope that awaited them, while we also affirm that they did not experience and, therefore, comprehend all that we experience and comprehend in Christ. For them, full disclosure awaited a later day.[6]

Peter captures both sides of this interpretive framework when he writes:

Concerning this salvation, the prophets who prophesied about the grace that was to be yours searched and inquired carefully, inquiring what person or time the Spirit of Christ in them was indicating when he predicted the sufferings of Christ and the subsequent glories. It was revealed to them that they were serving not themselves but you, in the things that have now been announced to you through those who preached the good news to you by the Holy Spirit sent from heaven, things into which angels long to look. (1 Pet. 1:10–12)

---

4   Jason S. DeRouchie, *How to Understand and Apply the Old Testament: Twelve Steps from Exegesis to Theology* (Phillipsburg, NJ: P&R, 2017), 72.

5   On this reading, see Brian A. Verrett, *The Serpent in Samuel: A Messianic Motif* (Eugene, OR: Resource, 2020), 143–77.

6   For similar conclusions, see Robert L. Plummer, "Righteousness and Peace Kiss: The Reconciliation of Authorial Intent and Biblical Typology," *SBJT* 14, no. 2 (2010): 54–61; G. K. Beale, "The Cognitive Peripheral Vision of Biblical Authors," *WTJ* 76, no. 2 (2014): 263–93. Beale writes, "There is always a related range of meaning that appropriately is an expansion of the explicit meaning that is expressed. . . . Old Testament authors may have had some inkling of how the meaning of their texts would be later interpreted in what would appear to us surprising interpretations" (265, 283). Cf. G. K. Beale and Benjamin L. Gladd, *Hidden but Now Revealed: A Biblical Theology of Mystery* (Downers Grove, IL: IVP Academic, 2014), 343, 359.

According to Peter, the Old Testament prophets were themselves studiers of earlier revelation, whether previously written biblical books or prophetic oracles they received by dreams or visions.[7] And under the guiding hand of the Spirit (2 Pet. 1:21), they "searched and inquired carefully" to know both *who* the Messiah would be and *when* he would appear, thus predicting Christ's sufferings and the days of the church.[8] While they did not know Jesus's name, they had a general sense of the type of person he would be and of when he would come, and they often learned this from studying the Scriptures (e.g., Ps. 119:2; Dan. 9:2; John 5:39; 7:52).[9] From this perspective, we can say that the Old Testament authors themselves (though not most of their contemporaries) already visualized much of the fulfillment that the New Testament identifies as culminating in Christ. While revelation did progress from the Old to New Testaments, the development was often from conscious, prospective prediction (whether direct or typological) to realized fulfillment and not simply prediction of which only God was originally aware but which we now recognize retrospectively.

This understanding of Old Testament texts is fueled when we consider how previous Scripture[10]—of which the prophets were searching and inquiring

7   For arguments that the "prophets" here are indeed *Old* Testament prophets, see Dan G. Mc-Cartney, "The Use of the Old Testament in the First Epistle of Peter" (PhD diss., Westminster Theological Seminary, 1989), 24–31; Mark Dubis, *Messianic Woes in First Peter: Suffering and Eschatology in 1 Peter 4:12–19*, StBibLit 33 (New York: Lang, 2002), 108–10.

8   In contrast to the NIV and CSB, the ESV is correct in identifying that the Old Testament prophets inquired about "what person or time" (similarly, see NRSV, NET, NASB). Peter always uses the Greek *tis* as a pronoun and *poios* as an adjective, which would result in a translation like "what person or what circumstances." See G. D. Kilpatrick, "Peter 1.11: TINA 'H POION KAIRON," *NovT* 28, no. 1 (1986): 91–92; Mark Dubis, *1 Peter: A Handbook on the Greek Text*, Baylor Handbook on the Greek New Testament (Waco, TX: Baylor University Press, 2010), 19.

9   Moyise concludes that the verbs for "searching and inquiring" in 1 Pet. 1:10 "refer to some sort of exegetical activity." Steve Moyise, *Evoking Scripture: Seeing the Old Testament in the New* (London: T&T Clark, 2008), 79. Similarly, Sargent states, "Peter stresses that the Old Testament prophets were studiers of all earlier revelation." Benjamin Sargent, *Written to Serve: The Use of Scripture in 1 Peter*, LNTS 547 (Edinburgh: T&T Clark, 2015), 22. Against Edward Gordon Selwyn, *The First Epistle of St. Peter: The Greek Text with Introduction, Notes and Essays*, 2nd ed., Thornapple Commentaries (Grand Rapids, MI: Baker, 1981), 134.

10 On this point, I agree with Kaiser that, before considering how subsequent revelation handles our passage, we must first use "all the divine revelation found in the books that *preceded* [historically] the selected text we are reading or studying as the context and 'informing theology' that could have the first input to 'thicken' the meaning." Walter C. Kaiser Jr., "Single Meaning, Unified Referents: Accurate and Authoritative Citations of the Old Testament by the New Testament," in *Three Views on the New Testament Use of the Old*, ed. Kenneth Berding and Jonathan

carefully—and the patterns in Israel's redemptive story[11] inform our reading, filling out implications of a text's meaning along with that which is explicitly stated. By "implications" I mean those subsidiary or implicit meanings that we can show fall within the author's "peripheral vision," though he may not have been conscious of them.[12] A proper reading of the Old Testament requires that we, for example, appreciate how Genesis 3:15 or 22:17–18 shapes and informs messianic hope in all the rest of the Bible, how associations between Yahweh and his Messiah (e.g., Hos. 3:5) may influence later readings elsewhere that only mention Yahweh (e.g., Hos.11:10–11), or how past types like sacrifice may guide a messianic reading within later texts (e.g., of the day of the Lord as sacrifice in Zeph. 2:7). The Old Testament prophets and New Testament authors seem to have read their Scriptures in this way.

Furthermore, when Peter says that "it was revealed to them that they were serving not themselves but you, in the things that have now been announced" (1 Pet. 1:12), he is highlighting that the Old Testament prophets were very aware that their searching and inquiring and writing were more for us than them. That is, they saw the things that God promised but merely "greeted them from afar," convinced "that apart from us they should not be made perfect" (Heb. 11:13, 40). Jesus testified that the Scriptures "bear witness about me" (John 5:39), and rebirth in Christ allows one to see him as the promised King (cf. John 3:3).[13] As Philip declared to Nathanael, "We

---

Lunde, Counterpoints: Bible and Theology (Grand Rapids, MI: Zondervan, 2008), 53 (emphasis original); cf. 72, 75. Similarly, though rightfully allowing for interaction with historically later works as well, Beale writes, "When a New Testament writer refers to an Old Testament passage, both the explicit and subsidiary understanding of the Old Testament author's meaning compose what we would call the New Testament writer's respect for the Old Testament contextual meaning. In addition to the explicit meaning from the specific text quoted and explicitly attended to by the New Testament author, this contextual meaning may include ideas from the immediate or nearby Old Testament context that are in mind, as well as ideas from other Old Testament books that are related to the meaning of the focus text." Beale, "The Cognitive Peripheral Vision of Biblical Authors," 273; cf. Beale and Gladd, *Hidden but Now Revealed*, 349.

11 See G. K. Beale, *Handbook on the New Testament Use of the Old Testament: Exegesis and Interpretation* (Grand Rapids, MI: Baker Academic, 2012), 96–102.

12 See especially Robert H. Stein, *A Basic Guide to Interpreting the Bible: Playing by the Rules*, 2nd ed. (Grand Rapids, MI: Baker Academic, 2011), 30–38; Robert H. Stein, "The Benefits of an Author-Oriented Approach to Hermeneutics," *JETS* 44, no. 3 (2001): 451–66; Beale, "The Cognitive Peripheral Vision of Biblical Authors," 263–93, esp. 266–70; Beale and Gladd, *Hidden but Now Revealed*, 344–47.

13 John frequently uses this statement to speak of a verbal testimony after a visible encounter (e.g., John 1:34; 3:11, 32; 19:35).

have found him of whom Moses in the Law and also the prophets wrote, Jesus of Nazareth" (John 1:45; cf. 5:46).

As in the case of Daniel (see chap. 2), the full meaning of some Old Testament texts can transcend the human author's understanding.[14] This is so because God's purposes often far exceed human understanding (Deut. 29:29; Eccl. 8:16–17; Isa. 55:8–9) and because he was authoring not simply individual books but *a* book (2 Tim. 3:16; 2 Pet. 1:21) whose parts were "incomplete" until Jesus "fulfilled" them by his coming (Matt. 5:17; 11:13; Rom. 10:4).[15] Nevertheless, while the coming of Christ certainly fills out the meaning of numerous Old Testament texts, the New Testament testifies that the Old Testament authors usually understood their end-times visions, had a true hope in the coming Messiah, and had some sense about the timing of his coming. Furthermore, interpreters should expect that the Old and New Testament

---

14 By "full meaning" I refer to both a Bible passage's sense and referent. Since E. D. Hirsch's landmark volume *Validity in Interpretation* (New Haven: Yale University Press, 1967), scholars have often limited meaning to *human* authorial intent, and I am highly sympathetic to this view. Numerous scholars, however, have offered fair critique of this perspective, seeing as one of Scripture's authors is God, whose purpose was not simply to write books but *a* book. See Philip B. Payne, "The Fallacy of Equating Meaning with the Human Author's Intention," *JETS* 20, no. 3 (1977): 243–52; Raju D. Kunjummen, "The Single Intent of Scripture—Critical Examination of a Theological Construct," *GTJ* 7, no. 1 (1986): 81–110; Peter Enns, "Apostolic Hermeneutics and an Evangelical Doctrine of Scripture: Moving Beyond a Modernist Impasse," *WTJ* 65, no. 2 (2003): 263–87; Jared M. Compton, "Shared Intentions? Reflections on Inspiration and Interpretation in Light of Scripture's Dual Authorship," *Them* 33, no. 3 (2008): 23–33; Vern S. Poythress, "The Presence of God Qualifying Our Notions of Grammatical-Historical Interpretation: Genesis 3:15 as a Test Case," *JETS* 50, no. 1 (2007): 87–103; Vern S. Poythress, "Dispensing with Merely Human Meaning: Gains and Losses from Focusing on the Human Author, Illustrated by Zephaniah 1:2–3," *JETS* 57, no. 3 (2014): 481–99; Douglas J. Moo and Andrew David Naselli, "The Problem of the New Testament's Use of the Old Testament," in *The Enduring Authority of the Christian Scriptures*, ed. D. A. Carson (Grand Rapids, MI: Eerdmans, 2016), 702–46. Significantly, Hirsch himself has refined his statements, affirming that his original line between "meaning" (which is textually bound) and "significance" (which is fluid) is not as fixed as he once thought. E. D. Hirsch, "Meaning and Significance Reinterpreted," *Critical Inquiry* 11, no. 2 (1984): 202–24; E. D. Hirsch, "Transhistorical Intentions and the Persistence of Allegory," *New Literary History* 25, no. 3 (1994): 549–67; cited in Darrell L. Bock, "Single Meaning, Multiple Contexts and Referents," in Berding and Lunde, *Three Views on the New Testament Use of the Old*, 123n15. On the question of the New Testament's use of the Old Testament, Kaiser is perhaps the strongest voice arguing that human authorial intent *exhausts* the full meaning of every Old Testament text, so that the New Testament authors are in *every instance* simply identifying what the Old Testament authors already meant in full. Walter C. Kaiser Jr., *The Uses of the Old Testament in the New* (Chicago: Moody, 1985); Kaiser, "Single Meaning, Unified Referents," 45–89. Stein is another evangelical following this basic approach to biblical interpretation. Stein, "The Benefits of an Author-Oriented Approach to Hermeneutics," 451–66; Stein, *A Basic Guide to Interpreting the Bible*.

15 So too, Moo and Naselli, "The Problem of the New Testament's Use of the Old Testament," 735.

uses of antecedent Scripture organically grow out of the earlier materials and never contradict them because all Scripture comes from God (2 Tim. 3:16) and because the prophets "searched and inquired carefully" (1 Pet. 1:10) and made Spirit-led interpretations (2 Pet. 1:20–21), learning from the Spirit and "interpreting spiritual truths to those who are spiritual" (1 Cor. 2:13).

The Rebels' Inability to Understand the Old Testament

The New Testament is clear that the blindness associated with the old covenant unbelieving rebel majority continued into Christ's day. We see this incapacity, for example, in the religious leaders, whom Jesus confronted numerous times. To Nicodemus he questioned, "Are you the teacher of Israel and yet you do not understand these things?" (John 3:10). And to other Jews he said, "You search the Scriptures because you think that in them you have eternal life; and it is they that bear witness about me, yet you refuse to come to me that you may have life" (John 5:39–40). Of the Pharisees he asserted through a parable, "If they do not hear Moses and the Prophets, neither will they be convinced if someone should rise from the dead" (Luke 16:31). The Jewish leaders were spiritually blind, unable to see how the Old Testament itself pointed to Christ.

Matthew highlights several episodes in Jesus's life where he treats those who were supposed to be masters of the Scriptures as though they didn't know how to read them. The Pharisees could not understand their own Scriptures:

> Have you not read what David did when he was hungry? . . . Or have you not read in the Law how on the Sabbath the priests in the temple profane the Sabbath and are guiltless? . . . If you had known what this means, "I desire mercy, and not sacrifice," you would not have condemned the guiltless. (Matt. 12:3, 5, 7)

> Have you not read that he who created them from the beginning made them male and female? (Matt. 19:4)

> Have you never read,

> "Out of the mouth of infants and nursing babies
>   you have prepared praise"? (Matt. 21:16)

Have you never read in the Scriptures:

> "The stone that the builders rejected
>   has become the cornerstone"? (Matt. 21:42)

And as for the resurrection of the dead, have you not read what was said to you by God? (Matt. 22:31)

The Gospels indicate the roots of such blindness. For example, Jesus again addresses the Pharisees and Sadducees, asserting, "You know how to interpret the appearance of the sky, but you cannot interpret the signs of the times. An evil and adulterous generation seeks for a sign!" (Matt. 16:3–4). At the core, their inability to interpret rightly was related to their innate evil and adultery against God. Similarly, Mark points to the leaders' "hardness" as the reason they refused to celebrate his coming: "And [Jesus] looked around at them with anger, grieved at their hardness of heart" (Mark 3:5). John further records Jesus's assertion, "Why do you not understand what I say? It is because you cannot bear to hear my word. You are of your father the devil, and your will is to do your father's desires" (John 8:42–44). Earlier John includes Jesus's statement:

> The Father who sent me has himself borne witness about me. His voice you have never heard. . . . I know that you do not have the love of God within you. . . . How can you believe, when you receive glory from one another and do not seek the glory that comes from the only God? Do not think that I will accuse you to the Father. There is one who accuses you: Moses, on whom you have set your hope. For if you believed Moses, you would believe me; for he wrote of me. But if you do not believe his writings, how will you believe my words? (John 5:37, 42–47)

The texts speak of innate wickedness that stands hostile to God, of hard hearts, of desires that are not submitted to God but that are aligned with the devil, and of a passion for man's praise over the glory that comes from God. The religious leaders of Christ's day loved being noticed in the public square and getting the best seats in the synagogues and at feasts (Matt. 23:6; Luke 11:43; 20:46). They were more concerned with their own exaltation than with God's. And the result was that they could not hear God's voice or savor God's beauty and purposes in the Scriptures. Thus, Jesus bemoaned over Jerusalem, "Would that you, even you, had known on this day the things that make for peace! But now they are hidden from your eyes" (Luke 19:42; cf. Isa. 54:13). The leaders were living in spiritual darkness, unable to grasp the Old Testament's testimony of God's glory in the face of Christ. And where the leaders went, the rest of the nation went also.

Speaking of the broader crowd that followed Jesus yet failed to exert saving faith, John writes,

> Though [Jesus] had done so many signs before them, they still did not believe in him, so that the word spoken by the prophet might be fulfilled:
>
> > "Lord, who has believed what he heard from us,
> >   and to whom has the arm of the Lord been revealed?"
>
> Therefore they could not believe. For again Isaiah said,
>
> > "He has blinded their eyes,
> >   and hardened their heart,
> > lest they see with their eyes,
> >   and understand with their heart, and turn,
> >   and I will heal them."
>
> Isaiah said these things because he saw his glory and spoke of him. (John 12:37–41)

Note that John stresses that the people's deafness and blindness were "that the word spoken by the prophet [Isaiah] might be fulfilled." God intended that his word through the prophets would be like a closed book until the time when the revealer of mysteries would come. Thus, quoting Isaiah 6:9–10, Jesus disclosed to his disciples the meaning of his teaching, declaring,

> To you has been given the secret [or "mystery"] of the kingdom of God, but for those outside everything is in parables, so that

"they may indeed see but not perceive,
  and may indeed hear but not understand,
lest they should turn and be forgiven." (Mark 4:12)

Paul echoes the realities we've seen thus far when he writes,

Israel failed to obtain what it was seeking. The elect obtained it, but the rest were hardened, as it is written,

"God gave them a spirit of stupor,
  eyes that would not see
  and ears that would not hear,
down to this very day." (Rom. 11:7–8)

The apostle draws the phrase "to this very day" from Moses's words in Deuteronomy 29:4 that "*to this day* the LORD has not given you a heart to understand or eyes to see or ears to hear." The rest he cites from Isaiah's statement regarding the ungodly:

The LORD has poured out upon you [Israel]
  a spirit of deep sleep,
and has closed your eyes. (Isa. 29:10)

Elsewhere, the apostle emphasizes, "The [Jews'] minds were hardened. For to this day, when they read the old covenant, that same veil remains unlifted, because only through Christ is it taken away" (2 Cor. 3:14). For Paul, Moses's veil that he wore after encountering the divine presence served as a parable of the people's spiritual emptiness. "To this day, whenever Moses is read a veil lies over their hearts. But when one turns to the Lord, the veil is removed" (2 Cor. 3:15–16). The old covenant bore a "ministry of condemnation" (2 Cor. 3:9), and only through Christ can one rightly see and celebrate how the Old Testament itself anticipates the superior new covenant's "ministry of righteousness" (2 Cor. 3:9). Through Jesus, God lifts the veil, disclosing how the old covenant had always magnified Christ's glory.

The old covenant age was one of ignorance and hardness (Acts 17:30; Eph. 4:18; 1 Pet. 1:14), with the devil keeping most of the world blind to

God's glories culminating in Christ. "If our gospel is veiled, it is veiled to those who are perishing. In their case, the god of this world has blinded the minds of the unbelievers, to keep them from seeing the light of the gospel of the glory of Christ, who is the image of God" (2 Cor. 4:3–4). But in Jesus new creation dawns, with gospel light breaking over the horizon and dispersing darkness and shadow. "God, who said, 'Let light shine out of darkness,' has shone in our hearts to give the light of the knowledge of the glory of God in the face of Jesus Christ" (2 Cor. 4:6).

Why would God purpose to extend such a season of hardness, ignorance, and blindness where the majority did *not* understand his word, cherish his precepts, heed his commands, or hope in his promises? Paul believes God purposed to move those receiving his mercy to marvel more at his manifold glory in Christ:

> What if God, desiring to show his wrath and to make known his power, has endured with much patience vessels of wrath prepared for destruction, in order to make known the riches of his glory for vessels of mercy, which he has prepared beforehand for glory—even us whom he has called, not from the Jews only but also from the Gentiles? (Rom. 9:22–24)

The Lord made the darkness so deep and the night so long so that we on whom the light has dawned may be able to savor even more the warmth, brilliance, and merciful glory of God bound up in his gift of Christ.

Some of the Remnant's Delayed Understanding of the Old Testament

The New Testament is clear that some were anticipating Christ's coming and rightly grasped his person and work. At the beginning of his Gospel, Matthew notes how a group of "wise men from the east" saw a star that they associated with the "king of the Jews" and came to worship him (Matt. 2:1–2). The Jewish leaders were then able to note from their Scriptures that the Messiah was to be born "in Bethlehem of Judah" (Matt. 2:5–6).

Similarly, with many allusions to Old Testament texts, Luke narrates how Gabriel told Mary that the son whom she was to call Jesus would "be great," "called the Son of the Most High," and reign on "the throne of his father David . . . over the house of Jacob forever" (Luke 1:32–33). With allusions back to Hannah's prediction of the messianic king (see 1 Sam. 2:1–10), Mary then praises God as the one who

has helped his servant Israel,
>   in remembrance of his mercy,
> as he spoke to our fathers,
>   to Abraham and to his offspring forever. (Luke 1:54–55)

Zechariah, too, recognized his own son John [the Baptizer] as a pointer to the coming Redeemer, who would be

> a horn of salvation for us
>   in the house of his servant David. (Luke 1:69)

Devout Simeon was "waiting for the consolation of Israel" (Luke 2:25) and for "the Lord's Christ" (2:26). Upon seeing Jesus, he declared,

> My eyes have seen your salvation
>   that you have prepared in the presence of all peoples,
> a light for revelation to the Gentiles,
>   and for glory to your people Israel. (Luke 2:30–32)

Not only this but he also appears to have anticipated Jesus's mission of suffering and how he would separate the righteous and unrighteous, when he told Mary, "Behold, this child is appointed for the fall and rising of many in Israel, and for a sign that is opposed (and a sword will pierce through your own soul also), so that thoughts from many hearts may be revealed" (Luke 2:34–35).[16] There were many in Jesus's day who were "waiting for the redemption of Jerusalem" (Luke 2:38).

Nevertheless, many of the disciples closest to Jesus failed to recognize fully who he was and all that their Scriptures anticipated about him. After noting that he was now revealing "the secret [or "mystery"] of the kingdom of God" to them (Mark 4:11), Jesus queried, "Do you not understand this parable?" (4:13). Later, following both his feeding of the five thousand and his calming of the storm, his disciples still "did not understand about the loaves, but their hearts were hardened" (Mark 6:52). Rather than recognizing that Jesus controlled

---

16 See John Nolland, *Luke 1–9:20*, WBC (Dallas: Word, 1989), 121–22; Robert H. Stein, *Luke*, NAC (Nashville: Broadman & Holman, 1992), 116–17; Joel B. Green, *The Gospel of Luke*, NICNT (Grand Rapids, MI: Eerdmans, 1997), 149–50.

creation and was their satisfier and supply, they still failed to see him for who he was. Jesus regularly charged the crowds to "hear" and "understand" (e.g., Mark 4:9, 23; 7:14), but he remained astonished that his closest followers did not grasp his meaning: "Then are you also without understanding? Do you not see?" (7:18). And again, "Do you not yet perceive or understand? Are your hearts hardened?" (Mark 8:17; cf. 8:21). We then read, "But they did not understand the saying, and were afraid to ask him" (Mark 9:32).

Significantly, Mark uses two parallel healing accounts to highlight the progressive growth of the disciples' understanding. Mark first compares Jesus's two-stage healing of the blind man (Mark 8:22–26) with Peter's partial understanding of Jesus's identity and mission. Peter rightfully confesses that Jesus is the Christ (Mark 8:27–30) but does not align with God's purposes for Jesus culminating in the cross (8:31–33). Next, Mark's account of Jesus's instantaneous and complete healing of blind Bartimaeus in Jericho signals how fuller understanding will come the more one embraces Jesus's mission of death and resurrection in Jerusalem (Mark 10:46–52).

Luke too emphasizes the disciples' lack of knowledge of the Old Testament. After his resurrection, Jesus challenged the two on the road to Emmaus, "O foolish ones, and slow of heart to believe all that the prophets have spoken! Was it not necessary that the Christ should suffer these things and enter into his glory?" (Luke 24:25–26). Even the closest followers of Jesus were culpable for failing to see. What mercy, then, is shown by Christ in disclosing himself by opening the Old Testament word to minds once closed. Following their encounter with the resurrected Christ, Christ's two students recalled, "Did not our hearts burn within us while he talked to us on the road, while *he opened to us the Scriptures*?" (Luke 24:32).[17] Christ made them wise to the Old Testament's meaning, thus fulfilling what both Isaiah and Daniel said would come to pass—that after a season of ignorance

> the deaf shall hear
>   the words of a book,
> and out of their gloom and darkness
>   the eyes of the blind shall see (Isa. 29:18)

---

17 See Dane C. Ortlund, "'And Their Eyes Were Opened, and They Knew': An Inter-Canonical Note on Luke 24:31," *JETS* 53, no. 4 (2010): 717–28.

and that at the time of the end "those who are wise shall understand" (Dan. 12:10).[18]

Luke further unpacks what the resurrected Christ enables with respect to the initial three-fourths of the Bible. After his encounter with the two men, he appeared to a group that included the eleven remaining apostles. We read, "Then he said to them, 'These are my words that I spoke to you while I was still with you, that everything written about me in the Law of Moses and the Prophets and the Psalms must be fulfilled.' Then *he opened their minds to understand the Scriptures*" (Luke 24:44–45). The resurrected Christ now allows the community associated with him to see things in the biblical text that were there all along but ungraspable without the correct light and lens. Jesus was revealing a "mystery" that was not totally new revelation (their gaining understanding of *the Scriptures*), but its full disclosure was to a significant extent hidden to them.[19] In Christ, God "enlightens" the eyes of our hearts (Eph. 1:18). He shines into our once darkened hearts "to give the light of the knowledge of the glory of God in the face of Jesus Christ" (2 Cor. 4:6). He grants "strength to comprehend" the love of God (Eph. 3:18–19), "revealing" Jesus to us (Matt. 13:16) and "giving us understanding" (2 Tim. 2:7).

John's Gospel in particular highlights how Christ's resurrection and glorification mark a turning point in the disciples' understanding of Scripture, providing a lens for reading rightly.[20]

18 Luke tells us that the meaning of Jesus's impending tribulation and resurrection is "concealed" (Luke 9:45) and "hidden" (18:34) from the disciples and that the eyes of those with Christ on the road to Emmaus "*were kept* from recognizing him" (24:16). In view of Jesus's stress that the Father and Son alone reveal truths about Jesus's person and work (Luke 10:21–22) and Luke's comments that the disciples' eyes "were opened" (24:31), Jesus "opened" the Scriptures to them (24:32), and Jesus "opened" their minds to grasp the Scripture's meaning (24:45), Tabb concludes, "*God* is ultimately the one who prevents the disciples from initially grasping Jesus's true identity. . . . Jesus brings *clarity* to the Bible's central message and gives his disciples the spiritual *capacity* to grasp his teaching. The word translated as 'opened' (*dianoigō*) is used three times (vv. 31, 32, 45) to highlight our dual need for *revelation* and *receptivity*." Brian J. Tabb, *After Emmaus: How the Church Fulfills the Mission of Christ* (Wheaton, IL: Crossway, 2021), 26 (emphasis in original).
19 Beale and Gladd, *Hidden but Now Revealed*, 30.
20 See especially D. A. Carson, "Understanding Misunderstandings in the Fourth Gospel," *TynBul* 33 (1982): 59–91; Ardel Caneday, "The Word Made Flesh as Mystery Incarnate: Revealing and Concealing Dramatized by Jesus as Portrayed in John's Gospel," *JETS* 60, no. 4 (2017): 751–65. Caneday notes the difference between the two articles as follows: "While Carson's focuses on the disciples' *reception* of Christ's revelation, my thesis accents Christ's revelatory *impartation*" (753, emphasis in original).

The Jews then said, "It has taken forty-six years to build this temple, and will you raise it up in three days?" But [Jesus] was speaking about the temple of his body. When therefore he was raised from the dead, his disciples remembered that he had said this, and they believed the Scripture and the word that Jesus had spoken. (John 2:20–22)

Jesus's resurrection moved the disciples to embrace in a fresh way both "the Scripture and the word that Jesus had spoken." Consider also the final comments in the verses below.

They took branches of palm trees and went out to meet him, crying out, "Hosanna! Blessed is he who comes in the name of the Lord, even the King of Israel!" And Jesus found a young donkey and sat on it, just as it is written,

"Fear not, daughter of Zion;
behold, your king is coming,
    sitting on a donkey's colt!"

His disciples did not understand these things at first, but when Jesus was glorified, then they remembered that these things had been written about him and had been done to him. (John 12:13–16)

Only when the Father glorified his Son did Christ's followers connect how the Old Testament Scriptures testified to Christ's triumphal entry.

Conclusion

The New Testament authors affirm that the Old Testament was written for Christians (Rom. 4:23–24; 15:4; 1 Cor. 10:11) and that the ancient prophets knew that they were writing for the benefit of new covenant saints (1 Pet. 1:12). Yahweh's prophets knew something about Christ and the time of his coming (1 Pet. 1:10–11; cf. John 8:56; Acts 2:30–31; Heb. 11:13), but the full meaning of an Old Testament text at times transcended the human author's understanding.

Fulfilling the prophecy of Isaiah (John 12:37–40; cf. Isa. 6:10; 53:1), the innate wickedness and hard-heartedness of most of the Jewish leaders and broader Jewish populous rendered them spiritually disabled. In judgment, God hardened them so that they were unable to understand his word or see his purposes culminating in Jesus (Rom. 11:7–8). Only "through Christ" is their blindness removed (2 Cor. 3:14).

As early as Jesus's birth, some like Simeon properly understood that the Christ's triumph would only come through tribulation (Luke 2:25–38). However, full understanding of Scripture's testimony about Jesus's death, resurrection, and global mission came to most of his disciples only after his resurrection (Luke 24:45–47; cf. John 2:20–22; 12:13–16).

Review and Reflection

1. According to the New Testament authors, for whom was the Old Testament written? What texts are the most significant in making this point?
2. What is one example of a New Testament author applying the Old Testament to believers today? For each of the examples given, how is the New Testament author using the Old Testament text?
3. Use a couple of New Testament texts to clarify how much of the meaning the Old Testament prophets understood about their own messages.
4. Describe the significance of 1 Peter 1:10–12 for our grasp of how the Old Testament prophets went about their task, why they engaged in it, and what they were seeking to know in relation to Christ.
5. What evidence does the New Testament give that the spiritual disability of old covenant Israel continued into Jesus's day? Among what groups was the disability present?
6. What significant truth does Romans 11:7–8 teach, and to what Old Testament texts does it quote or allude?
7. What important insight does 2 Corinthians 3:14–16 provide regarding how to read the Old Testament as God intended?
8. What special significance does the author see in how Mark uses the two accounts of Jesus's healing a blind man? How did their healings symbolically depict the disciples' growth in understanding?
9. What event enabled Jesus's disciples to understand their Scriptures rightly? What does this imply for us to fully understand the Old Testament today?
10. What was the greatest insight you gained in reading this chapter? What is your greatest takeaway?

2

The Old Testament's Audience and Comprehension

Old Testament Perspective

You will understand this.

JEREMIAH 30:24

THE NEW TESTAMENT AUTHORS RECOGNIZE that the Old Testament is Christian Scripture and that the Old Testament authors knew that a full understanding of their words would only come in the messianic age. This chapter shows that the Old Testament itself affirms these views.

The seers, sages, and songwriters who gave us the Old Testament testify that they were speaking and writing not merely for old covenant saints but also for new covenant believers—those who would enjoy relationship with God in the days of the Messiah and the new creation after Israel's exile. This chapter demonstrates this through four Old Testament examples: Moses, Isaiah, Jeremiah, and Daniel. At the conclusion, it considers some further implications of this fact for new covenant members approaching the Old Testament today.

Moses Anticipates an Age When Those Yahweh Restores Will Heed Moses's Law[1]

Moses's three most frequently used words to characterize Israel were "stubborn" (Deut. 9:6, 13; 10:16; 31:27), "unbelieving" (1:32; 9:23; cf. 28:66), and

---

1 The English term "law" routinely if inadequately translates the Hebrew noun torah. Moses's "law" (Deut. 4:44; cf. 1:5; 3:8; 17:18; 31:9, 11, 24) contains a blending of religious and societal

"rebellious" (9:7, 24; 31:27; cf. 1:26, 43; 9:23). His immediate audience was wicked (Deut. 9:4–6, 27), and he affirmed, "I know how rebellious and stubborn you are. Behold, even today while I am yet alive with you, you have been rebellious against the LORD. How much more after my death! . . . I know that after my death you will surely act corruptly and turn aside from the way that I have commanded you" (31:27, 29). Thus, Yahweh promised that the people's defiance would result in the outpouring of his curses on them:

> When you father children and children's children, and have grown old in the land, if you act corruptly by making a carved image in the form of anything and by doing what is evil in the sight of the LORD your God, so as to provoke him to anger, I call heaven and earth to witness against you today, that you will soon utterly perish from the land that you are going over the Jordan to possess. You will not live long in it, but will be utterly destroyed. And the LORD will scatter you among the peoples, and you will be left few in number among the nations where the LORD will drive you. And there you will serve gods of wood and stone, the work of human hands, that neither see, nor hear, nor eat, nor smell. (Deut. 4:25–28)

And again:

> This people will rise and whore after the foreign gods among them in the land that they are entering, and they will forsake me and break my covenant that I have made with them. Then my anger will be kindled against them in that day, and I will forsake them and hide my face from them, and they will be devoured. (Deut. 31:16–17; cf. 28:15–68)

Deuteronomy 29 tells the ultimate reason why Moses's immediate audience would not heed his words: "You have seen all that the LORD did before your eyes in the land of Egypt. . . . But to this day the LORD has not given you a heart to understand or eyes to see or ears to hear" (Deut. 29:2, 4).

instructions captured under terms like "testimonies" (6:20), "rituals/statutes" and "rules/judgments" (4:45; 5:1; 11:32), "commandments" (5:10, 29; 6:2, 17; 7:9; 8:2, 6, 11; 10:13; 11:1, 13, 27), "commandment" (5:31; 6:1, 25; 7:11; 8:1; 11:8, 22), and "charge/restriction" (11:1).

Israel was spiritually ignorant of God's ways, blind to his glories, and deaf to his word. They had been rebellious from the day Moses first met them (Deut. 9:24), and their stubbornness was still present and would continue into the future, resulting in their death (9:6; 31:27, 29).[2] In Moses's day, Yahweh had not overcome the resistance of the majority's hearts, and in alignment with his sovereign purposes for salvation history, he created the old covenant to bear a "ministry of death" and a "ministry of condemnation" so that through Christ a superior new covenant might bear a "ministry of righteousness" (2 Cor. 3:7, 9).[3]

Yahweh determined that he would not overcome Israel's crookedness and twistedness (Deut. 32:5; Acts 2:40; Phil. 2:15) until the prophet like Moses would rise to whom they should and could listen (Deut. 18:15; 30:8; cf. Matt. 17:5). In the age of restoration, Yahweh would change the remnant's hearts and enable their love. "The LORD your God will circumcise your heart . . . so that you will love the LORD your God with all your heart and with all your soul" (Deut. 30:6). In this end-times period, the

2   Block believes that Deut. 29:4 teaches that, "whereas the exodus generation as a whole did not grasp the revelatory, redemptive, and covenantal significance of Yahweh's actions (9:1–24; cf. 1:19–46), this generation knows; through Moses's final pastoral addresses Yahweh has given Israel a heart to know, eyes to see, and ears to hear." Daniel I. Block, *Deuteronomy*, NIVAC (Grand Rapids, MI: Zondervan, 2012), 676. This reading, however, fails to account for many factors: (1) Elsewhere in the book the phrase "until this day" never implies change (Deut. 2:22; 3:14; 10:8; 11:4; 34:6). See Paul A. Barker, *Triumph of Grace in Deuteronomy: Faithless Israel, Faithful Yahweh in Deuteronomy* (Eugene, OR: Wipf and Stock, 2007), 118–19. (2) Moses explicitly notes elsewhere that Israel's stubbornness persists in the present and will continue (Deut. 31:21, 27), thus forcing Block himself to admit that "Moses shares Yahweh's pessimistic view of the spiritual state of the people." Block, *Deuteronomy*, 734. (3) Both Isa. 6:10 and Jer. 5:21 stress that the triad of spiritual disability in "heart, eyes, and ears" continued in these prophets' days, and Paul alludes to Moses's "until this day" (Deut. 29:4) in both Rom. 11:8 and 2 Cor. 3:14, showing that Israel's hardness continued into the New Testament era. (4) The prophets believed that God would only reverse the majority's disability related to "heart, eyes, ears" in the day when the messianic "king will reign in righteousness" (Isa. 32:1, 3–4). Recognizably, the remnant, which would have included the prophets, had "hearts, eyes, and ears" that were responsive to God (Ezek. 40:4), already having "the eyes of [their] hearts enlightened" (Eph. 1:18). For an extended survey of interpretations of Deut. 29:4, see Michael A. Grisanti, "Was Israel Unable to Respond to God? A Study of Deuteronomy 29:2–4," *BSac* 163 (2006): 176–96. Grisanti's own proposal rightly affirms the presence of a remnant in the Old Testament who had their "hearts, eyes, and ears" enabled, but he fails to appreciate that the triad of metaphors refers to regeneration, which gives rise to faith rather than follows it (see John 3:3, 8).

3   Jason S. DeRouchie, "From Condemnation to Righteousness: A Christian Reading of Deuteronomy," *SBJT* 18, no. 3 (2014): 87–118; cf. Jason S. DeRouchie, "The Use of Leviticus 18:5 in Galatians 3:12: A Redemptive-Historical Reassessment," *Them* 45, no. 2 (2020): 240–59.

age we now identify with the new covenant and church (cf. Rom. 2:29; 2 Cor. 3:6), Moses's message in Deuteronomy would finally be heard and heeded: "And you will turn and you will hear the voice of the Lord and do all his commandments that I am commanding you today" (Deut. 30:8, author's translation). Moses believed that his instruction in Deuteronomy would serve those in the age of heart circumcision far more than the unbelieving rebels of his own day.[4]

---

4   Deuteronomy 30:11–14 does not present a counterargument to this claim. While contemporary English versions and most commentators treat 30:11–14 as expressing Israel's present ability to keep God's law, the greater context of the book does not support this reading (Deut. 29:4; cf. 4:25–28; 9:6; 10:16; 30:1; 31:16–18, 27–29). Moreover, the subordinate connection *ki* in 30:11 most naturally provides a reason ("for, because") for the *preceding* future predictions, thus suggesting that the verbless clauses in 30:11–14 should all be translated as futures and that Moses's statement that all he commanded "today" in 30:11 would align with the similar statements in 30:2 and 8. Thus 30:11–14 *predictively* clarifies why Israel will "listen" to Yahweh's voice (30:2, 8, 10; cf. 30:12, 13) and "do" (30:8, 10; cf. 30:12, 13, 14) his word in the future when they were not able to do so in the present. On this reading, Paul in Rom. 10:6–8 would be identifying the fulfillment of this prediction in Christ, and his contrast between Lev. 18:5 in Rom. 10:5 and Deut. 30:11–14 in Rom. 10:6–8 would be between texts addressing two different eras in redemption history. In support of this exegetical conclusion, see Colin J. Smothers, *In Your Mouth and in Your Heart: A Study of Deuteronomy 30:12–14 in Paul's Letter to the Romans* (Eugene, OR: Pickwick, 2022); cf. John H. Sailhamer, *The Pentateuch as Narrative: A Biblical-Theological Commentary*, Library of Biblical Interpretation (Grand Rapids, MI: Zondervan, 1992), 473; J. Gary Millar, *Now Choose Life: Theology and Ethics in Deuteronomy*, NSBT 6 (Downers Grove, IL: InterVarsity Press, 1998), 94, 174–75; Steven R. Coxhead, "Deuteronomy 30:11–14 as a Prophecy of the New Covenant in Christ," *WTJ* 68, no. 2 (2006): 305–20; Barker, *Triumph of Grace in Deuteronomy*, 168–90; Bryan D. Estelle, "Leviticus 18:5 and Deuteronomy 30:1–14 in Biblical Theological Development: Entitlement to Heaven Foreclosed and Proffered," in *The Law Is Not of Faith: Essays on Works and Grace in the Mosaic Covenant*, ed. Bryan D. Estelle, J. V. Fesko, and David VanDrunen (Phillipsburg, NJ: P&R, 2009), 123–37. While Moo chooses to render Deut. 30:11–14 as present time, he does admit, "I wish I could interpret Deut 30:11–14 in this way: it would, indeed, considerably diminish the apparent dissonance between this text and Paul's application." Douglas Moo, "Paul's Reading of Deuteronomy: Law and Grace," in *For Our Good Always: Studies on the Message and Influence of Deuteronomy in Honor of Daniel I. Block*, ed. Jason S. DeRouchie, Jason Gile, and Kenneth J. Turner (Winona Lake, IN: Eisenbrauns, 2013), 408. Significantly, the only reason that keeps Moo from this reading is that "most interpreters of Deuteronomy argue that the characteristic language of 'today' in v. 11 suggests that the implied tense in vv. 11–14 shifts back to the present," but this understanding fails to account for the uses of "today" in the immediate future contexts of 30:2 and 8 and for the most natural rendering of *ki* in 30:11. Furthermore, Moo himself notes that "most commentators do not even mention the [future] alternative" (408n56), suggesting that they likely were simply following the majority of English versions and did not wrestle in detail with the text itself. Using Paul's words, the overwhelming view of Deuteronomy is that the function of the old covenant in redemptive history was to bear "a ministry of death" and "a ministry of condemnation" (2 Cor. 3:7, 9),

Isaiah Anticipates a Day When Those Once
Spiritually Deaf Will Hear His Words

Israel's threefold spiritual disability (heart, eyes, ears) continued in the days of Isaiah, whom Yahweh called to

> make the heart of this people dull,
>> and their ears heavy,
>> and blind their eyes. (Isa. 6:10; cf. Deut. 29:4)

Thus, the prophet was to preach,

> Keep on hearing, but do not understand;
> keep on seeing, but do not perceive. (Isa. 6:9)

This would be the prophet's judgment cry until his land was laid waste, his people were destroyed, and all that remained was a "stump" or "holy seed" (Isa. 6:11–13; cf. 11:1; 53:2).[5] Speaking of God's servant-nation, Isaiah later says,

> He sees many things, but does not observe them;
>> his ears are open, but he does not hear. (Isa. 42:20)

> Bring out the people who are blind, yet have eyes,
>> who are deaf, yet have ears! (Isa. 43:8)

"They know not, nor do they discern, for he has shut their eyes, so that they cannot see, and their hearts, so that they cannot understand" (Isa. 44:18). Yahweh purposed that Israel's history would be characterized by "deep sleep" and the inability to "read" the word. It was as if Isaiah's words and

---

all so that "God, desiring to show his wrath and to make known his power, has endured with much patience vessels of wrath prepared for destruction, in order to make known the riches of his glory for vessels of mercy, which he has prepared beforehand for glory" (Rom. 9:22–23).

5   For more on this text, see Craig A. Evans, *To See and Not Perceive: Isaiah 6.9–10 in Early Jewish and Christian Interpretation* (Sheffield: JSOT, 1989); cf. Craig A. Evans, "Isa 6:9–13 in the Context of Isaiah's Theology," *JETS* 29, no. 2 (1986): 139–46.

the rest of the Scriptures were a sealed book to the bulk of the prophet's contemporaries. As Isaiah states in 29:9–11,

> Astonish yourselves and be astonished;
> blind yourselves and be blind!
> . . . .
> For the LORD has poured out upon you
> a spirit of deep sleep,
> and has closed your eyes (the prophets),
> and covered your heads (the seers).

And the vision of all this has become to you like the words of a book that is sealed. When men give it to one who can read, saying, "Read this," he says, "I cannot, for it is sealed."

Isaiah's audience could neither comprehend nor appropriate God's word because Yahweh had hardened them. Paul stresses this point when he brings together Isaiah 29:10 with Deuteronomy 29:4 in Romans 11:7–8:

Israel failed to obtain what it was seeking. The elect obtained it, but the rest were hardened, as it is written,

> "God gave them a spirit of stupor,
> eyes that would not see
> and ears that would not hear,
> down to this very day."

Similarly, when Paul turned away from the hard-hearted Jews in Rome to preach to the Gentiles, he identified the lasting impact of Isaiah's mission to harden in Isaiah 6:9–10 (Acts 28:26–27).

We can rejoice that salvation history did not end in darkness and silence. As Isaiah further notes, Yahweh promised,

> In that day the deaf shall hear
> the words of a book,

and out of their gloom and darkness
    the eyes of the blind shall see. (Isa. 29:18)

Because God instructed Isaiah to write his words in a book for a perpetual witness and because most of his own audience could not grasp these words, his book writing was principally for a later generation that would have hearts to know, eyes to see, and ears to hear.

> And now, go, write it before them on a tablet
>   and inscribe it in a book,
> that it may be for the time to come
>   as a witness forever. (Isa. 30:8)

> Your Teacher will not hide himself anymore, but your eyes shall see your Teacher. And your ears shall hear a word behind you, saying, "This is the way, walk in it." (Isa. 30:20–21)

Similarly, we are told that in the day when the messianic "king will reign in righteousness" (Isa. 32:1),

> Then the eyes of those who see will not be closed,
>   and the ears of those who hear will give attention.
> The heart of the hasty will understand and know. (Isa. 32:3–4;
>   cf. 35:5)

And again, of the Spirit-empowered, royal servant, God would declare,

> I will give you as a covenant for the people,
>   a light for the nations,
>   to open the eyes that are blind,
> to bring out the prisoners from the dungeon,
>   from the prison those who sit in darkness. (Isa. 42:6–7)

There was a small remnant of Isaiah's contemporaries who understood his message, at least at some level: "Bind up the testimony; seal the teaching among my disciples [lit., my taught ones]" (Isa. 8:16). Nevertheless,

God promised that one day there would be a broad acceptance of such knowledge: "My people shall know my name" and "shall know that it is I who speak" (Isa. 52:6). "All your children shall be taught by the LORD" (Isa. 54:13). Yahweh's law would go forth in "the latter days," and its recipients would include many from the "nations/peoples" (Isa. 2:3; 51:4–5). That is, while most Israelites from the time of Isaiah through the time of Jesus and the early church did not believe what they heard but rebelled, having their spiritual senses dull (Isa. 53:1 with John 12:38 and Rom. 10:16; Isa. 65:2 with Rom. 10:21), the prophet envisioned that God would one day disclose himself to many who never sought him (Isa. 65:1 with Rom. 10:20) and that kings from many nations would see "that which had not been told them" and understand "that which they have not heard" (Isa. 52:15 with Rom. 15:21). Isaiah associates the proclamation of this end-times instruction with the teaching and rule of the royal servant (Isa. 42:1, 4), who would

> sustain with a word
> him who is weary. (Isa. 50:4; cf. Matt. 11:28–30; 28:20)[6]

Building on this Old Testament context, Jesus indicated that through his own teaching God was fulfilling these promises by drawing a multi-ethnic people to himself. Jesus declared, "No one can come to me unless the Father who sent me draws him. And I will raise him up on the last day. It is written in the Prophets, 'And they will all be taught by God.' Everyone who has heard and learned from the Father comes to me" (John 6:44–45; cf. Isa. 54:13). Christ's sheep would include some not from the Jewish fold (John 10:16), yet all his sheep would "believe," "hear" his voice, and follow (10:27). To these awakened and responsive believers, the Lord would supply

> the secret of the kingdom of God, but for those outside everything is in parables, so that

---

6 Cf. Charles E. Hill, "God's Speech in These Last Days: The New Testament Canon as an Eschatological Phenomenon," in *Resurrection and Eschatology: Theology in Service of the Church; Essays in Honor of Richard B. Gaffin Jr.*, ed. Lane G. Tipton and Jeffrey C. Waddington (Phillipsburg, NJ: P&R, 2008), 203–54.

"they may indeed see but not perceive,
  and may indeed hear but not understand,
lest they should turn and be forgiven." (Mark 4:11–12; citing
    Isa. 6:9–10)

Isaiah himself saw that his writings would benefit a future transformed, multiethnic generation more than they would the spiritually disabled of his own day. In short, Isaiah would have agreed with Paul that he wrote his book for Christians.

Now, living on this side of the cross, we are the ones who can enter with Isaiah into the throne room and tremble at the sound of "Holy, holy, holy is the LORD" (Isa. 6:3). We are the ones who can testify that a people walking "in darkness have seen a great light" (Isa. 9:2)—a light emanating from a person whose very identity is "God with us" (7:14) and whose characterization through his eternal and universal reign is

Wonderful Counselor, Mighty God,
  Everlasting Father, Prince of Peace. (Isa. 9:6)

We Christians are the ones who can truly begin to celebrate the portrait of Yahweh's incomparability in Isaiah 40. And we are the ones—Jews and Gentiles in Christ—whom God's righteous royal servant has accounted righteous through his substitutionary atoning work portrayed in Isaiah 53. To the majority in Israel, the prophecies of Isaiah were like a sealed book until Yahweh's Spirit came upon this servant-hearted, royal God-man, and he began to proclaim the good news of provision to the poor, of healing to the sick, of freedom to the captives, and of comfort and joy—full joy— to those who mourn (Isa. 61:1–2; cf. Luke 4:18–19).

Jeremiah Anticipates Days When His Book Will Guide Those Who Know Yahweh

As he did with Isaiah (Isa. 30:8), Yahweh told Jeremiah that his writing was specifically intended for a future, postexilic, restored community of God.

Thus says the LORD, the God of Israel: Write in a book all the words that I have spoken to you. For behold, days are coming, declares the LORD, when I will restore the fortunes of my people, Israel and Judah, says the Lord, and I will bring them back to the land that I gave to their fathers, and they shall take possession of it. (Jer. 30:2–3)

While there was the potential that some of Jeremiah's contemporaries would repent upon hearing his words read (Jer. 36:2–3), God told Jeremiah that most would not heed his voice, for they would retain the same stubbornness that characterized previous generations (7:23–28; cf. 22:21). Moreover, 30:2–3 stress that the reason Jeremiah needed to write his words in a book (cf. Jer. 36:2, 4, 17–18, 28–32) was because the *future* generations would need them. While his verbal sermons condemned those in his days, his written words were less for his present generation and more for the generations of the restored community.

The prophet further notes that only in the latter days would full understanding of his writings come.

> "The fierce anger of the Lord will not turn back
>> until he has executed and accomplished
>> the intentions of his mind.
> *In the latter days you will understand this.*"

At that time, declares the Lord, I will be the God of all the clans of Israel, and they shall be my people." (Jer. 30:24–31:1; cf. 23:19–20)

The "you" in this passage is plural and refers to the members of the restored new covenant community in the latter days.[7] This is the most natural referent

---

7 Jack Lundbom notes that the Medieval Jewish rabbi Joseph Kimḥi (AD 1105–1170) identified the time of "understanding" in Jer. 30:24 with the messianic era (see Dan. 2:28; Hos. 3:5; cf. Gen. 49:1, 8–9; Num. 24:14, 17–19; Deut. 4:30–31; 31:29; Isa. 2:2; Jer. 23:20; 48:47; 49:39; Ezek. 38:16; Dan. 10:14; Mal. 4:1), but Lundbom himself follows the majority critical view that "eschatological meaning is not present in the pre-exilic use of this expression." Jack R. Lundbom, *Jeremiah 21–36: A New Translation with Introduction and Commentary*, AB (New Haven: Yale University Press, 2004), 198; cf. Horst Seebass, "אַחֲרִית *'acharîth*," *TDOT* 1:210–11; Ernst Jenni, "אחר *'ḥr* after," *TLOT* 1:87–88. Even the conservative J. A. Thompson says Jeremiah's day of understanding "is in the not too distant future; it is not an eschatological concept." J. A. Thompson, *The Book of Jeremiah*, NICOT (Grand Rapids, MI: Eerdmans, 1980), 563. However, Jeremiah's association of the following phrase, "at that time," with the covenant formula ("I will be the God of all the clans of Israel, and they shall be my people," Jer. 31:1) links the period

for two reasons: (1) It is the group about which Jeremiah was just prophesying (Jer. 30:18–22), and the statement, "I will be the God of all the clans of Israel, and they shall be my people" (Jer. 31:1) recalls the same declaration in 30:22, which is associated with the promised "ruler" (Jer. 30:21; cf. 23:5–6; 33:14–26). (2) Jeremiah 31:1 also anticipates 31:33, which restates the covenant formula in direct connection to the "new covenant": "For this is the [new] covenant that I will make with the house of Israel after those days, declares the Lord: I will put my law within them, and I will write it on their hearts. And I will be their God, and they shall be my people" (Jer. 31:33).

Jeremiah's "latter days" of "understanding" are connected (1) to Israel/Judah's restoration from exile and reconciliation with God (Jer. 30:10–11, 17, 18–22; 31:1–40; cf. 23:6–7), (2) to God's punishment of the enemy nations (Jer. 30:11, 16), (3) to the rise of a ruler from the people's midst (Jer. 30:21; cf. 23:5), and (4) to the incorporation of foreigners into the one people of God who too will be surrendered to "the Lord their God and David their king" (Jer. 30:8–9; cf. 3:16–18; 12:14–17; Hos. 3:5).[8] Christ and his church are now fulfilling Jeremiah's new covenant hopes (Luke 22:20; 2 Cor. 3:6; Heb. 8:13; 9:15), which include every covenant member enjoying forgiveness of sins (cf. Heb. 10:12–18) and having a new knowledge: "No longer shall each one teach his neighbor and each his brother, saying, 'Know the Lord,' for they shall all know me, from the least of them to the greatest, declares the Lord. For I will forgive their iniquity, and I will remember their sin no more" (Jer. 31:34). This new knowledge aligns with the earlier promise of "understanding" (Jer. 30:24) and recalls Isaiah's promise that, following the work of the suffering royal servant, "all your children shall be taught by the Lord" (Isa. 54:13). God has "taught" all who have come to Christ so that every Christian "knows" God in a personal way (John 6:45; cf. Matt. 11:27).

Ignorance prevailed in Jeremiah's day, but true knowledge of God and understanding of his Old Testament teaching would characterize the new covenant community. In Jeremiah, knowledge of God relates to an

---

of understanding with both the age of the messianic "prince" (30:21) and the "new covenant," which is when the reinstituted covenant relationship will be realized (31:31, 33). Cf. G. K. Beale, "Eschatology," *DLNT* 330–31.

8 For Jeremiah's vision of how Yahweh will incorporate Gentiles into his one people, see Jason S. DeRouchie, "Counting Stars with Abraham and the Prophets: New Covenant Ecclesiology in Old Testament Perspective," *JETS* 58, no. 3 (2015): 462–65.

experiential involvement in the Lord's commitment to steadfast love, justice, and righteousness (Jer. 9:24; 22:15–16). John later stressed how the knowledge for which Jeremiah longed is now enjoyed by *all* who are in Christ. "You all have knowledge. I write to you, not because you do not know the truth, but because you know it, and because no lie is of the truth" (1 John 2:20–21; cf. 2:27–29; 1 Thess. 4:9).

Daniel Anticipates the Time of the End When the Wise Will Understand All of His Prophecies

The book of Daniel is filled with symbolic dreams, visions, and declarations—"mysteries" (Dan. 2:18–19, 27–30, 47; 4:9)—some of which God reveals to Daniel so that we are told "he understood the word and had understanding of the vision" (Dan. 10:1; cf. 10:11–14). Indeed, Daniel grasped something of both the person and time of the Messiah's ministry (Dan. 9:24–25; cf. 1 Pet. 1:10–11).[9] Nevertheless, there are elaborations on these latter-day prophecies related to the kingdoms of God and mankind so that Daniel asserts, "I was appalled by the vision and did not understand it" (Dan. 8:27), and again, "I heard, but I did not understand" (12:8). He even pursues clarification, yet the Lord tells his prophet to "shut up the words and seal the book, until the time of the end" (Dan. 12:4). The "end" is God's appointed period in salvation history when he would fully disclose his purposes to the wise.[10]

[The divine messenger said,] "And many of those who sleep in the dust of the earth shall awake, some to everlasting life, and some to shame and everlasting contempt. And those who are wise shall shine like the brightness of the sky above; and those who turn many to righteousness,

9   The most satisfying interpretation of Dan. 9:24–27 is found in "The New Covenant in Daniel's Seventy Weeks," in Peter J. Gentry and Stephen J. Wellum, *Kingdom through Covenant: A Biblical-Theological Understanding of the Covenants*, 2nd ed. (Wheaton, IL: Crossway, 2018), 599–643. Gentry's discussion in this second edition is a substantial advance on his previous studies. See also Sam Storms, *Kingdom Come: The Amillennial Alternative* (Fearn, Scotland: Mentor, 2013), 71–133.

10 For more on "mystery" in Daniel and its implications for our understanding of continuity and discontinuity between the Testaments, see G. K. Beale and Benjamin L. Gladd, *Hidden but Now Revealed: A Biblical Theology of Mystery* (Downers Grove, IL: IVP Academic, 2014), 29–46. Cf. Benjamin L. Gladd, *Revealing the Mysterion: The Use of Mystery in Daniel and Second Temple Judaism with Its Bearing on First Corinthians*, BZNW 160 (Berlin: de Gruyter, 2008).

like the stars forever and ever. But you, Daniel, shut up the words and
seal the book, until the time of the end. Many shall run to and fro, and
knowledge shall increase." . . . And someone said . . . , "How long shall it
be till the end of these wonders?" And I heard the man . . . [say] that it
would be for a time, times, and a half a time, and that when the shattering
of the power of the holy people comes to an end all these things would be
finished. I heard, but *I did not understand.* Then I said, "O my lord, what
shall be the outcome of these things?" He said, "Go your way, Daniel, for
the words are shut up and sealed until the time of the end. Many shall
purify themselves and make themselves white and be refined, but the
wicked shall act wickedly. And none of the wicked shall understand, but
those who are wise shall understand. . . . But go your way till the end.
And you shall rest and shall stand in your allotted place at the end of the
days." (Dan. 12:2–4, 6–10, 13)

Daniel envisioned that only at "the time of the end" or at the appointed
last "hour" (as the phrase is rendered in the Greek translation of Dan. 8:17,
19; 10:14; 11:35, 40; 12:1) would some people grasp the full meaning of his
revelations regarding God's kingdom. That is, the hiddenness of the Old
Testament's meaning would be temporary for the remnant ("those who are
wise") but permanent for the rebels ("the wicked"). From a New Testament
perspective, the first coming of Christ has inaugurated the promised latter
days of realization when the wise can both hear and understand God's words
in this book. For example, after speaking of "the abomination of desolation
spoken of by the prophet Daniel" (cf. Dan. 11:31; 12:11), Matthew adds
an intrusive parenthetical comment: "Let the reader understand" (Matt.
24:15). Matthew believes his readers can begin to grasp the mysteries of
Daniel. Similarly, John records that "in the days of the trumpet call to be
sounded by the seventh angel, the mystery of God would be fulfilled, just
as he announced to his servants the prophets" (Rev. 10:7). Echoing Daniel
12:2–3 and its context, Jesus notes,

Truly, truly, I say to you, an hour is coming, and is now here, when the
dead will hear the voice of the Son of God, and those who hear will live.
. . . Do not marvel at this, for an hour is coming when all who are in the
tombs will hear his voice and come out, those who have done good to

the resurrection of life, and those who have done evil to the resurrection of judgment. (John 5:25, 28–29)[11]

Conclusion

The biblical texts cited above from Deuteronomy, Isaiah, Jeremiah, and Daniel all suggest that Yahweh's Old Testament prophets knew, as Peter would say, "that they were serving not themselves" but us (1 Pet. 1:12), believers on whom has come the end of the ages and to whom has come the revelation of mysteries through Christ (1 Cor. 10:11; 1 Pet. 1:11). The various passages indicate that God withheld the full meaning of his intended messages in at least two ways.

First, Yahweh's prophets were convinced that the unbelieving majority among their contemporaries could not (due to God's punishment) and would not (due to their sinfulness) hear or heed any of the prophets' words (Deut. 29:4; Isa. 6:9–10; 29:10–11). Nevertheless, they also envisioned a day when Yahweh would overcome spiritual disability, thus enabling a sensory, life-changing encounter with the living God (Deut. 30:6, 8; Isa. 29:18; Jer. 30:24). Most people in the Old Testament period were spiritually disabled—blind to the beauties of God, deaf to his laws, and ignorant of both their sin and its remedy. Because they ignored their depravity, they didn't grieve over their rebellion, lean on Yahweh, or long for his Messiah. However, at the rise of the child-King (Isa. 9:6–7), "the people who walked in darkness" would see "a great light" (Isa. 9:2; cf. Matt. 4:15–16).

In that day the deaf shall hear
  the words of a book,
and out of their gloom and darkness
  the eyes of the blind shall see. (Isa. 29:18)

Then "all [Jerusalem's] children shall be taught by the LORD," and their peace will be great (Isa. 54:13; cf. John 6:44–45).

Second, Yahweh's prophets themselves did not always fully grasp the meaning of their predictions and declarations. Thus, Daniel could both

---

11 Cf. Mark 13:11; John 4:23; 12:23; 16:32; 17:1; Acts 2:17; 1 Cor. 10:11; Heb. 1:2; 9:26; 1 Pet. 1:20; 1 John 2:18. See G. K. Beale, "The Old Testament Background of the 'Last Hour' in 1 John 2,18," *Bib* 92, no. 2 (2011): 231–54.

"understand" some words and visions (Dan. 10:1) while not "understand-ing" others (12:8). The remnant of the faithful would only fully comprehend God's intended meaning in "the latter days" (Jer. 30:24) or "the time of the end" (Dan. 12:4, 9–10). Thus, Jesus could say, "Many prophets and kings desired to see what you see, and did not see it, and to hear what you hear, and did not hear it" (Luke 10:24; cf. Matt. 13:17). Christians see more clearly today what the righteous ones of old longed to see but could not.

So, while the prophets understood most of their mysteries, some of their understanding was only partial. Moreover, most of their listeners' spiritual disability rendered them completely unresponsive to Yahweh's voice, un-able to follow his ways, and incapable of seeing and savoring his beauty and purposes culminating in Christ. As Paul would later say, "The mind that is set on the flesh is hostile to God, for it does not submit to God's law; indeed, it cannot" (Rom. 8:7). And again, "The natural person does not accept the things of the Spirit of God, for they are folly to him, and he is not able to understand them because they are spiritually discerned" (1 Cor. 2:14). A supernatural healing and revelation would be required to create fresh responsiveness to the Lord, thus awakening the heart to God's intended meaning of the Old Testament Scriptures. "Now we have received not the spirit of the world, but the Spirit who is from God, that we might understand the things freely given us by God" (1 Cor. 2:12).

Review and Reflection

1. How did Moses characterize Israel, and what did Moses envision for Israel's future?
2. What does Deuteronomy 29:4 say was the ultimate reason for Israel's spiritual disability, and what does this tell you about God's long-term purpose for the old covenant?
3. What hope did Moses have for a change in the people, with what person did he associate this hope, and when did he envision it happening? What role would his teaching play at this time?
4. What evidence is there in Isaiah that Israel's spiritual disability continued among most of his contemporaries?
5. For whom did Isaiah write his book, and when did he believe it would be heard (with spiritual ears) and heeded?
6. How did Jesus see his ministry fulfilling Isaiah's declarations?

7. For what period did Jeremiah write his words in a book, and when did he believe they would be understood by God's people?

8. How does the New Testament indicate the fulfillment of Jeremiah's hopes?

9. What did Daniel indicate would happen at the time of the end in relation to comprehending the full meaning of all his visions?

10. What was the greatest insight you gained in reading this chapter? What is your greatest takeaway?

3

Christ as Light and Lens for
Interpreting the Old Testament

God's mystery, which is Christ.

COLOSSIANS 2:2

WHILE THE OLD TESTAMENT prophets themselves appear to have understood most of what they declared, God did not allow the majority of those in the old covenant to understand his prophets' words (Deut. 29:4; Isa. 6:9–10; 29:10–11). And as a judgment, the people's blindness continued forward into the days of Christ (Mark 4:12; cf. Matt. 13:13–15). Nevertheless, fulfilling what the Old Testament predicts (e.g., Deut. 30:8; Isa. 29:18; Jer. 30:24; Dan. 12:10), Jesus's teaching and work began disclosing to his disciples truths that remained distant from the crowds:

To you has been given the secret [Greek *mystērion*] of the kingdom of God, but for those outside everything is in parables, so that

"they may indeed see but not perceive
   and may indeed hear but not understand,
lest they should turn and be forgiven." (Mark 4:11–12)

The embedded citation is from Isaiah 6:9–10 and highlights how the spiritual disability of Isaiah's day continued into Jesus's for some. The spiritual disability in both periods should be seen as punishment from God.

The New Testament's "mystery" language appears to grow out of the book of Daniel, where the Greek translation of Daniel 2 uses the term *mystērion* ("mystery") to render the Aramaic *raz* (Dan. 2:18–19, 27–30, 47[2x]; cf. 4:9).[1] King Nebuchadnezzar has a troubling dream about a towering image, of which he has partial knowledge (Dan. 2:31–35). He then looks to Daniel for the interpretive revelation that includes full knowledge (Dan. 2:36–45). The "mystery" that God revealed to Daniel (Dan. 2:19) included both the initial dream and its interpretation, as the God in heaven "who reveals *mysteries* . . . made known to King Nebuchadnezzar what will be in the latter days" (2:28; cf. 2:47). When Jesus alludes to this text by speaking about the mystery/secret of the kingdom (Mark 4:11–12), he indicates that the Old Testament's kingdom message would remain permanently hidden for some (cf. 1 Cor. 2:8–9 with Isa. 64:4; Eph. 1:17–18) but only temporarily hidden for others (see Dan. 12:8–9, 12; Matt. 11:25).[2]

Mystery in the New Testament

The New Testament employs the word *mystery* twenty-eight times as a technical term for an end-time reality that was largely (though not entirely) hidden in the Old Testament but that God now discloses more fully through Christ.[3] All the New Testament occurrences deal with the end times and are in some way linked to the Old Testament.[4]

What was this mystery? In the Synoptic Gospels, the "mystery" (Mark 4:11) or "mysteries" of the kingdom (Matt. 13:11; Luke 8:10) relate to the unexpected,

---

1   Benjamin L. Gladd, *Revealing the Mysterion: The Use of Mystery in Daniel and Second Temple Judaism with Its Bearing on First Corinthians*, BZNW 160 (Berlin: de Gruyter, 2008); G. K. Beale and Benjamin L. Gladd, *Hidden but Now Revealed: A Biblical Theology of Mystery* (Downers Grove, IL: IVP Academic, 2014), 29–46; Benjamin L. Gladd, "Mystery," *DNTUOT*, 551–55.

2   Gladd notes, "Temporary hiddenness operates on a redemptive-historical plane and concerns the unveiling of end-times events, whereas permanent hiddenness refers to the persistent inability to understand revelation even after the mystery has been revealed." Gladd, "Mystery," 551–55; cf. D. A. Carson, "Mystery and Fulfillment: Toward a More Comprehensive Paradigm of Paul's Understanding of the Old and New," in *The Paradoxes of Paul*, vol. 2 of *Justification and Variegated Nomism*, ed. D. A. Carson, Peter T. O'Brien, and Mark A. Seifrid (Grand Rapids, MI: Baker Academic, 2004), 432; Beale and Gladd, *Hidden but Now Revealed*, 60–63.

3   See esp. Carson, "Mystery and Fulfillment," 393–436.

4   Beale and Gladd, *Hidden but Now Revealed*, 321, 325–26; Gladd, "Mystery," forthcoming. See Matt. 13:11; Mark 4:11; Luke 8:10; Rom. 11:25; 16:25; 1 Cor. 2:1, 7; 4:1; 13:2; 14:2; 15:51; Eph. 1:9; 3:3–4, 9; 5:32; 6:19; Col. 1:26–27; 2:2; 4:3; 2 Thess. 2:7; 1 Tim. 3:9, 16; Rev. 1:20; 10:7; 17:5, 7.

gradual, already-but-not-yet fulfillment of God's end-times reign. While many Old Testament texts clearly anticipate that Yahweh's reign would come through his anointed servant-king (e.g., Gen. 49:8–10; Num. 24:17–19; Isa. 9:6–7; 11:10; 52:13–15; Dan. 2:44; 7:13–14; Zech. 14:9), the same texts do not as plainly identify an extended period when the remnant that is part of God's kingdom will coexist with the rebel community (cf. Ps. 110:1; Zeph. 3:8–20).[5]

In Paul's epistles, which include twenty-one of the term's New Testament occurrences, the revealed "mystery" or "mysteries" refer to insight into God's end-times purposes (1 Cor. 4:1; 13:2; 14:2; Eph. 1:9) most directly associated with more fully understanding Christ and the gospel (Rom. 16:25; 1 Cor. 2:1, 7; Eph. 3:3–4, 9; 6:19; Col. 2:2; 4:3; 1 Tim. 3:9, 16). This knowledge included grasping better what the gospel implies for end-times suffering (2 Thess. 2:7), for a multistage resurrection (1 Cor. 15:51), and for the people of God both as a multiethnic, adopted community (Rom. 11:25; Eph. 3:3; Col. 1:26–27) and in relation to Christ (Eph. 5:32).[6] Some elements in the gospel's advance are ironic and somewhat unexpected, as in how the God-man reigns in death (1 Cor. 1–2; cf. Isa. 52:13–53:12; Dan. 9:25–26; Zech. 12:10; 13:1), how God's saving Gentiles intersects with his saving Jews (Rom. 11:25–26; cf. Deut. 32:21; Jer. 3:16–18; 30:8–10), and how Gentiles join with Jews as full heirs of all God's promises yet apart from the Mosaic law (Eph. 3:3–4, 9; cf. Isa. 56:3–8; Jer. 3:14–17; Zech. 14:16–19). Through Christ's person and work, God reveals the meaning of every mystery and, by this, clarifies how we are to understand God (theology), salvation (soteriology), the church (ecclesiology), the last days (eschatology), and the like.

Finally, in Revelation "mystery" occurs four times. "The prophets" of old (like in Dan. 11:29–12:13) announced that the "mystery of God would be fulfilled" (Rev. 10:7). This "mystery" relates to the nature of the church (Rev. 1:20) and the self-destructive nature of Babylon (17:5, 7), both elements that Paul's letters also identify (see above).

Israel's spiritual blindness and deafness could be healed only through Jesus. "[The Jews'] minds were hardened. For to this day, when they read the old covenant, that same veil remains unlifted, because only through Christ is it

---

5   For more, see Beale and Gladd, *Hidden but Now Revealed*, 56–83. See also the synthesis in Gladd, "Mystery," forthcoming.

6   For a full survey of these texts in Paul, see Beale and Gladd, *Hidden but Now Revealed*, 85–259; cf. Carson, "Mystery and Fulfillment," 412–25. For a briefer synthesis, see Gladd, "Mystery," forthcoming.

taken away" (2 Cor. 3:14; cf. John 5:39–40; Rom. 11:7–8). Apart from Jesus, the Jews could not fully see and savor the beauty and purposes of God in the Old Testament. But through Christ, God lifts the veil, and the greater glory of the new covenant clarifies the meaning and purpose of the old covenant texts.

What Mystery Implies for Interpreting the Old Testament

Jesus, Paul, and John speak of God revealing a "mystery" to capture the idea of how in Christ we gain full disclosure of things that God significantly hid from most in the old covenant era.[7] Strikingly, the very mystery that is now revealed in and through Christ is also now made known to all nations *through* the Old Testament itself:

> Now to him who is able to strengthen you according to my gospel and the preaching of Jesus Christ, according to the revelation of the *mystery* that was kept secret for long ages but has now been disclosed and *through the prophetic writings has been made known to all nations*, according to the command of the eternal God, to bring about the obedience of faith—to the only wise God be glory forevermore through Jesus Christ! Amen. (Rom. 16:25–27)

From this framework, Paul can also say, "But now the righteousness of God has been manifested apart from the law *to which the Law and the Prophets testify*" (Rom. 3:21, author's translation). In the coming of Christ, an era of understanding replaces an era of ignorance as light overcomes darkness and as God grants a fresh perspective on old truths.

Similarly, Paul writes elsewhere, "You can perceive my insight into the *mystery* of Christ, which was not made known to the sons of men in other generations *as* [Greek *hōs*] it has now been revealed" (Eph. 3:4–5). On this

---

7   The most thorough assessment of these texts is Beale and Gladd, *Hidden but Now Revealed*; cf. Carson, "Mystery and Fulfillment," 393–436. Beale and Gladd write, "The revelation of the mystery is not a totally new revelation but the full disclosure of something that was to a significant extent hidden." Beale and Gladd, *Hidden but Now Revealed*, 30. Similarly, writing with respect to John's Gospel, Carson elsewhere asserts, "Thus we come by another route to something analogous to the dominant notion of μυστήριον ["mystery"] in the Pauline corpus: the gospel is simultaneously said to be hidden in times past but now disclosed, and prophesied in times past and now fulfilled." D. A. Carson, "Reflections on a Johannine Pilgrimage," in *What We Have Heard from the Beginning: The Past, Present, and Future of Johannine Studies*, ed. Tom Thatcher (Waco, TX: Baylor University Press, 2007), 91–92.

text, Benjamin Gladd asserts, "The term 'as' [*hōs*] is key here, for it seems to indicate that OT authors had *some* insight into the unveiled mystery that was disclosed to Paul."[8] We have seen elsewhere that the Old Testament prophets did indeed usually have understanding of their declarations, but Paul here may be referring not to the comprehension of the prophets themselves (which may have been complete) but to the minimal understanding of the broader public, due to their hardness.

Regardless, Beale and Gladd are correct when they affirm that "full or 'complete' meaning is actually 'there' in the Old Testament text; it is simply partially 'hidden' or latent, awaiting a later revelation, whereby the complete meaning of the text is revealed to the interpreter."[9] Likewise, D. A. Carson observes, "Paul thinks of the gospel he preaches as simultaneously something that has been predicted in times past, with those predictions now fulfilled, and something that has been hidden in times past, and now revealed."[10] These parallel truths bear at least three implications for interpreting the Old Testament as Christian Scripture: (1) Only those with spiritual sight can interpret the Old Testament correctly. (2) Jesus's life, death, and resurrection provide a necessary lens for fully understanding the Old Testament's meaning. (3) There is an organic relationship between the Old Testament's testimony and the meaning the New Testament authors attribute to it.

A Relationship with Christ Is Necessary to Understand the Old Testament Rightly

Jesus claimed, "Unless one is born again he *cannot see* the kingdom of God" (John 3:3) and "whoever is of God hears the words of God" (8:47). It is Jesus's sheep who believe, hear his voice, and follow him, whereas those who are not his sheep do not believe (John 10:26–27). John also notes,

They could not believe. For again Isaiah said,

"He has blinded their eyes
and hardened their heart." (John 12:39–40)

---

8   Gladd, "Mystery," forthcoming.
9   Beale and Gladd, *Hidden but Now Revealed*, 330.
10   Carson, "Mystery and Fulfillment," 425.

Similarly, Paul asserts, "For the mind that is set on the flesh is hostile to God, for it does not submit to God's law; indeed, *it cannot*" (Rom. 8:7). He also claims, "The natural person does not accept the things of the Spirit of God, for they are folly to him, and he is *not able to understand* them because they are spiritually discerned" (1 Cor. 2:14). The Scriptures are nothing less than the interpretation of "spiritual truths to those who are spiritual" (1 Cor. 2:13; cf. 2 Pet. 1:20–21). Yet to those who are perishing, the gospel ever remains "veiled," for "the god of this world has blinded the minds of the unbelievers, to keep them from seeing the light of the gospel of the glory of Christ who is the image of God" (2 Cor. 4:3–4).

Regarding many of his Jewish contemporaries, Paul declares, "Their minds were hardened. For to this day, when they read the old covenant, that same veil remains unlifted, because only through Christ is it taken away. Yes, to this day whenever Moses is read a veil lies over their hearts. But when one turns to the Lord, the veil is removed" (2 Cor. 3:14–16). Those who understand "God's mystery, which is Christ" (Col. 2:2; cf. 4:3; Eph. 3:4) are those for whom God "has shown in our hearts to give the light of the knowledge of the glory of God in the face of Jesus Christ" (2 Cor. 4:6). Christ supplies the necessary "light" for properly understanding what God has made known through the prophetic writings (Rom. 16:25–26; cf. 1:1–3). Indeed, he is "the radiance of the glory of God" (Heb. 1:3) and "the light of the world" (John 8:12; cf. 1:4–5, 9), who by his Spirit enlightens the eyes to see what the Old Testament revealed all along (Eph. 1:17–18; cf. John 9:5; 12:35; 14:26; 15:26).

The Old Testament prophets had this light; therefore, they too understood, at least in part, what they proclaimed. Jesus thus declared, "Your father Abraham rejoiced that he would see my day. He saw it and was glad" (John 8:56).[11] Similarly, Peter notes how the "prophet" David "foresaw and spoke about the resurrection of the Christ," having known "that God had sworn with an oath to him that he would set one of his descendants on his throne" (Acts 2:30–31). Thus, Jesus affirmed, "Many prophets and kings

---

11 For more on Abraham's sight of the coming Christ, see Jason S. DeRouchie, "Lifting the Veil: Reading and Preaching Jesus' Bible through Christ and for Christ," *SBJT* 22, no. 3 (2018): 167–77; Jason S. DeRouchie, "Redemptive-Historical, Christocentric Approach," in *Five Views of Christ in the Old Testament*, ed. Andrew M. King and Brian J. Tabb, Counterpoints: Bible and Theology (Grand Rapids, MI: Zondervan Academic, 2022), 191–99.

desired to see what you see, and did not see it, and to hear what you hear, and did not hear it" (Luke 10:24; cf. Matt. 13:17). "These all died in faith, not having received the things promised, but having seen them and greeted them from afar, and having acknowledged that they were strangers and exiles on the earth" (Heb. 11:13).

To have the "mystery" of God's kingdom purposes revealed means, in part, that one's spiritual eyes have been opened to properly understand what the Old Testament was proclaiming all along. Hence, the apostle can say of the sacred Old Testament writings that they "are able to make you wise for salvation *through faith in Christ Jesus*" (2 Tim. 3:15). Through rebirth we become spiritual people who can spiritually discern and rightly understand spiritual truths (1 Cor. 2:13–14). The meaning we now understand by the Spirit in the Old Testament is not foreign to the original meaning but is the full testimony of Christ's person and time that "the Spirit of Christ in [the Old Testament prophets] was indicating when he predicted the sufferings of Christ and the subsequent glories" (1 Pet. 1:11; cf. Acts 3:18, 24). True Christians are the only ones who can rightly grasp all that God intends to communicate through the Old Testament.

Christ's Person and Work Clarify More Fully the Old Testament's Meaning

The Old Testament is filled with declarations, characters, events, and institutions that bear meaning in themselves but that also find that meaning enhanced and clarified in Christ's person and work. For example, the portraits of figures like Adam, Melchizedek, and David develop when we meet Jesus, who stands as the "last Adam" (1 Cor. 15:45; cf. Rom. 5:14), a new priest in the order of Melchizedek (Heb. 5:6, 10), and David's royal heir (Luke 1:32). Similarly, the meanings of events like the exodus or objects like the sacrificial lamb are amplified when the New Testament treats Christ's saving work as an "exodus" (Luke 9:31)[12] and calls him "the Lamb of God, who takes away the sin of the world" (John 1:29; cf. 1 Cor. 5:7; Heb. 9:26; 10:12). Jesus's triumph secured his appointment as "the Son of God

---

12 Luke tells us that, during the transfiguration, Moses and Elijah "appeared in glory and spoke of his departure [Greek *exodus*], which he was about to accomplish in Jerusalem" (Luke 9:31; cf. 2 Pet. 1:15). On Scripture's association of Christ's saving work with a new exodus, see Rikki E. Watts, "Exodus," *NDBT* 478–87.

in power" (Rom. 1:4) and validated him as the ultimate object of all Old Testament hopes. This, in turn, transformed the apostles' reading of the Old Testament. "When therefore he was raised from the dead, his disciples remembered that he had said this, and *they believed the Scripture* and the word that Jesus had spoken" (John 2:22). And again, "His disciples did not understand these things at first, but when Jesus was glorified, then they remembered that *these things had been written about him* and had been done to him" (John 12:16).

The Old Testament lays out types or figures that give rise to patterns, all of which terminate in Christ, who elucidates what comes before. Perhaps using terms from mathematics will help here. If the Old Testament indicates that 2 is followed by 4, then we often need the New Testament to clarify what comes next (2, 4, ?). Hence, when the New Testament signals that the Old Testament finds its fulfillment in Christ as the digit 6, then we know not only the final answer but also that the Old Testament problem was 2 + 4. If, however, the New Testament establishes that the next digit is 8, then we know both the answer and that the Old Testament problem was 2 x 4. Christ's coming supplies the answer key and the algorithm that clarify how the divine author desired all along for us to read the Old Testament. Christ becomes the lens for rightly interpreting his Bible as God intended.[13]

In this respect, some have helpfully compared Scripture to "double narratives" like detective stories. Peter Leithart writes,

> Detective novels tell two stories at once: the story on the surface and the real story unveiled to the gathered suspects in the final chapter. Once the detective gives his solution to the crime, the reader cannot go back to the first narrative; the second completely overshadows it. . . . Under the circumstances, reading backwards is not merely a preferred reading strategy; it is the only sensible course of action for a reasonable person.[14]

---

13   Moo and Naselli assert, "The most basic of all New Testament 'hermeneutical axioms' . . . is the authors' conviction that the God who had spoken in the Old Testament continued to speak to them and that it was this final divine context for all of Scripture that determines the meaning of any particular text." Douglas J. Moo and Andrew David Naselli, "The Problem of the New Testament's Use of the Old Testament," in *The Enduring Authority of the Christian Scriptures*, ed. D. A. Carson (Grand Rapids, MI: Eerdmans, 2016), 737.

14   Peter J. Leithart, *Deep Exegesis: The Mystery of Reading Scripture* (Waco, TX: Baylor University Press, 2009), 66, following historian David Steinmetz. Leithart sees later texts actually altering

The point is *not* that the mysteries of the Old Testament were something that the most enlightened saints could have fully solved. No, only God could reveal the mysteries that he hid there. He did so partially to some in the Old Testament age, but he does so fully only through Christ. Whether God revealed to the prophets a mystery directly by vision, dream, or impression (as in Daniel's case; see Dan. 2:19) or through agency by their searching and inquiring carefully (1 Pet. 1:10–11; cf. 2 Pet. 1:21), the remnant understood many of God's mysteries, and those who did not comprehend were culpable before God for their lack of understanding. Other mysteries, however, God chose not to disclose until Jesus came (Dan. 12:8–10), and this fact indicates that the Bible's last "chapter" (the New Testament) supplies us with the necessary lens for reading the initial three-fourths the way God intends us to read it. Through Christ we can see and savor elements in the Old Testament's plotline, content, and structure that were there all along but that were not clear apart from him.

In this regard, Darrell Bock helpfully notes, "Later revelation can complete and fill meaning that was initially, but not comprehensively, revealed in the original setting, so that once the progress of revelation emerges, the earlier passage is better and more comprehensively understood."[15] He continues, "The force of earlier passages in God's plan becomes clearer and more developed as more of the plan is revealed in later events and texts. This increase in clarity often involves the identification of new referents, to which the initial referents typologically point forward."[16] While a type's predictive nature was innately present from the beginning (see 1 Cor. 10:6, 11), interpreters may only recognize the anticipatory elements in retrospect.[17]

---

the very nature of an earlier text's meaning. Leithart, *Deep Exegesis*, 40, 43. In contrast, it is better to speak of layers of meaning and about how later interpreted events or messages *illuminate*, *enhance*, and *extend* the single meaning God intended from the beginning but that was only realized progressively through greater revelation and realized fully with the tribulation and triumph of Jesus Christ. Such a view alone maintains the organic link between type and antitype and the unified, omniscient, and omnipotent working of the single divine author.

15 Darrell L. Bock, "Response to Kaiser," in *Three Views on the New Testament Use of the Old*, ed. Kenneth Berding and Jonathan Lunde, Counterpoints: Bible and Theology (Grand Rapids, MI: Zondervan, 2008), 92.

16 Darrell L. Bock, "Single Meaning, Multiple Contexts and Referents," in Berding and Lunde, *Three Views on the New Testament Use of the Old*, 114.

17 For an example of typology that is viewed to be primarily retrospective and not prospective, see Andrew David Naselli, *From Typology to Doxology: Paul's Use of Isaiah and Job in Romans 11:34–35* (Eugene, OR: Pickwick, 2012).

Nevertheless, once Paul met the resurrected Christ, he never read the Old Testament the same way. Indeed, as an Old Testament preacher, he declares, "I decided to know nothing among you except Jesus Christ and him crucified" (1 Cor. 2:2). At no point in interpreting the Old Testament should Christians act as if Jesus has not come.[18] Reading from the beginning through Scripture gets us to Christ, but once we find him, we must interpret all the Old Testament through him. Properly grasping how the whole Bible progresses, integrates, and climaxes in Jesus requires that we read Scripture forward, backward, and then forward again.[19]

The Way God Discloses the Mystery of Christ Signals Organic Connections between the Old and New

When Paul asserts that "the mystery that was kept secret for long ages . . . has now been disclosed and *through the prophetic writings has been made known* to all nations" (Rom. 16:25–26), he implies that the New Testament's use of the Old Testament is natural and unforced, aligning with the Old Testament's own innate meaning, contours, structures, language, and flow. Addressing Jesus's assertion in Luke 24:44 that "everything written about me in the Law of Moses and the Prophets and the Psalms must *be fulfilled*," D. A. Carson notes,

> [Jesus] himself, and all the major New Testament writers, speak of the events of his life as *fulfilling* what the Old Testament says, not as adding brand new meaning to what the Old Testament says. . . . The "fulfillment" terminology [the biblical authors] deploy is too rich and varied to allow us to imagine that they are merely reading in what is in fact not there. They would be the first to admit that *in their own psychological history* the recognition of Jesus came before their understanding of the Old Testament; but they would see this as evidence of moral blindness. As a result, they would be the first to insist, with their transformed hermeneutic (not least the reading of the sacred text in salvation-historical sequence), that *the*

---

18 Note especially my critique of Longman's two-readings proposal in Jason S. DeRouchie, "Response to Tremper Longman III (The Redemptive-Historical, Christocentric Approach)," in King and Tabb, *Five Views of Christ in the Old Testament*, 112–17.

19 Similarly, Schreiner writes, "We read the scripture both front to back and back to front. We always consider the developing story as well as the end of the story." Thomas R. Schreiner, "Preaching and Biblical Theology," *SBJT* 10, no. 2 (2006): 28.

Scriptures themselves can be shown to anticipate a suffering Servant King, a Priest-King, a new High Priest, and so forth.[20]

The New Testament authors are making organic connections with the whole of Scripture on its own terms and in alignment with God's originally intended meaning.

As Paul says elsewhere, the biblical authors are *"interpreting* spiritual truths to those who are spiritual" (1 Cor. 2:13). Yet as Peter notes, the interpretations that shape the prophecies of Scripture are not of human origin, "for no prophecy was ever produced by the will of man, but men spoke from God as they were carried along by the Holy Spirit" (2 Pet. 1:20–21). "The prophets who prophesied about the grace that was to be yours searched and inquired carefully, inquiring what person or time the Spirit of Christ in them was indicating when he predicted the sufferings of Christ and the subsequent glories" (1 Pet. 1:10–11). With the Spirit's help, the prophets were exegeting antecedent revelation, including Scripture, when "God foretold" through them "that his Christ would suffer" (Acts 3:18) and "proclaimed these days" (3:24).[21] In Abner Chou's words,

> Since the prophets are exegetes and theologians, they can engage in theological development of a variety of topics including the Messiah. Thus, Christ in the Old Testament is not something that has to be read into the Old Testament from the New, but rather it is what the prophets themselves advance just as our Lord says (cf. Luke 24:25–27).[22]

One's hermeneutical framework must affirm that God spoke of his Messiah "by the mouth of his holy prophets from of old" (Luke 1:70) and have a category for Paul "testifying to the kingdom of God and trying to convince them about Jesus both from the Law of Moses and from the Prophets" (Acts 28:23).

---

20 D. A. Carson, *Collected Writings on Scripture* (Wheaton, IL: Crossway, 2010), 282–83 (emphasis in original).

21 So, too, Steve Moyise, *Evoking Scripture: Seeing the Old Testament in the New* (London: T&T Clark, 2008), 79; Benjamin Sargent, *Written to Serve: The Use of Scripture in 1 Peter*, LNTS 547 (Edinburgh: T&T Clark, 2015), 22.

22 Abner Chou, "'They Were Not Serving Themselves, but You': Reclaiming the Prophets' Messianic Intention," *The Master's Seminary Journal* 33, no. 2 (2022): 231.

These things affirmed, the move in salvation history from promise to fulfillment and anticipation to realization does create some level of discontinuity between what the prophets envisioned and what we today now perceive. While Abraham saw Christ's day and was glad (John 8:56), "Many prophets and righteous people longed to see what you see, and did not see it, and to hear what you hear, and did not hear it" (Matt. 13:17; cf. Luke 10:24; Heb. 11:13). From this perspective, New Testament authors' interpretations clarify more fully God's intent for earlier texts, just as the New Testament testimony supplies the final revelation through Jesus's person and work.

On this, Beale writes,

> It is quite possible that the Old Testament authors did not exhaustively understand the meaning, implications, and possible applications of all that they wrote. Subsequently, the New Testament Scripture interprets the Old Testament Scripture by expanding its meaning, seeing new implications in it and giving it new applications. . . . This expansion does not contravene the integrity of the earlier texts but rather develops them in a way which is consistent with the Old Testament author's understanding.[23]

Regarding the revealed mystery's meaning, Beale and Gladd add,

> Since this new meaning was really "there" in the Old Testament, the original context is never completely severed. Certainly, the meaning of some Old Testament quotations is "newer" or more creative than others, but if the biblical model of mystery is upheld, the original context is to some degree retained.[24]

I would qualify that the meaning itself is *not* "newer" but is only understood in fuller ways now that the full object of hope is realized in space and time and clarified through God's special revelation.

The Old Testament prophets often envisioned the very form we now enjoy, not only seeing the shadow but also embracing the substance that

---

23 G. K. Beale, "Did Jesus and His Followers Preach the Right Doctrine from the Wrong Texts? An Examination of the Presuppositions of Jesus' and the Apostles' Exegetical Method," *Them* 14, no. 3 (1989): 91. Reprinted in G. K. Beale, ed., *The Right Doctrine from the Wrong Texts? Essays on the Use of the Old Testament in the New* (Grand Rapids, MI: Baker Academic, 1994), 393.

24 Beale and Gladd, *Hidden but Now Revealed*, 335.

is Christ (Col. 2:16–17), though perhaps more like an acorn or sapling anticipates a great oak.[25] Yahweh's work in their lives provided them *light* for seeing truths God did not disclose to others, but it was not enough to clarify everything. The *lens* of salvation history climaxing in Jesus would be necessary for full disclosure. As Beale states,

> When there is a divine understanding that transcends the conscious intention of the human author, the divine understanding is still organically related to the human author's understanding or "willed type." What God knew more fully than the prophet consciously knew would be an interpretive implication that would fit within the human author's "willed type," and, if asked later, the prophet would say, "Yes, I see how that is the wider, thicker meaning of what I intended originally to say."[26]

Even if the Old Testament authors were not fully aware of all God was speaking through them, they would have affirmed retrospectively the trajectories that later biblical authors identify.[27]

Christ as Light and Lens

The Scripture calls us to see both an organic unity and a progressive development between the Old and New Testaments. The move from Old

---

25 William Sanford LaSor once stated, "An ordinary seed contains in itself everything that will develop in the plant or tree to which it is organically related: every branch, every leaf, every flower. Yet no amount of examination by available scientific methods will disclose to us what is in that seed. However, once the seed has developed to its fullness, we can see how the seed has been fulfilled." William Sanford LaSor, "Prophecy, Inspiration, and Sensus Plenior," *TynBul* 29, no. 1 (1978): 55–56. Balancing out this statement, Beale writes, "Contrary to the consensus opinion both inside and outside evangelical scholarship, Old Testament authors may have had some inkling of how the meaning of their texts would be later understood in what would appear to us to be surprising interpretations." G. K. Beale, "The Cognitive Peripheral Vision of Biblical Authors," *WTJ* 76, no. 2 (2014): 283; Beale and Gladd, *Hidden but Now Revealed*, 359. Multiple texts indicate that a fuller awareness was even more common than either LaSor or Beale suggest (e.g., Dan. 10:1; Matt. 13:17; Luke 10:24; John 8:56; Heb. 11:13; cf. John 1:45; 5:39, 46; Acts 3:18, 24; 10:43; Heb. 3:5; 1 Pet. 1:10–12).

26 Beale, "The Cognitive Peripheral Vision of Biblical Authors," 283; cf. Beale and Gladd, *Hidden but Now Revealed*, 358.

27 Against Tremper Longman, who claims, "The Old Testament writers themselves would often have been surprised at how their writings anticipated Jesus, the suffering and victorious Messiah." Tremper Longman III, "Christotelic Approach," in King and Tabb, *Five Views of Christ in the Old Testament*, 74.

to New is like the development from acorn or oak sapling to mature oak tree. There is a natural and purposeful connection between what the Old Testament human authors intended and what the New Testament human authors saw fulfilled in Jesus, but comprehension of the Old Testament's meaning is now often fuller, expanded, or deeper because through Christ God reveals the mystery. Jesus's saving work supplies the spiritual *light* that enables one's spiritual senses to see and savor rightly, and his saving work provides the interpretive *lens* for properly understanding and applying the Old Testament itself in a way that most completely magnifies God in Christ.

Figure 3.1 unpacks what is happening with respect to Scripture's progressive revealing of Old Testament meaning. The horizontal axis represents the progress of revelation from the Old Testament to the New Testament eras through Christ, and the vertical axis distinguishes the unregenerate from the regenerate in both periods. In the Old Testament age, the remnant of faithful (like Abraham and Moses, Rahab and Hannah, David and Isaiah) had light for seeing and savoring God's purposes that would climax in Christ, but they did not have the full lens for discerning the full significance of what they saw. They knew something of Christ's person and time (1 Pet. 1:10–11; cf. John 8:56), but they could only greet him and his day from afar (Heb. 11:13; cf. Matt. 13:17; Luke 10:24). In contrast, the unregenerate, which included the majority of old covenant Israel, had neither light nor lens due to their hardness of heart and spiritual disability. Now, with Christ's coming, God is enlightening more eyes and has supplied the full lens for reading the Old Testament faithfully, but the unregenerate continue to live in the dark, having the lens of Christ available but not the light of Christ to see. The "mystery" continues permanently hidden for some (cf. 1 Cor. 2:8–9 with Isa. 64:4; Eph. 1:17–18) but is only temporarily hidden for others (see Dan. 12:8–9, 12; Matt. 11:25).

Figure 3.2 elucidates further the way Christ operates as a lens, supplying us a developed understanding of the Old Testament's inherent meaning. In Christ, the New Testament (1) interprets and clarifies Old Testament visions and declarations, (2) indicates the realization or fulfillment of the Old Testament's direct promises and predictions, (3) gives substance to the various types or shadows (persons, events, things/institutions), and (4) identifies the ultimate *goal* or *end* (Greek *telos*) of the law of Moses in Christ and the law associated with him.

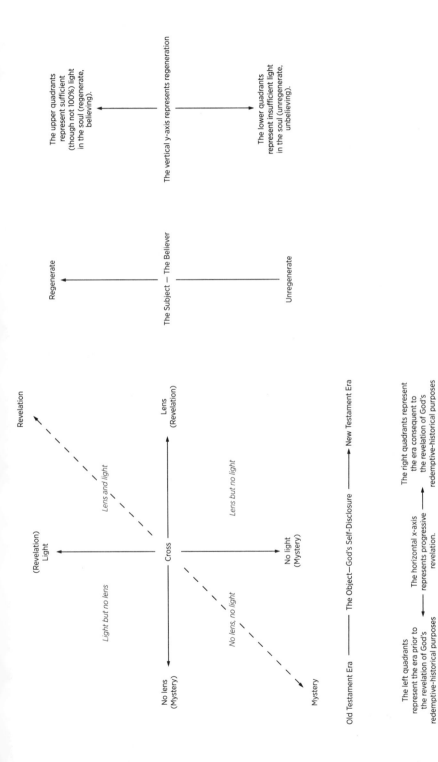

Figure 3.1   The Bible's progressive revelation of Old Testament mystery

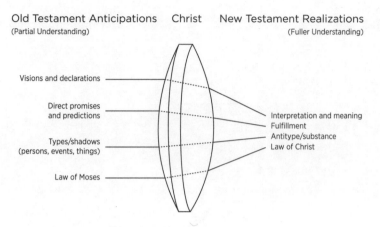

Figure 3.2   Interpreting the Old Testament through the lens of Christ

Conclusion

When Saul encountered the resurrected Christ, the blind man gained sight, the murderer became a missionary, and a Jewish Pharisee became an apostle of Jesus to the Gentiles whose interpretation of Scripture was forever changed. By means of the resurrected Jesus's appearing, a veil was lifted that now allowed Paul to read the old covenant materials with fresh eyes and in the way God originally intended (2 Cor. 3:14–16), and in them he found a clear message of the suffering and triumphant Messiah and the mission he would spark (Acts 26:22–23; cf. Luke 24:47). This Old Testament preacher could now assert, "I decided to know nothing among you except Jesus Christ and him crucified" (1 Cor. 2:2; cf. 1:23), for everything now bore connections with the cross. The gospel, which is of "first importance" (1 Cor. 15:3), supplied the light and lens for all Paul's teaching and transformed his approach to the Old Testament.

The Old Testament is Christian Scripture, and God intends that we interpret it as such and not as if Christ has not come. We must read the Scripture forward, then backward, and then forward again. The Old Testament prophets knew they were writing for new covenant saints living in the days of the Christ (1 Pet. 1:12; cf. Deut. 30:8; Isa. 30:8; Jer. 30:2–3, 24; Dan. 12:8–10). Bound up in the gospel of Jesus Christ is the revelation of a "mystery that was kept secret for long ages but has now been disclosed and through the prophetic writings has been made known to all nations" (Rom. 16:25–26). Through Christ we gain both receptivity and revelation.[28]

A relationship with Jesus is essential for rightly interpreting the Old Testament, for through him God enables hearts to understand, eyes to see, and ears to hear (Mark 4:9; 2 Cor. 4:6; 2 Pet. 1:19). In turning to Christ "the veil is removed" (2 Cor. 3:16). In Christ, the acorn or oak sapling becomes a mighty oak, shadows give rise to substance (Col. 2:16–17; cf. Heb. 8:5; 10:1), and every promise becomes "Yes" (2 Cor. 1:20). The *light* of Christ supplies us the needed spiritual sight for understanding the things of God (1 Cor. 2:12–13; 2 Cor. 3:14), and the *lens* of Christ's life, death, and resurrection provides the needed perspective for fully grasping the Old Testament's meaning (Matt. 5:17–18; Mark 4:11; Rom. 16:25–26). God wrote the Old Testament for Christians, and God enables believing interpreters to grasp more fully than others both the meaning and intended effect of the initial three-fourths of the Christian Scriptures.

Review and Reflection

1. What is the meaning of "mystery" in Scripture? What about the story of King Nebuchadnezzar's dream clarifies the term's sense? What does Jesus's use of "mystery/secret" in Mark 4:11–12 indicate?

2. What scriptural support is there for the claim that a relationship with Christ is necessary to understand the Old Testament rightly?

3. Give an example of how Christ's person and work clarify more fully the Old Testament's meaning.

4. How is Scripture like and unlike the "double narratives" of detective novels?

5. The author claims that when the New Testament authors cite the Old Testament they are making "organic connections." What does this mean, and why is this important?

6. In what ways is Christ both light and lens for interpreting the Old Testament text?

7. What does it mean to read the Scripture forward, then backward, then forward again?

---

28 So Brian J. Tabb, *After Emmaus: How the Church Fulfills the Mission of Christ* (Wheaton, IL: Crossway, 2021), 26.

8. Read Romans 16:25–26 and 2 Corinthians 3:14–16 and clarify how they contribute to the point of this chapter.

9. What was the greatest insight you gained in reading this chapter? What is your greatest takeaway?

10. How might reading the Old Testament through the light and lens of Christ help us to see Jesus in the Old Testament, to claim Old Testament promises, and to apply Old Testament laws? These are the primary topics in parts 2–4 of this book.

PART 2

SEEING WELL

How Jesus's Bible Testifies about Him

And he said to them, "O foolish ones, and slow of heart to believe
all that the prophets have spoken! Was it not necessary that
the Christ should suffer these things and enter into his glory?"
And beginning with Moses and all the Prophets, he interpreted
to them in all the Scriptures the things concerning himself.

LUKE 24:25–27

Then he said to them, "These are my words that I spoke to you
while I was still with you, that everything written about me
in the Law of Moses and the Prophets and the Psalms must
be fulfilled." Then he opened their minds to understand the
Scriptures, and said to them, "Thus it is written, that the Christ
should suffer and on the third day rise from the dead, and
that repentance and forgiveness of sins should be proclaimed
in his name to all nations beginning from Jerusalem."

LUKE 24:44–47

> *You search the Scriptures because you think that in them you*
> *have eternal life; and it is they that bear witness about me.*
>
> JOHN 5:39

Jesus indicated that his Hebrew Bible, what we call the Old Testament, included many things concerning him (Luke 24:25–27). Indeed, "to understand the Scriptures" means that one will see a portrait of the Messiah's tribulation and triumph and the global saving mission he would generate (Luke 24:44–47). Is that what you see when you read the Old Testament?

The Lord testified that "the Scriptures . . . bear witness about me" (John 5:39). Earlier, John records Philip declaring to Nathanael, "We have found him of whom Moses in the Law and also the prophets wrote, Jesus of Nazareth" (John 1:45). Peter also later claimed, "What God foretold by the mouth of all the prophets, that his Christ would suffer, he thus fulfilled" (Acts 3:18). Indeed, "all the prophets . . . proclaimed these days" of the church's rise (Acts 3:24), even as "all the prophets bear witness that everyone who believes in [Jesus] receives forgiveness of sins through his name" (10:43). As Paul claims, the very "gospel of God" that we celebrate today was "promised beforehand through his prophets in the holy Scriptures, concerning his Son" (Rom. 1:1–3). Old covenant messengers like Amos, Zephaniah, and Haggai foretold the good news of Jesus's coming.

Now, having embraced Jesus as the necessary light and lens, we are able to begin interpreting the Old Testament for what it is—Christian Scripture. When we do this, we find that Jesus is at its center, standing not only as the one *through whom* we read the Old Testament but also as the one *for whom* we read it. God's Spirit guided the Scriptures' writing (2 Pet. 1:21; cf. Mark 12:36; Acts 1:16), and the unchanging Spirit always works to glorify the Son (John 16:13–14; cf. 1 Pet. 1:11). And as we encounter him with unveiled eyes, "beholding the glory of the Lord," we "are being transformed into the same image from one degree of glory to another" (2 Cor. 3:18; cf. 3:14–16).

Part 2 of this book considers how the Old Testament relates to Jesus, and it proposes that seeing and celebrating Christ in the Old Testament requires a multiform approach that accounts for Jesus's place within all of

God's purposes in salvation history. Chapter 4 overviews the biblical storyline, highlighting how it climaxes in Christ. Chapter 5 initially supplies five principles modeled by Christ and the apostles for interpreting the Old Testament and then notes Scripture's three overlapping contexts that should guide all biblical interpretation. Finally, it adds an additional six potential ways to magnify Jesus faithfully from the Old Testament." Chapter 6 surveys Genesis to show how one Old Testament book bears foundational witness to Christ (John 5:39).

Significantly, the redemptive-historical, Christocentric model I am proposing does *not* appeal "to a hidden divine layer of meaning on top of the biblical writers' intent."[1] An approach that is *redemptive-historical* is one that accounts for how God's work and purposes in Scripture progress, integrate, and climax in Christ, and how all faithful biblical interpretation must account for the way Jesus's life, death, and resurrection inform and influence everything God is doing in space and time (Luke 16:16; Gal. 3:23–26). Through Jesus, God discloses mysteries (Mark 4:10; Rom. 16:25–26); allows shadows to reach their substance (Col. 2:16–17); and inaugurates a new creation (2 Cor. 5:17; Gal. 6:15), new covenant (Luke 22:20; Heb. 9:15), and new law (1 Cor. 9:21; Gal 6:2). A redemptive-historical approach requires that we consider every text in view of its close, continuing, and complete contexts within Scripture as a whole to fully discern what God meant in any passage.

By *Christocentric* I mean that our biblical interpretation and application must in some way be tied to the cross for it to be Christian (1 Cor. 2:2). I also mean that we are to interpret Scripture *through* Christ and *for* Christ. To interpret through Christ means that we start our reading as those believing in Jesus, with God having awakened our spiritual senses to see and hear rightly (1 Cor. 2:14; 2 Cor. 4:6). It also means that we recognize the way Christ's life, death, and resurrection inform the message of what is already present in the Old Testament itself (Rom. 16:25–26; 2 Cor. 3:14). To interpret *for Christ* means that we recognize that Old Testament history, prophecy, law, and promises point to Jesus (Mark 1:14; Acts 3:18; Rom. 10:4; 2 Cor. 1:20); that he fulfills all of them

---

1   Against Abner Chou's portrayal of a "Christocentric hermeneutic." Abner Chou, "'They Were Not Serving Themselves, but You': Reclaiming the Prophets' Messianic Intention," *The Master's Seminary Journal* 33, no. 2 (2022): 219.

(Matt. 5:17–18); and that the Spirit who inspired the biblical text is working to glorify the Son through it all (John 16:13–14; cf. 1 Pet. 1:11). Christian biblical interpretation reaches its end only after we have beheld Jesus's glory and found him transforming us into his image (2 Cor. 3:18).

4

The Story of God's Glory in Christ

The time is fulfilled.

MARK 1:15

"WHEN THE FULLNESS OF TIME HAD COME, God sent forth his Son" (Gal. 4:4), and now we are living at "the end of the ages" (1 Cor. 10:11; cf. Rom. 13:11). Jesus opened his ministry by "proclaiming the gospel of God, and saying, 'The time is fulfilled, and the kingdom of God is at hand; repent and believe in the gospel'" (Mark 1:15). Isaiah anticipated the good news of God's end-times reign through his royal servant and anointed conqueror (Isa. 40:9–11; 52:7–10; 61:1–3), and Jesus saw his own ministry realizing it. His kingdom message continued after his resurrection (Acts 1:3) and was shaped by the testimony that to faithfully "understand the Scriptures" means that we will see the Old Testament forecasting the Messiah's death and resurrection and his mission to save the nations: "Thus it is written, that the Christ should suffer and on the third day rise from the dead, and that repentance for the forgiveness of sins should be proclaimed in his name to all nations, beginning from Jerusalem" (Luke 24:45–47; cf. Acts 1:3, 8; 3:18, 24; 10:43).[1]

Paul, too, believed the Old Testament announced God's kingdom in Christ and the church he would build (Acts 26:22–23; cf. 20:25; 28:23).

---

1 On the central role of these verses for the theology of Luke-Acts, see Brian J. Tabb, *After Emmaus: How the Church Fulfills the Mission of Christ* (Wheaton, IL: Crossway, 2021).

The apostle proclaimed "the gospel of God . . . concerning his Son," and he recognized that God "promised [it] beforehand through his prophets in the holy Scriptures" (Rom. 1:1–3; cf. Gal. 3:8). The Old Testament first anticipated, foreshadowed, and foretold the good news that we now enjoy—that the reigning God would eternally save and satisfy sinners who believe through Christ's life, death, and resurrection (cf. John 1:45; 5:39, 46; 8:56; Heb. 11:13; 1 Pet. 1:10–11). The progress from creation to the fall to redemption to consummation is in a very real sense *his*-story, and it is this kingdom program that provides the framework for exalting Christ in the Old Testament.

Christ Is Central to God's Creative and Salvation-Historical Purposes

Salvation history is the progressive unfolding of God's redemptive purposes disclosed from Genesis to Revelation, all of which grow out of and culminate in God's commitment to glorify himself in Christ. Scripture progresses through five distinct but overlapping covenants and through various peoples, events, and institutions, all of which culminate in Jesus's person and work. Indeed, all God's purposes in space and time begin and end with Christ. We thus read,

> By [the Son] all things were created, in heaven and on earth, visible and invisible. . . . All things were created through and for him. And he is before all things, and in him all things hold together. And he is the head of the body, the church. He is the beginning, the firstborn from the dead, that in everything he might be preeminent. (Col. 1:16–18)

Furthermore, we learn that "the mystery of [God's] will" is "according to his purpose, which he set forth in Christ as a plan for the fullness of time, to unite all things in him, things in heaven and things on earth" (Eph. 1:9–10). God's creative and salvation-historical purposes climax in Christ.

The Old Testament's laws, history, prophecy, and wisdom point to Jesus (Matt. 5:17–18; Mark 1:15; Acts 3:18; 1 Cor. 1:23–24), and the entire storyline pivots on him. He thus declared, "The Law and the Prophets were until John; since then the good news of the kingdom of God is preached" (Luke 16:16). Paul, too, noted, "For Christ is the end of the law for righteousness to everyone who believes" (Rom. 10:4). "The law was our guardian until Christ came. . . . But now that faith has come, we are no longer under a guardian" (Gal. 3:24–26; cf. Heb. 8:6, 13). "All the promises of God find their Yes in him" (2 Cor. 1:20).

By disclosing Christ as the Old Testament's goal, the Father also illuminates his intent for the earlier parts. And in turn, those earlier parts then clarify the meaning of Jesus's person and work. In Christ, all the problems the Old Testament raises find their solution (Eph. 1:10; Col. 1:20), and all that the Old Testament anticipates is fully and finally realized. In Christ, shadow gives rise to substance (Col. 2:16–17), types move to antitype (e.g., Rom. 5:14; 1 Cor. 10:6, 11), and what God promised he now fulfills (Luke 24:44; 2 Cor. 1:20). In Christ, light triumphs over darkness (Matt. 4:15–16; 2 Cor. 4:6). The new creation, new age, and new covenant overcome the old creation, old age, and old covenant.

The flow of God's saving purposes in history demands that Christian Old Testament interpretation starts and ends with Christ. He is the hub around which all else turns and the measure upon which all else is weighed. As the means and focus of God's self-revelation through his Scriptures, the divine Son must operate as the heart of all exegesis and theology. Because Jesus stands at the beginning and end of all God's creative and redemptive purposes, we must interpret the Old Testament *through* Christ and *for* Christ.

God's Kingdom Program[2]

The kingdom Christ proclaimed and fulfilled (Luke 4:43; Acts 1:3) relates to God's reign over God's people in God's land for God's glory.[3] God reigns, saves, and satisfies through covenant for his glory in Christ. This theme stands at the core of God's purposes from Genesis to Revelation.

When the Old and New Testaments are read alongside one another, at least seven historical stages are apparent in God's kingdom program. The

---

2 What follows updates material that originally appeared in Jason S. DeRouchie, "Question 2: What Is Scripture's Storyline?," in Jason S. DeRouchie, Oren R. Martin, and Andrew David Naselli, *40 Questions about Biblical Theology* (Grand Rapids, MI: Kregel, 2020), 29–40. Published by Kregel, Inc. Used with permission.

3 While Graeme Goldsworthy does not front the importance of God's *reign* for understanding *kingdom* language in the New Testament, he does similarly note that God's kingdom is characterized by "God's people in God's place under God's rule." Graeme Goldsworthy, *The Goldsworthy Trilogy* (Exeter, UK: Paternoster, 2000), 112.

initial five are the foundation that is ultimately fulfilled in the last two. The acronym KINGDOM allows for easy memorization (see table 4.1).

Table 4.1   Stages in God's KINGDOM plan

Old Testament Narrative **Foundation**	K	Kickoff and rebellion	Creation, fall, and flood
	I	Instrument of blessing	Patriarchs
	N	Nation redeemed and commissioned	Exodus, Sinai, and wilderness
	G	Government in the land	Conquest and kingdoms
	D	Dispersion and return	Exile and initial restoration
New Testament Narrative **Fulfillment**	O	Overlap of the ages	Christ's work and the church age
	M	Mission accomplished	Christ's return and kingdom consummation

The major plot developments through this salvation story are marked by five overlapping covenants, the progression of which detail God's global purposes with humanity (Adamic/Noahic → Abrahamic → Mosaic → Davidic → new). The interrelationship of the covenants is like an hourglass, with the most universal scope occurring at the two ends and the work of Christ at the center (see fig. 4.1[4]). The titles of the initial four relate to their

---

4   The divisions in figure 4.1 between "narrative" and "commentary" relate to Scripture's different types of book groupings. Following the three-part arrangement of Jesus's Hebrew Bible (see Luke 24:44), the historical "narrative" books of the Old Testament begin with the Law (Genesis–Deuteronomy), continue through the Former Prophets (Joshua, Judges, Samuel, Kings), and end in the Latter Writings (Daniel, Esther, Ezra-Nehemiah, Chronicles). Here the story of redemption is told. In contrast, the groupings of prophetic and poetic books in the Latter Prophets (Jeremiah, Ezekiel,

human covenant head or mediator, whereas the title *new* covenant signals how it contrasts with and supersedes the *old* Mosaic administration (see Jer. 31:31–34; Heb. 8:6–13).[5]

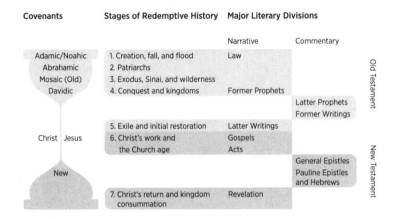

Figure 4.1   Salvation history in the context of Scripture

Scripture's story indicates that Yahweh's ultimate goal through his kingdom program is to display himself as the supreme Savior, sovereign, and satisfier of the world, ultimately through his messianic representative. As such, the Bible tells *the story of God's glory in Christ*.[6] Alongside the

---

Isaiah, the Twelve) and Former Writings (Ruth–Psalms, Job, Proverbs, Ecclesiastes, Song of Songs, Lamentations) provide theological "commentary" on the storyline by informing and guiding our reading of it. Similarly, the "narrative" in the New Testament is told in the Gospels (Matthew, Mark, Luke, John) and Acts and then ends with the prophetic narrative in Revelation. The "commentary" books are again in the middle making up the General Epistles (James, 1–2 Peter, 1–3 John, Jude), the Pauline Epistles (Romans, 1–2 Corinthians, Galatians, Ephesians, Philippians, Colossians, 1–2 Thessalonians, 1–2 Timothy, Titus), and Hebrews. The salvation-historical narrative frames both the Old and New Testaments and supplies the framework for interpreting everything. See Jason S. DeRouchie, "Question 16: Is the Order of the Canon Significant for Doing Biblical Theology?," in DeRouchie, Martin, and Naselli, *40 Questions about Biblical Theology*, 157–70; Jason S. DeRouchie, "The Hermeneutical Significance of the Shape of the Christian Canon," in *The Law, the Prophets, and the Writings: Studies in Evangelical Old Testament Hermeneutics in Honor of Duane A. Garrett*, ed. Andrew M. King, Joshua M. Philpot, and William R. Osborne (Nashville: B&H Academic, 2021), 29–53.

5   For more on the progress and interrelationship of the covenants, see Jason S. DeRouchie, "Question 22: What Is a Biblical Theology of the Covenants?," in DeRouchie, Martin, and Naselli, *40 Questions about Biblical Theology*, 215–26; Jason S. DeRouchie, "An Arc of the Covenants: Tracing How the Bible's Storyline Climaxes in Christ," *SBJT* 26, no. 1 (2022): 10–45; Jason S. DeRouchie, "Covenant," *DNTUOT*, 144–50.

6   See John Piper, "The Goal of God in Redemptive History," in *Desiring God: Meditations of a Christian Hedonist*, 3rd ed. (Sisters, OR: Multnomah, 2003), 308–21; John Piper, *Providence*

KINGDOM acronym, a set of images will help clarify the flow of God's purposes from creation to consummation (see fig. 4.2).

Figure 4.2   God's KINGDOM plan through images

1. *Kickoff and Rebellion (Creation, Fall, and Flood)*

God the Creator deserves highest praise in the world (1 Chron. 29:11; Rev. 4:11). He created humans to image him and commissioned them to "fill the earth and subdue it, and have dominion" (Gen. 1:28). Humans were to reign over God's world as his vice regents, but they failed to honor God rightly

---

(Wheaton, IL: Crossway, 2020), 47–201; Thomas R. Schreiner, "A Biblical Theology of the Glory of God," in *For the Fame of God's Name: Essays in Honor of John Piper*, ed. Sam Storms and Justin Taylor (Wheaton, IL: Crossway, 2010), 215–34.

and submitted to the authority of Satan (Gen. 3:1–6), who in turn became the ruler of this world (John 12:31; 2 Cor. 4:4; 1 John 5:19). Because in his rebellion Adam acted as a covenantal head, God now counts all the rest of humanity as having sinned in Adam (Rom. 5:12, 18–19). From conception we are condemned sinners under God's just wrath (John 3:36; Eph. 2:1–3), and the result is that all rebel and thus fall short of glorifying God (Rom. 1:21–23; 3:23). God called our first parents to heed his voice lest they die (Gen. 2:17), and when they sinned, Yahweh drove them from his presence outside his garden-sanctuary (3:24).

Before subjecting the world to futility (Gen. 3:16–19; Rom. 8:20–21), Yahweh promised to reestablish cosmic order through a human deliverer, who would decisively overcome the curse and the power of evil (Gen. 3:15). The sustained human sin after the fall resulted in the flood (Gen. 6:7–8), but God preserved a remnant whose hope was in the coming Redeemer. He reaffirmed through Noah his covenant with creation, thus providing a context in which saving grace would become operative (Gen. 6:12–13, 18; 8:21–9:1, 9–11). At the Tower of Babel, however, such mercy was matched by mankind exalting themselves over God, resulting in Yahweh punishing humanity once again by dispersing them and confusing their tongues (Gen. 11:1–9).

2. Instrument of Blessing (Patriarchs)

I ♠ ✾ ▣ 🌐

To the praise of his glorious grace, God elected and created a people for himself (Isa. 43:6–7; 49:3; Jer. 13:11; Eph. 1:4–6). From one of the seventy families dispersed throughout the earth at Babel (Gen. 10:32), Yahweh chose Abraham as the instrument through whom he would reverse the global curse with blessing. God himself was believable, and his promises were desirable, thus compelling the patriarch to leave Mesopotamia by faith (Acts 7:2; Heb. 11:8), heeding Yahweh's commission:

> *Go* from your country and your kindred and your father's house to the land that I will show you so that I may make of you a great nation, and may bless you, and may make your name great. And there, *be a blessing,*

> so that I may bless those who bless you, and him who dishonors you I may curse. And the result will be that in you all the families of the ground will be blessed. (Gen. 12:1–3, author's translation)

The commands "go" and "be a blessing" indicate two phases in the Abrahamic covenant: (1) In going to the land, Abraham would become a great nation (fulfilled in the Mosaic covenant). (2) Through one of Abraham's representatives (i.e., the Messiah), God would restore a relationship of blessing with some from all the earth's nations (fulfilled in the new covenant).

Though the patriarch's wife was barren (Gen. 11:30) and though he realized Yahweh's promises would take a miracle, Abraham believed God could do for him what he could not do on his own, and God counted his faith in the offspring promise as righteousness (15:6; cf. 18:13–14). To exalt his faithfulness and anticipate future mercy, Yahweh vowed to fulfill his land promise to Abraham's offspring (Gen. 15:17–18) and provided a substitute sacrifice in the place of Isaac (22:12–14). He also reaffirmed that he would bless the nations through a royal representative, now known to be from Judah, who would destroy evil and reestablish world peace (Gen. 22:17–18; 24:60; 49:8–10). Through this individual and by means of spiritual adoption, Abraham would become a father of a multitude of nations (Gen. 17:4–6), and the promised land (Gen. 17:8) would expand to lands (Gen. 22:17; 26:3–4), resulting in Abraham's inheriting the world (Rom. 4:13). For such ultimate good, God sent Joseph to Egypt to keep the children of Jacob/Israel alive amid famine while they awaited the promised land (Gen. 45:7–8; 50:20, 24–25; cf. Ps. 105:16–17).

3. Nation Redeemed and Commissioned (Exodus, Sinai, and Wilderness)

God fulfilled his promises by sustaining and multiplying Israel through four hundred years of Egyptian oppression (Ex. 1:7; cf. Gen. 15:13–14). For the sake of his name and reputation, God brought the plagues on Egypt and redeemed Israel from slavery (Ex. 7:5; 9:15–16; 14:4; 2 Sam. 7:23).

Yahweh gave Israel his old covenant law through Moses to mediate his presence and to display his holiness among the nations (Ex. 19:5–6).

Through lives of radical love overflowing in sustained obedience (Lev. 19:18; Deut. 6:4–5; 10:16–19), Israel could bear witness to the worth and excellencies of God to a watching world (Deut. 4:5–8). Yahweh would consider their perfect surrender as righteousness (Deut. 6:25), and they would enjoy lasting life (Deut. 4:1; 8:1; 16:20; cf. Lev. 26:3–13; Deut. 28:1–14). Yahweh provided a means of atonement so that they could be near him, and he declared that his presence alone would distinguish them from the nations (Ex. 33:16; 34:6–9; Lev. 9:3–6; 10:3). He also restated his promise that a royal deliverer would arise from Jacob who would exercise international influence (Num. 24:7–9, 17–19).

Nevertheless, the majority were stubborn, rebellious, and unbelieving (Deut. 9:6–7, 23–24). Yahweh did not overcome their hard-heartedness (Deut. 29:4; cf. Rom. 11:7–8) but foretold how they would continue to rebel and suffer exile (Deut. 4:25–29; 30:1; 31:16–17, 27–29). Nevertheless, out of his compassion (Deut. 4:31), he would also restore them to the land (30:3–5); raise up a new covenant-mediating prophet like Moses (18:15–19); punish their enemies (30:7; 32:35); incorporate some from the nations (32:21, 43; 33:19); and cause all his people to love Yahweh, hear his voice, and heed his new prophet's teaching (4:30; 30:1–2, 6, 8–14).

4. Government in the Land (Conquest and Kingdoms)

G ⚰ ♛ ⧈ ⚔

Through Israel's conquest of the promised land, Yahweh exalted himself before the nations as the only true God. In the words of Rahab the Canaanite, "The LORD your God, he is God in the heavens above and on the earth beneath" (Josh. 2:11; cf. 8:24; 1 Sam. 4:8). Yahweh was completely faithful to his promises (Josh. 21:43–45). As with Adam in Eden, he brought Israel into a new paradise (Ex. 15:17–18), and in a foreshadow of the messianic Savior's greater work (Heb. 4:8 with Matt. 11:28), God used Joshua to give them rest (Josh. 1:13; 11:23; 21:44).

Nevertheless, the majority soon forgot Yahweh and progressively became Canaanized: "They abandoned the LORD, the God of their fathers, who had brought them out of the land of Egypt. They went after other gods, from among the gods of the people who were around them, and bowed down to them. And they provoked the Lord to anger" (Judg. 2:12), resulting in their ruin. Without a faithful king, the people did what was right in their own eyes (Judg. 21:25), and God's word became rare (1 Sam. 3:1). The people sought a king, which God granted, but they wanted one who would replace rather than represent Yahweh (1 Sam. 8:7). Ultimately, because the leaders and community refused to listen to God's gracious appeal via his prophets, the united empire was divided (1 Kings 11:11, 13), and both the northern and southern kingdoms came to a ruinous end—exile and a destroyed temple (2 Kings 17:14–15, 18; 25:1–20).

Despite all the darkness and rebellion of Israel's rise and fall, Yahweh graciously renewed his promise of a coming royal Redeemer (1 Sam. 2:10, 35). King David foreshadowed this deliverer, and God declared that he would fulfill his universal kingdom purposes through David (2 Sam. 7:12, 16). One of David's offspring would be God's royal "Son" who would possess and bless the nations and destroy God's enemies (Pss. 2:7–9; 72:17; cf. 2 Sam. 7:14). God would establish and uphold David's throne with justice and righteousness (Isa. 9:7; cf. Luke 1:32). Bearing the name "Israel," this new representative servant-king would "bring back the preserved of Israel," the people, and be "a light to the nations," thus extending Yahweh's saving reign to the end of the earth (Isa. 49:3, 6). The anticipated savior-king would proclaim Yahweh's end-times reign—the year of his favor and the day of his vengeance (Isa. 52:7; 61:2; cf. Luke 4:18–19). While himself guiltless (Isa. 50:9; 53:9), he would also satisfy God's wrath against sinners through a substitutionary death and would, by his righteousness, "make many to be accounted righteous" (Isa. 53:5, 10–11; cf. John 11:50–52; Rom. 5:19; 2 Cor. 5:21).

5. Dispersion and Return (Exile and Initial Restoration)

D ⊘ ▥ ⚑

Yahweh cast Israel from the promised land because they failed to live for him and heed his voice (2 Kings 17:7; 2 Chron. 36:16). And from the depths of exile, Daniel pleaded,

> Open your eyes and see our desolations, and the city that is called by your
> name. For we do not present our pleas before you because of our righ-

teousness, but because of your great mercy. O Lord, hear; O Lord, forgive. O Lord, pay attention and act. Delay not, *for your own sake*, O my God, because your city and your people are called by your name. (Dan. 9:18–19)

Yahweh is a God whose "steadfast love . . . never ceases" and whose "mercies never come to an end" (Lam. 3:22–23). Out of his boundless kindness, God promised that, in the latter days, "the God of heaven will set up a kingdom that shall never be destroyed" (Dan. 2:44) and that "one like a son of man" would receive "dominion and glory and a kingdom, that all peoples, nations, and languages should serve him" (7:13–14). Hence, *for his own sake*, Yahweh would sustain Israel through exile and would ultimately use them as witnesses to his greatness in the world (Isa. 48:9, 11; Ezek. 36:22–23; cf. Acts 1:8).

Yahweh preserved his people. He prevented enemies from annihilating them (see Esther), and he restored them to the land (see Ezra-Nehemiah). He commanded the Jews to rebuild the temple "that I may be glorified" (Hag. 1:8), and he also charged them to "honor" and "fear" him as the "great King" over all things (Mal. 1:6, 14). Yet the story of God's glory still awaited its consummation.

The seventy-year exile that Jeremiah foretold (Jer. 25:12; 29:10; cf. Ezra 1:1; Dan. 9:2) came to an end in relation to Cyrus's decree that the people could return to the land (Isa. 44:26–28; 2 Chron. 36:20–23). Yet the royal servant who would reconcile sinners to God had yet to arrive (Isa. 49:6; 53:11; Dan. 9:24). Numerous features indicate that the end of the Old Testament era was not the end of God's kingdom program:

- The land had not returned to an Edenic state (Isa. 51:3; Ezek. 36:33–36).
- The nation was not fully reunited (Jer. 23:6; 31:31; Ezek. 37:22) with believing Gentiles in their midst (Isa. 2:2–4; 49:6; Jer. 12:16; 30:8–9).
- The Jews were still slaves (Ezra 9:8–9; Neh. 9:36), and the Davidic king was not yet reigning (Isa. 9:6–7; Jer. 23:5; 30:9; Ezek. 37:24).
- God's people did not enjoy a new covenant of universal, everlasting peace (Isa. 61:8–9; Jer. 31:31–34; 32:40; Ezek. 37:26).
- God's people did not have new internal dispositions to love and obey Yahweh (Deut. 30:6, 8; Isa. 2:3; 42:4; Jer. 31:33; 32:39–40; Ezek. 36:26–27).

- God's people did not fully enjoy his presence (Ezek. 36:27; 37:27–28).

Yahweh had not yet fully realized his kingdom purposes. The king who was to bring global blessing still needed to come.

6. *Overlap of the Ages (Christ's Work and the Church Age)*

O 🛡️📖🌐✨

As we move into the New Testament, one of the mysterious parts of God's kingdom program was the way Jesus's first coming was as suffering servant, and only in his second coming would he show himself fully as conquering King (Heb. 9:28). In his initial appearing, he brought the future into the middle of history. He proclaimed "the year of the LORD's favor," but only later will he bring "the day of vengeance of our God" (Isa. 61:2; cf. Luke 4:19). Today we live in an overlap of the ages: Christ has delivered us from "the present evil age" (Gal. 1:4) yet only in a way that lets us taste "the powers of the age to come" (Heb. 6:5).

Hence, "the sufferings of this present time are not worth comparing with the glory that is to be revealed to us" (Rom. 8:18).

> For the grace of God has appeared, bringing salvation for all people, training us to renounce ungodliness and worldly passions, and to live self-controlled, upright, and godly lives in the present age, waiting for our blessed hope, the appearing of the glory of our great God and Savior Jesus Christ. (Titus 2:11–13)

Already we have been "born again to a living hope through the resurrection of Jesus Christ from the dead," and that hope points to "an inheritance that is imperishable, undefiled, and unfading, kept in heaven for you, who by God's power are being guarded through faith for a salvation ready to be revealed in the last time" (1 Pet. 1:3–5; cf. Eph. 1:3–14). Figure 4.3 visualizes the *already-not-yet* aspects of the kingdom that are *already* fully initiated but *not yet* finally consummated in this overlap of the ages.[7]

---

7   At one level, the old and new covenants do not actually overlap, for Jesus "makes the first one obsolete" (Heb. 8:13) and "does away with the first in order to establish the second" (Heb. 10:9). At another

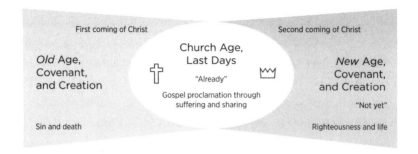

Figure 4.3   Salvation history and the overlap of the ages

In the fullness of time, "God sent forth his Son" (Gal. 4:4), as the very Word that was God "became flesh and dwelt among us" (John 1:14). And "by sending his own Son in the likeness of sinful flesh and for sin, [God] condemned sin in the flesh, in order that the righteous requirement of the law might be fulfilled in us" (Rom. 8:3–4). The kingdom is *already* here because Jesus came to earth to appease God's wrath against the sin of Israel and the world. Jesus is the Christ, the promised royal deliverer, who came "to give his life as a ransom for many" (Mark 10:45). He is "the Lamb of God, who takes away the sin of the world" (John 1:29), and by his life, death, and resurrection he inaugurated the new covenant (Luke 22:20; Heb. 9:15) and new creation (2 Cor. 5:17). In the great exchange of the ages, God counts every believer's sin to Christ and Christ's righteousness to every believer (Isa. 53:11; Rom. 5:18–19; 2 Cor. 5:21; Phil. 3:9).

Jesus lived for the glory of his Father (John 7:18; 17:4). His death and resurrection vindicated God's righteousness and exalted God's glory (John 12:27–28; 17:1). "God put forward [Jesus Christ] as a propitiation by his blood, . . . so that he might be just and the justifier of the one who has faith in Jesus" (Rom. 3:25–26). "Christ redeemed us from the curse of the law by becoming a curse for us . . . so that in Christ Jesus the blessing of Abraham might come to the Gentiles" (Gal. 3:13–14). God's glory raised Christ from the dead (Rom. 6:4) and through this act magnified Christ (Heb. 2:9; 1 Pet. 1:21).

---

level, however, because the old (Mosaic) covenant represents the age of death in Adam, the writer of Hebrews can add, "And what is becoming obsolete and growing old is ready to vanish away" (Heb. 8:13), noting that while "the end of the ages" is already upon us (Heb. 9:26), the consummation of "the age to come" has yet to be realized (Heb. 6:5; cf. 2 Cor. 3:11).

Jesus and his apostles proclaimed the good news of God's kingdom (Luke 4:43; Acts 1:1–3; 20:25; 28:23), a testimony that announced God's end-times reign displayed through "the glory of God in the face of Jesus Christ" (2 Cor. 4:6; cf. 1 Tim. 1:11). The good news is the message "that Christ died for our sins in accordance with the Scriptures, that he was buried, that he was raised on the third day in accordance with the Scriptures, and that he appeared to Cephas, and then to the twelve" (1 Cor. 15:3–5). By means of faith-filled, Spirit-empowered disciples bearing witness to Christ, God's reign and glory have spread from Jerusalem to Judea and Samaria and to the end of the earth (Acts 1:8). Under Christ's universal authority, the church must make disciples of all nations for the sake of Christ's name, ever trusting the powerful presence of the reigning King to guard his servants and open hearts to the gospel (Matt. 28:18–20; Rom. 1:5).

7. Mission Accomplished (Christ's Return
and Kingdom Consummation)

M 🌾 👑 🌍 ✨ ✝ ⛪

God's mercy, wrath, and power make known "the riches of his glory for vessels of mercy, which he has prepared beforehand for glory" (Rom. 9:22–23). Jesus came to satisfy our deepest longing and to help us see and celebrate his glory (John 6:35; 17:24). His return will be glorious (Matt. 16:27; 25:31), for we will "see the Son of Man coming on the clouds of heaven with power and great glory" (Matt. 24:30). Only those who "fear God and give him glory" (Rev. 14:7) will escape divine wrath when the Son of Man returns to be glorified in his saints (2 Thess. 1:9–10; cf. Matt. 16:27; 24:30; 25:31; John 17:24).

Even now, those around the throne of the conquering Lion and slain Lamb are declaring him worthy to carry out God's decreed purposes to punish and save (Rev. 5:5–6, 9–10). And the redeemed mixed multitude will one day cry together, "Salvation belongs to our God who sits on the throne, and to the Lamb!" (Rev. 7:10). In that day, "[God] will dwell with them, and they will be his people, and God himself will be with them as their God. He will wipe away every tear from their eyes, and death shall be no more, neither shall there be mourning, nor crying, nor pain anymore, for the former things have passed away" (Rev. 21:3–4). And "the glory of God" will give the city light—a glory that will be localized in none other than "the Lamb" (Rev. 21:23). And "by its light will the nations walk, . . . and there will be no night there" (Rev. 21:24–25). "No longer will there be anything accursed, but the throne of God and of the Lamb will be in it, and his servants will worship him. . . . They will need no light or lamp or sun, for the Lord God will be their light, and they will reign forever and ever" (Rev. 22:3, 5), thus fulfilling their original call to reflect, resemble, and represent God on earth (Gen. 1:26–28).

In view of these realities, Jesus proclaims, "I am the root and the descendant of David, the bright and morning star. . . . Surely I am coming soon" (Rev. 22:16, 20). And we say with John, "Amen. Come, Lord Jesus!" (Rev. 22:20).

Conclusion

From Genesis through Revelation and from creation to consummation, God is guiding a kingdom program that culminates in Jesus. Both the Old and New Testaments are framed by *his*-story—a story of God's glory in Christ. In the Old Testament, God identifies the key players and problems and makes kingdom promises; in the New Testament God then supplies the solution and fulfills the promises, ultimately through King Jesus. All salvation history points to Christ, and through him God fulfills all earlier hopes, to the praise of his glorious grace (Eph. 1:6, 12).

Tracing the Old Testament's salvation-historical trajectories supplies one important way to see and celebrate Christ in all of Scripture. The next chapter will detail six other ways to exalt Jesus that grow directly out of the Bible's overarching kingdom program.

Review and Reflection

1. Jesus associated "the gospel of God" with "the kingdom of God," and he saw his own ministry realizing it (Mark 1:15). How did Isaiah characterize the end-times gospel (Isa. 40:9–11; 52:7–10; 61:1–3), and how does his vision inform our understanding of Jesus's mission?
2. In what ways can we say of Jesus that Scripture's salvation drama from creation to consummation is *his*-story? Give some examples of how Jesus stands at the center of Scripture.

3. According to the author, what theme stands at the core of God's purposes from Genesis to Revelation?

4. Without looking, try to write down each of the seven stages in God's KING-DOM plan. Now walk through the story with someone by describing each of the thirty images, one at a time.

5. Write down twenty-five random people and events from the Old Testament. Now identify in which of the initial five KINGDOM stages each occurs. If you don't know, find someone who can help, so that you can begin to grasp better how the whole Bible progresses, integrates, and climaxes in Jesus.

6. In what foundational passage in Genesis did God promise to reestablish order in the cosmos through a human deliverer who would overcome curse and the power of evil?

7. What are the two phases by which God fulfills the Abrahamic covenant promises?

8. What are some features indicating that the Old Testament ends demanding a sequel and that God's kingdom purposes were not yet finished?

9. How is the church today living in the "overlap of the ages," and what does this imply for our mission?

10. What was the greatest insight you gained in reading this chapter? What is your greatest takeaway?

5

Seeing and Celebrating Christ
in All of Scripture

And beginning with Moses.

LUKE 24:27

"AND BEGINNING WITH MOSES and all the Prophets, he interpreted to them in all the Scriptures the things concerning himself" (Luke 24:27). The only Bible Jesus had was what we call the Old Testament, and he believed that his Scriptures bore witness about him (John 5:39), that Abraham saw his day and was glad (John 8:56), that Moses wrote of him (John 5:46), that prophets, righteous people, and kings longed for his coming (Matt. 13:17; Luke 10:24), and that everything the Old Testament said concerning him would be fulfilled (Luke 24:27, 44).

Christ's followers should be intent to properly magnify Jesus where he is evident. As the Puritan theologian John Owen wrote, "The revelation . . . of Christ . . . deserves the severest of our thoughts, the best of our meditations and our utmost diligence in them."[1] To accomplish this faithfully, one must employ a multifaceted approach that accounts for the way Jesus is central to all God is doing in history.

The previous chapter noted one important way that we can faithfully exalt Christ in our interpretation of the Old Testament. Scripture's storyline

---

1 John Owen, "Meditations on the Glory of Christ," in *The Works of John Owen*, ed. William H. Goold (Edinburgh: T&T Clark, 1862), 1:275. The quote dates to AD 1684.

91

progresses from creation to the fall to redemption to consummation and highlights Jesus's work as the decisive turning point in salvation history (Luke 16:16; Gal. 3:24–26). The five major divine-human covenants that guide God's kingdom program all terminate in Christ.

- In fulfillment of the *Adamic/Noahic covenant*, Jesus is the Son of Man, last Adam, and image of God (Mark 10:45; 14:62; 1 Cor. 15:45; 2 Cor. 4:4).
- In fulfillment of the *Abrahamic covenant*, Jesus is the offspring of Abraham and agent of universal blessing (Gen. 22:17–18; Acts 3:25–26; Gal. 3:16).
- In fulfillment of the *Mosaic (old) covenant*, Jesus represents Israel and stands as God's Son, Yahweh's servant, the embodiment of wisdom, the one who fulfilled the law's demands, and the substance of all covenant shadows (Ex. 4:22–23; Isa. 49:3, 5–6; Matt. 3:17; 11:2, 19; 12:42; 13:54; John 2:19–21; Acts 3:25–26; Rom. 5:19; Col. 2:17; Heb. 9:9–12; 10:1).
- In fulfillment of the *Davidic covenant*, Jesus is the King of the Jews, the Son of David, and the builder of the true temple (Matt. 2:1; 16:18; 21:9; Luke 1:32–33; Eph. 2:19–21).
- In fulfillment of the *new covenant* promises, Jesus is the prophet like Moses who was to come, the only true mediator between God and man, and the one who grants new hearts and the indwelling Spirit (Deut. 18:15, 18; Luke 7:16; 22:20; Acts 3:22–26; 7:37; Rom. 2:29; 2 Cor. 3:3; 1 Tim. 2:5; Heb. 8:6; 9:15; 10:16; 12:24).

Across the storyline, various themes also develop or progress as God gradually reveals more of himself and his ways through biblical revelation. Some of the main themes include covenant, God's kingdom, law, temple and God's presence, atonement, and mission, all of which find focus in Jesus. So we can see and celebrate Christ when we recognize how he stands as the climax of all the Old Testament's redemptive-historical trajectories.

How to Engage in Christ-Centered Old Testament Interpretation

In considering the relationship of the Testaments and Scripture's unity centered on the divine Son, G. K. Beale has identified five principles that are rooted in the Old Testament's own story of salvation history and that guided the New Testament authors' Old Testament interpretive conclusions:[2]

1. The New Testament authors always assume *corporate solidarity*, in which one can represent the many (e.g., Rom. 5:18–19).
2. Christ *represents the true (remnant) Israel of the old covenant and the true (consummate) Israel, the church*, of the new covenant (Isa. 49:3, 6 with Luke 2:32 and Acts 26:23; Gal. 3:16, 29).
3. God's wise and sovereign plan *unites salvation history* in such a way that earlier parts correspond to later parts (Luke 16:16; cf. Isa. 46:9–10; Eph. 1:11; Rev. 22:13).
4. Christ has initiated (though not consummated) *the age of end-times fulfillment* (Mark 1:15; Luke 16:16; Acts 2:17; Gal. 4:4; 1 Cor. 10:11; Heb. 1:2; 9:26; 1 John 2:18).
5. Christ and his glory stand as the end-time center and goal of history such that his life, death, and resurrection provide *the key to interpreting the earlier portions of the Old Testament and its promises.*

These principles directed the way Jesus and the apostles interpreted Scripture, and they should guide every Christian approach to the Old Testament.

Furthermore, the fact that God authored Scripture and gives it an overarching unity demands that all exegesis and theology in Old Testament interpretation consider three distinct but overlapping contexts:[3]

1. The *close context* focuses on a passage's immediate literary setting within the whole book. Here we observe carefully what and how the text communicates, accounting for both the words and the theology that shapes those words.

---

2 G. K. Beale, "Did Jesus and His Followers Preach the Right Doctrine from the Wrong Texts?," *Them* 14, no. 3 (1989): 90. Reprinted in G. K. Beale, ed., *The Right Doctrine from the Wrong Texts? Essays on the Use of the Old Testament in the New* (Grand Rapids, MI: Baker Academic, 1994), 392; G. K. Beale, *Handbook on the New Testament Use of the Old Testament: Exegesis and Interpretation* (Grand Rapids, MI: Baker Academic, 2012), 52–53, 95–102. I have added all the scriptural references.

3 These heading titles are drawn from Trent Hunter and Stephen J. Wellum, *Christ from Beginning to End: How the Full Story of Scripture Reveals the Full Glory of Christ* (Grand Rapids, MI: Zondervan, 2018), 42–69. The categories are similar to but not identical with the textual, epochal, and canonical "horizons" found in Richard Lints, *The Fabric of Theology: A Prolegomenon to Evangelical Theology* (Grand Rapids, MI: Eerdmans, 1993), 293–310.

2. The *continuing context* considers the passage within God's story of salvation. We examine how an Old Testament text is informed by antecedent Scripture (e.g., the Old Testament use of the Old Testament) and contributes to God's unfolding kingdom drama, whether by progressing the covenants or developing a biblical theme or typological pattern that culminates in Christ.

3. The *complete context* concerns a text's placement and use within the broader canon. We consider whether and how later Scripture uses or builds on this passage. We also keep in mind revelation's progressive nature, the way Christ's work influences all history, and how the divine authorship of Scripture allows later passages to clarify, enhance, or deepen the meaning of earlier texts.

Only by considering all three contexts will Christian interpreters be able to fully grasp God's intended meaning of Old Testament passages and understand how those texts point to Christ.

Six More Ways to See and Celebrate Christ in the Old Testament[4]

Christ fulfills the Old Testament in varied ways, and he holds together Scripture's vast diversity by varied means. The Christian interpreter must, therefore, carefully follow Scripture's signals to properly magnify the Messiah and his work. Along with tracing Scripture's kingdom program climaxing in Jesus (chap. 4), the salvation-historical, Christocentric model presented here proposes at least six other ways God exalts Jesus in the Old Testament:

See and Celebrate Christ through the
Old Testament's Direct Messianic Predictions

Peter stresses, "What God foretold by the mouth of *all* the prophets, that his Christ would suffer, he thus fulfilled" (Acts 3:18). Every one of the

---

4 Much of what follows adapts and extends material first published in Jason S. DeRouchie, "Question 3: How Does Biblical Theology Help Us See Christ in the Old Testament?," in Jason S. DeRouchie, Oren R. Martin, and Andrew David Naselli, *40 Questions about Biblical Theology* (Grand Rapids, MI: Kregel, 2020), 41–47. Published by Kregel, Inc. Used with permission. For related overviews, see, e.g., Sidney Greidanus, *Preaching Christ from the Old Testament: A Contemporary Hermeneutical Method* (Grand Rapids, MI: Eerdmans, 1999); Abner Chou, "'They Were Not Serving Themselves, but You': Reclaiming the Prophets' Messianic Intention," *The Master's Seminary Journal* 33, no. 2 (2022): 231–36.

prophets from Moses onward anticipated the Messiah's work and mission (Acts 3:22–24; 10:43). The Old Testament is loaded with explicit and implicit direct messianic predictions.

For example, Moses records that Yahweh promised Abraham that a single, male offspring would "possess the gate of his enemies" and that "all the nations of the earth" would regard themselves "blessed" in him (Gen. 22:17–18). Paul, then, notes how in Christ Jesus God fulfilled his promise to bring blessing to the Gentiles (Gal. 3:8, 14). Indeed, "the promises were made to Abraham and to his offspring . . . who is Christ. . . . And if you are Christ's, then you are Abraham's offspring, heirs according to promise" (Gal. 3:16, 29).

Operating as a prophet, David spoke of his messianic Lord's exaltation. Hence, citing Psalm 110:1, Jesus queried about the Sadducees,

> How can they say that the Christ is David's son? For David himself says in the Book of Psalms,
>
> > "The Lord said to my Lord,
> > 'Sit at my right hand,
> >   until I make your enemies your footstool.'"
>
> David thus calls him Lord, so how is he his son? (Luke 20:41–44; cf. Acts 2:30, 34; Heb. 1:13)

Speaking of how Yahweh's servant would suffer as a substitute for many, Isaiah foresaw,

> He was pierced for our transgressions;
>   he was crushed for our iniquities;
> upon him was the chastisement that brought us peace,
>   and with his wounds we are healed. (Isa. 53:5)

Later, Peter indicates how Jesus Christ fulfilled the prediction: "He himself bore our sins in his body on the tree, that we might die to sin and live to righteousness. By his wounds you have been healed" (1 Pet. 2:24).

Similarly, Yahweh promised through Ezekiel, "I will set up over them one shepherd, my servant David, and he shall feed them" (Ezek. 34:23).

Then in John 10, Jesus declared, "I am the good shepherd" (John 10:11), and again, "There will be one flock, one shepherd" (10:16). At times, the element of prediction-fulfillment is even more pronounced, as when Micah 5:2 foretells the birth of the royal deliverer in Bethlehem, and then Matthew 2:6 explicitly asserts that it happened just as the prophet wrote.

Christ fulfills the Old Testament as the specific focus or goal of direct Old Testament messianic predictions and redemptive-historical hopes. So, when you read the Old Testament's direct messianic predictions, see and celebrate how the divine Son realizes these hopes.

See and Celebrate Christ through Similarities and Contrasts of the Old and New Ages, Creations, and Covenants

Jesus's saving work creates both continuities and discontinuities between the old and new ages, creations, and covenants. For example, while the new covenant and old covenant contain a similar structure (i.e., God first redeems and then calls his people to obey), only the new covenant supplies freedom from sin and power for obedience to *all* covenant members (Jer. 31:33–34); the old covenant did not change hearts (Deut. 29:4; Rom. 8:3). Similarly, whereas Adam disobeyed and brought death to all, Christ obeys and brings life to many (Rom. 5:18–19). Whereas God used the blood of bulls and goats to picture atonement in the old covenant, Christ's own substitutionary sacrifice provides the ground for eternal redemption (Heb. 9:11–14). Whereas access to Yahweh's presence in the temple was restricted to the high priest on the Day of Atonement, Christ's priestly work opens the way for all in him to enjoy God's presence (Heb. 9:24–26; 10:19–22). Whereas the nations needed to come to the tabernacle/temple to encounter the Lord's presence in the old covenant, the Spirit of Christ now empowers the church in its witness to the nations from Jerusalem to the ends of the earth (Matt. 28:18–20; Acts 1:8). These kinds of similarities and contrasts between the old and new ages, creations, and covenants encourage a messianic reading of the Old Testament within the redemptive-historical approach. We can see and celebrate Christ's work by identifying the patterns and transformations.

See and Celebrate Christ through the Old Testament's Typology

The author of Hebrews says the Old Testament law was "a shadow of the good things to come" (Heb. 10:1), and Paul claims that clean and unclean food laws, the Jewish festivals and monthly sacrificial calendar, and even the Sabbath were each "a shadow of the things to come, but the substance belongs to Christ" (Col. 2:16–17). The New Testament calls these anticipations and pointers "types" or "examples" (Rom. 5:14; 1 Cor. 10:6) that in turn find their counterpart, or "antitype," in Jesus as their ultimate realization. G. K. Beale defines *typology* as

> the study of analogical correspondences among revealed truths about persons, events, institutions, and other things within the historical framework of God's special revelation, which, from a retrospective view, are of a prophetic nature and are escalated in their meaning.[5]

Significantly, Abner Chou is correct that typology is *not* an interpretive strategy or reading technique but is instead established through "a linguistic association found objectively in the text. . . . While typology does not always need to use the word 'type,' the only valid type is one that comes from the meaning of Scripture, from the author's intent."[6] Exegetical warrant is necessary to establish any type.

Andrew Naselli notes that every true type includes at least four elements: (1) *analogy:* the type and antitype are analogous; (2) *historicity:* the type and antitype occur in real history; (3) *foreshadowing:* God sovereignly designed the type to foreshadow the antitype; (4) *escalation:* the antitype escalates the type from shadow to reality by climaxing in Jesus.[7] God structured the progressive development of salvation history in such a way that certain Old Testament characters (e.g., Adam, Melchizedek, Moses, David), events (e.g., the flood, the exodus, the return to the land), and institutions or objects (e.g., the Passover lamb, the temple, the priesthood) bear meanings that clarify, color, and predictively anticipate the Messiah's life and work. Without attempting to be exhaustive, here are some examples of Old Testament types that find their fulfillment in Christ:

TYPOLOGICAL PERSONS

- Adam was a type of Christ as the ultimate human (Rom. 5:12–21; 1 Cor. 15:45–49).

5 Beale, *Handbook on the New Testament Use of the Old Testament*, 14.
6 Chou, "'They Were Not Serving Themselves, but You,'" 230.
7 Andrew David Naselli, "Question 8: How Should Biblical Theology Approach Typology?," in DeRouchie, Martin, and Naselli, *40 Questions about Biblical Theology*, 81–88.

- Melchizedek was a type for Christ's eternal royal priesthood (Gen. 14:18–24; Heb. 5:5–9; 6:20; 7:1–10, 17).
- Moses was a type for Christ's prophetic role (Deut. 18:15–19; Acts 3:19–26) and faithfulness (Heb. 3:1–6).
- Aaron was a type for Christ's high priesthood (Heb. 5:1–5).
- Israel as God's corporate son (Ex. 4:21–22) and servant (Isa. 42:18–20) typified Christ as the representative Son (Matt. 4:1–4) and servant (Isa. 49:3, 6; cf. 42:1–3 with Matt. 12:15–21).
- David as Israel's king and God's royal son typified Christ's representative kingship and sonship (2 Sam. 7:14–16; Ps. 2:7; Matt. 21:9; Heb. 1:5).
- Jonah's time in and departure from the belly of the fish made him a type for Christ's death, burial, and resurrection (Jonah 2; Matt. 12:40).

TYPOLOGICAL EVENTS OR ACTS

- Every one of God's major creative or redemptive acts in the Old Testament anticipates Christ's work of salvation. Creation gives rise to new creation; the original exodus points to the second exodus; the destruction of Samaria and Jerusalem on the day of the Lord finds culmination at the cross and final day of judgment; the initial restoration to the land prepares for the ultimate reconciliation with God.
- The elevation of the bronze serpent typified the crucifixion of Christ (where he became sin and bore our curse) and its resulting benefits (Num. 21:4–9; John 3:14).
- The flood and Red Sea deliverances typified baptism (1 Cor. 10:2; 1 Pet. 3:20–21).
- The smiting of the rock typified Christ's substitutionary, life-giving sacrifice (1 Cor. 10:4).
- Other events in Israel's wilderness years were types to benefit Christians (1 Cor. 10:11).

TYPOLOGICAL INSTITUTIONS OR OBJECTS

- The earthly tabernacle and all its furniture (Ex. 25:9, 40) were but "a copy and shadow of the heavenly things" (Heb. 8:5; cf. 8:2; 9:11, 24). This included "the mercy seat" (Ex. 25:21–22; Lev. 16:14–15) that points directly to Christ as the one upon whom atonement is realized (Rom. 3:24–26).

- The earthly temple typified Christ (John 2:19–21; cf. 1:14) and his church (1 Cor. 6:19).
- The Old Testament priesthood (Zech. 3:8) anticipated Christ as the high priest (Heb. 2:17; 9:11; cf. 9:24) and the church as priests (1 Pet. 2:5, 9).
- The Passover lamb (Ex. 12:3) typified Christ's substitutionary death (Isa. 53:7; John 1:29; Acts 8:32; 1 Cor. 5:7; 1 Pet. 1:19).
- The substitutionary sacrifices in Leviticus typified Christ's own substitutionary sacrifice (Isa. 53:4–5, 8, 10–12; Heb. 9:12–14; 10:1–4, 10; 1 John 1:9–2:2; 10; cf. Col. 2:13–14).
- Clean and unclean food laws and the Jewish festivals and monthly sacrificial calendar typologically pointed to Christ (Col. 2:16–17; cf. Rom. 14:5–6; Gal. 4:9–10).
- The Sabbath typologically anticipated the rest that Christ's resurrection inaugurated (Matt. 11:28–12:8; Col. 2:16–17; Heb. 4:1–11).

When you identify Old Testament types that clarify and anticipate Christ's person and work, see and celebrate the divine Son as the substance of all earlier shadows.[8]

See and Celebrate Christ through Yahweh's Identity and Activity

When we meet Yahweh in the Old Testament, we are catching glimpses of the coming Christ. Recall that Jesus said that "no one has ever seen God" the Father except the Son (John 1:18; 6:46) but that "whoever has seen me has seen the Father" (John 14:9). Similarly, Paul speaks of the Father as "the invisible God" (Col. 1:15) "who dwells in unapproachable light, whom no one has ever seen or can see" (1 Tim. 6:16). Minimally, this means that those who saw God in the Old Testament (e.g., Ex. 24:11; 33:11; Isa. 6:1) were enjoying preliminary and partial glimpses of his glory (Ex. 33:18–23), at

---

8 For more on the concept of typology, see Dennis E. Johnson, *Him We Proclaim: Preaching Christ from All the Scriptures* (Phillipsburg, NJ: P&R, 2007); Mitchell Chase, *40 Questions about Typology and Allegory* (Grand Rapids, MI: Kregel, 2020); James M. Hamilton, *Typology—Understanding the Bible's Promise-Shaped Patterns: How Old Testament Expectations Are Fulfilled in Christ* (Grand Rapids, MI: Zondervan, 2022).

times through visions with figurative images (Dan. 7:9–10). It also implies that, at least in some instances where Yahweh becomes embodied in a human form in the Old Testament, we are likely meeting the preincarnate Son. Such is possible in the stories of Abraham's third guest (Gen. 18:22), Jacob's wrestling opponent (Gen. 32:24–30), Joshua's "commander of the LORD's army" (Josh. 5:13–15), Ezekiel's exalted king (Ezek. 1:26), Daniel's "son of man" (Dan. 7:13–14), and the numerous manifestations of the "angel/messenger of Yahweh."[9] John tells us that we also see Jesus's glory in Isaiah's vision of the Lord seated on the throne (John 12:41; cf. Isa 6:1).[10] Each of these revelations provides potential glimpses of the promised Christ who would come as the God-man.

Additionally, with allusions to Yahweh's declaration, "I AM WHO I AM" (Ex. 3:14), John emphasizes how Jesus explicitly linked himself to Yahweh by his identity statements and his actions. Thus, he declared, "Before Abraham was, I am" (John 8:58).

- Jesus is the calmer of storms: "*I am*; do not be afraid" (John 6:20).[11]
- He is the all-satisfying one: "*I am* the bread of life" (John 6:35).
- He is the ultimate guide and enabler: "*I am* the light of the world" (John 8:12).
- He is the one in whom you must be saved: "Unless you believe that *I am*, you will die in your sins" (John 8:24).
- He is the one whom people will link with Yahweh after his death and resurrection: "When you have lifted up the Son of Man, then you will know that *I am*" (John 8:28). "I am telling you this now, . . . that when [the resurrection] does take place you may believe that *I am*" (John 13:19).
- He is the only entry to refuge: "*I am* the door of the sheep" (John 10:7, 9).
- He is the ultimate provider and protector: "*I am* the good shepherd" (John 10:11, 14).

9   E.g., Gen. 16:7–13; 22:11–18; Ex. 3:2; Num. 20:16; 22:22–35; Judg. 2:1–4; 5:23; 6:11–12, 21–22; 13:3, 13–21; 2 Sam. 24:16; 1 Kings 19:7; 2 Kings 1:3, 15; 19:35; Dan. 3:24–25, 28.
10 Cf. 1 Kings 22:19.
11 In some of these texts from John, the ESV renders the Greek *egō eimi* slightly differently (e.g., "I am he"; "it is I"). I have rendered every instance of the expression here as "I am."

- He is the one who provides eternal life and access to the Father: "*I am* the resurrection and the life" (John 11:25). "*I am* the way, and the truth, and the life. No one comes to the Father except through me" (John 14:6).
- He is the one who helps us grow: "*I am* the true vine. . . . Whoever abides in me and I in him, he it is that bears much fruit" (John 15:1, 5).
- He is the one whose identity demands homage: "When Jesus said to them, '*I am*,' they drew back and fell to the ground" (John 18:6).

When we hear Yahweh speaking or see him acting in the Old Testament as the object of people's faith, we are encountering the very one who would embody himself in the incarnate Christ. The Word who was "in the beginning . . . with God . . . was God" (John 1:1–2). The very Son who would be named Jesus "was in the form of God" (Phil. 2:6), was the very "image of the invisible God" (Col. 1:15), and was "the radiance of the glory of God and the exact imprint of his nature" (Heb. 1:3). Thus, the author of Hebrews could attribute Moses's reproach for *God's* sake as a reproach endured for *Christ*: "He considered the reproach of Christ greater wealth than the treasures of Egypt, for he was looking to the reward" (Heb. 11:26). This is also why Jude could identify Israel's deliverer at the exodus as *Jesus*: "Now I want to remind you . . . that Jesus, who saved a people out of the land of Egypt, afterward destroyed those who did not believe" (Jude 5). Who fought for Israel and rescued them at the exodus? Was it not Yahweh? Yes! And it was *Jesus*!

Anticipating the messianic era, Isaiah declares that "a voice" cried out: "In the wilderness prepare the way of the Lord" (Isa. 40:3), and each of the Gospel writers identifies this with John the Baptizer's pointing to Jesus's coming (Matt. 3:3; Mark 1:3; Luke 3:4; John 1:23). Similarly, Joel proclaims, "Everyone who calls on the name of the Lord shall be saved" (Joel 2:32), and Paul applies this verse to *Jesus* in Romans 10:13. Finally, Malachi asserts that a new Elijah would arrive and then "the Lord whom you seek will suddenly come to his temple" (Mal. 3:1; 4:5). Jesus claimed that John the Baptizer was this Elijah (Matt. 11:11–15; 17:10–13), who himself pointed to Christ as the anticipated Lord (Matt. 3:11–12) who embodies God's presence (John 1:14; 2:21).

Christ's words bear unparalleled authority (Mark 1:22), and he did what only God can do—commanding demons and healing the sick (Mark 1:34;

3:10–11, 22), forgiving sins (Mark 2:7, 10–11), and raising the dead (Mark 5:35–36, 41–43). Jesus said that if we have seen him, we have seen the Father (John 14:9), and that the Father was working through him (John 14:10). Every Old Testament manifestation of Yahweh's punishment, pardon, retribution, and reconciliation directly foreshadows and ultimately flows from the work of God's Son, "whom he appointed the heir of all things, through whom he created the world," who "is the radiance of the glory of God and the exact imprint of his nature," and who "upholds the universe by the word of his power" (Heb. 1:2–3). The very Word that "was God . . . became flesh and dwelt among us, and we have seen his glory, glory as of the only Son from the Father, full of grace and truth" (John 1:1, 14; cf. Ex. 33:18; 34:6).

When we meet Yahweh in the Old Testament, we are catching glimpses of the coming Christ. Thus, when you revel in Yahweh's identity and activity, see and celebrate the divine Son.

See and Celebrate Christ through the Ethical Ideals of Old Testament Law and Wisdom

The Old Testament is filled with stories of sinners who needed a savior. Moses's law stressed the importance for Christ in the way it characterized and multiplied sin (Rom. 3:20; 5:20; cf. 7:7–12; Gal. 3:19), imprisoned the sinful (Rom. 3:19–20; 8:2–3; Gal. 3:10, 13, 22), and showed everyone's need for atonement. The law by its nature, therefore, predicted Christ as "the end of the law for righteousness to everyone who believes" (Rom. 10:4).

Jesus is the perfect embodiment of God's character and the ideal image of dependence, law keeping, wisdom, praise, and perseverance. Paul stresses both that in the law we have "the embodiment of knowledge and truth" (Rom. 2:20) and that "the law is holy, and the commandment is holy and righteous and good" (Rom. 7:12). The same can be said of Christ, who remained sinless (2 Cor. 5:21; Heb. 4:15; 1 Pet. 2:22; 1 John 3:5) and "became to us wisdom from God, righteousness and sanctification and redemption" (1 Cor. 1:30).

To those whom God calls, Christ is "the power of God and the wisdom" (1 Cor. 1:24). With allusions to Proverbs 8:22–31, Paul speaks of Jesus as "the image of the invisible God, the firstborn of all creation" in whom "all things hold together" (Col. 1:15, 17). "Wisdom is justified by her deeds"

(Matt. 11:19), and while Solomon's wisdom was great, in Christ "something greater than Solomon is here" (Matt. 12:42).

> Who has wrapped up the waters in a garment?
>   Who has established all the ends of the earth?
> What is his name, and what is his son's name?
>   Surely you know! (Prov. 30:4; cf. 3:19–20)

Paul stresses, "But now the righteousness of God has been manifested apart from the law, although the Law and the Prophets bear witness to it—the righteousness of God through faith in Jesus Christ for all who believe" (Rom. 3:21–22). Figures like Moses, David, and Isaiah anticipated the righteousness displayed through the gospel (Rom. 1:16–17). It's bound up in Christ's perfect obedience climaxing in his death on the cross (Rom. 3:22–26; Phil. 2:8), through which we are justified by faith (Rom. 3:27–30; 5:1). Jesus incarnated the portrait of the worshiping sufferer and victorious king of the Psalms. He perfectly kept his Father's commandments and abided in his love (John 15:10). Through Christ's substitutionary work, God canceled "the record of debt that stood against us with its legal demands" (Col. 2:14). He "condemned sin in the flesh, in order that the righteous requirement of the law might be fulfilled in us" (Rom. 8:3–4).

As God's Word made flesh, Jesus manifests in his person the essence of every ethical ideal aligned with Yahweh's revealed will, and it is this perfection that is then imputed to believers. "Therefore, as one trespass led to condemnation for all men, so one act of righteousness leads to justification and life for all men. For as by the one man's disobedience the many were made sinners, so by the one man's obedience the many will be made righteous" (Rom. 5:18–19; cf. 8:4). Paul views himself as being "found in" Christ, "not having a righteousness of my own that comes from the law, but that which comes through faith in Christ, the righteousness from God that depends on faith" (Phil. 3:9). "For our sake he made him to be sin who knew no sin, so that in him we might become the righteousness of God" (2 Cor. 5:21).

Every law and every wise saying in the Old Testament is a source for magnifying the greatness of Christ on our behalf. Therefore, when you observe how the Old Testament law and wisdom express ethical ideals, see and celebrate the justifying work of the divine Son.

See and Celebrate Christ by Using the Old Testament to Instruct Others

The New Testament authors recognized that the Old Testament law was "imposed until the time of reformation" (Heb. 9:10) and that "the law was our guardian until Christ came. . . . But now that faith has come, we are no longer under a guardian" (Gal. 3:24–25). Nevertheless, Paul has no hesitation declaring that "all Scripture [which in context principally meant the Old Testament] is . . . profitable for teaching, for reproof, for correction, and for training in righteousness" (2 Tim. 3:16). In this context, the apostle could even charge Timothy, "Preach the word" (2 Tim. 4:2), urging this Christian pastor to help his people find hope in the gospel mostly from the Old Testament Scriptures.

For Paul and the other apostles, while the old covenant law and wisdom no longer bore direct authority in the Christian's life, they still bore indirect authority when read through the mediation of Christ. Thus, Paul could say to Timothy about the Old Testament, "From childhood [as a Jew; see Acts 16:1; 2 Tim. 1:5] you have been acquainted with the sacred writings [i.e., the Old Testament], which are able to make you wise for salvation *through faith in Christ Jesus*" (2 Tim. 3:15). The Old Testament continues to matter for Christians, but we must approach it through the light and lens of Jesus. Only through him can we see, hope, and live as God intended. Jesus's coming unlocks the significance of the Old Testament text, and through him we now have access to a massive amount of Scripture that can clarify how to love God and love our neighbor (Rom. 16:25–26; 2 Cor. 3:14).

Some of the Old Testament promises that "find their Yes in [Christ]" (2 Cor. 1:20) are those that predicted how new covenant believers would live out God's law in the day when hearts were circumcised (Deut. 30:6, 8) and when God would put his Spirit in his transformed people (Ezek. 36:27; Jer. 12:16). In that day of restoration, all God's children "shall be taught by the LORD" (Isa. 54:13; cf. John 6:44–45), and having the law written on their hearts, "they shall know [the LORD], from the least of them to the greatest" (Jer. 31:33–34; cf. 1 John 2:20–21, 27).

In Christ, God now empowers us to keep the "precepts" of the law, as we live with circumcised hearts by the power of the Spirit (Rom. 2:26, 29; cf. 2:14–15; see Deut. 30:10; Ezek. 36:27). We fulfill the law as we love our neighbor (Rom. 13:8–10; cf. Matt. 7:12; Gal 6:2). Christ is our teacher

(Isa. 42:4; 51:4; Matt. 17:5; 28:20), and his own law fulfillment now clarifies for us what it means to follow God (Matt. 5:17–19; cf. 1 Cor. 9:21; James 1:25; 2:8, 12). In Christ we find a new pattern for surrender and service (Phil. 2:5–7; Heb. 12:1–3; 1 Pet. 2:21; 1 John 2:6), and in Jesus we experience true pardon (Rom. 3:23–26; 5:8–9, 18–19; 8:3–4; 2 Cor. 5:21), which in turn supplies both power to obey (Rom. 1:16; 6:22; 8:13; 1 Cor. 1:18; 15:10) and promises that motivate this obedience (2 Cor. 1:20; 7:1; 2 Pet. 1:4; 1 John 3:3; cf. Isa. 41:10; Phil. 1:6; 1 Thess. 5:23–24; Heb. 13:20–21). When we use the Old Testament to instruct or guide others, calling them to love and thus fulfill the law, we can see and celebrate the sanctifying work of the divine Son.[12]

Conclusion

This chapter and the previous one have supplied seven ways to see and celebrate Christ in the Old Testament. Not all operate at the same time, but each of these provides readers and teachers of Scripture fresh avenues to make much of Jesus. See and celebrate the divine Son by:

- Considering the Old Testament's salvation-historical trajectories;
- Seeing the Old Testament's direct messianic predictions;
- Recognizing similarities and contrasts within salvation history;
- Identifying Old Testament types;
- Reveling in Yahweh's identity and activity;
- Observing the Old Testament's ethical ideals; and
- Using the Old Testament to instruct others.

Furthermore, the very presence of the Bible testifies to a God who does not immediately wipe out unbelieving rebels. Although the Lord was speaking before the fall of humanity into sin, he did not have this sacred text written until after sin entered the world. Rather than definitively destroying all of humankind as we deserved, he by grace initiated a history of salvation culminating in Christ. Every word, indeed, every letter of the Bible testifies to the reality of divine grace, and we enjoy all grace only because of Jesus's substitutionary sacrifice (see e.g., Gen. 8:20–21; John 3:16–17; 1 Tim. 4:10; 1 John 2:2). All things, including the very letters of Scripture

---

12 For more on the Christian's relationship to old covenant law, see chaps. 10–13 in this book.

(Matt. 5:18), are from the divine Son, through the divine Son, and for the divine Son (Col. 1:16). With this, the Spirit who inspired the biblical text is always working to magnify the Son (John 16:14). If, after evaluating any given Old Testament text through the seven above ways, you still don't find a bridge to magnifying the Messiah, then recognize that we can see and celebrate Christ in the mere fact that we have the written word. God is speaking through the Old and New Testaments, and he is speaking only because Jesus purchased both common and saving grace; Jesus purchased the grace that allows sinners to receive the sacred text.

I have sought to show how biblical theology helps us see and celebrate Christ in the Old Testament. Jesus identified that his Bible was about him—his death and resurrection and the mission he would generate (Luke 24:44–47; Acts 26:22–23). By reading Old Testament texts in view of how Scripture progresses, integrates, and climaxes in Jesus, Christ's person and work become apparent in multifaceted ways. Once the apostles met the resurrected Christ, they *never* interpreted their Bible in the same way. Jesus supplies both a light and a lens for rightly reading what was present in the Old Testament all along (Rom. 16:25–26; 2 Cor. 3:14). May we increasingly learn to faithfully proclaim "Jesus Christ and him crucified" (1 Cor. 2:2) from the initial three-fourths of the Christian Scriptures.[13]

Review and Reflection

1. List from memory the five major divine-human covenants that guide God's kingdom program, and then clarify how Christ fulfills each.

2. List the five principles that guide the New Testament authors' Old Testament interpretive conclusions.

3. What are the three distinct but overlapping contexts that should direct all Old Testament exegesis and theology?

---

13 For more on this redemptive-historical, Christocentric approach to Christ in the Old Testament that interacts with other major perspectives and engages in case studies (on Gen. 15:1–6; 22:1–19; Prov. 8:22–31; Isa. 42:1–4), see Jason S. DeRouchie, "Lifting the Veil: Reading and Preaching Jesus' Bible through Christ and for Christ," *SBJT* 22, no. 3 (2018): 157–79; Jason S. DeRouchie, "Redemptive-Historical, Christocentric Approach," in *Five Views of Christ in the Old Testament*, ed. Andrew M. King and Brian J. Tabb, Counterpoints: Bible and Theology (Grand Rapids, MI: Zondervan Academic, 2022), 181–211, 234–37; cf. 56–62, 112–17, 163–69, 284–89. See also the entire issue of *SBJT* 22, no. 3 (2018) on "Preaching Christ from the Old Testament" and King and Tabb, *Five Views of Christ in the Old Testament*.

4. Chapter 4 traced salvation history to Christ. List from memory the additional six ways this chapter proposes for seeing and celebrating Jesus in the Old Testament. Which one of the six stands out to you most as a new potential way you could savor Christ in the Old Testament?

5. Which of the seven ways of seeing and celebrating Christ in the Old Testament would most naturally align with each of the following texts?

- Genesis 15:1–6
- Exodus 12:1–7
- Deuteronomy 22:1–3
- Judges 2:11–15
- 2 Kings 17:14–18

- Psalm 110
- Proverbs 8:22–31
- Proverbs 10:6–11
- Ezekiel 37:24–28
- Micah 5:2–4

6. What is an Old Testament "type"? Supply one example each of a character, event, and institution/object that serve as types for Christ in the Old Testament.

7. What are some of Jesus's "I am" statements, and how are they significant in relation to the Old Testament? What do they tell us about Jesus's self-identity?

8. In what ways do the Old Testament's ethical ideals anticipate Christ? How do they help us celebrate justification by grace alone through faith alone in Christ alone?

9. What was the last passage you worked through in the Old Testament? How might this chapter help you see and celebrate Christ from there?

10. What was the greatest insight you gained in reading this chapter? What is your greatest takeaway?

6

The Message of Genesis and the Hope for Christ

He shall bruise your head.

GENESIS 3:15

PHILIP ASSERTED TO NATHANAEL, "We have found him of whom Moses in the Law and also the prophets wrote, Jesus of Nazareth" (John 1:45). Jesus also charged the Jewish leaders, saying, "There is one who accuses you: Moses, on whom you have set your hope. For if you believed Moses, you would believe me, for he wrote of me" (John 5:45–46). Finally, the author of Hebrews notes: "Moses was faithful in all God's house as a servant, to testify to the things that were to be spoken later" (Heb. 3:5). Moses longed for and wrote of the coming royal deliverer and his days.

This chapter provides a case study of Genesis through the light and lens of Christ and sketches how this book's message testifies to Moses's hope. As summarized in table 6.1, the previous two chapters overviewed seven possible ways to see and celebrate Christ in the Old Testament.

Table 6.1   Seven ways to see and celebrate Christ in the Old Testament

1. Consider the Old Testament's salvation-historical trajectories.
2. See the Old Testament's direct messianic predictions.
3. Recognize similarities and contrasts within salvation history.
4. Identify Old Testament types.
5. Revel in Yahweh's identity and activity.
6. Note the Old Testament's ethical ideals.
7. Use the Old Testament to instruct others.

While overviewing Genesis's messianic hope, this chapter highlights examples of each of these seven ways.

Introduction

In Genesis, Yahweh introduces his kingdom program by highlighting the need for universal blessing and how he would restore it. Not only does the book clarify the world's problem (sin, curse), it also instills hope for the solution. Genesis describes the initial two KINGDOM stages: Kickoff and Rebellion (creation, fall, flood) and Instrument of Blessing (the patriarchs). In the process, it also details the initial two major biblical covenants: the Adamic/Noahic covenant with creation and the Abrahamic covenant.

While Exodus through Deuteronomy establish the old Mosaic covenant and detail Israel's calling as a kingdom of priests and a holy nation (Ex. 19:5–6), Genesis clarifies the global context of Israel's calling and the hope of the male royal deliverer. Sin has resulted in worldwide curse, which gave rise to a global flood catastrophe. Abraham and his offspring—climaxing in a single, male, royal descendant in the line of Judah—would be the means for Yahweh's blessing to overcome the curse.

Arrangement and Thought Flow

Genesis opens with a preface in 1:1–2:3 that highlights God's commission to his male and female image bearers to "fill the earth and subdue it" (Gen. 1:28). Genesis then comprises ten units, each with a heading including the phrase "the generations of" (Hebrew *toledot*). This phrase is linked to a named character, from whom flows either a historical narrative or genealogy (Gen. 2:4; 5:1; 6:9; 10:1; 11:10, 27; 25:12, 19; 36:1[+

36:9]; 37:2). For example, a ten-member genealogy stretching from Adam to Noah (Gen. 5:1–32) follows the title "the book of the generations of Adam" (5:1), and the title "the generations of Jacob" (37:2) introduces an extended story, principally focused on Jacob's sons (37:2–50:26). The "generations" headings progressively direct the reader from progenitor (i.e., the ancestor) to progeny (i.e., offspring) and narrow the readers' focus from all the world to Israel, through whom the royal offspring will rise to bless the world.

The choice of "generations" as the structuring term was intentional, for Genesis is dominated by the theme of "seed/offspring," with the term itself (Hebrew *zera'*) occurring 59 times (26 percent of the total 229 Old Testament occurrences) and referring to plant seed (10 times), animal seed (2 times, though figurative for humans displaying serpent-like hostility to God in Gen. 3:15), and human seed/offspring (47 times), the latter cluster of which includes at least 11 references to a single, male deliverer.[1]

Significantly, while not evident in the ESV, the ten "generations" headings are grouped into five units by the fronting of the Hebrew conjunction *waw* (often translated "and") (see table 6.2). Furthermore, building off the contrast between the serpent's "offspring" and the woman's "offspring" in Genesis 3:15, seven of the headings introduce units focused on the remnant who hope in God's promise of the offspring, and three address the rebel nations who were still in need of Yahweh's blessing. We have, therefore, a contrast between those enjoying Yahweh's blessing (the missionaries/the chosen) and those needing it (the mission field/the rejected).

Of the seven positive units, five introduce narrative histories: Genesis 2:4–4:26 (heavens and earth); 6:9–29 (Noah); 11:27–25:11 (Terah); 25:19–35:29 (Isaac); 37:2–50:26 (Jacob). Two introduce linear narrative genealogies (i.e., A gave birth to B; B gave birth to C; C gave birth to D):

1   The references to human "offspring/seed" in Genesis are to (1) natural offspring in general (13x in Gen. 9:9; 15:3; 16:10; 17:12; 19:32, 34; 21:13; 38:8–9[3x]; 46:6–7[2x]; 48:11), (2) special natural offspring as a people (23x in Gen. 4:25; 12:7; 13:15–16[3x]; 15:13, 18; 17:7–10[5x], 19; 21:12; 24:7; 26:24; 28:4, 13–14[3x?]; 32:13; 35:12; 48:4), and (3) special natural offspring as a person (11x in Gen. 3:15; 15:5; 22:17–18[3x]; 24:60; 26:3–4[4x]; 48:19). For an article that considers the relationship of the single male offspring to the special offspring people in both the old and new covenants and that includes a chart cataloging all of the Bible's uses, see Jason S. DeRouchie, "Counting Stars with Abraham and the Prophets: New Covenant Ecclesiology in Old Testament Perspective," *JETS* 58, no. 3 (2015): 445–85 (chart on 448–49). This earlier study catalogs seven of the above "offspring as a person" references differently.

5:1–6:8 (Adam); 11:10–26 (Shem). The remaining three "generations" headings front segmented genealogies, whose disjointed nature forces the reader to slow down and consider their significance (i.e., A gave birth to B and C; B gave birth to E, F, G; C gave birth to H, I, J): 10:1–11:9 (Noah's sons); 25:12–18 (Ishmael); 36:1–8, 9–37:1 (Esau).[2]

Table 6.2   The "these are the generations" structure of Genesis

Part	Section	The Preface and "Generations" Units	Genre
1		Preface: Biblical worldview foundations (1:1–2:3)	
2	i	These are the generations of the heavens and the earth (2:4–4:26)	N (+LG/SG)
3A	ii	This is the book of the generations of Adam (5:1–6:8)	LG (+N)
	iii	These are the generations of Noah (6:9–9:29)	N
		And these are the generations of Noah's sons (10:1–11:9)	SG (+N)
3B	iv	These are the generations of Shem (11:10–26)	LG
		And these are the generations of Terah (11:27–25:11)	N (+SG)
		And these are the generations of Ishmael (25:12–18)	SG

2   For a full discussion of the "generations" headings and what they contribute to the message of Genesis, see Jason S. DeRouchie, "The Blessing-Commission, the Promised Offspring, and the *Toledot* Structure of Genesis," *JETS* 56, no. 2 (2013): 219–47; cf. Jason S. DeRouchie, *How to Understand and Apply the Old Testament: Twelve Steps from Exegesis to Theology* (Phillipsburg, NJ: P&R, 2017), 107–9.

(Table 6.2 continued)

		And these are the generations of Isaac (25:19–35:29)	N
		And these are the generations of Esau (36:1–8, 9–37:1)	SG (+N+SG)
	v	These are the generations of Jacob (37:2–50:26)	N (+SG+N)

KEY: N = Narrative; LG = Linear Genealogy; SG = Segmented Genealogy

This structure highlights many significant features: First, the most extended literary grouping runs from Genesis 11:10 to 37:1 and gives prominence to the account of Yahweh's covenant with the patriarchs (809 of 1,533 verses—that is, 56 percent of the book). The size of the narrative suggests that the plot development, divine charges, and patriarchal covenant promises related to land, offspring, blessing, and divine presence highly contribute to Genesis's overall message.[3]

Second, the five major sections (i–v in table 6.2) shift from the heavens and earth (Gen. 2:4) to Adam (5:1) to Noah (6:9) to Shem (11:10) and to Jacob (37:2) and thus indicate a movement from (1) all creation to (2) humanity in general to (3) all living humanity (after the execution of the rest) to (4) a subset of living humanity (through a shift in genealogical focus) and finally to (5) Israel.[4] Genesis, therefore, signals a progressive narrowing that places focus on the line of promise and the centrality of Israel in God's kingdom purposes to restore blessing to the world.

Third, Genesis's overarching flow of thought is as follows: The book opens with a preface (Gen. 1:1–2:3) that elevates the blessing-commission (1:28) by focusing on God's desire for his image-bearing humans to reproduce and then reflect, resemble, and represent his glory to the ends of the earth (1:28). We then get the only "generations" heading in the book that does

---

3   For a catalog of all the patriarchal promises with references, see chap. 7.
4   Matthew A. Thomas, *These Are the Generations: Identity, Promise and the Toledot Formula*, LHBOTS 551 (New York: Bloomsbury T&T Clark, 2011), 73.

not include a human name (part 2 in table 6.2). Both this and the context suggest that the section devoted to "the generations of the heavens and the earth" (2:4–4:26) introduces the redemptive story that follows. The section clarifies the world's *need for blessing*, as it (1) celebrates humanity's covenantal purpose in the global context (2:4–25); (2) details humanity's sin, God's curse on the world, and its immediate aftermath (3:1–4:26); and (3) highlights Yahweh's merciful kingdom promise of a curse-overcoming offspring (3:15).

After this, the two linear genealogies unpacking the sections related to Adam (Gen. 5:1–6:8) and Shem (11:10–26) introduce two parallel units— 3A and 3B in table 6.2—that develop the world's *hope for blessing* and how Yahweh will mercifully preserve and provide (5:1–11:9; 11:10–50:26). Part 3A (table 6.2) opens by reporting the perpetual kingdom hope from Adam to Noah, all in the context of threat (5:1–6:8). It then uses a mixture of narrative and genealogy to describe how Yahweh protected the promised line and mercifully renewed his covenant with creation in the context of the flood punishment and its aftermath (6:9–11:9). Part 3B (table 6.2) shows the perpetuation of kingdom hope from Shem to Terah and clarifies how God will use Abraham and his offspring, climaxing in a single deliverer (15:4–6; 22:17–18) to extend kingdom blessing to the world's nations (11:10–37:1). It then closes with an extended narrative (37:2–50:26) that recounts the promised line's preservation in Egypt while also stressing the developing of kingdom hope for a royal deliverer, now known to be from the tribe of Judah (49:8–10).

An Outline of Genesis's Thought Flow

I. Preface—God's blessing-commission (1:1–2:3): God purposes that humanity rule his world as his image bearers

II. The need for blessing (2:4–4:26): humanity rebels and God curses the world yet promises a curse overcoming offspring

III. The hope for blessing (5:1–50:26): God preserves humanity and provides a way for the world to enjoy kingdom blessing

A. God reaffirms humanity's blessing-commission (5:1–11:9)

1. God perpetuates kingdom hope from Adam to Noah in the context of threat (5:1–6:8)

2. God protects the promised line and restores humanity's kingdom purpose in the context of punishment (6:9–11:9)

B. God declares how his kingdom blessing will reach the world
(11:10–50:26)

1. God perpetuates kingdom hope from Shem to Terah and
elevates Abraham and his offspring as the agents for bringing
kingdom blessing to the world (11:10–37:1)

2. God preserves the promised line through famine in Egypt
and develops kingdom hope for a royal deliverer from Judah
(37:2–50:26)

When read within its close, continuing, and complete contexts, Genesis details gospel hope climaxing in Christ. Within this framework, *the book's main idea* is this: despite humanity's losing the blessing of eternally reigning over a very good world under God as his image bearers and spreading God's heavenly kingdom to the ends of the earth, Yahweh will restore this blessing to all the nations when they place their faith in the victorious, royal offspring of the woman, who will descend from Abraham, Isaac, Jacob, and Judah and who will crush the serpent and claim all lands.

An Overview of Major Movements in Genesis
The Preface (Gen. 1:1–2:3)

"In the beginning, God created the heavens and the earth" (Gen. 1:1). As the climax to his creative work, God shapes humans in his image (1:26–27) and charges his male and female representatives to "be fruitful and multiply and fill the earth and subdue it, and have dominion" (1:28). From the start, God's covenant with creation through Adam stresses the themes of progeny, property, and power (rule), all themes that resurface at each period in Scripture's covenantal progression culminating in Christ.[5] The narrator characterizes the commission as a blessing, meaning that mankind would only increase and rule as God's representatives on the earth if he graciously empowered it to happen. Proper image bearing demands dependence.

---

5   See Paul Kyuwook Kim, "From Biblical Coherence to Systematic Theology: A Critical Reinterpretation of Covenant Theology" (ThD diss., South African Theological Seminary, 2020),
especially the overview on 13–15.

See and Celebrate Christ in the Old Testament

Way 5: Revel in Yahweh's identity and activity

God's role as Creator (Gen. 1:1) allows us to see and celebrate Christ, who was "in the beginning with God" and without whom "was not any thing made that was made" (John 1:2–3; cf. Col. 1:16).

The Generations of the Heavens and the Earth (Gen. 2:4–4:26)

Yahweh set the first man as head over his creation (Gen. 2:15–17) and then provided him a wife from his own body (Gen. 2:21–25). She would, therefore, stand as his glory (1 Cor. 11:7) and would help him as a partner in God's calling (Gen. 2:18; cf. 1:28). When Adam rebelled (Gen. 3:1–6), he secured his own death and the death of those he represented (Gen. 2:17; Rom. 5:12). He also transferred the world's rule to the evil serpent (2 Cor. 4:4; Eph. 2:2; 1 John 5:19). A new "Adam" figure, operating as a new covenantal head, would be the only one to reverse such a curse (John 12:31; Rom. 5:18–19).

See and Celebrate Christ in the Old Testament

Way 4: Identify Old Testament types

Paul notes that Adam "was a type of the one who was to come. . . . For as by the one man's disobedience the many were made sinners, so by the one man's obedience the many will be made righteous" (Rom. 5:14, 19).

Specifically, Yahweh subjected creation to "futility," but he did so "in hope" (Rom. 8:20), for when he cursed the serpent, he promised,

I will put enmity between you and the woman,
    and between your offspring and her offspring;
he shall bruise your head,
    and you shall bruise his heel. (Gen. 3:15)

C. John Collins has shown that an adjective or pronoun's number (i.e., singular or plural) makes explicit whether the Hebrew term for "offspring" refers to one or many.[6] The singular pronoun "he" (Hebrew *hu'*) in Genesis 3:15, therefore, clarifies that the woman's "offspring" is indeed a male individual (cf. 2 Sam. 7:12–13), who would, through personal tribulation, triumph over the evil serpent, thus reversing the curse and bringing new creation.

> **See and Celebrate Christ in the Old Testament**
>
> *Way 2: See the Old Testament's direct messianic predictions*
>
> Genesis 3:15 is direct messianic prophecy anticipating Christ, and Revelation 12:1–6, 17 recalls the verse with respect to Jesus.

In the narrative that follows, Adam names Eve "the mother of all living" (Gen. 3:20). By doing this, he expressed faith that, through the promises of conquest (3:15) and childbirth (3:16), life and a line of offspring identified with it would overcome the curse of death. Furthermore, Eve praised God for a male child when Cain was born (Gen. 4:1). She then praised Yahweh for supplying Seth as an "offspring" to replace Abel (4:25), whom Cain killed (4:8). Cain's act proved that he was an offspring of the serpent and not the woman (1 John 3:12, 15; cf. John 8:33, 39–44).

The Generations of Adam, Noah, and Noah's Sons (Gen. 5:1–11:9)

That Adam's son Seth was "in his own likeness, after his image" (Gen. 5:3) highlights how closely being made in God's "likeness" (5:1) is related to sonship. It also reinforces how Yahweh sought to shape a worldwide kingdom

---

6   The Hebrew authors make explicit whether the collective singular noun *zera'* ("seed/offspring") bears a singular or plural referent by including singular or plural adjectives and/or pronouns (whether independent, object, or suffix pronouns). C. John Collins, "A Syntactical Note (Genesis 3:15): Is the Woman's Seed Singular or Plural?," *TynBul* 48, no. 1 (1997): 139–48, esp. 142–44. Cf., e.g., *singular* in Gen. 4:25; 22:17b; 21:13; *plural* in 15:13; 17:7–9; 48:11–12. Abernethy and Goswell deny that pronoun number is determinative, but in their three examples the pronouns modify rather than stand equivalent to the "seed," and all can legitimately be interpreted as bearing singular referents (Lev. 11:37–38; 26:16; Deut. 31:21). Andrew T. Abernethy and Gregory Goswell, *God's Messiah in the Old Testament: Expectations of a Coming King* (Grand Rapids, MI: Baker Academic, 2020), 13, 15.

community radiating his glory, like a son exhibits the characteristics of his father (cf. Eph. 4:24; Col. 3:10). Such would be true of Christ, who is the very "image of God" (2 Cor. 4:4; cf. Col. 1:15), "the radiance of the glory of God and the exact imprint of his nature" (Heb. 1:3; cf. Phil. 2:6).

> **See and Celebrate Christ in the Old Testament**
>
> *Way 4: Identify Old Testament types*
>
> Along with being the "last Adam" (1 Cor. 15:45), Christ is the antitypical human, who perfectly images God (2 Cor. 4:4; Col. 1:15).

The linear genealogy and extended human ages from Adam to Noah highlight how God was preserving the "living," whose hope was in the one to come. In typological foreshadowing of the fulfillment of Genesis 3:15, Lamech optimistically declared that his son (Noah) would serve as a curse overcomer (Gen. 5:29). Because "Noah found favor/grace in the eyes of the Lord," he "was a righteous man" (Gen. 6:8–9), and he, his family, and the animals on the ark were the only land creatures to survive Yahweh's flood punishment (7:21–23). Through Noah, God also reaffirmed his blessing-commission (Gen. 9:1, 7) and his covenant with creation (6:18; 9:9–17), which provided a context for his saving grace through the coming deliverer to be operative. By substitutionary atonement (Gen. 8:20–22), which itself anticipated Christ's saving work, Yahweh purchased the common grace to make "his sun rise on the evil and on the good" (Matt. 5:45). He then highlighted that the offspring of Noah's son Shem would be his agent of oversight in the world (Gen. 9:25–27).

> **See and Celebrate Christ in the Old Testament**
>
> *Way 7: Use the Old Testament to instruct others*
>
> That "Noah walked with God" and "was a righteous man, blameless in his generation" (Gen. 6:8–9) magnifies Christ as the one whose sanctifying power makes justified saints holy—even Old Testament saints—thus providing us an example by which to live (Heb. 11:7).

Following the flood, the evil intentions of human hearts (Gen. 8:21) led them to rebel again (11:1–6). So Yahweh overcame their pride by confusing their languages and dispersing them throughout the earth (Gen. 11:7–9). Specifically, those that spread abroad after the flood were the three "clans/families" of Shem, Ham, and Japheth, which together shaped seventy "nations" (Gen. 10:32; 11:7–9). Yahweh would incorporate a remnant of these "families" (Gen. 12:3; 28:14) and "nations" (18:18; 22:18; 26:4) into his global kingdom purposes.

The Generations of Shem, Terah, Ishmael, Isaac, Esau, and Jacob (Gen. 11:10–50:26)

THE GENERATIONS OF SHEM AND TERAH (GEN. 11:10–26; 11:27–25:11)

The heading "the generations of Shem" (Gen. 11:10) recalls his elevation among his brothers in Yahweh's kingdom program (9:26–27), and Shem's linear genealogy to Terah again highlights how Yahweh preserved "living" ones in every generation who were hoping in the coming offspring (11:10–26). The progenitor in the next "generations" heading is Terah (11:27) because Moses wanted to devote much of the next section to the story of Abram, later named Abraham. The barrenness of the patriarch's wife Sarai (11:30), later named Sarah, increases narrative tension in a book so focused on offspring.

The plot then develops significantly as Yahweh commissions the patriarch to "go" to the land of Canaan and there "be a blessing." These two coordinated commands (Gen. 12:1b, 2d) are each followed by one or more conditional promises (12:2abc, 3ab), and the second command-promise unit includes the ultimate promissory result: global blessing (12:3c) (see table 6.3).[7] The two command-promise units indicate how God would reverse the punishments of property and progeny from Genesis 3:14–19.[8]

---

7   On this structure, cf. Gen. 17:1–2. See also Paul R. Williamson, *Sealed with an Oath: Covenant in God's Unfolding Plan*, NSBT 23 (Downers Grove, IL: InterVarsity Press, 2007), 78–79; William J. Dumbrell, *Covenant and Creation: An Old Testament Covenant Theology*, 2nd ed. (Milton Keynes, UK: Paternoster, 2013), 73–76; DeRouchie, *How to Understand and Apply the Old Testament*, 209–11, 247–50; Peter J. Gentry and Stephen J. Wellum, *Kingdom through Covenant: A Biblical-Theological Understanding of the Covenants*, 2nd ed. (Wheaton, IL: Crossway, 2018), 266–70.

8   James M. Hamilton Jr., "The Seed of the Woman and the Blessing of Abraham," *TynBul* 58, no. 2 (2007): 253–73.

He would do so as the patriarch or his representative would "go" to the land and there "be a blessing."

See and Celebrate Christ in the Old Testament

Way 7: Use the Old Testament to instruct others

Hearing the commands and believing that the promises were desirable and that the promise maker was trustworthy, "Abraham went" (Gen. 12:4) and by this provided a model of faith and obedience for every believer (Heb. 11:8). We can follow the patriarch's pattern only through Jesus, who is "the founder and perfecter of our faith" (Heb. 12:2).

Table 6.3   The command-promise structure of Genesis 12:1–3 (author's translation)

	And Yahweh said to Abram,	1a
Phase 1: Realized in the Mosaic covenant	"Go from your land and your kindred and your father's house to the land that I will show you,	b
	so that I may make you into a great nation,	2a
	and may bless you,	b
	and may make your name great.	c
Phase 2: Realized in the new covenant	Then be a blessing,	d
	so that I may bless those who bless you,	3a
	but him who dishonors you I will curse,	b
	with the result that in you all the families of the ground may be blessed."	c

The command-promise units also foresee two major phases in God's saving drama.[9] Phase 1 relates to Abraham fathering one nation with a kingdom
centered in Canaan. Yahweh would fulfill this through the Mosaic covenant
after Egypt afflicted Israel four hundred years (Gen. 15:13, 18; 17:8).[10] God gave
Canaan to Israel for the twelve tribes during the days of Joshua (Josh. 11:23;
21:43–45; cf. Gen. 17:8), but it was not until David and Solomon reigned that
Israel's realm stretched from the river of Egypt to the Euphrates River (2 Sam.
7:1; 1 Kings 4:20–21; cf. Gen. 15:18). Phase 2 would occur when Abraham's
representative would "bless" the "clans/families" Yahweh dispersed (Gen.
12:2d–3; cf. 10:32). This would happen only when Abraham's offspring would
perfectly obey (Gen. 18:18–19)—something realized only through Abraham's
ultimate offspring who blesses the world (Gen 22:18; Acts 3:26; Gal. 3:14, 16,
29). Jesus does this through his perfect life of obedience culminating in his death
and resurrection (Rom. 5:18–19; Phil. 2:8; 1 Pet. 2:22), by which he created the
new covenant community (Luke 1:54–55, 72–73).[11] "The Scripture, foreseeing
that God would justify the Gentiles by faith, preached the gospel beforehand
to Abraham, saying, 'In you shall all the nations be blessed.' . . . In Christ Jesus
the blessing of Abraham . . . [comes] to the Gentiles" (Gal. 3:8, 14).

See and Celebrate Christ in the Old Testament

*Way 1: Consider the Old Testament's
salvation-historical trajectories*

Through the two commands—"go" and "be a blessing"—in Genesis
12:1–3, Yahweh sets a salvation-historical trajectory that moves
through Abraham's becoming a father of one nation (the old covenant, Gen. 17:7–8) to Christ's saving work that makes Abraham the
father of many nations (the new covenant, 17:4–6).

9   DeRouchie, *How to Understand and Apply the Old Testament*, 209–11; cf. Thomas Edward Mc-
Comiskey, *Covenants of Promise: A Theology of the Old Testament Covenants* (Grand Rapids, MI:
Baker Books, 1985), 172–74, 195–210; Meredith G. Kline, *Kingdom Prologue: Genesis Founda-
tions for a Covenantal Worldview* (Eugene, OR: Wipf & Stock, 2006), 332–40; Daniel I. Block,
"Covenance: A Whole Bible Perspective," in *The Triumph of Grace: Literary and Theological
Studies in Deuteronomy and Deuteronomic Themes* (Eugene, OR: Cascade, 2017), 65–66.
10 Cf. Ex. 2:24; 6:4–5, 8; 33:1; Deut. 1:8; 9:5.
11 Gentry and Wellum, *Kingdom through Covenant*, 775–82; cf. Jeffrey J. Niehaus, *The Special Grace
Covenants (Old Testament)*, vol. 2 of *Biblical Theology* (Bellingham, WA: Lexham, 2017), 123–29.

Yahweh promised Abraham an offspring-*people* or nation that would inherit both the land of Canaan (Gen. 13:15–16; 17:7–8) and a broader territory (15:18). Yet the patriarch was also certain that God would raise up through him an offspring-*person* who would become as numerous as the stars (Gen. 15:3–5; cf. 3:15) and make Abraham "the father of a multitude of nations" (17:5; cf. 35:11). With a barren wife, the patriarch had to believe Yahweh could do for him what he could not do on his own, and Yahweh counted Abraham's faith in the offspring promise as righteousness (Gen. 15:6).[12]

See and Celebrate Christ in the Old Testament

Way 6: Note the Old Testament's ethical ideals

"Righteousness" was the ethical goal of law keeping (Deut. 6:25). Yet God credits righteousness to Abraham by faith apart from works (Gen. 15:16), thus justifying the ungodly (Rom. 4:5) based on Christ's perfect righteousness, which leads to "justification and life for all men" (Rom. 5:18; cf. 3:21–26).

With its focus on the male organ of reproduction, the covenant of circumcision (Gen. 17:10–14) once again made fulfillment of the offspring promise contingent on the need to obey (17:1–2).[13] God would overcome the curse and bless the nations through Abraham (Gen. 18:18), but it would come through his offspring's obedience (18:19).

---

12 For this reading, see Jason S. DeRouchie, "Lifting the Veil: Reading and Preaching Jesus' Bible through Christ and for Christ," *SBJT* 22, no. 3 (2018): 167–77.

13 Meredith G. Kline, *By Oath Consigned: A Reinterpretation of the Covenant Signs of Circumcision and Baptism* (Grand Rapids, MI: Eerdmans, 1968); Jason S. DeRouchie, "Circumcision in the Hebrew Bible and Targums: Theology, Rhetoric, and the Handling of Metaphor," *BBR* 14 (2004): 182–89; John D. Meade, "The Meaning of Circumcision in Israel: A Proposal for a Transfer of Rite from Egypt to Israel," *SBJT* 20, no. 1 (2016): 35–54.

See and Celebrate Christ in the Old Testament

Way 5: Revel in Yahweh's identity and activity

Abraham's third guest speaks as Yahweh (Gen. 18:1–33) and likely supplies an example where the "invisible God" (Col. 1:15) who "dwells in unapproachable light" (1 Tim. 6:16) and whom "no one has ever seen" (John 1:18) manifests himself through his preincarnate Son, whose words of hope regarding the coming offspring made Abraham rejoice (John 8:56).

Through Isaac God would affirm his covenant and name the promised offspring (Gen. 17:19, 21; 21:12). This one would serve as Abraham's greater "son," through whom, by his substitutionary sacrifice, "the LORD will provide" pardon for many (Gen. 22:13–14; cf. Rom 8:32). By becoming numerous, this singular "offspring" will conquer his enemies' gate (Gen. 22:17; 24:60; cf. 26:3) and stand as the one in whom all nations count themselves blessed (22:18; cf. 26:4), thus expanding the patriarch's fatherhood (17:4).[14] Upon Abraham's death, Yahweh blessed Isaac (Gen. 25:11).

14 For my messianic reading of Gen. 22:1–19, see Jason S. DeRouchie, "Redemptive-Historical, Christocentric Approach," in *Five Views of Christ in the Old Testament*, ed. Andrew M. King and Brian J. Tabb, Counterpoints: Bible and Theology (Grand Rapids, MI: Zondervan Academic, 2022), 191–99; cf. T. Desmond Alexander, "Further Observations on the Term 'Seed' in Genesis," *TynBul* 48, no. 2 (1997): 363–67; Andrew E. Steinmann, "Jesus and Possessing the Enemies' Gate (Genesis 22:17–18; 24:60)," *BSac* 174, no. 693 (2017): 13–21. I read the hithpael of *brk* here as an estimative-declarative reflexive, following Chee-Chiew Lee, "גוים in Genesis 35:11 and the Abrahamic Promise of Blessings for the Nations," *JETS* 52, no. 3 (2009): 472. Scripture uses the hithpael form only where the singular offspring-deliverer is explicitly in view, and the reflexive identifies how his coming marks the ability to specifically regard oneself as blessed in him (Gen. 22:18; 26:4). In contrast, the passive niphal of *brk* always occurs where the text identifies a patriarch and, at times, his plural offspring-nation as the agents of God's blessing (and the ones from whom the messianic deliverer would rise: Gen. 12:3; 18:18; 28:14). Cf. Michael B. Shepherd, *The Text in the Middle*, StBibLit 162 (New York: Lang, 2014), 22.

> ### See and Celebrate Christ in the Old Testament
>
> *Ways 2 and 4: See the Old Testament's direct messianic predictions, and identify Old Testament types*
>
> The account of Abraham's near sacrifice of Isaac and Yahweh's response in Genesis 22:1–19 typologically anticipates God sacrificially giving his own Son for us all (Gen. 22:2; Rom. 8:32) and directly predicts Abraham's individual offspring, Christ (Gen. 22:17–18), who would possess enemy gates (Matt. 16:18) and in whom the nations would regard themselves blessed (Gal. 3:8, 16, 29; cf. Acts 3:25–26).

THE GENERATIONS OF ISHMAEL, ISAAC, AND ESAU
(GEN. 25:12–18; 25:19–35:29; 36:1–37:1)

At this point the narrative includes a segmented genealogy devoted to "the generations of Ishmael" (Gen. 25:12–18), whom Hagar bore to Abraham and whom Yahweh said would become a great nation but not as the agent of his covenant (22:20–21). The various peoples arising from him represent those living under curse in need of the blessing Abraham's promised offspring would supply.

With the narrative associated with "the generations of Isaac" (Gen. 25:19–35:29), Yahweh reaffirmed and developed his patriarchal promises. Rebekah's twins would be rival "nations/peoples" (Edom and Israel) with the older serving the younger (Gen. 25:23; cf. Mal. 1:2–5), a reality soon anticipated when the elder Esau sold his birthright to Jacob (Gen. 25:29–34). Furthermore, in commissioning Isaac to sojourn in the singular "land," God promised his presence ("I will be with you") and blessing, which would include the "offspring" through whom "all the nations of the earth shall be blessed" inheriting plural "lands" (Gen. 26:3–4; cf. 22:18). Earlier God referred to both the limited "Canaan" and the larger suzerain state with the singular "land" (Gen. 15:18; 17:8), so the plural "lands" suggests that God's earthly kingdom would indeed spread out to control enemy turf (Gen. 22:17). God would overcome the world's curse, and Abraham would inherit "the world" (Rom. 4:13; cf. Ps. 2:8; Dan. 2:35; Matt. 5:5; Eph. 6:3). Quoting the lands promise in Genesis 26:3 with an allusion to 22:17–18 (cf. Gen. 13:15; 17:8; 24:7; 28:4), Paul identifies Christ as the "offspring" that blesses the world (Gal. 3:16; cf. 3:8, 14). He then notes that all who belong to him become "Abraham's offspring, heirs according to promise" (Gal. 3:29).[15]

See and Celebrate Christ in the Old Testament

Way 3: Recognize similarities and contrasts within salvation history

The continuity and discontinuity between the "land" (singular in Gen. 12:1–2; 15:18; cf. Josh. 21:43; 1 Kings 4:21) and "lands" (plural in Gen. 26:3–4; "world" in Rom. 4:13) magnifies Christ as the one in whom this salvation-historical development happens, culminating in the new heavens and earth.

Through Jacob's trickery, he received his father's blessing, which passed on the patriarchal promises to him and his line. Peoples and nations would serve him, with those cursing him being cursed and those blessing him being blessed (Gen. 27:29; cf. 12:3). Furthermore, he would multiply and become a company of peoples (28:3; cf. 1:28). Yahweh then affirmed that Jacob would spread out across the world and that in him and his offspring "shall all the families of the earth be blessed" (28:14). Upon Jacob's marriages to Rachel and Leah and his return to the promised land from Haran, Yahweh changed his name to "Israel" (32:28), thus bestowing on him a new identity and establishing the title of the nation that would arise from him.

Yahweh reaffirmed how Jacob/Israel was to fulfill the original blessing-commission ("be fruitful and multiply") and that from him would come "a nation and a company of nations" that would include kings (Gen. 35:11–12). We then learn of Rachel and Isaac's deaths just before two extended segmented genealogies associated with "the generations of Esau," the content of which again details those surrounding Israel who needed

15 C. John Collins, "Galatians 3:16: What Kind of Exegete Was Paul?," *TynBul* 54, no. 1 (2003): 75–86; Jason S. DeRouchie and Jason C. Meyer, "Christ or Family as the 'Seed' of Promise? An Evaluation of N. T. Wright on Galatians 3:16," *SBJT* 14, no. 3 (2010): 36–48; DeRouchie, "Counting Stars with Abraham and the Prophets," 478–85.

Yahweh's blessing. The narrator supplies a final note that Jacob dwelt in Canaan (36:1–37:1).

THE GENERATIONS OF JACOB (GEN 37:2–50:26)

The book's final chapters are all devoted to "the generations of Jacob" (Gen. 37:2–50:26), detailing the preservation of his twelve sons and their descendants who would become the nation of Israel and through whom the promised offspring-deliverer would rise. While Joseph was the eleventh-born son, his father treated him as the firstborn (Gen. 37:3–4; cf. 1 Chron. 5:1–2), and the narrative anticipates that he will rise above his brothers (Gen. 37:5–11). Yet his brothers sold him into slavery in Egypt, and his father thought he was dead (Gen. 37:28–36).

At this, the narrative pauses to chronicle a story significantly focused on "offspring" in the life of Judah, Jacob's fourth oldest son (Gen. 38). Judah had three sons, the oldest of whom was married to Tamar, but he was so wicked that God killed him (Gen. 38:6–7). Following the custom, Judah gave his second son to Tamar "to raise up offspring" for his brother, but he refused, so Yahweh put him to death also (Gen. 38:8–10). Because his third son was too young for marriage and because Judah feared that "he would die, like his brothers," Judah sent Tamar to her father's house until the youngest son was grown (38:11). In due course, his youngest son grew up, but Judah did not give him to Tamar in marriage (38:14). Therefore, after Judah's wife died, Tamar pretended to be a prostitute and became pregnant by Judah, receiving his signet, cord, and staff as pledge of payment (38:17–18). She then gave birth to twins, with the son Perez coming out first (Gen. 38:27–30). Significantly, the mention of "offspring" recalls the patriarchal hope and anticipates that Judah's line through Perez has something to do with the coming deliverer (cf. Ruth 4:12, 18–22), even though we have already learned that Joseph will be elevated above his brothers.

The narrative returns to Joseph, who over the course of thirteen years moved from being a prisoner in Egypt to second in command over the land (Gen. 39:1–41:40). Yahweh used Joseph's wisdom and position to provide for Egypt and the surrounding lands during a famine and to save his family. Joseph declared, "God sent me before you to preserve life" (Gen. 45:5), and "God sent me before you to preserve for you a remnant on earth, and to keep alive for you many survivors" (45:7). Once the seventy persons of

Jacob's house were enjoying refuge in Egypt (Gen. 47:26–27), Jacob recalled how Yahweh promised to make him "fruitful," to raise up a "company of peoples" through him, and to give the promised land to his offspring (48:4). He then blessed Joseph's sons, advancing the younger Ephraim over the older Manasseh (Gen. 48:15–22).

Through another blessing, Jacob also foretold how Yahweh would bless Joseph's offspring in a special manner (Gen. 49:22–26; cf. Deut. 33:13–17). Historically, one way this was realized was in Yahweh's choosing Ephraim's city Shiloh as the promised land's first central sanctuary (Josh. 18:1). Jacob also declared why the wicked actions of Reuben, Simeon, and Levi, the three eldest sons, moved Yahweh to pass over them (Gen. 49:3–7). Yet with Judah, Jacob declared that his brothers would praise and bow to him, that he would overcome his enemies, and that kingship would remain in his line until the promised one comes and enjoys both the obedience of the peoples and bounty (Gen. 49:8–12). The text, therefore, indicates that, though Joseph retained the blessing of the firstborn, Judah would be the one through whom the offspring-deliverer would rise who would bless the world "in days to come" (Gen. 49:1). The shift of significance from Joseph to Judah becomes evident through two events: (1) when the wickedness of the Shiloh priests causes the loss of the ark of the covenant and the downfall of the central shrine (1 Sam. 2:30–36; 4:1–22) and (2) when David brings the ark to Jerusalem, thus establishing a new central sanctuary (2 Sam. 6), and then enjoys Yahweh's covenant (2 Sam. 7; cf. Ps. 78:56–72).

See and Celebrate Christ in the Old Testament

Way 2: See the Old Testament's direct messianic predictions

Yahweh's promise that "the scepter shall not depart from Judah" and that a king would rise to whom "shall be the obedience of the peoples" (Gen. 49:10) directly predicts the rise of Jesus Christ, who is "the son of David, the son of Abraham" (Matt. 1:1), who will reign on "the throne of his father David," and "of his kingdom there will be no end" (Luke 1:32–33).

Genesis concludes by turning attention toward the promised land, in which Yahweh would fulfill phase 1 of the Abrahamic covenant promises. Following his father's request (Gen. 49:29–30), Joseph and his brothers buried their father in Canaan where Abraham, Sarah, Isaac, Rebekah, and Leah were buried (50:1–14). Back in Egypt, Joseph then reassured his brothers that what they meant for evil "God meant . . . for good, to bring it about that many people should be kept alive, as they are today" (Gen. 50:20). He requested to be buried in the promised land when Yahweh allowed them to return, and then he died (Gen. 50:22–26).

New Testament Realization

The New Testament opens by recalling Genesis's "generations" structure: "The book of the genealogy of Jesus, the son of David, the son of Abraham" (Matt. 1:1). In doing so, it sets Jesus up as both a new Adam figure (cf. Gen. 5:1) and the promised offspring in the line of Judah (Gen. 3:15; 22:17–18; 49:8–10). This selective genealogy is then followed by an extended linear genealogy that begins with Abraham, Isaac, Jacob, Judah, and Perez by Tamar and then carries all the way to Jesus, thus identifying Christ as the ultimate, long-awaited offspring of promise (Matt. 1:2–16). Luke, too, opens his Gospel recalling Genesis's promises, but he does so by letting Mary and Zechariah celebrate God's faithfulness to his word to Abraham by helping Israel (Luke 1:54–55) and by delivering his people from their enemies (1:73–74). Luke then includes a genealogy that stretches from Jesus through Perez, Judah, Jacob, Isaac, Abraham, and Terah—all the way back to "Adam, the son of God" (Luke 3:23–38). Even the sonship language recalls the offspring promise in Genesis 3:15.

Often the New Testament indicates the identity of Abraham's true "offspring." Jesus told the Jewish leaders, "If you were Abraham's children, you would be doing the works Abraham did. . . . Your father Abraham rejoiced that he would see my day. He saw it and was glad" (John 8:39, 56). With echoes of the curse in Genesis 3:15, he also told them, "You are of your father the devil, and your will is to do your father's desires. He was a murderer from the beginning" (John 8:44). At Pentecost after Jesus's resurrection, Peter recalled for the Jews how God told Abraham, "And in your offspring shall all the families of the earth be blessed" (Acts 3:25). The apostle then pointed to Jesus as the offspring, asserting, "God, having raised up his servant, sent him to you first, to bless you by turning every one of you from your wickedness" (Acts 3:26). Paul, apostle to the Gentiles, went further. He notes, "The Scripture, foreseeing that God would justify the Gentiles by faith, preached the gospel beforehand to Abraham saying, 'In you shall all the nations be blessed'" (Gal. 3:8). Then he explicitly states, "Now the promises were made to Abraham and to his offspring. It does not say, 'And to offsprings,' referring to many, but referring to one, 'And to your offspring,' who is Christ" (Gal. 3:16; cf. Gen. 26:3 with Gen. 22:18). Finally, he clarifies, "And if you are Christ's, then you are Abraham's offspring, heirs according to promise" (Gal. 3:29).

Abraham's faith in God progressively led to obedience, and this feature of his life models for believers how the root of saving faith always bears fruit in heeding God's voice (Heb. 11:8–13). Yahweh's counting the patriarch's faith as righteousness in Genesis 15:6 stresses for Christians how God justifies the ungodly by faith alone in Christ alone and not by works (Rom. 4:1–5; cf. Rom. 9:30–10:4). The patriarch's offering up Isaac on the altar "completed" his faith and "fulfilled" God's earlier declaration of righteousness that Abraham enjoyed by faith alone (James 2:22–23).

Conclusion

The blessing-commission in Genesis 1:28 and the promise of an offspring-deliverer in 3:15 help shape the plotline of Genesis. The book develops over ten "generations" sections in five groupings made up of narratives or genealogies. These groupings progressively narrow the reader's focus from the whole world to Israel and heighten hope in the male promised offspring of the woman, Abraham, and Judah. Through numerous rebellions, punishments, and obstacles, Yahweh preserves a line of those hoping in the coming one. The need for blessing (Gen. 2:4–4:26) gives rise to the hope for blessing, which includes Yahweh's reaffirmation of humanity's blessing-commission (5:1–11:9) and his declaration that his kingdom blessing would reach the world (11:10–50:26). When reading Genesis within its close, continuing, and complete contexts, its *main idea* is this: despite mankind's losing the blessing of eternally reigning over a very good world under God as his image bearers and spreading God's heavenly kingdom to the ends of the earth, Yahweh will restore this blessing to all the nations when they place their faith in the victorious, royal offspring of the woman, who will descend from Abraham, Isaac, Jacob, and Judah and who will crush the serpent and claim all lands.

This chapter has attempted to show how an Old Testament book like Genesis is Christian Scripture that Yahweh supplied to help readers see and celebrate the Messiah and the gospel's hope. Observing carefully, understanding rightly, and evaluating fairly every Old Testament book should allow prayerful Christian study to enjoy similar results.

Review and Reflection

1. Briefly describe the initial two stages of God's KINGDOM plan that occur in Genesis.

2. What elements guide the structure of Genesis, and what features does the structure highlight?

3. How does the author describe the main idea of Genesis?

4. What key text in Genesis 3 indicates that "the creation was subjected to futility . . . *in hope*" (Rom. 8:20)? According to Genesis, what is the nature of that hope?

5. The author states that Genesis 12:1–3 anticipates two major phases in God's saving drama. What suggests this, and how are these phases fulfilled in salvation history in relation to the Abrahamic covenant?

6. What do the stories of Abraham and Isaac contribute to the hope of the coming deliverer?

7. In what ways does "the generations of Jacob" section (Gen. 37:2–50:26) draw attention to Judah to heighten the book's messianic hope?

8. How does the New Testament's opening recall Genesis and indicate that Jesus is the promised offspring? In what other ways does the New Testament point to Jesus as the deliverer promised in Genesis?

9. Recall the seven ways the author suggests that Christians can see and celebrate Christ in the Old Testament and provide one example of each from the book of Genesis.

10. What was the greatest insight you gained in reading this chapter? What is your greatest takeaway?

PART 3

HOPING WELL

How Jesus Secures Every Divine Promise[1]

This is my comfort in my affliction,
that your promise gives me life.

PSALM 119:50

Since we have these promises, beloved, let us cleanse
ourselves from every defilement of body and spirit,
bringing holiness to completion in the fear of God.

2 CORINTHIANS 7:1

Beloved, we are God's children now, and what we will be has
not yet appeared; but we know that when he appears we shall

---

1   Much of part 3 updates material first published in Jason S. DeRouchie, "Is Every Promise 'Yes'? Old Testament Promises and the Christian," *Them* 42, no. 1 (2017): 16–45. Used by permission. Cf. Jason S. DeRouchie, "Question 37: How Should a Christian Relate to Old Testament Promises?," in Jason S. DeRouchie, Oren R. Martin, and Andrew David Naselli, *40 Questions about Biblical Theology* (Grand Rapids, MI: Kregel, 2020), 355–64; DeRouchie, "Promises," *DNTUOT*, 630–35.

> *be like him, because we shall see him as he is. And everyone*
> *who thus hopes in him purifies himself as he is pure.*
>
> 1 JOHN 3:2-3

God's promises play a vital role in helping believers grow in sanctification and suffer with hope. What we dread or hope for tomorrow changes who we are today. As Peter states, "He has granted to us his precious and very great promises, so that through them you may become partakers of the divine nature, having escaped from the corruption that is in the world because of sinful desire" (2 Pet. 1:4). The promises of God motivate holiness and awaken expectation and confidence in our pursuit of him.

But which biblical promises are for Christians? Should believers today claim all Old Testament promises as their own, seeing as God gave those promises to a different people and under a different covenant? Part 3 of this book considers why and how *every* promise is "Yes" in Christ (2 Cor. 1:20). Its thesis is this: through Jesus, God empowers Christians to appropriate Old Testament promises faithfully without abusing them.

Chapter 7 considers the importance and challenge of claiming Old Testament promises. It overviews the Bible's major promises, considers the misuse of Old Testament promises by prosperity teachers, and then highlights how the New Testament indeed applies Old Testament promises to Christians. Chapter 8 lays out five principles that guided New Testament authors when appropriating their Scripture's promises. Chapter 9 then concludes the unit by considering four different ways Jesus's coming influences past promises.

7

The Importance and Challenge of Claiming Old Testament Promises

Your promise gives me life.

PSALM 119:50

TO PROMISE IS TO ASSURE that one will do a particular thing or that a certain thing will happen. God's promises of blessing and curse play a key role in helping believers grow in sanctification (2 Pet. 1:4; cf. 2 Cor. 7:1; 1 John 3:2–3) and suffer with hope (Ps. 119:50). Promises are one of Scripture's unifying motifs, and some scholars have even argued that divine promise is *the* theological center of the Christian canon.[1] This chapter considers the language and form of biblical promises, overviews the major divine promises in Scripture, and considers both the challenge and need for Christians to hope in Old Testament promises.

The Importance of God's Promises for the Christian

The apostle Peter declares, "[God] has granted to us his precious and very great promises, so that through them you may become partakers of the divine nature, having escaped from the corruption that is in the world because of sinful desire" (2 Pet. 1:4; cf. Rom. 4:18–21; 15:13). John makes

---

1 Walter C. Kaiser Jr., *Toward an Old Testament Theology* (Grand Rapids, MI: Zondervan, 1978); Walter C. Kaiser Jr., *The Promise-Plan of God: A Biblical Theology of the Old and New Testaments* (Grand Rapids, MI: Zondervan, 2008).

a similar claim: "Beloved, we are God's children now, and what we will be has not yet appeared; but we know that when he appears we shall be like him, because we shall see him as he is. And everyone who thus hopes in him purifies himself as he is pure" (1 John 3:2–3). Whether the promises relate to blessing or curse, believing God's promises creates hope or dread, and what we anticipate tomorrow changes who we are today.

Stated differently, a fundamental way that we as Christians are to pursue holiness and overcome sinful cravings is by embracing higher, more beautiful desires.[2] Sin makes deceitful promises that lure us away from God, and we battle the desires of the flesh by trusting God's promises for a better tomorrow. We put our faith in the Lord's promise of future grace, and in doing so we gain fresh power in our pursuit of godliness, at the end of which is life in God's presence. "Blessed are the pure in heart, for they shall see God" (Matt. 5:8). "Strive . . . for the holiness without which no one will see the Lord" (Heb. 12:14). "But now that you have been set free from sin and have become slaves of God, the fruit you get leads to sanctification and its end, eternal life" (Rom. 6:22).

God's promises confront a whole host of sins. Examples of such promises are as follows:

1. If we are *anxious* about having enough, we turn from worry and heed Jesus's call to "seek first the kingdom of God and his righteousness," confident that "all these things [food, clothing, shelter] will be added to you" (Matt. 6:33). We engage in "prayer and supplication with thanksgiving," trusting that God's peace "will guard [our] hearts and [our] minds in Christ Jesus" (Phil. 4:6–7) and that "my God will supply every need of yours according to his riches in Christ Jesus" (Phil. 4:19).

2. When *covetousness* rises in our souls, we nurture contentment and keep our lives free from the love of money by recalling promises like, "I will never leave you nor forsake you" (Heb. 13:5).

2 This is the primary thesis of John Piper, *Future Grace: The Purifying Power of the Promises of God*, 2nd ed. (Colorado Springs, CO: Multnomah, 2012). When Peter speaks of God's "promises," he appears to be referring both to anticipated future *blessings* (e.g., 1 Pet. 3:9, 14) and potential future *curses*. That the latter is included is clear when he asserts of the coming of future salvation of the righteous *and* punishment of the wicked, "The Lord is not slow to fulfill his promise as some count slowness, but is patient toward you, not wishing that any should perish, but that all should reach repentance" (2 Pet. 3:9).

3. In our passion for sexual purity, we fight *lust* by remembering the promise, "Blessed are the pure in heart, for they shall see God" (Matt. 5:8). We also recall Jesus's words:

> If your right eye causes you to sin, tear it out and throw it away. For it is better that you lose one of your members than that your whole body be thrown into hell. And if your right hand causes you to sin, cut it off and throw it away. For it is better that you lose one of your members than that your whole body go into hell. (Matt. 5:29–30)

4. Similarly, to overcome seeds of *bitterness*, we remember Jesus's warning: "If you do not forgive others their trespasses, neither will your Father forgive your trespasses" (Matt. 6:15). Also, Paul motivates his charge to "repay no one evil for evil" and to "never avenge yourselves" by promising that God takes seriously all sins against his own people and will repay: "Leave it to the wrath of God, for it is written, 'Vengeance is mine, I will repay, says the Lord'" (Rom. 12:17, 19).

5. We fight *fear of man* by heightening our fear of God, recalling how valuable we are to him and recognizing that the consequence of not living for his pleasure is far greater than anything man can do to us.

> And do not fear those who kill the body but cannot kill the soul. Rather fear him who can destroy both soul and body in hell. Are not two sparrows sold for a penny? And not one of them will fall to the ground apart from your Father. But even the hairs of your head are all numbered. Fear not, therefore; you are of more value than many sparrows. (Matt. 10:28–31)

6. Assurance that God is already 100 percent for us in Christ is fundamental to battling *fear of condemnation* and to pursuing holiness. The only sins that we can overcome are forgiven ones, for we must move ahead in the power of blood-bought grace. Those in Christ Jesus trust that "there is . . . now no condemnation" (Rom. 8:1), for "Christ Jesus is the one who died—more than that, who was raised—who is at the right hand of God, who indeed is interceding for us" (Rom. 8:34; cf. 8:32; John 10:27–30).

7. Finally, to battle *fear of failure*, we believe promises like, "He who began a good work in you will bring it to completion at the day of Jesus Christ" (Phil. 1:6; cf. Jer. 32:40; 1 Thess. 5:23–24).

Christians must recognize the importance of God's promises not only for our pursuit of holiness but also for supplying hope amid affliction. The psalmist declares,

> This is my comfort in my affliction,
> > that your promise gives me life. (Ps. 119:50)

When we face suffering, God's promises in Scripture supply one of the bulwarks of hope for Christians.[3] We trust that God *will* be faithful to his word and that in his good time he *will* act on behalf of his own.

When tears flow, we call to mind that

> he heals the brokenhearted
> > and binds up their wounds.
> . . . .
> The LORD lifts up the humble;
> > he casts the wicked to the ground. (Ps. 147:3, 6)

When the darkness lingers, we believe,

> The steadfast love of the LORD never ceases;
> > his mercies never come to an end;
> they are new every morning. (Lam. 3:22–23)

So we

> sing praises to the LORD . . .
> > and give thanks to his holy name.
> For his anger is but for a moment,

---

3   I say, "*one* of the bulwarks of hope," because God's character and disposition toward the broken also give us hope: "O Israel, hope in the LORD! / For with the LORD there is steadfast love, / and with him is plentiful redemption" (Ps. 130:7; cf. Ex. 32:6–7; Deut. 10:17–18).

and his favor is for a lifetime.
Weeping may tarry for the night,
> but joy comes in the morning. (Ps. 30:4–5)

When fear assaults, we remember God's words,

Fear not, for I am with you;
> be not dismayed, for I am your God;
I will strengthen you, I will help you,
> I will uphold you with my righteous right hand. (Isa. 41:10)

When worry grips the soul and we feel alone, Yahweh's pledge rings out:

When you pass through the waters, I will be with you;
> and through the rivers, they shall not overwhelm you;
when you walk through the fire you shall not be burned,
> and the flame shall not consume you.
For I am the Lord your God,
> the Holy One of Israel, your Savior. (Isa. 43:2–3)

And finally, when death's shadow draws near, our souls find rest knowing,

The Lord is my shepherd
. . . .
Even though I walk through the valley of the shadow of death,
> I will fear no evil,
for you are with me. (Ps. 23:1, 4)

All of the biblical texts quoted above are rich with divine promise, but these last several promises of hope amid suffering are from the Old Testament. Paul declares in 2 Corinthians 1:20 that "all the promises of God find their Yes in [Jesus]." But was he talking about the Old Testament promises too—like those given to Adam, Noah, the patriarchs, and national Israel? Before answering this question, let's survey the forms and types of promises we are talking about.

The Language and Form of Biblical Promises

The Old Testament employs a form of the verb *dbr* ("to speak") or, less commonly, a form of the verb *'mr* ("to say") in the sense of "to promise." Foster McCurley and Walter Kaiser have identified the use of *dbr* in relation to the promises of land (Ex. 12:25; Deut. 9:28; 12:20; 19:8; 27:3; Josh. 23:5, 10), blessing (Deut. 1:11; 15:6), the multiplication of Israel (Deut. 6:3; 26:18), rest (Josh. 22:4; 1 Kings 8:56), all good things (Josh. 23:15), and a Davidic dynasty and throne (2 Sam. 7:28; 1 Kings 2:24; 8:20, 24–25; 1 Chron. 17:26; 2 Chron. 6:15–16; Jer. 33:14).[4] Scripture also employs the noun *dabar* ("word, thing") in relation to Yahweh's promise to/through Abraham (Ps. 105:42) and Moses (1 Kings 8:56). The Greek Old Testament rarely uses the verb *epangellomai* ("to promise") and noun *epangelia* ("promise") (but see LXX Esth. 4:7; Ps. 55:9; Prov. 13:12; Amos 9:6). Nevertheless, they are common in the New Testament, often in relation to the promises God gave the patriarchs and Israel in the Old Testament (see Rom. 9:4; 15:8; Eph. 2:12; Heb. 7:6; 11:17; cf. 2 Cor. 1:20; Heb. 6:12), which in turn are made better in the new covenant through Christ (Heb. 8:6; 10:23). For example, the verb occurs in relation to God's varied promises to Abraham (Acts 7:5; Rom. 4:21; Gal. 3:19; Heb. 6:13; 11:11) and to his promises of eternal life (Titus 1:2; James 1:12; 1 John 2:25), his kingdom inheritance (James 2:5), and the day of his appearing as judge (Heb. 12:26). Kevin Conway convincingly argues that Paul was unique in his exclusive use of *epangelia* for divine promises and that the conceptual and linguistic correspondence with *euangelion* ("gospel") grounded in the Abrahamic promises drove the apostle's application.[5]

God's Major Promises in Scripture

God's promises throughout Scripture commonly relate to life and death, blessing and curse. Divine provision, protection, and presence character-

---

4 Foster R. McCurley Jr., "The Christian and the Old Testament Promise," *LQ* 22, no. 4 (1970): 402n2; Kaiser, *Toward an OT Theology*, 33.
5 Kevin P. Conway, *The Promises of God: The Background of Paul's Exclusive Use of "Epangelia" for the Divine Pledge*, BZNW 211 (Berlin: de Gruyter, 2014). Prior to his establishing the old covenant with Israel, Yahweh promised hope and dread without any evident prophetic mediation. From Moses forward, however, human agents arbitrate most divine promises. Individuals commonly heighten promises into oaths by invoking a divine witness and/or expressing expected punishment if the promised reality does not come to pass (Heb. 6:13–14; cf. Gen. 22:16; 26:3; 1 Chron. 16:15–18; Ps. 105:9; Jer. 11:5). Hebrew can formally signal an oath by the niphal verb *shb'* ("to swear"), whereas Greek uses the verb *omnyō*. Speakers can also use truncated oath formulas, in which a portion of an oath represents the whole.

ize the blessing of life, whereas Yahweh removes all three of these in the curse of death.

God's first explicit promise in Scripture stresses the result that would occur if the first couple ate of the tree of the knowledge pertaining to good and evil: "In the day that you eat of it you shall surely die" (Gen. 2:17). Following their disobedience, Adam and Eve's spiritual death and God's exiling them from the garden proved Yahweh's faithfulness to his word (Gen. 3:22–24). But even prior to punishing them, Yahweh also cursed the serpent and promised him enmity with the woman and between his offspring and her offspring. He also promised that one of her male descendants would, through tribulation, triumph over him, thus reconstituting creation under God (Gen. 3:15). As we began to see in chapter 6, from this point forward, salvation history discloses a progressive hope in this coming offspring and in the age of global reconciliation with God that he would ignite.

While there are earlier foreshadowings (e.g., Gen. 9:25–27), Scripture next anticipates the curse's reversal in God's promises to the patriarchs, which relate to (1) offspring, (2) land, (3) blessing or curse, and (4) divine presence:

1. *Offspring.* God will grow the patriarchs into a great nation (Gen. 12:2; 18:18; 46:3), multiply their offspring (15:5; 17:2, 6; 22:17; 26:4, 24; 28:3, 14; 48:4, 16), and raise up kings from their midst who will exert influence over nations (17:6, 16; 25:23; 35:11; 49:10). In time, Abraham's fatherhood will expand adoptively to include not only the single nation of Israel but also the nations more broadly (Gen. 17:4–6, 16) when a single, male descendant will rise and bless the world (Gen. 22:18; cf. Acts 3:25–26; Gal 3:14, 16, 29).[6]

2. *Land.* Yahweh committed to give the patriarchs the land of Canaan as their central state (Gen. 17:8) with their broader kingdom

---

6 C. John Collins, "A Syntactical Note (Genesis 3:15): Is the Woman's Seed Singular or Plural?," *TynBul* 48, no. 1 (1997): 139–48; C. John Collins, "Galatians 3:16: What Kind of Exegete Was Paul?," *TynBul* 54, no. 1 (2003): 75–86; T. Desmond Alexander, "Further Observations on the Term 'Seed' in Genesis," *TynBul* 48, no. 2 (1997): 363–67; Jason S. DeRouchie and Jason C. Meyer, "Christ or Family as the 'Seed' of Promise? An Evaluation of N. T. Wright on Galatians 3:16," *SBJT* 14, no. 3 (2010): 36–48; Jason S. DeRouchie, "Counting Stars with Abraham and the Prophets: New Covenant Ecclesiology in Old Testament Perspective," *JETS* 58, no. 3 (2015): 445–85.

reaching from the river of Egypt to the Euphrates (Gen. 15:18–21; cf. Deut. 1:7; 1 Kings 4:20–21; Ps. 80:11). But he also promised that a royal deliverer would expand the kingdom turf to include the rest of the world (Gen. 22:17–18; 26:3–4; 28:14; cf. Ps. 2:7; Matt. 5:6; Rom. 4:13; Eph. 6:3)—realities that are now inaugurated in Christ's first coming and will be consummated in the new heavens and new earth.[7]

3. *Blessing and curse.* God promised to bless Abraham and his offspring through Sarah (Gen. 12:2; 17:16; 22:17; 24:1; 25:11; 26:3, 12, 24, 29; 27:27–29; 28:3–4; 32:29; 48:3, 16, 20; 49:25–26). Moreover, Yahweh would bless those who bless the patriarchs or those associated with them, whereas he would curse those who curse them (Gen. 12:3; 27:29). Ultimately, Yahweh would use a single, male offspring from Abraham to overcome God's enemies (Gen. 22:17; 24:60; cf. 3:15) and to bless some from all the families/nations of the earth (12:3; 18:18; 22:18; 26:4; 28:14).[8]

4. *Divine presence.* From the beginning, Scripture associates God's blessing with humanity's ability to represent God rightly in the world (Gen. 1:28). God's favor alone provides a context for flourishing; curse brings only tragedy. In such a setting, Yahweh affirmed that

---

7   See esp. Oren R. Martin, *Bound for the Promised Land: The Land Promise in God's Redemptive Plan*, NSBT 34 (Downers Grove, IL: IVP Academic, 2015). See also Paul R. Williamson, "Promise and Fulfillment: The Territorial Inheritance," in *The Land of Promise: Biblical, Theological and Contemporary Perspectives*, ed. Philip S. Johnston and Peter W. L. Walker (Downers Grove, IL: InterVarsity Press, 2000), 15–34; T. Desmond Alexander, "Beyond Borders: The Wider Dimensions of Land," in Johnston and Walker, *The Land of Promise*, 35–50; Peter W. L. Walker, "The Land in the Apostles' Writings," in Johnston and Walker, *The Land of Promise*, 81–99; Peter W. L. Walker, "The Land and Jesus Himself," in Johnston and Walker, *The Land of Promise*, 100–120; O. Palmer Robertson, "A New-Covenant Perspective on the Land," in Johnston and Walker, *The Land of Promise*, 121–41; G. K. Beale, *A New Testament Biblical Theology: The Unfolding of the Old Testament in the New* (Grand Rapids: Baker Academic, 2011), 750–52; Peter J. Gentry and Stephen J. Wellum, *Kingdom through Covenant: A Biblical-Theological Understanding of the Covenants*, 2nd ed. (Wheaton, IL: Crossway, 2018), 824–38; Oren R. Martin, "The Land Promise Biblically and Theologically Understood," in *Progressive Covenantalism: Charting a Course between Dispensational and Covenant Theologies*, ed. Stephen J. Wellum and Brent E. Parker (Nashville: B&H Academic, 2016), 255–74; Oren R. Martin, "Question 29: What Is a Biblical Theology of Land?," in Jason S. DeRouchie, Oren R. Martin, and Andrew David Naselli, *40 Questions about Biblical Theology* (Grand Rapids, MI: Kregel, 2020), 283–89.

8   Eckhard J. Schnabel, "Israel, the People of God, and the Nations," *JETS* 45, no. 1 (2002): 35–57; Jason S. DeRouchie, "The Blessing-Commission, the Promised Offspring, and the *Toledot* Structure of Genesis," *JETS* 56, no. 2 (2013): 219–47.

he would be present with the patriarchs and their offspring (Gen. 9:27; 28:15, 20; 31:3, 4, 42; 46:4; 48:21).

One scholar tags Genesis 12:1–3 "the keystone passage in all of Scripture for the promises of God" and rightly notes that these promises significantly color the New Testament's depiction of the gospel.[9] Indeed, nearly all other biblical promises from Genesis to Revelation in some way relate to these patriarchal promises. God fulfills some promises in a single event (e.g., the coming of a specific offspring), whereas others he realizes progressively (e.g., the claiming of the land[s] promise and blessing reaching the nations) (cf. Heb. 11:13, 33, 39). Most of the patriarchal promises are initially and partially fulfilled in the Mosaic covenant (e.g., nationhood in the promised land with various material blessings to neighboring nations), but all are only ultimately and completely fulfilled through Christ and the new covenant (e.g., God's overcoming the curse with universal blessing and a global kingdom in the new heavens and new earth).

Some Reflections on Prosperity Theology[10]

If "all the promises of God find their Yes in [Jesus]" (2 Cor. 1:20), should we as Christians claim as our own the various promises God gave before Jesus's time to specific individuals under different covenants? In the West, a popular gospel song goes,

---

9 Conway, *The Promises of God*, 48, 145–223.

10 By "prosperity theology" I mean a type of teaching (1) that disregards a new covenant expectation of suffering, (2) that prioritizes present-day health and wealth and the exploitation of others, and (3) that denigrates a true relationship with Christ that counts all else as loss in relation to knowing him. By "prosperity theology" I do *not* mean speaking and working to see people move from material, social, emotional, and spiritual poverty to dependence on God and self-sustainability, for such a desire is God honoring and stands as a natural fruit of the gospel in one's life. See Timothy Keller, "The Gospel and the Poor," *Them* 33, no. 3 (2008): 8–22; cf. Craig L. Blomberg, *Neither Poverty nor Riches: A Biblical Theology of Possessions*, NSBT 7 (Downers Grove, IL: InterVarsity Press, 1999); Steve Corbett and Brian Fikkert, *When Helping Hurts: How to Alleviate Poverty without Hurting the Poor—and Yourself*, 2nd ed. (Chicago: Moody, 2012); Wayne Grudem and Barry Asmus, *The Poverty of Nations: A Sustainable Solution* (Wheaton, IL: Crossway, 2013); Brian Fikkert and Russell Mask, *From Dependence to Dignity: How to Alleviate Poverty through Church-Centered Microfinance* (Grand Rapids, MI: Zondervan, 2015). My own overseas ministry among the poor has shown that microsavings groups empower participants and have far more success than microfinance groups, for the borrower is a slave to the lender (Prov. 22:7).

> *Ev'ry* promise in the book is mine,
> *Ev'ry* chapter, ev'ry verse, ev'ry line;
> *All* are blessings of his love divine,
> *Ev'ry* promise in the book is mine.[11]

Should we sing these words? Do they demand any qualification? Prosperity preachers claim that for all who have faith, Christ has already secured every spiritual *and* physical blessing (health and wealth) for us to enjoy *today.* In contrast Richard Schultz helpfully cautions that a biblical promise is not ours if "it is limited to a particular addressee or time or if it depends on a condition that I am unwilling or unable to fulfill. . . . Keeping the original context of the promise in mind can help to guard us against misusing the text."[12] I will argue that every biblical promise for God's people is indeed ours but that such promises are only received through Christ and fully realized at the consummation of the kingdom.

Health and Wealth

Consider Moses's words in Deuteronomy 28 and 30:

> And if you faithfully obey the voice of the LORD your God, . . . blessed shall you be in the city, and blessed shall you be in the field. Blessed shall be the fruit of your womb and the fruit of your ground and the fruit of your cattle, the increase of your herds and the young of your flock. Blessed shall be your basket and your kneading bowl. Blessed shall you be when you come in, and blessed shall you be when you go out. (Deut. 28:1, 3–6)

> If you obey the commandments of the LORD your God that I command you today, by loving the LORD your God, by walking in his ways, and by keeping his commandments and his statutes and his rules, then you shall live and multiply, and the LORD your God will bless you in the land that you are entering to take possession of it. . . . I call heaven and earth

11 "Every Promise in the Book Is Mine," in *Glad Gospel Songs* (Winona Lake, IN: Harry W. Von Bruch, 1937), no. 93 (emphasis added). The song's author is unknown.

12 Richard L. Schultz, *Out of Context: How to Avoid Misinterpreting the Bible* (Grand Rapids, MI: Baker Books, 2012), 81, 83.

to witness against you today, that I have set before you life and death, blessing and curse. Therefore choose life, that you and your offspring may live. (Deut. 30:16, 19)

Are these blessings from Deuteronomy something that we in Christ can or even should claim as ours today, already, by faith?

Prosperity author Gordon Lindsay says,

> Just as clearly as the Word of God shows that healing and health are blessings of the Lord, so sickness and disease are shown to be curses. In Deuteronomy 28 God lists various diseases that will come upon the Israelites if they do not obey the voice of the LORD. It is not difficult to recognize many of them as those we see inflicting people today. . . . Some contend . . . that sickness was spoken of as a curse *then*, but since today we are under a different covenant, the situation concerning sickness and healing is reversed. . . . How ridiculous! The New Testament teaches divine health for the believer just as much as the Old Testament does.[13]

Similarly, in his book *Your Best Life Now*, prosperity preacher Joel Osteen recalls Moses's charge to "choose life" in Deuteronomy 30:19 and then stresses, "This is not a once-and-for-all matter. It's a choice we have to make on a moment-by-moment basis. We must choose to dwell on the positive, choose to dwell on the good."[14] He further emphasizes that we must start claiming Jesus's affirmation that "all things are possible for one who believes" (Mark 9:23).[15] Osteen writes,

> With God on your side, you cannot possibly lose. He can make a way when it looks as though there is no way. . . . My question to you is: Will you believe? . . . We serve the Most High God, and His dream for your life is so much bigger and better than you can even imagine. It's time to enlarge your vision![16]

13 Gordon Lindsay, *The Bible Secret of Divine Health* (Santa Ana, CA: Trinity Broadcasating Network, 1987), 19–20, 21–22.
14 Joel Osteen, *Your Best Life Now: 7 Steps to Living at Your Full Potential* (New York: Warner Faith, 2004), 115.
15 Osteen, *Your Best Life Now*, 11.
16 Osteen, *Your Best Life Now*, 10, 12.

The "Good" Life

Health and wealth advocate Oral Roberts declares of many Christians,

> They do not seem to understand the full measure of their abundant life in Jesus here in this lifetime, BEFORE they go to heaven. They haven't understood how great and how good God is and that He provided for them spiritually, physically, and financially. They don't know God wants them to have some of Heaven to go to Heaven in. They don't understand that God's Word teaches that He wants to bless and prosper them in the now of their lives.[17]

Thus, he urges his readers to begin working out this principle with their finances: "If you sow it, God will grow it."[18] In support, he points to three foundational texts for prosperity teaching:[19]

- "Give, and it will be given to you. Good measure, pressed down, shaken together, running over, will be put into your lap. For with the measure you use it will be measured back" (Luke 6:38).
- "He who supplies seed to the sower and bread for food will supply and multiply your seed for sowing and increase the harvest of your righteousness" (2 Cor. 9:10).
- "Whatever one sows, that will he also reap" (Gal. 6:7).

Reflecting on verses like these, Osteen says, "If you give with a dump truck, you're going to get dump truck loads of blessings in your life. . . . If you're not satisfied with where you are in life, increase the amount of seed you are sowing."[20] The principle of sowing and reaping is biblical, but do these texts indeed promise increases of material wealth or status as the blessing for which we are to hope?

Jesus stressed that God will bless the giver, and in Galatians 6:8–9 Paul characterized at least some of the blessings. "The one who sows to the Spirit

---

17　Oral Roberts, *If You Need to Be Blessed Financially Do These Things* (Tulsa, OK: Oral Roberts Evangelistic Association, 1982), 8.
18　Roberts, *If You Need to Be Blessed Financially Do These Things*, 5.
19　Roberts, *If You Need to Be Blessed Financially Do These Things*, 15–16.
20　Osteen, *Your Best Life Now*, 255.

will from the Spirit reap *eternal life*" (Gal. 6:8). Hence, he urges, "And let us not grow weary of doing good, for in due season we will reap, if we do not give up" (Gal. 6:9).

Similarly, in 2 Corinthians Paul introduces his discussion of sowing and reaping this way: "Though [our Lord Jesus Christ] was rich, yet for your sake he became poor, so that you by his poverty might become rich" (2 Cor. 8:9). It is from this framework that Paul then says, "Whoever sows sparingly will also reap sparingly, and whoever sows bountifully will also reap bountifully" (2 Cor. 9:6). Health and wealth types assume that riches and poverty here mean material gain or lack and that reaping bountifully speaks of an accumulation of wealth. The context, however, points in a different direction.

First, when Paul speaks of Jesus's shift from rich to poor, he refers not to a change in Christ's economic status but to his incarnation and his willingness to die that we might gain life. Elsewhere Paul notes, "Though he was in the form of God, [Christ Jesus] did not count equality with God a thing to be grasped, but emptied himself, by taking the form of a servant, being born in the likeness of men" (Phil. 2:6–7). Servanthood is Christ's poverty. Or, as Paul declares in 2 Corinthians: "For our sake [God] made him to be sin who knew no sin, so that in him we might become the righteousness of God" (2 Cor. 5:21). Our gain in Christ is not first material riches; it is right standing with God. Jesus entered our broken world so that we who were separated from God and under his wrath could enjoy the blessing of reconciliation with God. This is our riches.

Indeed, the ones to whom Paul was talking in 2 Corinthians gave to the poor out of "their abundance of joy and their [own] extreme poverty" (2 Cor. 8:2). Their giving did not secure for them more wealth in this life, but it did testify to the hope they had in the gospel (2 Cor. 9:13) and to the surpassing grace God had poured out on them (2 Cor. 9:14; cf. 1 Cor. 1:4–8).

Second, with respect to sowing and reaping, what Paul means is that, as you give to others, God will make you "abound in every good work" (2 Cor. 9:8). The harvest is not more money or bigger businesses or more servants but righteousness and increased thanksgiving to God: "He who supplies seed to the sower and bread for food will supply and multiply your seed for sowing and increase the harvest of your righteousness. You will be enriched in every way to be generous in every way, which through us will produce thanksgiving to God" (2 Cor. 9:10–11). Paul does not envision Christians working to get nicer clothes and better cars and more power. Rather, the Lord gives to us so that we can serve as his hands and feet to others, regardless of whether our material poverty remains.

From another perspective, Jesus promised,

> Truly, I say to you, there is no one who has left house or brothers or sisters or mother or father or children or lands for my sake and for the gospel, who will not receive a hundredfold *now in this time*, houses and brothers and sisters and mothers and children and lands, *with persecutions*, and *in the age to come* eternal life. (Mark 10:29–30)

Of this verse, Lindsay asserts,

> There can be no mistake, the promise includes temporal wealth, "houses and lands . . . in this time." How much? An hundredfold! In other words he who gives up thousands in following Christ is eligible to receive hundreds of thousands! Not in the age to come, but this age. *Here then is the master key to prosperity!*[21]

In contrast, far from encouraging material gain in this age, Jesus's statement comes directly after his calling the rich man to let go of his quest for *earthly* riches, to allow his funds to fall to the poor, and to seek "treasure *in heaven*" (Mark 10:21). The "hundredfold . . . houses . . . and lands" that Christ's follower will enjoy "now in this time" are no more his material property than the "hundredfold . . . brothers and sisters and mothers and children" are his biological relatives. No, the present enjoyment Christ promises is that the disciple who gives up all will be provided for "now in this time" through the benevolence of his new spiritual family in Christ and, after "persecutions," he will gain "eternal life" in "the age to come." It is because of this truth that Jesus declared of the rich man and to all prosperity preachers, "How difficult it will be for those who have wealth to enter the kingdom of God!" (Mark 10:23).

God promises to "supply every need" of Christians "according to his riches in glory in Christ Jesus" (Phil. 4:19). Yet as Paul stresses earlier, we must be

---

21 Gordon Lindsay, *God's Master Key to Prosperity* (Dallas: Christ for the Nations, 1998), 85 (emphasis in original).

willing to let the Lord define our needs, learning how "to be brought low and . . . how to abound" (Phil. 4:12). Today believers look to the Lord for daily bread (Matt. 6:11), trusting that he values his people and will give food, drink, and clothing in due measure to those who "seek first the kingdom of God and his righteousness" (Matt. 6:25–26, 31–33). We also rest confident in Jesus's command and promise, "Give, and it will be given to you. Good measure, pressed down, shaken together, running over, will be put into your lap" (Luke 6:38). Yet as was clear in Paul's own life, having great faith in the truth of these promises does not secure a life free of beatings, stonings, ship-wrecks, dangers, toil and hardship, sleepless nights, hunger and thirst, cold and exposure (2 Cor. 11:23–28).[22] Indeed, like Abraham, God may have us die "in faith, not having received the things promised" (Heb. 11:13).

The Pain-Free Life

Jesus often healed physical sickness and charged his disciples to do the same (Matt. 4:23; 10:6–8; Mark 2:8–12). Indeed, after a series of Jesus's healings (Matt. 8:16–17), Matthew cites Isaiah 53:4–5, stating, "This was to fulfill what was spoken by the prophet Isaiah: 'He took our illnesses and bore our diseases'" (Matt. 8:17). From these verses, Lindsay stresses, "If Christ paid for our sins, then we do not need to carry them. If He paid for our sicknesses, then we do not have to be sick."[23] He continues, "Divine health is God's plan; healing is God's second best for His people. . . . We must recognize sickness as a curse, the work of Satan and something to be banished from our lives, or we will succumb to it."[24]

Lindsay points to two texts in Exodus for what he calls God's "covenant of health" with his people:[25]

If you will diligently listen to the voice of the LORD your God, and do that which is right in his eyes, and give ear to his commandments and keep

---

22 Walter Kaiser observes, "Prosperity teachers tend to equate 'your Father knows what you need before you ask' (Matt 6:8) with 'everything our Li'l ol' heart wants.' But Jesus only pointed to three needs: food, drink, and clothing (Matt 6:8–32). Paul advises, 'If we have food and clothing, with these we will be content' (1 Tim 6:8)." Walter C. Kaiser Jr., "The Old Testament Promise of Material Blessings and the Contemporary Believer," *TJ* 9, no. 2 (1988): 165.

23 Gordon Lindsay, *The Bible Secret of Divine Health*, 12.

24 Lindsay, *The Bible Secret of Divine Health*, 5–6.

25 Lindsay, *The Bible Secret of Divine Health*, 9–12, 17–22.

all his statutes, I will put none of the diseases on you that I put on the Egyptians, for I am the LORD, your healer. . . . You shall serve the LORD your God, and he will bless your bread and your water, and I will take sickness away from among you. (Ex. 15:26; 23:25; cf. Deut. 7:15)

Lindsay concludes, "God promises if we truly serve Him, He will send His angel before us. He will bless our bread and our water, and take sickness from our midst."[26] And again, "God has promised health for Christians. . . . Even under the law, the obedient believer was promised deliverance from sickness. . . . In the New Testament the same standard of health is indicated."[27] In support, Lindsay points to John's words: "Beloved, I pray that all may go well with you and that you may be in good health, as it goes well with your soul" (3 John 2).[28]

Yet John's words are a prayer, not a promise. Furthermore, in Jesus's first coming he mostly restricted his ministry to the Jews (Matt. 10:6–8), and we only know of his raising three people from the dead: the ruler's daughter (Mark 5:35–36, 41–43), the son of the widow of Nain (Luke 7:12–15), and Lazarus (John 11:38–46). He did not yet right all the wrongs or relieve all pains (Luke 4:16–21; 7:18–23). There is a tension we must hold in this already-but-not-yet period. Believers today must recognize the truth of Christ's declaration that "some of you they will put to death," while always trusting that "not a hair of your head will perish" and "by your endurance you will gain your lives" (Luke 21:16, 18–19).[29]

Paul too healed only sporadically and does not appear to have expected that all would be healed in this age. He healed the crippled man in Lystra (Acts 14:10), the demonized girl in Philippi (16:18), many people in Ephesus

---

26 Lindsay, *The Bible Secret of Divine Health*, 18.

27 Lindsay, *God's Master Key to Prosperity*, 70–71.

28 Lindsay, *The Bible Secret of Divine Health*, 34–35; cf. 6, 22; Lindsay, *God's Master Key to Prosperity*, 71.

29 Reflecting on Jesus's non-universal healings in his first coming, Kaiser notes, "Even if our LORD did perform a series of healing ministries as a fulfillment of what was spoken by Isaiah, was this more than a foretaste of the total restoration that was to come when our LORD returned the second time in all history? . . . We conclude that there is healing in the atonement; we only contest how and when it is fully applicable. We think that believers will be finally delivered from the dread of disease only when our Lord has put all enemies under his feet, even death itself." Kaiser, "The Old Testament Promise of Material Blessings and the Contemporary Believer," 167.

(19:12), and Eutychus who died after falling out of a window (20:9–10). However, he couldn't gain relief from his "thorn," whether it be sickness or persecution (2 Cor. 12:7), and he couldn't heal himself from the ailment that he had when he preached in Galatia (Gal. 4:13–14). He also evidently couldn't stop Epaphroditus's sickness from becoming life-threatening (Phil. 2:26–27), and he couldn't heal Timothy from his stomach ailments (1 Tim. 5:23) or Trophimus whom he "left ill at Miletus" (2 Tim. 4:20). God calls Christians to pray for healing (James 5:14–15; 3 John 2), but the physical wholeness that Christ purchased for us (Matt. 8:16–17) may not come until we enjoy our resurrection bodies (Rom. 6:5; 8:11; 1 Cor. 15:20, 23, 51, 52; Phil. 3:20–21).

Living in the Overlap of the Ages

At present we live in the overlap between the old and new ages. In Christ, our hope is real, and our inheritance is secure. Yet our physical bodies still rest firmly in the old, cursed creation. Believers are to expect suffering, tribulation, and affliction of all sorts. Jesus said, "If they persecuted me, they will persecute you" (John 15:20). He also stressed, "In the world you will have tribulation. But take heart; I have overcome the world" (John 16:33). Discipleship comes at great cost (Luke 14:33; John 12:25). Just as Christ had to endure the cross before enjoying his resurrection body, so too the believer in Christ must carry his cross, identifying with Christ in his suffering, before receiving his resurrection body (Mark 8:34; 1 Pet. 4:13). God's discipline nurtures holiness and righteousness in our lives (Heb. 12:7–11; cf. Lev. 26:18, 21, 23–24, 27–28), and we endure today knowing that something better is coming tomorrow (Heb. 10:34; 13:12–14; 1 Pet. 1:6–7).

Paul said, "Through many tribulations we must enter the kingdom of God" (Acts 14:22). God has granted that we "should not only believe in [Christ] but also suffer for his sake" (Phil. 1:29). We are "destined" for "afflictions" (1 Thess. 3:3), and "all who desire to live a godly life in Christ Jesus will be persecuted" (2 Tim. 3:12). Paul himself experienced trials far broader than persecution—"afflictions, hardships, calamities, beatings, imprisonments, riots, labors, sleepless nights, hunger" (2 Cor. 6:4–5; cf. 11:23–28). As he did, he said, "In any and every circumstance, I have learned the secret of facing plenty and hunger, abundance and need. I can do all things through him who strengthens me" (Phil. 4:12–13).

If you are united to Christ by faith, you should boldly claim God's promises in *all* of Scripture, following the pattern of the New Testament authors. Every promise is truly ours already, but those we tangibly experience now are those related to God's presence, favor, power, and pleasure as they come to us today by the Spirit of Christ. All other promises addressing more physical, material provision and protection are already ours truly, but they will be realized fully in space and time only at the consummation of the new heavens and new earth. Then we will receive our resurrection bodies, and there will be no more tears, death, mourning, crying, or pain (Rev. 21:4).

The psalmist declares,

> With the LORD there is steadfast love,
> and with him is plentiful redemption. (Ps 130:7)

In view of his character, God may still be pleased at any moment to bring our future hope into the present through a miraculous act of power. We must, therefore, continue to help others find relief from poverty and become self-sustaining (Deut. 10:17–19; 15:11; Ps. 41:1; Gal. 2:10; 1 John 3:17) and to pray that God would heal those sick and suffering (James 5:13–15; 3 John 2; cf. 1 Cor. 12:9), all for God's glory and his kingdom's advance. God is pleased to magnify his power, but he can do this either by removing the pain or by sustaining us through it. The Lord will bring relief according to his timetable, manner, and degree, but we can trust that he will work all things out for our good (Rom. 8:28) and that the day is coming when he will restore all things and when God's people will never again hunger or thirst (Rev. 7:16).

Synthesis

The point in all of this is to stress that as Christians we must live our lives trusting God's promises and that the "living hope" into which God has "caused us to be born again" relates "to an inheritance that is imperishable, undefiled, and unfading, kept in heaven for you" (1 Pet. 1:3–4). As we will develop in the next chapter, the Spirit and his accompanying blessings are *already* ours, but the full enjoyment of the inheritance is *not yet* (Eph. 1:3, 13–14; cf. 2 Cor. 1:22). Prosperity theology advocates are wrong in thinking that more faith will bring health and wealth today. They are also wrong—not because they assert that old covenant blessings apply to Christians—but because their understanding of the end times is over-realized. They want to bring the future into the present too quickly.[30]

The New Testament's Application of
Old Testament Promises to Christians

While the reflections on prosperity preachers are relevant, the larger purpose of part 3 of this book is not to critique health and wealth teaching but to equip Christians to think through the lasting significance of Old

---

30 For two helpful, balanced, recent critiques of prosperity theology, see John Piper, "Introduction to the Third Edition," in *Let the Nations Be Glad: The Supremacy of God in Missions*, 3rd ed. (Grand Rapids, MI: Baker Academic, 2010), 15–32; Michael Otieno Maura, Conrad Mbewe, Ken Mbugua, John Piper, and Wayne Grudem, *Prosperity? Seeking the True Gospel* (Nairobi: Africa Christian Textbooks Registered Trustees, 2015). As an initial response, I would say that a conscious or unconscious imbalanced belief in retribution theology—"what you sow you will reap in the here and now"—often bears devastating effects. The worldliness of prosperity theology is seen at least in the ways it (1) nurtures an entitlement mentality, (2) places undue guilt, (3) misrepresents God's character, and (4) minimizes Christ's saving work while exalting some individuals at the expense of others. *First*, in my life and in the lives of many who are part of Western evangelical churches, prosperity theology perspectives show up when we have wealth or health, expect to keep it, and get angry at God or at least very anxious when he takes it away. We feel entitled to a certain level of physical provision and protection right now. Oh, that we with Paul would live out the truth, "In any and every circumstance, I have learned the secret of facing plenty and hunger, abundance and need. I can do all things through him who strengthens me" (Phil. 4:12–13). *Second*, another subtle version of "health and wealth" thinking occurs when parishioners carry unjustified guilt or burden because they believe that their hardship or ailment must be due to their own lack of spiritual fervor. While possible (e.g., 1 Cor. 11:29–30), both the story of Job and Jesus's own teaching stress that some brokenness has nothing to do with our sin or the sins of our parents (Job 2:3; John 9:2–3). *Third*, prosperity preaching becomes full grown when popular personalities in North America, South America, Africa, and parts of Asia become rich by promoting a shallow, paralyzing, unqualified health and wealth message. They promise material riches or bodily wholeness for the here and now if one has enough faith. But in doing so, as with idolatry in the Old Testament age, they misrepresent God's character and commitments, treating him as someone we can manipulate and viewing material blessing as an earned wage (e.g., Hos. 2:12; 9:1; Mic. 1:7) (somewhat comparable to the Eastern religious principle of *karma*). In contrast, the Lord "is not partial and takes no bribe," and he "executes justice for the fatherless and the widow, and loves the sojourner, giving him food and clothing" (Deut. 10:17–18). *Fourth*, health and wealth teaching often fails to address the gospel's true core—that by Christ Jesus's life, death, and resurrection the reigning God saves and satisfies sinners who believe. In failing to address sin and the need for a Savior, they fail to clarify the only means of relief from eternal suffering. And in the end, the worldview repays little, except into the pockets of those who are not at all grieved over the ruin before them (Amos 6:6). God is not pleased with these destructive teachers, and to such as these he declared through Amos, "Prepare to meet your God!" (Amos 4:12). "Woe to you who desire the day of the LORD! / Why would you have the day of the LORD? / It is darkness, and not light!" (Amos 5:18).

Testament promises. Yet, in responding to prosperity theology or in grasping for ourselves how Old Testament promises relate to believers, we must not say, "We are part of the new covenant; therefore, old covenant promises do not apply to the church," for the New Testament apostles are very quick to cite Old Testament promises and to apply lasting significance to them!

For example, consider Paul's charge: "Never avenge yourselves, but leave it to the wrath of God, for it is written, 'Vengeance is mine, I will repay, says the Lord'" (Rom. 12:19). The apostle cites the promise from Deuteronomy 32:35, which Yahweh declares against all who would oppress his people (cf. Heb. 10:30). Paul believes that we gain power to love our enemies today when we trust that God will indeed judge rightly in the future. And we believe this because of an Old Testament promise.

Similarly, the author of Hebrews declares,

> Keep your life free from love of money, and be content with what you have, for he has said, "I will never leave you nor forsake you." So we can confidently say,

> "The Lord is my helper;
>   I will not fear;
> what can man do to me?" (Heb. 13:5–6)

Here the author combines a promise to Joshua with an expression of confidence from Psalms. The psalmist proclaims Godward trust during a time of distress (Ps. 118:6), and the author of Hebrews asserts that every believer today can rest assured with the same truths. As for the promise, he claims that we should not look to money for security *because* God has promised to be with us always! He draws on the pledge that Moses gave to Joshua and that Yahweh reaffirmed to Joshua just before Israel's conquest of Canaan: "It is the Lord who goes before you. He will be with you; he will not leave you or forsake you" (Deut. 31:8); "just as I was with Moses, so I will be with you. I will not leave you or forsake you" (Josh. 1:5). Somehow, Christians can and should legitimately use this promise to help us battle giants like covetousness in our own lives.[31]

---

31 For more on this promise, see chap. 9.

Conclusion

God's promises of provision and protection, including those from the Old Testament, are vital for helping us in our pursuit of godliness. Yet Christians need a framework for benefiting from Old Testament promises in a way that does not produce abuses, like those seen in prosperity teaching. The next chapter will consider five principles that inform how Christians relate to Old Testament promises.

Review and Reflection

1. What is one of the most recent biblical promises in which you have trusted in your pursuit of holiness or as you have faced suffering?
2. Give some scriptural examples of how God's promises help us battle sins like anxiety, covetousness, lust, bitterness, and fear.
3. Provide some scriptural examples of how God's promises help us face suffering with hope.
4. What are the four types of promises God made to the patriarchs, and what function do these promises have in Scripture? Supply one example of how each of the four is related to the gospel of Jesus Christ.
5. Clarify from the immediate context why interpreters should not read 2 Corinthians 8:9 and 9:6 as referring to material gain.
6. Does the fact that Jesus "took our illnesses and bore our diseases" (Isa. 53:4–5; Matt. 8:17) mean that Christians should expect a pain-free life today? Why or why not?
7. What does the author mean when he says that we live in the overlap of the ages, and how does this fact help us respond to the claim that Christians should expect health and wealth in the present?
8. What are some Old Testament promises that you have claimed in the past? Give an example of an Old Testament promise that you think some may have abused.
9. What questions do you have about how Christians should rightly claim Old Testament promises?
10. What was the greatest insight you gained in reading this chapter? What is your greatest takeaway?

8

Relating Old Testament
Promises to Christians

Heirs according to promise.

GALATIANS 3:29

PAUL CLAIMS, "*All* the promises of God find their Yes in [Jesus]" (2 Cor. 1:20), but is he referring only to New Testament promises or to Old Testament promises as well? After citing a list of Old Testament promises later in the epistle (2 Cor. 6:16–18), he urges the Corinthian believers to pursue holiness "since we have these promises" (7:1). For Paul, both the Old and New Testament promises belong to Christians, yet this is only so *in Jesus*. What follows are five principles that shape how the New Testament authors relate Old Testament promises to Christians.

1. Christians Benefit from Old Testament
Promises Only through Christ

In Galatians 3, Paul confronts claims that, for Gentiles to become full inheritors of God's Old Testament promises, they need to submit to circumcision and, with that, the Mosaic law. In contrast, the apostle asserts that, while the old covenant law served as a "guardian until Christ came, . . . now that [the age of] faith has come, we are no longer under a guardian" (Gal. 3:24–25). Furthermore, he stresses that only identifying with Christ Jesus by faith secures inheritance rights for Jew and Greek alike. All must receive "adoption as sons" (Gal. 4:5).

155

In his argument, Paul fluctuates freely between the singular "promise" of inheritance that includes God's Spirit (Gal. 3:14, 17–19, 22, 29; cf. 3:8) and the plural "promises" of offspring, land, and international blessing that God gave to Abraham and his offspring (Gal. 3:16, 21). With texts like Genesis 12:3 and 18:18 in mind, he writes,

> Know then that it is those of faith who are sons of Abraham. And the Scripture, foreseeing that God would justify the Gentiles by faith, preached the gospel beforehand to Abraham, saying, "In you shall all nations be blessed." So then, those who are of faith are blessed along with Abraham, the man of faith." (Gal. 3:7–9)

Paul then says that this blessing is enjoyed by all in Christ Jesus (Gal. 3:14; cf. Gen. 22:18; 26:4).[1] Furthermore, Paul is apparently thinking of the promise of lands in Genesis 26:3, and using an allusion to Genesis 22:17–18 (cf. Gen 13:15; 17:8; 24:7; 28:4), when he says, "Now the promises were made to Abraham and to his offspring. It does not say, 'And to offsprings,' referring to many, but referring to one, 'And to your offspring,' who is Christ" (Gal. 3:16). Paul recognizes that Genesis places the hope of the world not on a corporate Israel but on a single, representative, male, royal messianic deliverer. "And your offspring shall possess the gate of *his* enemies, and *in your offspring* shall all the nations of the earth regard themselves blessed" (Gen. 22:17–18, author's translation). And now that this offspring has come, "if you are Christ's, then you are Abraham's offspring, heirs according to promise" (Gal. 3:29; cf. Rom. 15:8–9). For Paul, only in Christ Jesus can anyone inherit the Old Testament's promised blessings (see fig.

---

1   Genesis speaks of all "the *families* of the ground" (author's rendering) being blessed in Abraham (Gen. 12:3) and in Jacob and his offspring (28:14) and of all "the *nations* of the earth" being blessed in Abraham (18:18). It speaks of all "the *nations* of the earth" considering themselves blessed in Abraham's offspring (Gen. 22:18) and in Isaac's offspring (26:4). As already noted, the passive niphal of *brk* ("blessed") occurs where the text identifies a patriarch and, at times, his plural offspring-people as the agents of God's blessing (Gen. 12:3; 18:18; 28:14), whereas the estimative-declarative reflexive hithpael of *brk* ("regard themselves blessed") happens where the singular offspring-deliverer is in view (22:17–18; 26:3–4). For this use of the hithpael, see Chee-Chiew Lee, "גוים in Genesis 35:11 and the Abrahamic Promise of Blessings for the Nations," *JETS* 52, no. 3 (2009): 472. For the different roles of the niphal and hithpael, see Michael B. Shepherd, *The Text in the Middle*, StBibLit 162 (New York: Lang, 2014), 22.

8.1).[2] This is what Paul means when he declares that in Christ alone all of God's promises find their "Yes" (2 Cor. 1:20).[3]

God makes promises to Abraham and his seed.	►	Christ is the seed.	►	Faith unites us to Christ.	►	Union with Christ makes us seed with him.	►	We become heirs of the promises.

Figure 8.1   Old Testament promises reach believers only through Christ

2. All Old Covenant Curses Become New Covenant Curses

With a heart full of hope, Moses wrote, "And the LORD your God will circumcise your heart and the heart of your offspring, so that you will love the LORD your God with all your heart and with all your soul, that you may live. And the LORD your God will put all these curses on your foes and enemies who persecuted you" (Deut. 30:6–7). Notice here that in the age of new covenant heart circumcision (now realized today in the church; see Rom. 2:28–29; Phil. 3:3), Yahweh will take Deuteronomy's curses—the very ones that served as warnings to old covenant national Israel (see table 8.1[4])—and he will pour them out on the enemies of God's restored community. This suggests that the old covenant curses become new covenant curses, which Yahweh brings not on the members of the new covenant but on their enemies. As in the Abrahamic covenant, where Yahweh promised to curse anyone who dishonored the patriarch and those he represented—"him who dishonors you I will curse" (Gen. 12:3; cf. 27:29)— so too Yahweh will confront those who spurn his new covenant community.

---

2   For this framework, see John Piper, "Isaiah 41:10: Are the Old Testament Promises Made to Us?," Desiring God, July 12, 2016, http://www.desiringgod.org/; see also John Piper, "Which Old-Testament Promises Apply to Me?," Desiring God, November 30, 2016, http://www.desiring god.org/. For a helpful synthesis of promise, offspring, and inheritance in Gal. 3, see David Starling, "The Yes to All God's Promises: Jesus, Israel and the Promises of God in Paul's Letters," *RTR* 71, no. 3 (2012): 187–89. For Paul's use of Genesis in Gal. 3:16, see C. John Collins, "Galatians 3:16: What Kind of Exegete Was Paul?," *TynBul* 54, no. 1 (2003): 75–86; Jason S. DeRouchie and Jason C. Meyer, "Christ or Family as the 'Seed' of Promise? An Evaluation of N. T. Wright on Galatians 3:16," *SBJT* 14, no. 3 (2010): 36–48. See also Jason S. DeRouchie, "The Blessing-Commission, the Promised Offspring, and the *Toledot* Structure of Genesis," *JETS* 56, no. 2 (2013): 226–29; Jason S. DeRouchie, "Counting Stars with Abraham and the Prophets: New Covenant Ecclesiology in Old Testament Perspective," *JETS* 58, no. 3 (2015): 445–85.

3   For a helpful overview of Paul's promise theology, see Starling, "The Yes to All God's Promises," 185–204; Kevin P. Conway, *The Promises of God: The Background of Paul's Exclusive Use of "Epangelia" for the Divine Pledge*, BZNW 211 (Berlin: de Gruyter, 2014).

4   All references are from Lev. 26; Deut. 4; 28–32. No single prophetic book, except perhaps Isaiah, mentions all categories.

Both Romans 12:19 and Hebrews 10:30 reaffirm this fact by citing Deuteronomy 32:35–36 as present hope for Christians:

> "Vengeance is mine, and recompense,
>   for the time when their foot shall slip;
> for the day of their calamity is at hand,
>   and their doom comes swiftly."
> For the LORD will vindicate his people
>   and have compassion on his servants.

In all these passages God is the one who bears the responsibility to curse. The believer's responsibility is only to rest, trusting that God will work justice in the best time and in the best way. Sometimes initial expressions of his wrath come through the political state (Rom. 13:4; cf. 1 Thess. 4:6) or through death (Acts 5:5, 10; 12:23). Nevertheless, the ultimate manifestation will come at Christ's second appearing (2 Thess. 1:8–9; cf. Isa. 66:15).

Table 8.1   Mosaic covenant blessings, curses, and restoration blessings

Blessings	
1. Yahweh's presence / favor / loyalty (Lev. 26:11–12)	6. General and unspecified (Deut. 28:2, 6, 8, 12–13)
2. Confirmation of the covenant (Lev. 26:9)	7. Peace and security in the land with no fear:
3. Be a holy people to Yahweh (Deut. 28:9)	a. General (Lev. 26:5–6)
4. Rains in season (Lev. 26:4; Deut. 28:12)	b. From harmful animals (Lev. 26:6)
5. Abounding prosperity and productivity	c. From enemies (Lev. 26:6)
a. General (Deut. 28:12)	8. Victory over enemies (Lev. 26:7–8; Deut. 28:7)
b. Fruit of the womb (Lev. 26:9; Deut. 28:4, 11)	9. Freedom from slavery (Lev. 26:13)
c. Fruit of the livestock (Deut. 28:4, 11)	10. Global influence and witness (Deut. 28:1, 10, 12)
d. Fruit of the ground (Lev. 26:4–5, 10; Deut. 28:4, 8, 11)	

(Table 8.1 continued)

Curses

1. Anger and rejection from Yahweh (Lev. 26:17, 24, 28, 41; Deut. 4:24–25; 29:20, 24, 27–28; 31:17–18, 29; 32:16, 19–22, 30)
2. Rejection and destruction of the cult (Lev. 26:31)
3. War and its ravages
   a. General (Lev. 26:17, 25, 33, 37; 28:25, 49, 52; 32:23–24, 30, 41–42)
   b. Siege (Lev. 26:25–26, 29; Deut. 28:52–53, 55, 57)
4. Fear, terror, and horror (Lev. 26:16–17, 36–37; Deut. 28:66–67; 32:25)
5. Occupation and oppression by enemies and aliens (Lev. 26:16–17, 32; Deut. 28:31, 33, 43–44, 48, 68; 32:21)
6. Agricultural disaster and nonproductivity
   a. General (Lev. 26:20; Deut. 28:17–18, 22, 40; 29:23)
   b. Drought (Lev. 26:19; Deut. 28:22–24)
   c. Crop pests (Deut. 28:38–42)
7. Starvation / famine (Lev 26:26, 29; Deut 28:53–56; 32:24)
8. Illness, pestilence, and contamination (Lev. 26:16; Deut. 28:21–22, 27–28, 35, 59–61; 29:22; 32:24, 39)
9. Desolation
   a. Of holy places (Lev. 26:31)
   b. Of cities and towns (Lev. 26:31, 33)
   c. Of the land (Lev. 26:32–35, 43; Deut. 28:51; 29:23)
10. Destruction by fire (Deut. 28:24; 32:22)
11. Harm from wild animals (Lev. 26:22; Deut. 32:24)
12. Decimation and infertility
    a. Of family (Lev. 26:22; Deut. 28:18, 59)
    b. Of cattle (Lev. 26:22; Deut. 28:18, 51)
    c. Of population generally (Lev. 26:22, 36; Deut. 4:27; 28:62; 32:36)
13. Exile and captivity
    a. Of the people (Lev. 26:33–34, 36, 38–39, 41, 44; Deut. 4:27; 28:36–37, 41, 63–64, 68; 29:28; 30:4; 32:26)
    b. Of the king (Deut. 28:36)
14. Forced idolatry in exile (Deut. 4:28; 28:36, 64)
15. Futility (Lev. 26:16, 20; Deut. 28:20, 29–31, 33, 38–41)
16. Dishonor and degradation (Lev. 26:19; Deut. 28:20, 25, 37, 43–44, 68)
17. Loss of possessions and impoverishment (Deut. 28:31)
18. Loss of family (Deut. 28:30, 32, 41; 32:25)
19. Helplessness and stumbling (Lev. 26:36–37; Deut. 28:29, 32; 32:35–36; 38–39)
20. Psychological afflictions (Deut. 28:20, 28, 34, 65–67)
21. Lack of peace and rest (Deut. 28:65)
22. Denial of burial (Deut. 28:26)
23. Becoming like the cities of the plain (Deut. 29:23)
24. Death and destruction (Lev. 26:36, 39; Deut. 4:26; 28:20–22, 44, 48, 51, 61; 29:20; 30:15,18–19; 31:17; 32:25–26, 35, 39, 42)
25. General and unspecified (Deut. 4:30; 28:20, 24, 45, 59, 61, 63; 29:19, 21–22; 31:17, 21, 29; 32:23, 35)
26. General punishment, curse, and vengeance (Lev. 26:41, 43; Deut. 28:16, 20–21, 27; 30:19; 32:35, 41, 43)
27. Multiple punishments (Lev. 26:18, 21, 24, 28)

(Table 8.1 continued)

Restoration Blessings	
1. Renewal of Yahweh's presence, favor, and loyalty (Lev. 26:42, 45; Deut. 4:29, 31; 30:3, 9)	6. Restoration of general prosperity, well-being, and wealth (Deut. 30:3, 5, 9; 32:39)
2. Renewal of the covenant (Lev. 26:42, 44–45; Deut. 4:31)	7. Return from exile and repossession of the land (Deut. 30:3–5)
3. Restoration of true worship and ability to be faithful (Deut. 4:30; 30:6, 8)	8. Reunification (Deut. 30:3–4)
	9. Power over enemies and aliens (Deut. 30:7)
4. Population increase (Deut. 30:5, 9)	10. Freedom and restoration from death and destruction (Lev. 26:44; Deut. 30:6; 32:39)
5. Agricultural bounty (Lev. 26:42; Deut. 30:9)	

The New Testament displays new covenant curses as warnings against permanently falling away from Christ (i.e., apostasy) and against all who oppose God and his people (see Matt. 25:31–46; Luke 6:20–26; 2 Tim. 2:12; Heb. 10:26–27; cf. 10:29–30; 2 Pet. 2:1). Those in Christ will not experience curse in a punitive way, for Christ bears upon himself God's curse against all believers (Gal. 3:13; cf. John 3:14–15; 2 Cor. 5:21; 1 Pet. 2:24). While Christians still experience the Lord's fatherly discipline, no level of earthly discipline or consequence calls into question the eternal security of any believer (Rom. 5:9). Instead, new covenant curses serve as a means of grace to those in Christ to generate within them reverent fear of God leading to greater holiness (cf. Lev. 26:18, 21, 23, 27; Rom. 2:4; Heb. 12:11).

3. In the New Covenant, Christians Inherit the Old Covenant's Original and Restoration Blessings

As seen in table 8.1, the old covenant contained conditional promises of blessing (Lev. 26:3–13; Deut. 28:1–14) and curse (Lev. 26:14–39; Deut. 28:15–68). The condition was perfect obedience (Lev. 26:3, 14–15; Deut. 28:1, 15), and the blessings included both righteousness (Deut. 6:25; Rom. 9:31–32) and life (Lev. 18:5; Deut. 4:1; 8:1; Rom. 7:10; cf. Rom. 10:5; Gal. 3:12).[5] There were

---

5   For more, see Jason S. DeRouchie, "From Condemnation to Righteousness: A Christian Reading of Deuteronomy," *SBJT* 18, no. 3 (2014): 87–118; Jason S. DeRouchie, "The Use of

also restoration blessings (Lev. 26:40–45; Deut. 30:1–14) that point in part to the church age following the curse of exile.

As noted at the beginning of this chapter, at the end of 2 Corinthians 6, Paul uses a string of Old Testament promises to motivate Christians to "not be unequally yoked with unbelievers" (2 Cor. 6:14). Here he refers to one original Mosaic covenant blessing (Lev. 26:11–12 in 2 Cor. 6:16) and a series of restoration blessings associated with the the Davidic and everlasting/new covenants (Ezek. 37:27 in 2 Cor. 6:16; Isa. 52:11 and Ezek. 20:34 in 2 Cor. 6:17; 2 Sam. 7:14 and Isa. 43:6 in 2 Cor. 6:18).[6] The apostle believed all these promises are for Christians to aid our pursuit of holiness (2 Cor. 7:1).

Significant for our purposes is the first citation where the apostle writes,

What agreement has the temple of God with idols? For we are the temple of the living God; as God said,

"I will make my dwelling among them and walk among them,
    and I will be their God,
    and they shall be my people." (2 Cor. 6:16)

Paul combines citations from an original old covenant blessing (Lev. 26:11–12) and a restoration blessing (Ezek. 37:27). Table 8.2 compares the texts.

We begin with the restoration blessing in Ezekiel 37:27. The chapter opens with the vision of the valley of dry bones. Far from obeying the law and enjoying life (Ezek. 20:11, 13, 21; cf. Lev. 18:5), the nation of Israel had disobeyed Yahweh, resulting in their ruin.[7] Their exile was equivalent to their death, and any future would demand a resurrection and new creation.[8] Yahweh promised to work this for them, joining the bones, adding flesh, and then placing his Spirit within them so that they might live as if they were his temple

---

Leviticus 18:5 in Galatians 3:12: A Redemptive-Historical Reassessment," *Them* 45, no. 2 (2020): 240–59.

6 For further reflections on these texts, see Starling, "The Yes to All God's Promises," 191–93.

7 For a development of this contrast, see Preston M. Sprinkle, "Law and Life: Leviticus 18:5 in the Literary Framework of Ezekiel," *JSOT* 31, no. 3 (2007): 275–93.

8 So Kenneth J. Turner, *The Death of Deaths in the Death of Israel: Deuteronomy's Theology of Exile* (Eugene, OR: Wipf & Stock, 2011); Kenneth J. Turner, "Deuteronomy's Theology of Exile," in *For Our Good Always: Studies on the Message and Influence of Deuteronomy in Honor of Daniel I. Block*, ed. Jason S. DeRouchie, Jason Gile, and Kenneth J. Turner (Winona Lake, IN: Eisenbrauns, 2013), 189–220.

(Ezek. 37:1–14). And as in earlier days when the nations would come to see God's greatness at his temple (e.g., 1 Kings 8:41–43; 10:1), now the nations would see the people and be pointed to Yahweh's majesty (Ezek. 36:23; 37:28; cf. 36:27). Into this context, Yahweh declared, "My dwelling place shall be with them, and I will be their God, and they shall be my people" (Ezek. 37:27).

Table 8.2   Paul's use of the Old Testament in 2 Corinthians 6:16

2 Corinthians 6:16 (ESV) "What agreement has the temple of God with idols? For we are the temple of the living God; as God said, 'I will make my dwelling among them and walk among them, / and I will be their God, / and they shall be my people.'"	
Leviticus 26:3, 11–12 (NETS) *(translation from the Greek Old Testament)* "If you walk by my ordinances and observe my commandments and do them, . . . I will place my tent [lit., 'covenant'] among you, and my soul shall not abhor you. And I will walk about among you and will be your God, and you shall be for me a nation."	Ezekiel 37:27 (NETS) *(translation from the Greek Old Testament)* "And my encamping shall be among them, and I will be a god for them, and they shall be my people."
Leviticus 26:3, 11–12 (ESV) *(translation from the Hebrew Old Testament)* "If you walk in my statutes and observe my commandments and do them, . . . I will make my dwelling among you, and my soul shall not abhor you. And I will walk among you and will be your God, and you shall be my people."	Ezekiel 37:27 (ESV) *(translation from the Hebrew Old Testament)* "My dwelling place shall be with them, and I will be their God, and they shall be my people."

Whereas the Greek Old Testament reads, "My dwelling shall be with them," Paul's wording is "I will make my dwelling among them," and this difference suggests that the apostle is either quoting from memory or supplying his own rendering directly from the Hebrew. Regardless, the second half of the promise parallels closely the Greek translation. What is missing in Ezekiel, however, is any mention of God's "walking" among his people, and this suggests that along with Ezekiel 37:27 Paul also has in mind the original Mosaic covenant blessing in Leviticus 26:11–12.[9]

The Mosaic law conditioned the enjoyment of its original blessings on perfect obedience. Yahweh declared, "If you walk in my statutes and observe my commandments and do them, . . . I will make my dwelling among you, and my soul shall not abhor you. And I will walk among you and will be your God, and you shall be my people" (Lev. 26:3, 11–12). Paul's inclusion of the phrase "and walk among them" directly matches the promises in Leviticus 26:12, thus suggesting that the apostle had *both* Moses's and Ezekiel's words in mind.

Significantly, because Israel did not fully obey God's instructions, the Mosaic covenant resulted in curse and condemnation, not blessing (2 Cor. 3:9). Nevertheless, Paul says that all those in Christ are enjoying the inaugurated fulfillment of both the original and restoration blessings.[10] When Christ perfectly obeyed the Father, he satisfied God's demands for absolute loyalty and thus secured blessing for the elect he represents (cf. John 15:10; Rom. 5:18–19; 8:4; Eph. 1:3; Phil. 2:8; Heb. 5:8). The reason that we as the church are delighting in the presence of God today is because of what Jesus has done on our behalf and not because we have kept the law perfectly. In Paul's words elsewhere, the inheritance "depends on faith, in order that the promise may rest on grace and be guaranteed to all his offspring—not only to the adherent of the law [namely, Christ] but also to the one who shares the faith of Abraham, who is the father of us all" (Rom. 4:16).[11]

Two conclusions follow from how Paul applies Old Testament promises in 2 Corinthians 6:16: (1) The restoration blessings of the old covenant include all

---

9 For a similar view that Paul is conflating both Lev. 26:11–12 and Ezek. 37:27, see Peter Balla, "2 Corinthians," in *Commentary on the New Testament Use of the Old Testament*, ed. G. K. Beale and D. A. Carson (Grand Rapids, MI: Baker Academic, 2007), 772.

10 Balla writes, "Since all of these OT references [in 2 Cor. 6:16–18] are direct verbal prophecies or are set in a direct verbal prophetic context, Paul sees them having inaugurated fulfillment in the Corinthian community. Consequently, the Corinthians are the beginning of the prophesied end-time tabernacle or temple, and they are part of the dawning fulfillment of Israel's restoration prophecies." Balla, "2 Corinthians," 773.

11 For a development of this latter text, see Starling, "The Yes to All God's Promises," 193–95.

the original blessings but in escalation and without the chance of loss. The way Ezekiel's new covenant promise reasserts the original old covenant blessings from Leviticus 26 supports this claim. (2) Through Christ, the original old covenant blessings *and* the restoration blessings have direct bearing on Christians. Paul appears to draw together both texts, suggesting not only their close tie in the Old Testament but also that, along with the new covenant restoration blessings, the original old covenant blessings do indeed relate to believers.[12]

4. Christians Already Possess All Blessings of Their Inheritance but Will Enjoy Them Fully Only at Christ's Final Coming

Paul emphasizes,

> Blessed be the God and Father of our Lord Jesus Christ, who has blessed us *in Christ* with every spiritual blessing in the heavenly places. . . . *In him* you also, when you heard the word of truth, the gospel of your salvation, and believed in him, were sealed with the promised Holy Spirit, who is the guarantee of our inheritance until we acquire possession of it, to the praise of his glory. (Eph. 1:3, 13–14)

Most scholars believe that "every spiritual blessing" refers to all the blessings that Christ's Spirit secures for the saints, including those like election, adoption, redemption, forgiveness, sealing, and all that we will enjoy completely when we gain our full inheritance (cf. 2 Cor. 1:20, 22; 1 Pet. 1:3–4).[13]

All these blessings fulfill the Old Testament's end-times hopes associated with the promises of new covenant restoration (e.g., Deut. 30:6; Isa. 53:11;

---

12 Starling writes, "Paul indicates by the way in which he merges the citations together [in 2 Cor. 6:16–18] that the Sinaitic and Davidic covenant formulas are applied to his readers not directly but secondhand, refracted through the lens of the end-of-exile prophecies of Ezekiel and Isaiah." Starling, "The Yes to All God's Promises," 192.

13 E.g., Andrew T. Lincoln, *Ephesians*, WBC (Dallas: Word, 1990), 19; Gordon D. Fee, *God's Empowering Presence: The Holy Spirit in the Letters of Paul* (Peabody, MA: Hendrickson, 1994), 666–67; Klyne R. Snodgrass, *Ephesians*, NIV Application Commentary (Grand Rapids, MI: Zondervan, 1996), 46; Peter T. O'Brien, *The Letter to the Ephesians*, PNTC (Grand Rapids, MI: Eerdmans, 1999), 95. F. F. Bruce distinguishes the "spiritual" blessings from "material," but I do not see this as justified in light of the reference in Eph. 1:14 to our full inheritance, which will include a transformed material creation. F. F. Bruce, *The Epistles to the Colossians, to Philemon and to the Ephesians*, NICNT (Grand Rapids, MI: Eerdmans, 1995), 253. See also the citation of Ps. 34:12–16 in 1 Pet. 3:9–12.

Jer. 31:33–34; 32:40; Ezek. 36:27; Dan. 9:24). Yet while *all* God's promises already find there "Yes" for those in Christ (2 Cor. 1:20), a Christian's full enjoyment awaits the coming inheritance. "[He] has put his seal on us and given us his Spirit in our hearts as a guarantee" (2 Cor. 1:22).

Consider also how Peter asserts that the divine favor in Psalm 34:12–16 is lastingly relevant for the church:

Do not repay evil for evil or reviling for reviling, but on the contrary, bless, for to this you were called, that you may obtain a blessing. For

"Whoever desires to love life
    and see good days,
let him keep his tongue from evil
    and his lips from speaking deceit;
let him turn away from evil and do good;
    let him seek peace and pursue it.
For the eyes of the Lord are on the righteous,
    and his ears are open to their prayer.
But the face of the Lord is against those who do evil." (1 Pet. 3:9–12)

Psalm 34 holds out a vision of end-times blessing for the righteous ones (plural) who pursue good and not evil, and Peter claims that this hope still exists for believers today.[14] The retribution principle that stands behind the psalm (i.e., what you sow, you will reap) appears to build on the covenantal blessing-curse structure of Leviticus 26 and Deuteronomy 28, yet it colors these promises in eschatological hues. This future orientation is clear: the psalmist knew that in the present many afflictions would come to God's followers, and yet he was confident that "the Lord hears / and delivers them out of all their troubles" (Ps. 34:17) and that those who serve Yahweh and take refuge in him would not be condemned (34:22). In contrast, God will condemn those who hate the righteous one (singular), which likely refers to the messianic

---

14 Karen Jobes supplies the following list of allusions to Ps. 34 (Ps. 33 LXX) in the first half of Peter's letter: 1 Pet. 1:3 (Ps. 34:1); 1:6 (Ps. 34:19); 1:17 (Ps. 34:5, 7); 1:18; 2:16 (Ps. 34:5); 2:17 (Ps. 34:9, 11); 3:12 (Ps. 34:11). Karen H. Jobes, *1 Peter*, BECNT (Grand Rapids, MI: Baker Academic, 2005), 221–22. In 1 Pet. 3:10–12 the apostle follows the LXX in an adaptive fashion, writing in third person rather than second. See D. A. Carson, "2 Peter," in Beale and Carson, *Commentary on the New Testament Use of the Old Testament*, 1037.

King (Ps. 34:21; cf. 2:12). Peter also recognized that obedient Christians suffer (1 Pet. 2:19–23; 3:14, 17; 4:12–19), and he too remained certain that in time God would "restore, confirm, strengthen, and establish you" (1 Pet. 5:10).[15]

At one level, the "blessing" that is sought in 1 Peter 3:9 is something that God's followers already enjoy, for it is connected to the "living hope" into which saints are already born (1 Pet. 1:3; cf. 1:22–24; 5:1). We see the present nature of "blessing" in 1 Peter 4:14 when the apostle stresses, "If you are insulted for the name of Christ, *you are blessed*, because the Spirit of glory and of God rests upon you." From this perspective, Peter stresses that we experience numerous present expressions of divine favor as we pursue right conduct by faith and in God's power (1 Pet. 1:5).[16]

Nevertheless, while we truly enjoy all God's blessings now, we will only fully enjoy them in the future—truly now, fully later.

- Our battle with sin is still evident, but God has freed believers so that sin no longer enslaves and condemns (Rom. 6:16–18; 7:25; 12:2). Furthermore, rather than being given over to rebellion and a debased mind (Rom. 1:24, 26, 28), God now gives us over to obedience and a renewed mind (6:16–18; 12:2; cf. 7:22–23, 25).
- We also still battle brokenness and decay, but such sufferings only develop our dependent faith in God and heighten our longing for the future (Rom. 8:20–23; 2 Cor. 4:16–18).
- While death looms over us all, Christ removes its sting, and death itself becomes the channel to great reward (Phil. 1:21; cf. Rom. 5:17; 6:23; Rev. 22:4).

---

15 See John Piper, "Hope as the Motivation for Love: 1 Peter 3:9–12," *NTS* 26 (1980): 212–31.

16 Wayne Grudem finds no less than ten "blessings" in this life that according to 1 Peter result from a Christian's right conduct: (1) loving Christ leads to utterable joy (1 Pet. 1:8); (2) continuing faith leads to more benefits of salvation (1:9); (3) a holy life with fear leads to avoiding God's fatherly discipline (1:17); (4) partaking of spiritual milk leads to growing up toward salvation (2:2); (5) trusting and obeying God leads to God's approval (2:19–20); (6) wives submitting to their husbands leads to husbands won for Christ (3:1–2); (7) living considerately with one's wife leads to a husband's prayers not hindered (3:7); (8) enduring reproach for the name of Christ leads to a spirit of glory and of God resting on you (4:14); (9) casting one's cares on God leads to his caring for one's needs (5:7); (10) resisting the devil leads to God's restoring, confirming, strengthening, and establishing you (5:9–10). Wayne Grudem, *1 Peter: An Introduction and Commentary*, TNTC (Downers Grove, IL: InterVarsity Press, 1988), 157. To these I would add that humility before God leads to enjoyment of his grace (1 Pet. 5:5). Cf. Leonhard Goppelt, *A Commentary on 1 Peter*, ed. Ferdinand Hahn, trans. John E. Alsup (Grand Rapids, MI: Eerdmans, 1993), 230.

Christians have a "living hope . . . to an inheritance that is imperishable, undefiled, and unfading, kept in heaven for you" (1 Pet. 1:3–4). Our inheritance
relates to our faith resulting "in praise and glory and honor at the revelation
of Jesus Christ" (1 Pet. 1:7) and to "the unfading crown of glory" that we long
to receive (5:4). We see this future orientation in 1 Peter 3:14, which reads,
"But even if you should suffer for righteousness' sake, *you will be blessed.*"

5. All True Christians Will Persevere and Enjoy Their Full Inheritance

The last principle regarding how Christians relate to Old Testament promises concerns the role of Christian obedience for receiving what God has
promised. Speaking figuratively of people and using the language of old
covenant land, the author of Hebrews reasons, "The land that has drunk
the rain that often falls on it, and produces a crop useful to those for whose
sake it is cultivated, receives a blessing from God. But if it bears thorns and
thistles, it is worthless and near to being cursed, and its end is to be burned"
(Heb. 6:7–8).[17] He then asserts, however,

> Though we speak in this way, yet in your case, beloved, we feel sure of
> better things—things that belong to salvation. For God is not unjust so as
> to overlook your work and the love that you have shown for his name in
> serving the saints, as you still do. And we desire each one of you to show
> the same earnestness to have the full assurance of hope until the end, so
> that you may not be sluggish, but imitators of those who through faith
> and patience inherit the promises. (Heb. 6:9–12)

Because Hebrews 6:13 supplies a reason for the final claim (using the
subordinate conjunction "for" [Greek *gar*]) and refers to a time "when God

---

17 George Guthrie notes how the harsh warning of Heb. 6:7–8 falls "squarely in the context of
Deuteronomy's blessing and curse framework." George H. Guthrie, "Hebrews," in Beale and
Carson, *Commentary on the New Testament Use of the Old Testament,* 964. The passage echoes
several elements from Deuteronomy: (1) the blessing of the land drinking rain (Deut. 11:11;
cf. Heb. 6:7), (2) the blessed over against the cursed land (Deut. 28:12; 29:18, 23–27; cf. Heb.
12:15), (3) the burning of the land as an image of God's punishment (Deut. 4:24; 9:3; 29:20;
32:22; cf. Heb. 12:29), (4) and the nearness of God's judgment (Deut. 32:35; cf. Heb. 6:8; 10:30).
He adds that the "thorns and thistles" from Heb. 6:8 comes from the curse text in Gen. 3:18,
from which springs the imagery in Deuteronomy. Guthrie, "Hebrews," 962–63.

made a promise to Abraham," the promises to which the author refers in 6:12 include those in the Old Testament. The only people who will inherit these promises are those who persevere until the end by maintaining a believing heart and not giving in to sin's deceitfulness (Heb. 3:12–13). Such people alone are authentically part of the new covenant, for they truly share in the work of the new covenant priestly mediator: "For we have come to share in Christ, if indeed we hold our original confidence firm to the end" (Heb. 3:14; cf. 8:6–7, 13; 9:15).[18]

Like other New Testament teachers (e.g., Matt. 5:8; 2 Cor. 7:1; Rev. 21:27), the author of Hebrews emphasizes that "without [holiness] no one will see the Lord" (Heb. 12:14). Persevering fruitfulness is a necessary condition to enjoy the future inheritance, for future judgment will be in accord with (though not based on) deeds we do in this life (Matt. 16:27; Rom. 2:6; 2 Cor. 5:10; 1 Pet. 1:17; Rev. 2:23; 20:12). Thus, Paul urges Timothy, "Keep a close watch on yourself and on the teaching. Persist in this, for by so doing you will save both yourself and your hearers" (1 Tim. 4:16). And elsewhere Paul stresses, "If you live according to the flesh you will die, but if by the Spirit you put to death the deeds of the body, you will live" (Rom. 8:13; cf. 1 Cor. 6:9–10; Gal. 5:19–22; Eph. 5:5).

Elsewhere Paul makes clear that this new covenant call to persevere in faith is not like the old covenant's call to obey so that you may live: "If a person does [my statutes and rules], he shall live by them: I am the Lord" (Lev. 18:5; cf. Rom. 10:5; Gal. 3:12). Speaking predominantly to the unregenerate, the old covenant charged Israel to pursue righteousness (Deut. 16:20), and it declared that they would only be counted righteous and secure life if they met all the covenant's demands (Deut. 6:25; 8:1; cf. 4:1). Yet for Paul, "the very commandment that promised life proved to be death" (Rom. 7:10). "The law is holy, and the commandment is holy and righteous and good" (Rom. 7:12). Yet the majority in "Israel who pursued a law that would lead to righteousness did not succeed in reaching that law . . . because they did not pursue it by faith, but as if it were based on works" (Rom. 9:31–32). Paul can thus declare that "Christ is the end of the law for righteousness to everyone who believes" (Rom. 10:4), because by Christ's perfect obedience

---

18 Scripture appears to teach that there will be levels of reward in heaven based on the deeds one performs in this life (1 Cor. 3:8, 15; 4:4–5; 2 John 8; cf. Ps. 62:12; Matt. 10:41–42; 16:27; Rom. 2:6; 2 Cor. 5:10).

in life and death God frees believers from sin's condemning power (Rom. 5:18–19; 8:1; Col. 2:14), declares us righteous and reconciled (Rom. 5:9–10; 2 Cor. 5:21), and enables us to walk in newness of life (Rom. 6:4, 17, 22). That is, in the new covenant, righteousness and life become the foundation and not just the goal.[19]

From the perspective of Hebrews, Christ's priestly work as new covenant mediator provides an unprecedented "sure and steadfast anchor of the soul" (Heb. 6:19) and "a better hope" than that of the old covenant (7:19).[20] This is so for at least two reasons. First, unlike the sinful old covenant priests who themselves died, the high priest Jesus "always lives to make intercession" for those he saves (Heb. 7:25), which means that we can "with confidence draw near to the throne of grace" expecting to "receive mercy and find grace to help in time of need" (4:16). The one with all authority in heaven and on earth is working for his own! Furthermore, by his death he not only "redeems [all his saints] from the transgressions committed under the first covenant" (Heb. 9:15) but also "has perfected for all time those who are being sanctified" (10:14). Those in the new covenant start from the basis of being completely forgiven for all time (Heb. 10:17–18), and this new foundation places our pursuit of holiness on a completely different footing than that of the old covenant. With this, God now writes his laws on our minds (Heb. 10:16), moving us to follow his ways. Stated another way, because through Christ's single sacrifice "we have been sanctified" (Heb. 10:10) "with our hearts sprinkled clean from an evil conscience and our bodies washed with pure water" (10:22), we can now "hold fast the confession of our hope without wavering" (10:23). We gain fuel to persevere because God is already 100 percent for us in Jesus (Heb. 13:5) and because "he who promised is faithful" (10:23). We have already "come to Mount Zion and to the city of the living God, the heavenly Jerusalem" (Heb. 12:22), and he will "equip [us] with everything good that [we] may do his will, working in us that which is pleasing in his sight, through Jesus Christ, to whom be glory forever and ever" (13:21).

---

19 Again, for more on these principles, see DeRouchie, "From Condemnation to Righteousness," 108–13; DeRouchie, "The Use of Leviticus 18:5 in Galatians 3:12," 240–59, esp. 256–59.

20 See especially Stephen J. Wellum, "The New Covenant Work of Christ: Priesthood, Atonement, and Intercession," in *From Heaven He Came and Sought Her: Definite Atonement in Biblical, Historical, Theological, and Pastoral Perspective*, ed. David Gibson and Jonathan Gibson (Wheaton, IL: Crossway, 2013), 517–40.

All sins that true saints seek to conquer are ones that God has already forgiven in Christ. We will receive our future inheritance based on Christ's new covenant sacrifice alone. We must persevere and enjoy "the holiness without which no one will see the Lord" (Heb. 12:14). However, by means of our past pardon, Christ's present intercession, and the promises of future reward for the faithful and future punishment for those who fall away, God generates persevering faith, hope, and love and thus makes certain the endurance of all members of the new covenant.

Conclusion

The New Testament authors were guided by at least five principles when they related Old Testament promises to Christians: (1) Believers benefit from Old Testament promises only through Christ. (2) Old covenant curses become new covenant curses. (3) As part of the new covenant, Christians inherit the old covenant's original and restoration blessings. (4) Christians already possess all blessings of their inheritance but will enjoy them fully only at Christ's final coming. (5) All true Christians will persevere and enjoy their full inheritance. The next chapter will overview four ways Christ serves as a lens for claiming Old Testament promises as Christians.

Review and Reflection

1. What in the broader literary context of 2 Corinthians suggests that "all the promises of God find their Yes in [Jesus]" (2 Cor. 1:20) refers to both Old and New Testament promises?

2. Using Galatians 3 for your response, why is it true that Christians benefit from Old Testament promises only through Christ?

3. What Old Testament text suggests that old covenant curses become new covenant curses? What is meant by new covenant curses when Christ has already borne God's curse on behalf of Christians?

4. What two Old Testament texts does Paul draw from in 2 Corinthians 6:16, and why is this significant in considering the blessings that Christians inherit in Christ?

5. According to Ephesians 1:3–14, what spiritual blessings are for all who are in Christ?

6. What evidence in 1 Peter indicates that Christians already possess all blessing of their inheritance but will enjoy them fully only at Christ's final coming?

7. How does a present relationship with Jesus alter one's approach to sin, suffering, and death?

8. How does Christ's priestly work as new covenant mediator provide a "sure and steadfast anchor of the soul" for believers today (Heb. 6:19)?

9. Which of the five principles for relating Old Testament promises to Christians helped you most and why?

10. What was the greatest insight you gained in reading this chapter? What is your greatest takeaway?

9

Claiming Old Testament
Promises through Christ

The promises . . . Yes in him.

2 CORINTHIANS 1:20

YAHWEH'S PROMISES (OLD AND NEW) are vital for Christians. If we fail to trustingly embrace Old Testament promises, we will lose three-fourths of the life-giving words of truth that our trustworthy God has given us to nurture our hope. Yet we must appropriate them through Christ.

This Will Work Out for My Deliverance

Consider how Paul lived in hope by claiming promises that encouraged Job. The apostle opens his Philippian letter noting that he was in prison for Christ (Phil. 1:7) and for the defense of the gospel (1:16) but that this imprisonment had itself advanced the gospel's spread (1:12–13). He then asserts, "Yes, and I will rejoice, *for I know that* through your prayers and the help of the Spirit of Jesus Christ *this will turn out for my deliverance*" (Phil. 1:18–19). Was Paul claiming that he knew the Philippians' prayers of faith would result in his being freed from prison? Both his use of Scripture and his immediate context help answer this question.

With the phrase "this will turn out for my deliverance" (Phil. 1:19), Paul alludes to the Greek translation of Job 13:16, the only other place in Scripture where the clause occurs. Job declares,

173

> Though [God] slay me, yet will I hope in him;
>   I will surely defend my ways to his face.
> Indeed, *this will turn out for my deliverance.* (Job 13:15–16 NIV)

Paul is comparing his experience of persecution with Job's experience of physical suffering and loss. With full hope, Job anticipated that even death would not stop him from pleading his cause face-to-face before Yahweh and being saved. So, too, Paul declares, "For I know that . . . this will turn out for my deliverance," and then supplies the reason: "as it is my eager expectation and hope that I will not be at all be ashamed, but that with full courage now as always Christ will be honored in my body, whether by life or by death" (Phil. 1:19–20). Like Job, Paul was convinced that he would be delivered, but this salvation could even come "by death."

Along with alluding to Job 13:16, Paul's initial "for I know that" may also recall Job's later statement,

> For *I know that* my Redeemer lives,
>   and at the last he will stand upon the earth.
> And after my skin has been thus destroyed,
>   yet in my flesh I shall see God. (Job 19:25–26)

The Greek construction rendered "for I know that" occurs only five other times in Scripture, three of which are in Job (Deut. 31:29; Job 9:28; 19:25; 30:23; Rom. 7:18). The likelihood that Paul alludes to the suffering sage's resurrection hope in Job 13:16 heightens the probability that he also has Job 19:25 in mind and melds the two together in Philippians 1:19.[1]

Paul is Christ Jesus's servant (Phil. 1:1), and his sole hope for attaining "the resurrection" (3:11) was that he be found in Christ, "not having a righteousness of my own that comes from the law, but that which comes through faith in Christ" (3:9). The apostle, therefore, claims Job's promise through Jesus, whose own resurrection power (Phil. 3:10) made both Job's and Paul's hope possible.

Paul further declares, "It has been granted to you that for the sake of Christ you should not only believe in him but also suffer for his sake"

---

1   Cf. Moisés Silva who affirms that Paul is citing Job 13:16 but makes no mention of 19:25 in "Philippians," in *Commentary on the New Testament Use of the Old Testament*, ed. G. K. Beale and D. A. Carson (Grand Rapids, MI: Baker Academic, 2007), 836.

(Phil. 1:29). God purposes that Christians in this age suffer: "Through many tribulations we must enter the kingdom of God" (Acts 14:22). Yet in all, Paul's prayer and hope was that "Christ will be honored in my body whether by life or by death. For to me to live is Christ, and to die is gain" (Phil. 1:20–21).

With full courage, Paul sought that he would honor Christ in his body *by death*, for "to die is gain." In what way is dying gain? He tells us two verses later: "My desire is to depart and be with Christ, for that is far better" (Phil. 1:23). We honor Christ in death when we die believing that to be with him is far better than this life. Thus, Job could confidently say,

> And after my skin has been thus destroyed,
> yet in my flesh *I shall see God*. (Job 19:26)

Furthermore, with full courage, Paul sought to honor Christ in his body *by life*, for "to live is Christ." A little later Paul indicates his meaning: "But whatever gain I had, I counted as loss for the sake of Christ. Indeed, I count everything as loss because of the surpassing worth of knowing Christ Jesus my Lord. For his sake I have suffered the loss of all things and count them as rubbish, in order that I may gain Christ" (Phil. 3:7–8). Paul's quest was far different than that of prosperity preachers. He sought to know and gain Jesus, not to acquire goods or health or status or fame. He was in a prison rejoicing because the loss of all else was allowing him to gain Christ.

The very promises that kept Job fearing God through the fire were Paul's in Christ. And today they belong to all who are in Jesus.

Four Ways Jesus Makes Every Promise "Yes"

When Jesus fulfills the Old Testament Law and Prophets, he is actualizing what Scripture anticipated and achieving what God promised and predicted (Matt. 5:17; 11:13; Luke 16:16; 24:44). Truly *every* promise in Scripture is "Yes" in Christ (2 Cor. 1:20), and in him God secures *every* blessing for believers (Gal. 3:14; Eph. 1:3).

Yet Jesus fulfills the Old Testament's promises in more than one way, and this means Christians cannot approach Old Testament promises all in the same manner. Believers must claim Scripture's promises using a salvation-historical framework that has Jesus at the center. Christ is the lens that clarifies and focuses the lasting significance of all God's promises for us (see fig. 9.1).

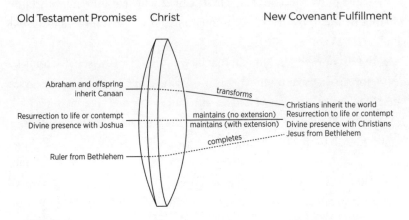

Figure 9.1   The fulfillment of Old Testament promises through the lens of Christ

1. Christ Maintains Some Old Testament Promises with No Extension

Christ *maintains* certain promises without extending them to further beneficiaries. Many of these are explicit restoration promises that include a vision of a global salvation after Israel's exile. Consider, for example, Daniel's prediction: "And many of those who sleep in the dust of the earth shall awake, some to everlasting life, and some to shame and everlasting contempt" (Dan. 12:2). Alluding to this passage, Jesus associated this same resurrection with his second coming: "An hour is coming when all who are in the tombs will hear [the Son of Man's] voice and come out, those who have done good to the resurrection of life, and those who have done evil to the resurrection of judgment" (John 5:28–29; cf. 11:11, 25; 1 Cor. 15:51–52).

Jesus noted that the Old Testament indicates that the Messiah's resurrection would precede and generate our own: "Thus *it is written* that the Christ should suffer and on the third day rise from the dead, and that repentance and forgiveness of sins should be proclaimed in his name to all nations, beginning from Jerusalem" (Luke 24:46–47; cf. 1 Cor 15:3–5).[2] The Old Testament portrays Yahweh as one who would raise the dead:

---

2   For more on the Old Testament predictions of Christ's third-day resurrection, see Mitchell Lloyd Chase, "Resurrection Hope in Daniel 12:2: An Exercise in Biblical Theology" (PhD diss., The

I kill and I make alive;
I wound and I heal. (Deut. 32:39; cf. 1 Sam. 2:7, 10)

Furthermore, speaking to a people that God had already torn and struck down, Hosea said,

After two days he will revive us;
on the third day he will raise us up,
that we may live before him. (Hos. 6:2; cf. 13:14; 1 Cor. 15:55)

The resurrection of God's people would come *on the third day*, and Yahweh and his King would generate it (Hos. 3:5). Isaiah further portrayed Yahweh's righteous servant triumphing in resurrection following his own substitutionary death; by this act he would bear the iniquities of many and account them righteous (Isa. 53:10–11).[3]

The resurrection from the dead and eternal judgment are two of "the elementary doctrine[s] of Christ" (Heb. 6:1–2). Christians should claim the promise of resurrection in Daniel 12:2 as our own. We do so, however, recognizing that we will only rise because Christ was first raised. "Christ has been raised from the dead, the firstfruits of those who have fallen

---

Southern Baptist Theological Seminary, 2013); Mitchell L. Chase, "The Genesis of Resurrection Hope: Exploring Its Early Presence and Deep Roots," *JETS* 57, no. 3 (2014): 467–80; Mitchell L. Chase, "'From Dust You Shall Arise': Resurrection Hope in the Old Testament," *SBJT* 18, no. 4 (2014): 9–29; Nicholas P. Lunn, "'Raised on the Third Day according to the Scriptures': Resurrection Typology in the Genesis Creation Narrative," *JETS* 57, no. 3 (2014): 523–35; Stephen G. Dempster, "From Slight Peg to Cornerstone to Capstone: The Resurrection of Christ on 'the Third Day' according to the Scriptures," *WTJ* 76, no. 2 (2014): 371–409; Joel R. White, "'He Was Raised on the Third Day According to the Scriptures' (1 Corinthians 15:4): A Typological Interpretation Based on the Cultic Calendar in Leviticus 23," *TynBul* 66, no. 1 (2015): 103–19; Jason S. DeRouchie, "Why the Third Day? The Promise of Resurrection in All of Scripture," *Midwestern Journal of Theology* 20, no. 1 (2021): 19–34.

3 David captured Christ's journey through tribulation unto triumph in Ps. 22, which opens with the king crying, "My God, my God, why have you forsaken me?" (Ps. 22:1; cf. Matt. 27:46). He is "scorned by mankind and despised by the people," with some mocking him and wagging their heads (Ps. 22:6–8; cf. 2:1; Matt. 27:39, 43). His strength and mouth are dried up (Ps. 22:15; John 19:28). He is encircled by evildoers who pierce his hands and feet and then cast lots for his clothing (Ps. 22:16–18; cf. Matt. 27:35; Luke 24:39–40; John 19:24), yet not one of his bones is broken (Ps. 22:17; 34:20; John 19:36). He declares, "You lay me in the dust of death" (Ps. 22:15), but he then proclaims, "You have rescued me from the horns of the wild oxen. / I will tell of your name to my brothers" (Ps. 22:21–22; cf. Matt. 28:10; Heb. 2:10–12).

asleep. . . . Christ the firstfruits, then at his coming those who belong to Christ" (1 Cor. 15:20, 23). As Jesus said, "I am the resurrection and the life. Whoever believes in me, though he die, yet shall he live" (John 11:25; cf. Rom. 6:5). This resurrection has an already-but-not-yet dimension, as the redeemed saints from both the Old and New Testament epochs benefit from it. Jesus maintains the Old Testament promise without altering those profiting from it.

2. Christ Maintains Some Old Testament Promises with Extension

When Christ fulfills some Old Testament promises, he extends the promise to all parties related to him. For example, consider how the Messiah's promised mission gets extended to the church. Isaiah portrayed the coming royal deliverer as speaking in first person and declaring that Yahweh called him from the womb, named him "Israel," and told him that his mission as God's servant was to save some from the people of Israel and the rest of the nations:

> It is too light a thing that you should be my servant
> > to raise up the tribes of Jacob
> > and to bring back the preserved of Israel;
> I will make you as a light for the nations,
> > that my salvation may reach to the end of the earth. (Isa. 49:6
> > > cf. 49:1, 3)[4]

---

4   Within Isa. 40–53, the term "servant" occurs twenty times, always in the singular. Sometimes it refers to God's sinful "servant-people" (e.g., Isa. 42:19, 22; 43:8, 10), but within the Servant Songs it always refers to the eschatological Messiah, God's "servant-person" (Isa. 42:1–9; 49:1–13; 50:4–11; 52:13–53:12). For arguments that the servant of Isaiah's Servant Songs is the promised messianic deliverer, see G. P. Hugenberger, "The Servant of the Lord in the 'Servant Songs' of Isaiah: A Second Moses Figure," in *The Lord's Anointed: Interpretation of Old Testament Messianic Texts*, ed. Philip E. Satterthwaite, Richard S. Hess, and Gordon J. Wenham (Grand Rapids, MI: Baker Academic, 1995), 108–11; Walter C. Kaiser Jr., "The Identity and Mission of the 'Servant of the Lord,'" in *The Gospel According to Isaiah 53: Encountering the Suffering Servant in Jewish and Christian Theology*, ed. Darrell L. Bock and Mitch Glaser (Grand Rapids, MI: Kregel Academic, 2012), 89–92; Jason S. DeRouchie, "Redemptive-Historical, Christocentric Approach," in *Five Views of Christ in the Old Testament*, ed. Andrew M. King and Brian J. Tabb, Counterpoints: Bible and Theology (Grand Rapids, MI: Zondervan Academic, 2022), 208–9. For a specific argument that the servant in Isa. 49:1–6 refers to the eschatological Messiah, see G. K. Beale, *A New Testament Biblical Theology: The Unfolding of the Old Testament in the New* (Grand Rapids, MI: Baker Academic, 2011), 656–57.

By this act God would fulfill his earlier promises to Abraham (Gen. 12:3; 22:18; cf. Isa. 51:1–4; 54:1–3).

Paul saw Jesus as the most immediate referent to Isaiah's servant-person, for he said he was "saying nothing but what the prophets and Moses said would come to pass: that the Christ must suffer and that, by being the first to rise from the dead, he would proclaim light both to our people and to the Gentiles" (Acts 26:22–23). Yet Paul also saw the Old Testament promises reaching further to the mission of all who are in Christ:

We are turning to the Gentiles. For so the Lord has commanded us, saying,

> "I have made you a light for the Gentiles,
>   that you may bring salvation to the ends of the earth."
>   (Acts 13:46–47)

A promise related to the messianic servant's work has now become a commission for all the servants identified with him.

As Isaiah himself anticipated, following the work of the royal, eschatological servant (singular) (Isa. 42:1; 49:3, 5–7; 50:10; 52:13; 53:11; cf. Acts 3:26; 4:27–30), God would commission many priestly "servants" (plural) from both Israel and other nations to carry on the Messiah's work (e.g., Isa. 54:17; 56:6; 63:17; 65:8–9, 13–15; 66:14). Paul saw himself as one of these ambassadors.[5] Jesus's cross work had purchased Paul's rescue from sin and from God's wrath, and now the apostle was bound as "a servant" of his Savior (cf. Rom. 1:1 with 6:20, 22) (see fig. 9.2).[6]

Figure 9.2   God maintains the promise of serving as a light while extending it to all in Christ

---

5   Cf. Isa. 42:6–7 with Acts 26:15–18, 22–23; Isa. 49:6 with Acts 13:45–48; Isa. 49:8 with 2 Cor. 6:1–4.

6   See also how the beautiful feet of the Messiah (Isa. 52:7) become the beautiful feet of the church (Rom. 10:15) and how the iron rod of the Messiah (Ps. 2:9; Rev. 12:5; 19:15) becomes the iron rod of his people (Rev. 2:26–27).

Second, as introduced in chapter 7, the author of Hebrews claims for Christians a promise that Moses and Yahweh made to Joshua just before he entered the promised land.[7] The prophet declared, "It is the LORD who goes before you. He will be with you; he will not leave you or forsake you" (Deut. 31:8). Later, Yahweh said, "Just as I was with Moses, so I will be with you. I will not leave you or forsake you" (Josh. 1:5). When Joshua received this promise, what was true for him would be true for all who followed him. As Moses himself asserted to the congregation: "Do not fear or be in dread . . . for it is the LORD your God who goes with you. He will not leave you or forsake you" (Deut. 31:6).

Yet from what framework does the writer of Hebrews apply this promise to Christians battling covetousness? He writes, "Keep your life free from love of money, and be content with what you have, for he has said, 'I will never leave you nor forsake you'" (Heb. 13:5). How does a promise for Israel's leader before the conquest of Canaan become a promise for Christians today?

In Hebrews, the Old Testament's wilderness and conquest narratives play an important role in magnifying the way Christ and the new covenant are better. Moses was faithful to God "as a servant," whereas Christ was faithful "as a son" (Heb. 3:5–6). Most in the exodus generation rebelled, hardening their hearts in unbelief, and because of this Yahweh declared, "They shall not enter my rest" (Heb. 3:7–11). Some like Joshua believed that God was able to secure rest, but all others died because of unbelief (Heb. 4:2). Later Joshua led Israel into the promised land, but the rest he secured was only temporary and predictive of the greater rest that the supreme Joshua (the Hebrew name *Joshua* is *Jesus* in Greek) would secure for all in him (Heb. 4:8).

So, if the Lord was with the first Joshua and all who followed him, how much more can we be assured that he will be with those identified with the greater Joshua![8] The original promise God gave to one man bore implications for the whole community, and now in the new covenant the same

7   For the proposal that the writer of Hebrews is citing Josh. 1:5, yet supplementing it with wording from Deut. 31:8, see Brooke Foss Westcott, ed., *The Epistle to the Hebrews: The Greek Text with Notes and Essays*, 3rd ed. (London: Macmillan, 1920), 434; William L. Lane, *Hebrews 9–13*, WBC (Dallas: Word, 1991), 519–20.

8   Lane, *Hebrews 9–13*, 520.

promise expands to all who are in Christ. We already share in Christ Jesus (Heb. 3:14) but do not yet fully enjoy all that God promised (6:12). But because God has pledged, "I will never leave you nor forsake you" (Heb. 13:5), Christians can rest secure knowing that we will one day fully enjoy the inheritance. It is truly ours now and will be fully enjoyed in the future.

In Joshua's day, Achan's covetous act led to his demise, such that he and his family were not able to enjoy the promised inheritance (Josh. 7:1, 20–25). In Christ, we are freed from the love of money and empowered to enjoy contentment and to live radically today in the hope of tomorrow (Heb. 13:5). Knowing that God is for us and with us helps us "lay aside every weight, and sin which clings so closely" (Heb. 12:1). We look "to Jesus, the founder and perfecter of our faith, who for the joy that was set before him endured the cross, despising the shame, and is seated at the right hand of the throne of God" (Heb. 12:2). And as we consider "him who endured from sinners such hostility against himself," we are helped to "not grow weary or fainthearted" (Heb. 12:3). God's presence and favor are our hope and our security. "For you had compassion on those in prison, and you joyfully accepted the plundering of your property, since you knew that you yourselves had a better possession and an abiding one" (Heb. 10:34). God's promise of his presence moves from the lesser (Joshua) to the greater (Jesus) and to all who are in him (see fig. 9.3).

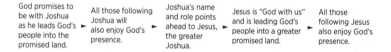

Figure 9.3   God maintains the promise of his presence while extending it to all in Christ

Third, Paul's use of Leviticus 26:11–12 in 2 Corinthians 6:16 provides another example of maintaining a promise with extension. In support of the claim that "we [the church] are the temple of the living God" (2 Cor. 6:16), Paul cites Moses's original covenant blessing that Yahweh would bestow a greater manifestation of his presence if Israel would perfectly obey: "If you walk in my statutes and observe my commandments and do them, . . . I will make my dwelling among you, and my soul shall not abhor you. And I will walk among you and will be your God, and you shall be my people"

(Lev. 26:3, 11–12). Because Yahweh was already "walking" in Israel's midst by inhabiting the tabernacle (Deut. 23:14), Moses appears to envision an enjoyment of Yahweh's presence beyond the physical structures of the tabernacle and temple, which were mere models of a heavenly pattern (Ex. 25:9; 1 Chron. 28:19; cf. Acts 7:44; Heb. 8:5). The earthly, man-made replicas bore a built-in obsolescence, for they would be replaced if the heavenly reality ever came to earth (cf. Heb. 9:11–12, 24). And according to Moses, this would only be possible when God's people (or their representative) would be perfectly obedient.

Significantly, following Ezekiel's vision of Yahweh's departure from Jerusalem (Ezek. 8–11) and his account of the city's destruction (Ezek. 33:21; cf. 2 Kings 25), he predicted a day when Yahweh would move his people from death to life and inhabit them with his Spirit (Ezek. 36:27; 37:14). Yahweh declared, "David my servant shall be their prince forever" (Ezek. 37:25), and then, with allusions back to the promise of Leviticus 26:11–12, God promised, "My dwelling place shall be with them, and I will be their God, and they shall be my people. Then the nations will know that I am the LORD who sanctifies Israel, when my sanctuary is in their midst forever" (Ezek. 37:27–28).[9] Of this new "temple," Haggai foresaw that it would be filled with glory and peace (Hag. 2:9), Zechariah said it would be built by the messianic king-priest with the help of foreigners (Zech. 6:12–13, 15), and Malachi says the messenger of the covenant would come to it on the day of the Lord (Mal. 3:2). Isaiah foretold that the Spirit enjoyed by God's restored people (Isa. 32:15; 44:3; cf. Joel 2:28) first rested on the royal servant himself (Isa. 11:2; 42:1; 59:21; 61:1).

Speaking of the divine Son, John declares, "The Word became flesh and dwelt among us, and we have seen his glory" (John 1:14). Jesus characterized himself as "the temple" (John 2:19–22), and all who believe in him become a "dwelling place for God by the Spirit" (Eph. 2:19–22; cf. 1 Cor. 3:16; 1 Pet. 2:5). Thus, Paul says, "We are the temple of the living God" (2 Cor. 6:16), and then indicates that, in the church, God is fulfilling his original promise to Israel from Leviticus 26:11–12. Through Jesus, who perfectly obeyed on our behalf (Rom. 5:18–19), we enjoy his tabernacling presence (John 1:14; 2:21) and become God's temple (1 Cor. 3:16; 2 Cor. 6:16).

9 The book's final extended vision of the new Jerusalem and of Yahweh's return (Ezek. 43:4–5; 48:35) supplies a symbolic portrayal of what Ezek. 36:27 and 34:14, 27 predict.

In Jesus, we are already associated with the heavenly Jerusalem (Gal. 4:26; Heb. 12:22), but we still await the day when the holy city itself will come down from heaven, when in its consummate state "the dwelling place of God is with man" (Rev. 21:2–3). Then the Most Holy Place will be all that we enjoy, for the temple of the city will be "the Lord God the Almighty and the Lamb" (Rev. 21:22). Then God will have made some "from every tribe and language and people and nation" into "a kingdom and priests to our God, and they shall reign on the earth" (Rev. 5:9–10) (see fig. 9.4).

| God promises to dwell and walk among his people as a moveable temple. | → | Christ is God's temple. | → | Faith unites us to Christ. | → | Union with Christ makes us God's temple. | → | God is presently building his temple, which will fill all things. |

Figure 9.4   God maintains the promise of his dwelling while extending it to all in Christ

Finally, numerous other promises that God gave to the broader old covenant community reach Christians today through Jesus. Two such promises that are deeply encouraging include

Fear not, for I am with you;
be not dismayed, for I am your God;
I will strengthen you, I will help you,
I will uphold you with my righteous right hand. (Isa. 41:10)

and

For I know the plans I have for you, declares the LORD, plans for welfare and not for evil, to give you a future and a hope. (Jer. 29:11)

Through Jesus, these promises that Yahweh gave to old covenant Israel extend to the church—not to any geopolitical people or territory but to the church. Because Jesus fully represents national Israel in every way (Gal. 3:16; cf. Isa. 49:3, 6) and because no one inherits blessings apart from faith in Christ (Gal. 3:7, 9), all those adopted into Christ by faith receive all the benefits of being part of his family, whether Jew or Gentile (Gal. 3:29; 4:5). Christians are all "one in Christ" (Gal. 3:28), "one new man" (Eph. 2:15), together enjoying "adoption . . . as sons" (Eph. 1:5) with equal partnership in the "inheritance of the saints" (Col. 1:12; cf. Gal. 3:18; Eph. 3:6) (see fig. 9.5).

This structure of inheritance rights is no different than how my own adopted children from Africa and biological children from North America together enjoy every benefit of being a DeRouchie. No child receives preferential treatment, for all bear the same family identity and are counted as true children. How much more is this true in the household of God, wherein *every* child of the king, both Jew and Gentile, is adopted into Christ. Yahweh foretold such realities when he declared how, in the new creation, foreigners would gain new birth certificates declaring their link with the new Jerusalem:

> Glorious things of you are spoken,
>> O city of God.   *Selah*
>
>
> Among those who know me I mention Rahab and Babylon;
>> behold, Philistia and Tyre, with Cush—
>> "This one was born there," they say.
> And of Zion it shall be said,
>> "This one and that one were born in her";
>> for the Most High himself will establish her.
> The LORD records as he registers the peoples,
>> "This one was born there."   *Selah* (Ps. 87:3–6)

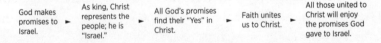

| God makes promises to Israel. | ► | As king, Christ represents the people; he is "Israel." | ► | All God's promises find their "Yes" in Christ. | ► | Faith unites us to Christ. | ► | All those united to Christ will enjoy the promises God gave to Israel. |

Figure 9.5   God maintains his promises to Israel while extending them to all in Christ

3. Christ Himself Completes or Uniquely Realizes Some Old Testament Promises

Some Old Testament promises Christ has already completed or uniquely realized. Such fulfillments prove that God will certainly keep the rest of his promises (Deut. 18:22; Ezek. 33:33; cf. Rom. 8:32). For example, the prophet Micah predicted that a long-prophesied ruler in Israel would rise from Bethlehem (Mic. 5:2), and Christ exclusively fulfilled that promise at his birth (Matt. 2:6). There is only one Christ, and he was born only once. Nevertheless, his birth was to spark a global return of "his brothers," and as King he would "shepherd his flock in the strength of the LORD," thus establishing lasting security and peace and enjoying a great name (Mic. 5:3–5). All these added promises continue to give Christians comfort and hope, and Christ's birth in Bethlehem validates for us the certainty of his permanent and global exaltation.

Another example is Yahweh's promise to Solomon that, because he asked for wisdom rather than long life, riches, or punishment on his enemies, God would give him wisdom, as well as riches and honor (1 Kings 3:11–13). This promise was "yes" in Christ in that on the cross Jesus purchased every divine bestowal of kindness, forbearance, and patience experienced in the realm of common grace (Gen. 8:20–21; Rom. 2:4; 3:25–26). Nevertheless, because the promise was contingent on one man's request and included blessing related to one man's specific reign, the promise's specificity indicates that this is not a promise that every believer always enjoys. Unlike Yahweh's promise to never leave nor forsake Joshua (Deut. 31:8; Josh. 1:5), which was true for all who followed him (Deut. 31:6), this promise was unique to Solomon himself, with others benefiting only from the wisdom, riches, and honor he himself enjoyed.

4. Christ Transforms Some Old Testament Promises

At times, Jesus transforms or develops the makeup and audience of an Old Testament promise. These promises relate most directly to shadows that clarify and point to a greater substance in Christ—that is, to Old Testament patterns or types that find their climax or antitype in Jesus.[10] The land that Yahweh promised to Abraham and his offspring as a lasting possession is of this kind (cf. Gen. 13:15; 17:8; 48:4; Ex. 32:13). The patriarch would serve as a father of a single nation who would dwell in the land of Canaan (Gen. 17:8) and oversee an even broader geopolitical sphere (Gen. 15:18). These realities are initially fulfilled in the Mosaic covenant (Ex. 2:24; 6:8; Deut. 1:8;

---

10 For an exceptional overview of typology and transformation as argued for here, see Brent E. Parker, "The Israel-Christ-Church Relationship," in *Progressive Covenantalism: Charting a Course between Dispensational and Covenant Theologies*, ed. Stephen J. Wellum and Brent E. Parker (Nashville: B&H Academic, 2016), 39–68.

6:10; 9:5; 30:20; 34:4) and realized in the days of Joshua (Josh. 11:23; 21:43) and Solomon (1 Kings 4:20–21). Nevertheless, Genesis already foresees Abraham becoming the father of not just one nation but *nations* (Gen. 17:4–6) and anticipates his influence reaching beyond the land (singular) to *lands* (plural) (26:3–4; cf. 15:18; 17:8). This would happen when the singular, royal offspring rose to possess the gate of his enemies and when, in him, all the earth's nations counted themselves blessed (Gen. 22:17–18; 24:60; cf. Ps. 2:7). Paul cites the Genesis lands promise (Gen. 26:3) and its allusion (22:17–18; cf. 13:15; 17:8; 24:7; 28:4) when he identifies Christ as the offspring to whom the promises were made (Gal. 3:16). The apostle then declares that all in Christ, whether Jew or Gentile, slave or free, male or female, "are Abraham's seed and heirs according to the promise" (Gal. 3:28–29). Paul also stresses that the Christian's inheritance (Gal. 3:18) was *not* the present Jerusalem associated with the Mosaic covenant but was instead the heavenly Jerusalem (Gal. 4:24–26), which both Isaiah and John associate with the new earth (Isa. 65:17–25; Rev. 21:1–22:5; cf. Heb. 12:22).[11]

In the new covenant, Christ transforms the type into the antitype by fulfilling the original land promise in himself and by extending it to the whole world through his people. In Paul's words, God promised "Abraham and his offspring that he would be heir of the *world*" (Rom. 4:13); at the consummation the new earth will fully realize the antitype. By extending the promised land to lands, Jesus transforms Israel's "everlasting possession" (Gen. 17:8; 48:4), realizing what God had already foretold to the patriarchs.

Similar New Testament declarations signal the same promissory extension. Jesus declared, "Blessed are the meek, for they shall inherit the earth" (Matt. 5:5). Paul, too, added motivation to his command to honor one's parents by drawing on the promise in Exodus 20:12: "that it may go well with you and that you may live long in the land" (Eph. 6:2–3).[12] Finally, in

---

11   Paul's explicit language of "inheritance" in Gal. 3:18 is most likely rooted in the Old Testament land promise (e.g., Num. 26:53–56; Josh. 11:23). So Thomas R. Schreiner, *Galatians*, ZECNT (Grand Rapids, MI: Zondervan, 2010), 230; cf. Ronald Y. K. Fung, *The Epistle to the Galatians*, NICNT (Grand Rapids, MI: Eerdmans, 1988), 155. Cf. Num. 18:20; 32:18–19; 33:54; 34:2; Deut. 4:21, 38; 12:9; 15:4; 19:14; 20:16; 24:4; 25:19; 26:1; Josh. 13:6–8; 24:28.

12   By omitting the clause "that the LORD your God is giving you," Paul appears to be supplying broader, more universal application to the promise. Andrew T. Lincoln, *Ephesians*, WBC (Dallas: Word, 1990), 405; F. F. Bruce, *The Epistles to the Colossians, to Philemon and to the Ephesians*, NICNT (Grand Rapids, MI: Eerdmans, 1995), 398.

Hebrews 11 we learn that Abraham "was looking forward to the city that has foundations, whose designer and builder is God" (Heb. 11:10). Indeed, people like Abel, Enoch, Noah, Abraham, and Sarah all recognized that their immediate earthly inheritance was *not* the ultimate hope. "They were strangers and exiles on earth. . . . They desire a better country, that is, a heavenly one. Therefore God is not ashamed to be called their God, for he has prepared for them a city" (Heb. 11:13, 16).

This "city" is none other than "Mount Zion . . . the city of the living God, the heavenly Jerusalem," to which all who are Christians have *already* come (Heb. 12:22; cf. Gal. 4:26). Nevertheless, we still await "a new heaven and a new earth" when the "new Jerusalem" will come "down out of heaven from God, prepared as a bride adorned for her husband" (Rev. 21:1–2). In that day, "the dwelling of God" will be with mankind. "He will dwell with them, and they will be his people, and God himself will be with them as their God" (Rev. 21:3). In this city, all nations will find healing and rest forevermore in God's presence (Rev. 22:1–2).[13]

Conclusion

God's promises are often associated with life or death and conditioned on whether his covenant partner obeys. Whereas the old Mosaic covenant was conditional and revocable (and thus temporarily considered Israel's disobedi-ence), the Abrahamic covenant was conditional and irrevocable. This means that God would indeed realize all the promises but would do so only through an obedient Son (cf. Gen. 12:3; 18:18–19; 22:17–18). Representing Abraham and Israel, Jesus actively obeyed and secured Old Testament promises for all who are in him. Christ maintains some promises without extension, maintains others with extension, completes some, and transforms others.

Isaiah declares that throughout the ages no ear has heard nor eye has seen a God like ours "who acts for those who wait for him" (Isa. 64:4). The call of the biblical text, therefore, is that we would trust in the promises of God. Just before Paul asserts that "all the promises of God find their Yes in [Christ]" (2 Cor. 1:20), he declares, "God is faithful" (1:18). As the psalmist declares,

---

13 For more on this approach to the land promises, see esp. Oren R. Martin, *Bound for the Prom-ised Land: The Land Promise in God's Redemptive Plan*, NSBT 34 (Downers Grove, IL: IVP Academic, 2015).

The LORD is faithful in all his words
    and kind in all his works. (Ps. 145:13; cf. 2 Thess. 3:3; 2 Tim. 2:11–13;
        1 Pet. 4:19; 1 John 1:9)

One day, God will complete all his promises to us in Christ. And we will say in that day,

Behold, this is our God; we have waited for him, that he might save us.
This is the LORD; we have waited for him;
let us be glad and rejoice in his salvation. (Isa. 25:9)

Review and Reflection

1. In Philippians 1:17–21 Paul draws on two Old Testament promises from Job 13:15–16 and Job 19:25–26. What truths did you find most helpful when considering how Paul uses Job?

2. What is meant by the claim that Christ maintains some Old Testament promises with no extension? What suggests that this category fits Daniel's promise regarding the resurrection in Daniel 12:2?

3. What New Testament texts suggest that God maintains the promise that his servant would serve as a light to the nations (Isa. 49:6) but that he extends it to all in Christ?

4. Compare the promise of beautiful feet in Isaiah 52:7 with Paul's citation in Romans 10:15. How can Paul justly apply a text that referred to the individual servant ("how beautiful . . . are the feet of *him*") to the whole church ("how beautiful are the feet of *those*")?

5. In recalling God's promise "I will never leave you nor forsake you" (Heb. 13:5), the author of Hebrews applies to Christians a promise God first gave Joshua before entering the promised land (cf. Deut. 31:8; Josh. 1:5). Clarify from within the book of Hebrews how this is justified and how Christ is the key for both maintaining the promise and extending it.

6. The author argues that all those who are united to Christ by faith enjoy all the promises God made to the nation of Israel. Explain in your own words why this is so.

7. What benefit remains for believers today of Old Testament promises that Christ himself completes or uniquely fulfills?

8. How does Genesis itself envision how Yahweh will transform the land promise in the day when Abraham becomes the father of a multitude? How does the New Testament see this fulfilled?
9. Go back to the devotional on Philippians 1:17–21 that opened the chapter. Which of the four ways that Jesus makes every promise "yes" appears operative in how Paul reaffirms for his own life and for other Christians the promises that guided Job?
10. What was the greatest insight you gained in reading this chapter? What is your greatest takeaway?

PART 4

LIVING WELL

How Jesus Makes Moses's Law Matter[1]

I have not come to abolish [the Law or the Prophets] but to fulfill them. For truly, I say to you, until heaven and earth pass away, not an iota, not a dot, will pass from the Law until all is accomplished. Therefore whoever relaxes one of the least of these commandments and teaches others to do the same will be called least in the kingdom of heaven, but whoever does them and teaches them will be called great in the kingdom of heaven.

MATTHEW 5:17–19

---

1   Much of Part 4 updates material first published in Jason S. DeRouchie, *How to Understand and Apply the Old Testament: Twelve Steps from Exegesis to Theology* (Phillipsburg, NJ: P&R, 2017), 427–59. Used by permission. Cf. Jason S. DeRouchie, "Making the Ten Count: Reflections on the Lasting Message of the Decalogue," in *For Our Good Always: Studies on the Message and Influence of Deuteronomy in Honor of Daniel I. Block*, ed. Jason S. DeRouchie, Jason Gile, and Kenneth J. Turner (Winona Lake, IN: Eisenbrauns, 2013), 415–40; Jason S. DeRouchie, "From Condemnation to Righteousness: A Christian Reading of Deuteronomy," *SBJT* 18, no. 3 (2014): 87–118; Jason S. DeRouchie, "The Use of Leviticus 18:5 in Galatians 3:12: A Redemptive-Historical Reassessment," *Them* 45, no. 2 (2020): 240–59; Jason S. DeRouchie, "Question 25: What Is a Biblical Theology of the Law?," in Jason S. DeRouchie, Oren R. Martin, and Andrew David Naselli, *40 Questions about Biblical Theology* (Grand Rapids, MI: Kregel, 2020), 245–56.

Sin will have no dominion over you, since you
are not under law but under grace.

ROMANS 6:14

Owe no one anything, except to love each other, for
the one who loves another has fulfilled the law.

ROMANS 13:8

While most people in Moses's old covenant audience were stubborn, rebellious, unbelieving, and spiritually disabled (Deut. 9:6–7, 23–24; 29:4), he anticipated a day when Yahweh's redeemed community would hear and heed all the words he was commanding in Deuteronomy: "And you shall again obey the voice of the LORD and keep all his commandments that I command you today" (30:8). This would happen after exile (Deut. 30:1) when Yahweh would circumcise the people's hearts, thus empowering them to love and live (30:6). The covenant-mediating prophet like Moses would rise, and his followers would listen to his words (Deut. 18:15; cf. Acts 3:22–26). He would extend the significance of Moses's original law into a new age (Deut. 30:8), and he would do so in a way that God's very word in his mouth (Deut. 18:18) would be in the mouths and hearts of his hearers (Deut. 30:14; cf. Isa. 59:21)—all realities fulfilled today in the church through Jesus (Rom. 10:6–9).[2]

Jesus came not "to abolish the Law or the Prophets . . . but to fulfill them" (Matt. 5:17–18). "Christ is the end of the law for righteousness to everyone who believes" (Rom. 10:4), so Christians today are "not under law but under grace" (Rom. 6:14). Nevertheless, while Moses's law no longer directly binds any Christian, Jesus's followers must still consider the law's lasting relevance as Scripture by assessing how Christ fulfills any given law, each of which we fulfill through love (Rom. 13:8; cf. Matt. 7:12).

---

2   For more on this reading, see Colin J. Smothers, *In Your Mouth and in Your Heart: A Study of Deuteronomy 30:12–14 in Paul's Letter to the Romans* (Eugene, OR: Pickwick, 2022); cf. Steven R. Coxhead, "Deuteronomy 30:11–14 as a Prophecy of the New Covenant in Christ," *WTJ* 68 (2006): 305–20.

Part 4 seeks to help Christians better understand their relationship to the Mosaic law-covenant so that we can celebrate Christ's justifying and sanctifying work more fully and receive God's intended guidance from the portrait of love found in the old covenant law. The thesis is this: The Mosaic law does not *directly* bind the Christian in a legal manner, but we treat all the Old Testament laws as profitable and instructive when we read them through the lens of Christ. Chapter 10 uses exegesis and biblical theology to discern the lasting relationship of the law to Christians. Chapter 11 then addresses the proposed threefold division of the law and confronts three unhelpful and perhaps dangerous perspectives on the Christian's relationship to Old Testament law. Chapter 12 opens by proposing a model for discerning the law's lasting relevance and then supplies two case studies in how Jesus maintains certain laws with and without extension. Chapter 13 adds two more case studies, noting how Jesus's saving work transforms and annuls certain laws.

10

Relating Moses's Law to Christians

Not under law.

ROMANS 6:14

THE ANGLICAN EVANGELICAL revivalist and hymnist John Berridge (1716–1793) thoughtfully averred:

> To run and work the law commands,
> Yet gives me neither feet nor hands;
> But better news the gospel brings:
> It bids me fly and gives me wings.[1]

Scripture normally uses the term *law* to speak of the body of written religious and legal commandments in the Mosaic covenant that together call people to love God and neighbor (Rom. 13:8–10; cf. Matt. 7:12; 22:37–40). Hence, Paul asserts, "The law, which came 430 years afterward, does not annul a covenant previously ratified by God, so as to make the promise [made to Abraham] void" (Gal. 3:17). In Matthew 5, Jesus uses "Law" as shorthand for the first canonical division of his Bible (i.e., the Pentateuch), when he states, "I have not come to abolish the Law or the Prophets . . . but to fulfill them" (Matt. 5:17). Immediately, though, he narrows his focus to

---

1 Quoted in Jason C. Meyer, *The End of the Law: Mosaic Covenant in Pauline Theology*, NAC Studies in Bible & Theology (Nashville: B&H Academic, 2009), 2.

the lasting significance of the commandments: "Until heaven and earth pass away, not an iota, not a dot, will pass from the Law until all is accomplished. Therefore whoever relaxes one of the least of these commandments and teaches others to do the same will be called least in the kingdom of heaven" (Matt. 5:18–19). Jesus saw lasting relevance for Christians in Moses's instruction when appropriated through his fulfillment (cf. Rom. 15:4; 2 Tim. 3:16). Nevertheless, Paul also made clear that, as a believer, he was not "under the law [of Moses]" yet was not "outside the law of God but under the law of Christ" (1 Cor. 9:20–21; cf. Rom. 6:14).

Moses's law is one expression of God's eternal law, which grows out of his unchanging, righteous character. The eternal law manifests itself in different institutional and covenantal forms through the timeline of salvation history. Indeed, those institutional and covenantal changes mark off one era of redemptive history from another. For example, God's command for the first couple not to eat from the tree of the knowledge pertaining to good and evil reveals the outworking of his eternal law at that moment, but it doesn't directly bind us today. We, thus, can't just say, "God's law is eternal, so let's apply that garden command directly to us." Rather, we need to do the tough work of figuring out how or in what sense such a law would apply.

As I will argue, the same principle applies to the Mosaic law, which clarified the way God's eternal law was to govern ancient Israel at that particular time in history. The law through Moses was distinctive from anything that governed previous generations, and God gave it to ancient Israel and not to every nation on earth. For Christians today, the question then becomes: How does the Mosaic law apply to Christians when so much has changed with Christ's coming, not least of which is that we are part of the new covenant and not the old? With a simple alliteration, Brian Rosner has captured well three principles that clarify the Christian's relationship to the Mosaic law covenant: *repudiate, replace,* and *reappropriate.*[2]

1. Biblical Authors *Repudiate* the Mosaic Law-Covenant

Through his written code, Yahweh called Israel to holiness (Lev. 20:26; cf. 19:2; 20:7; 21:8), such that their complete surrender would enable them

---

2   Brian S. Rosner, *Paul and the Law: Keeping the Commandments of God*, NSBT 31 (Downers Grove, IL: IVP Academic, 2013), 208–9, 217–22.

to mediate his presence and display his majesty to the nations (Ex. 19:5–6; Deut. 4:5–6). By perfectly obeying, they could enjoy righteous status (Deut. 6:25) and obtain life, resting in his provision and protection (Lev. 26:3–13; Deut. 28:1–14). Unpardoned disobedience, however, would bring death (Lev. 26:14–39; Deut. 28:15–68).

Israel was stubborn, rebellious, and unbelieving (Deut. 9:6–7, 23–24; 29:4), and both Yahweh and Moses declared that Israel's sin would only blossom to their own ruin (Deut. 4:25–28; 31:16–18, 27–29). History showed this to be true, and Paul, therefore, noted the Mosaic law-covenant bore a ministry of death and condemnation, which stands in contrast to the new covenant's ministry of righteousness (2 Cor. 3:7, 9; cf. Rom. 7:10). While "the law is holy" (Rom. 7:12; cf. 2:20), "the law is not of faith" (Gal. 3:12), meaning that the age of the Mosaic administration was characterized not by faith but by unbelief.[3]

By God's purposes, the Mosaic law multiplied transgression (Rom. 5:20; Gal. 3:19), exposed sin (Rom. 3:20), and brought wrath (Rom. 4:15) to show that "one is justified by faith apart from works of the law" (Rom. 3:28; cf. Gal. 3:10; James 2:10) and that only for "the one who does not work but believes in him who justifies the ungodly, his faith is counted as righteousness" (Rom. 4:5; cf. 9:30–32). Christians repudiate the Mosaic law-covenant, "for Christ is the end of the law for righteousness to everyone who believes" (Rom. 10:4). As the author of Hebrews declares, "In speaking of a new covenant, he makes the first one obsolete. And what is becoming obsolete and growing old is ready to vanish away" (Heb. 8:13). "The law made nothing perfect" (Heb. 7:19), but in Christ we find "a better hope" (7:19), "a better covenant" (7:22; cf. 8:6), "better promises" (8:6), "better sacrifices" (9:23), "a better possession" (10:34), "a better country" (11:16), "a better life" (11:35), and "a better word" (12:24).

2. Biblical Authors *Replace* Moses's Law with the New Covenant Law of Christ

The grace and truth Jesus Christ brings supersedes the grace God bestowed through the Mosaic law (John 1:16–17). Furthermore, Christ has broken

---

3   Jason S. DeRouchie, "Question 34: How Does Galatians 3:12 Use Leviticus 18:5?," in Jason S. DeRouchie, Oren R. Martin, and Andrew David Naselli, *40 Questions about Biblical Theology* (Grand Rapids, MI: Kregel, 2020), 327–37; Jason S. DeRouchie, "The Use of Leviticus 18:5 in Galatians 3:12: A Redemptive-Historical Reassessment," *Them* 45, no. 2 (2020): 240–59.

the condemning and controlling power of the law, such that Paul can say of believers, "You are not under law but under grace" (Rom. 6:14), and "you also have died to the law through the body of Christ, so that you may belong to another, to him who has been raised from the dead, in order that we may bear fruit for God" (Rom. 7:4). "There is . . . now no condemnation for those who are in Christ Jesus" (Rom. 8:1).

Elsewhere the apostle notes, "Before faith came, we were held captive under the law, imprisoned until the coming faith would be revealed. So then, the law was our guardian until Christ came, in order that we might be justified by faith. But now that faith has come, we are no longer under a guardian" (Gal. 3:23–25; cf. 5:18). Such truths impacted Paul's approach to ministry:

> To those under the law [i.e., unregenerate Jews] I became as one under the law (though not being myself under the law) that I might win those under the law. To those outside the law [i.e., unregenerate Gentiles] I became as one outside the law (not being outside the law of God but under the law of Christ) that I might win those outside the law. (1 Cor 9:20–21)

The old covenant law bore a "ministry of condemnation," whereas the new covenant bears a "ministry of righteousness" (2 Cor. 3:9). Moses recognized this distinction. On the one hand, he knew Israel's unrighteousness and stubbornness (Deut. 9:6) would result in the nation's progressive death through curse culminating in the exile (4:25–28; 31:16–18, 27–29). On the other hand, he also hoped for a day following the people's restoration to the land when Yahweh would raise up a new prophetic covenant mediator (Deut. 18:15–19), transform his people's hearts to love him and to listen to his word through the prophet (30:6, 8–14), curse his enemies (3:7), and incorporate many from the nations as worshipers (32:21, 43; 33:19).

Moses knew that Israel's system of worship was merely symbolic, which suggests that it would become obsolete when shadow moved to substance (Ex. 25:9, 40; Zech. 3:8–9; 6:12–13). In Christ, the substance has come (Col. 2:16–17; Heb. 9:11–12). Furthermore, Moses affirmed the need for a better covenant built on a different nature of grace—one in which Yahweh would accomplish for Israel what he did not do in the Mosaic covenant era.

In Moses's day he called them to hear his voice and love him with their all (Deut. 6:4–5), but he did not give them a heart to know or eyes to see or ears to hear (Deut. 29:4). The law could not give life (Gal. 3:21), weakened as it was by the flesh (Rom. 8:3). But in Christ God does what the law could not do, condemning sin in Christ's flesh in order that the righteous requirement of the law might be fulfilled in us (Rom. 8:3–4). Moses anticipated a day when God's people would listen to the voice of the new prophetic covenant mediator (Deut. 18:15) and when God would cause his people to love him with their all and to heed his commands (Deut. 30:6, 8). The prophets equally longed for the day when God would teach every member of the multiethnic, blood-bought community (Isa. 54:13), write his law on their hearts (Jer. 31:33), and cause them to walk in his statutes and obey his rules (Ezek. 36:27). These hopes are all realized today through the church as accomplished by Christ's person and work (John 6:44–45; Rom. 2:14–15, 25–29; Phil. 3:3).

As Christians, our "release from the law" (Rom. 7:6) in part means that the Mosaic law is no longer the direct and immediate guide or judge of the conduct of God's people.[4] The age of the Mosaic law-covenant has come to an end in Christ, so the law itself has ceased from having a central and determinative role among God's people (2 Cor. 3:4–18; Gal. 3:15–4:7).[5] "Christ is the end of the law for righteousness to everyone who believes" (Rom. 10:4). As a written legal code, not one of the 613 stipulations in the Mosaic law-covenant is directly binding on Christians (cf. Acts 15:10; Gal. 4:5; 5:1–12; Eph. 2:14–16). Instead, we are bound by the law of Christ (1 Cor. 9:20–21; Gal. 6:2), which is summarized in the call to love our neighbor and which James refers to as the perfect law, the law of liberty, and the royal law:

> But the one who looks into the perfect law, the law of liberty, and perseveres, being no hearer who forgets but a doer who acts, he will be blessed in his doing. . . . If you really fulfill the royal law according to the Scripture, "You shall love your neighbor as yourself," you are doing well.

---

4 So also Douglas J. Moo, "The Law of Christ as the Fulfillment of the Law of Moses: A Modified Lutheran View," in *Five Views on Law and Gospel*, ed. Wayne G. Strickland, Counterpoints: Bible and Theology (Grand Rapids, MI: Zondervan, 1996), 343; cf. 375.

5 Moo, "The Law of Christ as the Fulfillment of the Law of Moses," 359.

... So speak and so act as those who are to be judged under the law of liberty. (James 1:25; 2:8, 12)

Today, the direct authority for guiding Christians is not Moses's instructions but Christ's words through his apostles. Fulfilling Moses's prediction of a prophetic covenant mediator to whom others would listen, God declared of Jesus in Moses's sight, "This is my beloved Son, with whom I am well-pleased; listen to him" (Matt. 17:5; cf. Deut. 18:15). Everyone who hears Christ's words and acts on them is wise (Matt. 7:24–27), and the call to make disciples includes teaching others to obey Christ's teaching (Matt. 28:19–20). His instructions through his apostles now provide the essence for all Christian instruction (John 16:12–14; 17:8, 18, 20; 2 Thess. 2:15). The early church "devoted themselves to the apostles' teaching" (Acts 2:42), for the church is "built on the foundation of the apostles and prophets, Christ Jesus himself being the cornerstone" (Eph. 2:20).

> Christ has obtained a ministry that is as much more excellent than the old as the covenant he mediates is better, since it is enacted on better promises. . . . In speaking of a new covenant, he makes the first one obsolete. And what is becoming obsolete and growing old is ready to vanish away. (Heb. 8:6, 13; cf. 7:12; 10:9)

Christians are part of the new covenant, not the old, and are bound to Christ's law, not Moses's.

3. Biblical Authors *Reappropriate* Moses's Law through Christ

While the New Testament authors highlight the Mosaic law-covenant's condemning nature and stress that believers are now under the law of Christ, they also apply Old Testament laws to Christians based on Christ's justifying and sanctifying work. For example, by God's mercies shown in Christ (Rom. 12:1), Paul urges believers to fulfill the law by loving others:

> The commandments, "You shall not commit adultery, You shall not murder, You shall not steal, You shall not covet," and *any other commandment*,

are summed up in this word: "You shall love your neighbor as yourself." Love does no wrong to a neighbor; therefore love is the fulfilling of the law. (Rom. 13:9–10)

Paul cites four commands associated with the Ten Commandments that focus directly on valuing God's image in others.[6] Yet in adding "any other commandment" he shows that love fulfills all Moses's directives, even those beyond the Ten Commandments.[7]

The apostle stresses that, in this new covenant age, Gentile believers, to whom God did not give the written law of Moses, now "do what the law requires" and by this "show that the work of the law is written on their hearts" (Rom. 2:14–15; cf. Jer. 31:33) and that they are true Jews, having circumcised hearts by the power of the Spirit (Rom. 2:26–29; Phil. 3:3; cf. Deut. 30:6; Ezek. 36:27).[8] Also from this framework, the apostle uses Moses's law to stress that a workman is worthy of pay (1 Cor. 9:7–9; 1 Tim. 5:18; cf. Deut. 25:4). Similarly, he charges children to honor their parents, citing one of the Ten Commandments that contains a promise of life (Eph. 6:1–3; cf. Ex. 20:12). Peter, too, urges Christians to pursue holiness *because* God commands it in his Old Testament Scriptures (1 Pet. 1:15–16; cf. Lev. 19:2).

Although Moses's law does not *directly* bind Christians legally, we do not throw out the law itself. As Moses himself foresaw, in the day of heart

---

6   He follows the arrangement in the Greek translation of Deut. 5:17–21 but leaves out the command not to bear false witness (5:20) and leaves unspecified the two prohibitions (5:21). Whereas Ex. 20:1 refers to the Ten Commandments as "all these words," the rest of the Law calls them the "Ten Words" (i.e., the Decalogue; Ex. 34:28; Deut. 4:13; 10:4). Both Jesus and Paul indicate, though, that they are indeed "commandments" (Mark 10:19; Luke 18:20; Rom. 13:9; Eph. 6:2). For a discussion of their numbering and lasting relevance, see Jason S. DeRouchie, "Counting the Ten: An Investigation into the Numbering of the Decalogue," in *For Our Good Always: Studies on the Message and Influence of Deuteronomy in Honor of Daniel I. Block*, ed. Jason S. DeRouchie, Jason Gile, and Kenneth J. Turner (Winona Lake, IN: Eisenbrauns, 2013), 93–125; Jason S. DeRouchie, "Making the Ten Count: Reflections on the Lasting Message of the Decalogue," in DeRouchie, Gile, and Turner, *For Our Good Always*, 415–40.

7   So Douglas Moo, *The Letter to the Romans*, 2nd ed., NICNT (Grand Rapids, MI: Eerdmans, 2018), 832; contra Colin G. Kruse, *Paul's Letter to the Romans*, PNTC (Grand Rapids, MI: Eerdmans, 2012), 501.

8   For this reading of Rom. 2, see Simon J. Gathercole, "A Law unto Themselves: The Gentiles in Romans 2.14–15 Revisited," *JSNT* 24, no. 3 (2002): 27–49; A. B. Caneday, "Judgment, Behavior, and Justification according to Paul's Gospel in Romans 2," *JSPHS* 1, no. 2 (2011): 153–92; Thomas R. Schreiner, *Romans*, 2nd ed., BECNT (Grand Rapids, MI: Baker Academic, 2018), 136–45.

circumcision God's people would "turn and hear the voice of the Lord and keep all his commandments that I command you today" (Deut. 30:8, author's translation). Moses's instruction still matters for Christians. That is, along with *repudiating* the old covenant and *replacing* its law with the law of Christ, Christians must *reappropriate* (i.e., heed, embrace, affirm, follow, and/or obey) Moses's instruction (1) as a testimony to God's character and values, (2) as prophecy that anticipates the gospel of Jesus, and (3) as wisdom intended to guide new covenant saints in our pursuit of God.

All these aspects (revelation of God, prophecy realized, and wisdom as guide) relate to how Christ fulfills Moses's law and are evident in Christ's words: "The Law and the Prophets were until John [the Baptizer]; since then the good news of the kingdom of God is preached. . . . But it is easier for heaven and earth to pass away than for one dot of the Law to become void" (Luke 16:16–17). Jesus fulfills the Old Testament age of prediction (resulting in discontinuity between the old and new covenants), but all of Moses's words remain part of Christian Scripture and are therefore instructive (implying continuity between the old and new covenants).

Moses's Law Reveals God's Character and Values

The Mosaic law expresses God's character. Yahweh asserted, "You shall be holy, for I . . . am holy" (Lev. 19:2), and the way Israel would fulfill this charge was by heeding God's words. "Now therefore, if you will indeed obey my voice and keep my covenant . . . you shall be to me a kingdom of priests and a holy nation" (Ex. 19:5–6). And again, "So you shall remember and do all my commandments, and be holy to your God" (Num. 15:40). Paul stresses that the law is "the embodiment of knowledge and truth" (Rom. 2:20) and that "the law is holy, and the commandment is holy and righteous and good" (Rom. 7:12). Peter, too, asserts, "As obedient children, do not be conformed to the passions of your former ignorance, but as he who called you is holy, you also be holy in all your conduct, since it is written, 'You shall be holy, for I am holy'" (1 Pet. 1:14–16). Moses's law signals what Yahweh values and what he hates, what he delights in and what he detests. Christians learn about the character of the living God through Moses's law, and this in turn can clarify what it means to image him faithfully in the world (Gen. 1:26–28).

Moses's Law Anticipates the Gospel Concerning Christ

Jesus stressed that he came not "to abolish the Law and the Prophets" but "to fulfill them" (Matt. 5:17). By "fulfill" he meant in part that he supplies the end-times actualization of all that the Old Testament predicted.⁹ He does this through direct or typological prophecy and through the overarching salvation-historical trajectory. Thus, "all the Prophets and the Law prophesied until John" (Matt. 11:13), and the very "gospel of God . . . concerning his Son" was "promised beforehand through his prophets in the holy Scriptures" (Rom. 1:1–3). Jesus stood as the goal and end of Old Testament's hopes, pictures, and patterns.¹⁰

As the last Adam (1 Cor. 15:45; cf. Rom. 5:14), the representative of Israel (Isa. 49:1–6; Matt. 21:9; Luke 1:32–33), the true Passover lamb (John 1:29; 1 Cor. 5:7), the true temple (John 2:21), and so on, Christ is the substance of all old covenant shadows (Col. 1:16–17; Heb. 8:5; 10:1). His role as teacher and covenant mediator also fulfills Moses's own future hopes for a covenant-mediating "prophet" like him—one who would know God face-to-face, who would perform great signs and wonders, and to whom people would listen (Deut. 18:15–19; 34:10–12; cf. Luke 7:16; 9:35; Acts 3:22–26; 7:37).

Every Old Testament ethical ideal also pointed ahead to Christ's perfection on behalf of the elect. Deuteronomy 17:18–20 anticipates this when it stresses that Yahweh's ideal King will be a man of the book who never replaces Yahweh but represents him perfectly as he lives out the law. He will have his own copy of Moses's words, and he will read them daily, which will generate fear leading to obedience, humility, and a lasting kingdom.

9 Tom Wells and Fred G. Zaspel, *New Covenant Theology: Description, Definition, Defense* (Frederick, MD: New Covenant Media, 2002), 115; cf. 77–159. For an exceptional word study on *plēroō* ("to fulfill"), see Vern S. Poythress, *The Shadow of Christ in the Law of Moses* (Phillipsburg, NJ: Presbyterian and Reformed, 1991), 363–77; cf. 263–69 on Matt. 5:17–19. For other comparable approaches to Matt. 5:17–19, see Douglas J. Moo, "Jesus and the Authority of the Mosaic Law," *JSNT* 7, no. 20 (1984): 23–28; Douglas J. Moo, "Law," *DJG* 456–58; Moo, "The Law of Christ as the Fulfillment of the Law of Moses," 347–53; D. A. Carson, "Matthew," in *Matthew–Mark*, 2nd ed., EBC 9 (Grand Rapids, MI: Zondervan, 2010), 172–79.

10 Vern Poythress helpfully writes, "Jesus does not assert merely a static continuation of the force of the law, but rather a dynamic advance—in fact, the definitive fulfillment. What was temporary and shadowy in the form of the Old Testament law is superseded, now that God's glory and kingly power are being manifested in the very person of Jesus and in his ministry. The promise of the kingdom of heaven involves the intensification of all that served to manifest God in the Old Testament. All is transformed by the supremacy and weightiness of God Himself coming to save." Poythress, *The Shadow of Christ in the Law of Moses*, 265.

The divine servant that Isaiah describes embodies this ideal and can make "many to be accounted righteous" because he himself is "righteous" and bears the iniquity of the guilty (Isa. 53:11; cf. 1 John 1:9–2:1). Jesus was perfectly obedient (Rom. 5:19; 8:3–4; Phil. 2:8; Heb. 5:8) and sinless (Heb. 7:26; 1 Pet. 2:22; 1 John 3:5; cf. Isa. 50.5, 8–9; 53:9; John 8:46; 14:30–31), and for those in him, his life of perfect surrender provides freedom from the law's condemning power and the righteousness the law required. At the cross, God canceled "the record of debt that stood against us with its legal demands" (Col. 2:13–14; cf. Gal. 3:13). This he accomplished by counting our sins to Jesus, by pouring out his wrath against Jesus in our stead, and by counting Jesus's righteousness as ours: "For our sake [God the Father] made [Christ] to be sin who knew no sin, so that in him we might become the righteousness of God" (2 Cor. 5:21; cf. Rom. 5:18–19; Heb. 9:28). Through Jesus, God "condemned sin in the flesh, in order that the righteous requirements of the law might be fulfilled in us" (Rom. 8:3–4). This likely means that Christ's perfect statute keeping is counted to all who are in him, the proof of which is that we now walk by the Spirit.[11]

Moses's law also anticipated Jesus in the way it identified and multiplied sin (Rom. 3:20; 5:20; cf. 7:7–12; Gal. 3:19), imprisoned the sinful (Rom. 3:19–20; 8:2–3; Gal. 3:10, 13, 22), and by these disclosed everyone's need for atonement in Christ. The law, in this sense, predicted Christ, who is "the end of the law for righteousness to everyone who believes" (Rom. 10:4). As Paul states elsewhere,

> By works of the law no human being will be justified in [God's] sight, since through the law comes knowledge of sin. But now the righteousness of God has been manifested apart from the law, although the Law and the

11 The singular use of *dikaiōma* ("righteous requirement") in Rom. 5:18 strongly suggests that the singular use of the same term in 8:4 refers to *Christ's* perfect obedience—his righteousness—counted as ours through our incorporation into him rather than to the Christian's keeping of the law. On this, I agree with Moo, *Epistle to the Romans*, 504–8. Our walking by the Spirit is in turn evidence that we are justified, and Paul speaks of this walking both as fulfilling the law (Rom. 13:8, 10) and as keeping the law's "righteous requirements" (*dikaiōmata*, plural accusative of *dikaiōma*) through a circumcised heart and by the power of the Spirit (Rom. 2:26; cf. 2:29; Ezek. 36:27). For an alternative view of Rom. 8:4 that sees the "righteous requirement" as something we are empowered to do instead of what Christ did for us, see Kevin W. McFadden, "The Fulfillment of the Law's *Dikaiōma*: Another Look at Romans 8:1–4," *JETS* 52, no. 3 (2009): 483–97; Schreiner, *Romans*, 400–403.

Prophets bear witness to it—the righteousness of God through faith in Jesus Christ for all who believe. (Rom. 3:20–22)

Moses's Law Guides Christians in Love and Wise Living

Jesus stressed that all the commandments of Moses's law are still instructive for his followers but *only when read in the light of how he fulfills the law*.

> Do not think that I have come to abolish the Law or the Prophets; I have not come to abolish them but to fulfill them. For truly, I say to you, until heaven and earth pass away, not an iota, not a dot, will pass from the Law until all is accomplished. Therefore whoever relaxes one of the least of these commandments and teaches others to do the same will be called least in the kingdom of heaven, but whoever does them and teaches them will be called great in the kingdom of heaven. (Matt. 5:17–19)

By "these commandments," Jesus most likely refers to the directives and prohibitions of Moses's law itself.[12] He thus affirms that Moses's law remains a relevant guide for believers (continuity) but *only* when we engage it through the lens he supplies (discontinuity), which could result in the intensifying, transforming, extending, or annulling of any given law (see below). On these matters, Douglas Moo writes that Matthew 5:17–19 asserts "the enduring validity and usefulness of the law, *when seen in light of its fulfillment in Christ*. . . . The OT law is not to be abandoned. Indeed, it must continue to be taught (Matt 5:19)—but interpreted and applied in light of its fulfillment by Christ."[13] Similarly, D. A. Carson observes,

> The authority of the older revelation is not called into question, but its continuing power lies not in unchanging legal prescription but in that to which it points, its fulfillment. . . . The precise form of the Mosaic law may change with the crucial redemptive events to which it points. . . . The commandments of these Scriptures . . . must be practiced. But the

---

12 So too Moo, "Jesus and the Authority of the Mosaic Law," 28; Moo, "Law," 458; Moo, "The Law of Christ as the Fulfillment of the Law of Moses," 353; Poythress, *The Shadow of Christ in the Law of Moses*, 267–69; Wells and Zaspel, *New Covenant Theology*, 127; Carson, "Matthew," 179.

13 Douglas J. Moo, "The Law of Moses or the Law of Christ," in *Continuity and Discontinuity: Perspectives on the Relationship Between the Old and New Testaments; Essays in Honor of S. Lewis Johnson Jr.*, ed. John S. Feinberg (Westchester, IL: Crossway, 1988), 206 (emphasis in original).

nature of the practicing has already been affected by vv. 17–18. The law pointed forward to Jesus—his activity and his teaching—so it is properly obeyed by conforming to his word. As it points to him, so he, in fulfilling it, establishes what continuity it has, the true direction to which it points and the way it is to be obeyed.[14]

The "law of Christ" that we live out (1 Cor. 9:21; cf. Isa. 42:4; Matt. 28:20) is the law of love as fulfilled and taught by Jesus, which is the end-times realization of Moses's law in its original form. Jesus said that "all the Law and the Prophets" depend on the dual commands to love God and love neighbor (Matt. 22:37–40). Stressing how love for neighbor really proves whether we love God, Jesus went further, saying, "Whatever you wish that others would do to you, do also to them, for this is the Law and the Prophets" (Matt. 7:12). Similarly, Paul stresses that "the whole law is fulfilled in one word: 'You shall love your neighbor as yourself'" (Gal. 5:14). Significantly, not just a "moral" subset of the law but all the law—every commandment— is fulfilled in the call to love.

> Owe no one anything, except to love each other, for the one who loves another has fulfilled the law. For the commandments, "You shall not commit adultery, You shall not murder, You shall not steal, You shall not covet," and any other commandment, are summed up in this word: "You shall love your neighbor as yourself." Love does no wrong to a neighbor; therefore love is the fulfilling of the law. (Rom. 13:8–10)

In both the old and new covenants, love is *what* God's people are to do. All the other commandments simply clarify *how* to do it. From this perspective, while the Mosaic law does not bear direct or immediate guidance in a Christian's life, it does supply us a pattern for how deeply and widely love for God and neighbor should impact our lives.

Indeed, even within ancient Israel, the Old Testament's familial, social, economic, and political structures bore a testimonial purpose, which God intended to provide a contextual paradigm for all peoples in all times. Such is evident in the life of Abraham, whom Yahweh said "obeyed my voice

---

14 Carson, "Matthew," 175, 178–79.

and kept my charge, my commandments, my statutes, and my laws" (Gen. 26:5). Moses used the very language of the old covenant (see Deut. 30:10; 1 Kings 2:3; 2 Kings 17:13, 34) to describe Abraham's life of dependence, and this indicates the paradigmatic nature of the law.

Had Israel heeded Yahweh's voice, kept his covenant, and lived as his treasured possession, they would have borne witness to Yahweh's greatness amid the world (Ex. 19:5–6).[15] The nations would have seen the uprightness of God's law and viewed Israel as both wise and understanding (Deut. 4:5–8). The Mosaic law, therefore, served to shape for the world a clear picture of righteous living, the whole of which pointed back to the greatness of God and anticipated the person of Christ. We can learn much about how God calls us to love others by carefully considering the Mosaic law.[16]

Four Ways Christ Fulfills Moses's Law

While none of Moses's law directly binds Christians in a legal way, all the law is indirectly authoritative, profitable, and instructive for believers through the mediation of Christ (cf. Rom. 4:23; 13:9; 15:4; 1 Cor. 10:11; 2 Tim. 3:16–17). In Douglas Moo's words, "[Old covenant law] stands no longer as the *ultimate* standard of conduct for God's people, but must always be viewed through the lenses of Jesus' ministry and teaching."[17] Jesus is the

15 For including the "treasured possession" statement in the protasis ("if" section), see Jason S. DeRouchie, *How to Read and Apply the Old Testament: Twelve Steps from Exegesis to Theology* (Phillipsburg, NJ: P&R, 2017), 226–29; Jason S. DeRouchie, "Understanding and Applying Exodus 19:4–6: A Case Study in Exegesis and Theology," *JBTS* 6, no. 1 (2021): 92–95.

16 Many evangelicals follow either a principlizing or principlizing-paradigmatic approach to Old Testament law, but these models must work through a redemptive-historical, Christocentric framework to explain all that the New Testament authors are doing with the Mosaic law. For more on the principlizing approach, see Walter C. Kaiser Jr., *Toward Old Testament Ethics* (Grand Rapids, MI: Zondervan, 1983); Walter C. Kaiser Jr., "A Principlizing Model," in *Four Views on Moving beyond the Bible to Theology*, ed. Gary T. Meadors, Counterpoints: Bible and Theology (Grand Rapids, MI: Zondervan, 2009), 19–50; J. Daniel Hays, "Applying the Old Testament Law Today," *BSac* 158 (2001): 21–35; Jerram Barrs, *Delighting in the Law of the Lord: God's Alternative to Legalism and Moralism* (Wheaton, IL: Crossway, 2013). For more on the principlizing-paradigmatic approach, see Christopher J. H. Wright, *Old Testament Ethics for the People of God* (Downers Grove, IL: InterVarsity Press, 2004), 62–74, 182–211, 314–25; cf. Waldemar Janzen, *Old Testament Ethics: A Paradigmatic Approach* (Louisville: Westminster John Knox, 1994); Elmer A. Martens, "How Is the Christian to Construe Old Testament Law?," *BBR* 12, no. 2 (2002): 199–216; Peter T. Vogt, *Interpreting the Pentateuch: An Exegetical Handbook*, Handbooks for Old Testament Exegesis (Grand Rapids, MI: Kregel, 2009), 42–48; Daniel I. Block, "Preaching Old Testament Law to New Testament Christians," *STR* 3, no. 2 (2012): 195–221.

17 Moo, "The Law of Moses or the Law of Christ," 206.

lens that clarifies how to rightly appropriate the law of Moses, and he alone supplies the power to obey it.

Because Jesus fulfills various laws in different ways, we must consider each law on its own in view of Christ's work. This process helps clarify the breadth and depth of the "law of Christ" (1 Cor. 9:21; Gal. 6:2). The number of Old Testament laws that the New Testament addresses is minimal, yet the New Testament's examples guide our handling of other related commands or prohibitions and illuminate each law's lasting significance.

When Jesus is viewed as the lens for considering the lasting validity of Moses's instruction (fig. 10.1), some laws appear unchanged before and after Christ, whereas others hit the lens and get "bent" in various ways.[18] Jesus's coming maintains (with or without extension), transforms, and annuls various laws. Chapters 12–13 below will supply case studies for each of these various ways that Christ fulfills Moses's law.

- *Maintains (no extension):* When fulfilling Moses's prohibitions against murder, adultery, theft, coveting, and the like (e.g., Ex. 20:13–17), Christ maintains the law's essence without any extension from the old to new covenants (Matt. 15:18; 19:17–21; cf. Rom. 13:9). Obeying such laws looks the same in both eras.
- *Maintains (with extension):* When fulfilling Moses's charge not to muzzle an ox while it is threshing (Deut. 25:4), Christ's work extends the principle's application to include paying wages to ministers (1 Cor. 9:8–12; 1 Tim. 5:17–18; cf. Matt. 10:10). Similarly, the law on parapet building (Deut. 22:8) necessitates care for our neighbors in the way we handle all our personal property (e.g., fences around a swimming pool or a railing around a deck). Such extensions often occur in laws where their biblical moral instruction includes cultural or situational details that are different from our own; in such instances, we heed Jesus's words at the end of the parable of the good Samaritan and "do likewise" (Luke 10:37), though working out the principle in a new way.
- *Transforms:* When fulfilling laws like Yahweh's charge to observe the Sabbath (e.g., Deut. 5:12–15) or Moses's directions on capital

---

18 Refraction in convex lenses "bends" light rays "in" toward the lens axis.

punishment (e.g., Deut. 22:22), Christ transforms. On the one hand, he secures sustained rest for his followers and calls them to receive it (Matt. 11:28–12:8), and on the other hand, his work leads to applying the charge to "purge the evil person from your midst" to excommunication within the church (1 Cor. 5:13).

- *Annuls:* When fulfilling Moses's laws about unclean food (e.g., Lev. 20:25–26), Christ annuls them, declaring all foods clean (Mark 7:19; cf. Acts 10:14–15; Rom. 14:20). But though he rescinded the diet restrictions, we still benefit from the commands by considering what they tell us about God and how they magnify Jesus's work.

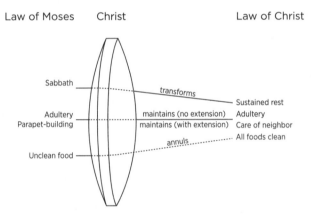

Figure 10.1   The law's fulfillment through the lens of Christ

In a real sense, even laws that Christ maintains (with or without extension) are intensified in the shift from the old to new covenant. This is so because Jesus's own life supplies believers an unparalleled pattern for living the godward life (Phil. 2:5–7; Heb. 12:1–3; 1 Pet. 2:21; 1 John 2:6) and an unparalleled power for the same (Rom. 1:16; 1 Cor. 1:18). Christians benefit from this pattern and power through Christ's blood-bought pardon (Rom. 6:6–7, 22; 8:10) and promises (Rom. 8:32; 2 Cor 1:20; 2 Pet 1:4) working through the Spirit on our new hearts (Rom. 2:29; Phil. 3:3; cf. Deut. 30:6; Jer. 31:33; Ezek. 36:27). Old Testament interpreters must assess every law on its own terms to properly discern how it applies today.

Another way to grasp how Christians should relate to Old Testament law is to visualize two riverbanks separated at varying distances by water (fig. 10.2). The two sides symbolize the old and new covenant laws, and Jesus is the "bridge" over which we move from one side to the other. The length of the bridge and our distance from the specific Mosaic legislation changes depending on the nature of the law itself. The distance is always great enough that we can't access the other side apart from Christ, but some laws are so similar on each side of the bridge that the distance seems almost nonexistent (e.g., murder, adultery, etc.). Other laws, however, disclose substantial distance or changes (e.g., Sabbath, food laws, etc.).

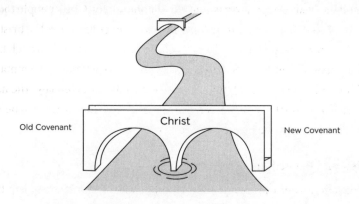

Figure 10.2   The law's fulfillment over the bridge of Christ

When approaching the Old Testament through the lens of Christ, *everything* in the Old Testament operates as Christian Scripture written "for our instruction" (Rom. 15:4; cf. 4:23; 1 Cor. 10:11) and remains "profitable for teaching, for reproof, for correction, and for training in righteousness" (2 Tim. 3:16). We access and apply Moses's law only through Christ and in view of the apostles' teaching, which together ground and sustain the church (Acts 2:42; Eph. 2:20; cf. Matt. 7:24–27; 17:5; 28:20; John 16:12–14; 17:8, 18, 20; 2 Thess. 2:15; Heb. 1:1–2).[19]

---

19 For more on this redemptive-historical approach to a Christian's relationship to Old Testament law, see David A. Dorsey, "The Law of Moses and the Christian: A Compromise," *JETS* 34, no. 3 (1991): 321–34; Poythress, *The Shadow of Christ in the Law of Moses*, 251–86; Moo, "The Law of Christ as the Fulfillment of the Law of Moses," 317–76; Wells and Zaspel, *New Covenant Theology*, 77–160, esp. 126–27, 157–60; Daniel M. Doriani, "A Redemptive-Historical Model," in Meadors, *Four Views on Moving beyond the Bible to Theology*, 51–56, 75–121, 205–9, 255–61; Meyer, *The End of the Law*; Jason C. Meyer, "The Mosaic Law, Theological Systems, and the Glory of Christ," in *Progressive Covenantalism: Charting a Course between Dispensational and Covenant Theologies*, ed. Stephen J. Wellum and Brent E. Parker (Nashville: B&H Academic,

Conclusion

Most often, "law" in Scripture points to the Mosaic law, which operated within the old covenant to identify and multiply sin and to condemn Israel. Jesus and the New Testament authors *repudiate* the Mosaic law-covenant, *replace* Moses's law with the law of Christ, and *reappropriate* Moses's law through Christ.[20] They do this to give us glimpses of God's character and values, to help us behold the perfect righteousness of Christ, and to guide us in wisdom and love. None of Moses's law operates as the ultimate or immediate legal or regulatory standard of conduct for God's people today (Rom. 7:4; Gal. 3:24–25), but it continues to impact us through Christ in both revelatory and pedagogical ways.[21] Christ is like a lens, and through him (and his New Testament revelation) we can recognize whether he maintains (with or without extension), transforms, or annuls any given law. The next chapter will evaluate some contemporary teachings that misconstrue the law's relationship to believers in various ways.

Review and Reflection

1. Explain in your own words what John Berridge meant by the poem that opens the chapter.
2. Point to some New Testament texts that clarify the destructive role the old law-covenant performed in God's saving purposes.
3. What does the author suggest that "the law is not of faith" means in Galatians 3:12?
4. Clarify some of the ways the author of Hebrews declares that the new covenant in Christ is "better."
5. What are some key texts to which you could point to show that the biblical authors replace Moses's law with the new covenant law of Christ.
6. What does the New Testament mean by the law of Christ (also called the perfect law, the law of liberty, or the royal law)?
7. What are the three ways by which Christians reappropriate Moses's law today?

2016), 66–99; Thomas R. Schreiner, *40 Questions about Christians and Biblical Law* (Grand Rapids, MI: Kregel, 2010); Rosner, *Paul and the Law*; William W. Combs, "Paul, the Law, and Dispensationalism," *DBSJ* 18, no. 1 (2013): 19–39; Stephen J. Wellum, "Progressive Covenantalism and the Doing of Ethics," in Wellum and Parker, *Progressive Covenantalism*, 215–33.

20 As already noted, this alliteration is borrowed from Rosner, *Paul and the Law*, 208–9, 217–22.

21 On these distinctions, see Dorsey, "The Law of Moses and the Christian," 325, 331.

8. What are some of the ways Moses's law anticipates or "prophesies" about the Christ?

9. Why must Christians view Moses's law through the lens of Christ to properly apply it today?

10. What was the greatest insight you gained in reading this chapter? What is your greatest takeaway?

11

Evaluating Alternative Proposals

We uphold the law.

ROMANS 3:31

THIS CHAPTER CONSIDERS alternative proposals to how Moses's law relates to Christians. It first tackles the common distinction between moral, civil, and ceremonial law, and then it confronts three defective and harmful approaches to the law that followers of Christ must avoid.

Assessing the Threefold Division of the Law

Historically, many evangelicals have distinguished three kinds of laws when considering the contemporary importance of Moses's instruction:[1]

- *Moral laws* are those fundamental ethical principles that are eternally applicable, regardless of the time or covenant.
- *Civil laws* related to Israel's political and social structures and supplied case-specific applications of the moral law in Israel's context.

---

1 For an affirmation of the threefold division of Moses's law, see the Westminster Confession of Faith 19.3–5. These are *theological* categories, in contrast to the *content* distinctions of criminal, civil, family, cultic/ceremonial, and compassion laws the next chapter addresses. Most scholars point to Thomas Aquinas as the first to utilize the threefold division as the basis for discerning continuity and discontinuity between the Old and New Testaments; Aquinas stressed the lasting validity of the "moral" law but viewed both the "civil" and "ceremonial" legislation as terminated in Christ.

- *Ceremonial laws* are those symbolic requirements related to Israel's religious rituals and cult worship that find their typological end in Christ.

Many classic covenant theologians (often associated with Presbyterian or Reformed churches) believe the "moral laws" alone (seen most clearly in the Ten Commandments) remain legally binding on Christians today, whereas the "civil" and "ceremonial" laws are time bound and no longer applicable.[2] For example, Michael Horton writes,

> Civil laws . . . are obviously in force only so long as the theocracy itself exists. Ceremonial laws . . . are similarly "canonical" only as long as the theocracy stands. . . . [B]ut the moral law, summarized in the Ten Commandments, is inscribed on our consciences by virtue of our being created in the image of God. . . . While the civil and ceremonial laws pertain exclusively to the theocracy and are no longer binding, the moral law is still in force.[3]

In contrast, theonomists assert that, because civil laws are situational applications of the moral laws, they too carry over through Christ and are to guide

---

2   Classic covenant theology is a theological system that sees one people of God in both Testaments and views all the historical covenants as progressive expressions of a single covenant of grace. For a brief synthesis of the view, see Benjamin L. Merkle, *Discontinuity to Continuity: A Survey of Dispensational and Covenantal Theologies* (Bellingham, WA: Lexham, 2020), 139–69. Some in the classic Reformed tradition do not follow the threefold division. For example, Vern Poythress, professor at Westminster Theological Seminary, notes, "No simple and easy separation between types of law will do justice to the richness of Mosaic revelation. . . . The entirety of this Mosaic revelation simultaneously articulates general moral principles and symbolic particulars: it points forward to Christ as the final and permanent expression of righteousness and penal substitution (with moral overtones) but is itself, in that very respect, a shadow (with ceremonial overtones)." Vern S. Poythress, *The Shadow of Christ in the Law of Moses* (Phillipsburg, NJ: Presbyterian and Reformed, 1991), 283. Similarly, Jerram Barrs, professor at Covenant Theological Seminary, writes, "These divisions are not hard and fast. For example, many of the ceremonial laws include moral and civil aspects. Many of the civil laws include moral aspects. A problematic consequence in this view, if it is held with systematic rigor, is that the beauties of the ceremonial and civil aspects of the law become lost to us during this present age." Jerram Barrs, *Delighting in the Law of the Lord: God's Alternative to Legalism and Moralism* (Wheaton, IL: Crossway, 2013), 314.
3   Michael Horton, *Introducing Covenant Theology* (Grand Rapids, MI: Baker Books, 2009), 177–78, 180; cf. John M. Frame, *The Doctrine of the Christian Life*, A Theology of Lordship (Phillipsburg, NJ: P&R, 2008), 203–36; Philip S. Ross, *From the Finger of God: The Biblical and Theological Basis for the Threefold Division of the Law* (Fearn, Ross-shire, Scotland: Mentor, 2010).

both the church and the state.[4] As Rousas Rushdoony asserts, "Every aspect of the Old Testament law still stands, except those aspects of the ceremonial and priestly law specifically fulfilled by the coming of Christ, and those laws specifically re-interpreted in the New Testament."[5] And again, "It is a serious error to say that the *civil law* was also abolished, but the *moral law* retained. What is the distinction between them? . . . It is clearly *only* the sacrificial and ceremonial law which is ended because it is replaced by Christ and his work."[6]

These different approaches to the proposed threefold division of the law helpfully celebrate that Christ stands as the antitype, substance, and end of all Old Testament shadows (Col. 2:16–17; Heb. 8:5–7) and that his coming alters some laws more than others. They also recognize that the laws called "moral" are those that Christians keep (Rom. 2:26) or fulfill (Rom. 13:8, 10; Gal. 5:14; 6:2) in a fashion most similar with their old covenant function.[7]

Nevertheless, neither model satisfies the biblical testimony concerning the nature and lasting significance of Moses's law. Against both approaches, the previous chapter argues that *none* of the Mosaic covenant is directly binding on Christians today (Rom. 10:4; 1 Cor. 9:20–21; Gal. 3:24–25)[8] but that *all* of it is still significant as revelation, prophecy, and wisdom when mediated through Christ (Matt. 5:17–19). Furthermore, as will be developed below, Scripture treats *all* the law as a single entity, *all* the law as

---

4 Both Christian reconstructionist and general equity theonomy stress the binding nature of Moses's moral and civil laws today. Christian reconstructionism teaches that Moses's moral and civil laws should be used to reconstruct the church and every society in every time. General equity stresses that Moses's law supplies lasting principles of justice that apply in all contexts and times, beginning with the church and extending to all levels of society.

5 Rousas John Rushdoony, *The Roots of Reconstruction* (Vallecito, CA: Ross, 1991), 553.

6 Rousas John Rushdoony, *The Institutes of Biblical Law*, 3 vols. (Phillipsburg, NJ: P&R, 1973), 1:10.

7 Even Christian reconstructionist theonomist Greg Bahnsen, who affirms the lasting validity of the old covenant's "civil" legislation, recognizes redemptive-historical and cultural discontinuities between the old and new covenant eras. Greg L. Bahnsen, "The Theonomic Reformed Approach to Law and Gospel," in *Five Views on Law and Gospel*, ed. Wayne G. Strickland, Counterpoints: Bible and Theology (Grand Rapids, MI: Zondervan, 1996), 100–108.

8 To support his claim for one, undifferentiated law of God, Bahnsen ("The Theonomic Reformed Approach to Law and Gospel") limits the New Testament's derogatory statements regarding the "law" to Jewish legalism (e.g., Gal. 2:19 [p. 96]), ceremonial requirements (1 Cor. 9:20–21 [pp. 107–8]; Gal. 3:23–25 [p. 99]; Eph. 2:14–15 [p. 104]), or spiritual bondage and impotence (e.g., Rom. 6:14 [pp. 106–7]). However, Douglas Moo compellingly shows that "law" in the New Testament refers to the Mosaic law unless there are clear signs in the context to the contrary. Douglas Moo, "The Law of Christ as the Fulfillment of the Law of Moses," in Strickland, *Five Views on Law and Gospel*, 319–76.

moral in nature, and *all* the law as having devotional benefit for believers. After addressing these latter three issues, I will summarize some additional problems with theonomy.[9]

The Bible Treats All the Law as a Single Entity

The Old Testament distinguishes types of laws based on content (i.e., criminal, civil, family, cultic/ceremonial, and compassion laws; see tables 12.1 and 12.2 in chap. 12). In this framework, the call to love was always considered more foundational than ritual (e.g., Deut. 6:5; 10:12; 1 Sam. 15:22–23; Isa. 1:11–17; Hos. 6:6; Amos 5:21–24; Mic. 6:8). At times, people applied the law in fresh ways (1 Chron. 15:12–15 with Num 7:9 and Deut. 10:8; 2 Chron. 30:2–3 with Num. 9:9–13), adapted it to new contexts (2 Chron. 29:34, 36 with Lev. 1:5–6; 2 Chron. 30:17–20; 35:5–6 with Ex. 12:21), or even developed it (2 Chron. 8:12–15; 29:25–30). There are even instances where God did not hold people guilty though they failed to fulfill ceremonial obligations (Lev. 10:16–20) or engaged in ceremonially unlawful activity (1 Sam. 21:3–6; cf. Lev. 22:10; Matt. 12:4).

Nevertheless, the Old Testament never distinguishes moral, civil, and ceremonial laws in the way the threefold division proposes. Leviticus 19, for example, shows little distinction between laws, mixing calls to love one's neighbor (Lev. 19:11–12, 17–18) with various commands related to family (19:3, 29), corporate worship (19:3–8, 26–28, 30–31), business practice (19:9–10, 13, 19, 23–25, 34–36), care for the needy and disadvantaged (19:9–10, 13–14, 33–34), criminal and civil disputes (19:15–16, 35), and ritual matters (19:19). Moses made no attempt to elevate certain laws over others.

---

9   For further reflections on why the division of the law into moral, civil, and ceremonial laws is not preferable, see David A. Dorsey, "The Law of Moses and the Christian: A Compromise," *JETS* 34, no. 3 (1991): 329–31; D. A. Carson, "The Tripartite Division of the Law: A Review of Philip Ross, *The Finger of God*," in *From Creation to New Creation: Essays on Biblical Theology and Exegesis*, ed. Daniel M. Gurtner and Benjamin L. Gladd (Peabody, MA: Hendrickson, 2013), 223–36; William W. Combs, "Paul, the Law, and Dispensationalism," *DBSJ* 18, no. 1 (2013): 26–28; Brian S. Rosner, *Paul and the Law: Keeping the Commandments of God*, NSBT 31 (Downers Grove, IL: IVP Academic, 2013), 36–37; Jason C. Meyer, "The Mosaic Law, Theological Systems, and the Glory of Christ," in *Progressive Covenantalism: Charting a Course between Dispensational and Covenant Theologies*, ed. Stephen J. Wellum and Brent E. Parker (Nashville: B&H Academic, 2016), 87–89; Stephen J. Wellum, "Progressive Covenantalism and the Doing of Ethics," in Wellum and Parker, *Progressive Covenantalism*, 218–21; Joshua M. Greever, "Paul and the Tripartite View of the Law of Moses," *SBJT* 26, no. 1 (2022): 46–66.

Following the Old Testament prophets before him (e.g., 1 Sam. 15:22; Hos. 6:6; Mic. 6:6–8), Jesus did distinguish "weightier" and "lighter" matters of the law (Matt. 23:23; cf. 9:13; 12:7). Yet when he confronted hypocrites who were willing to tithe on their spice rack but unwilling to engage in the more difficult tasks of "justice and mercy and faithfulness," he emphasized, "These you ought to have done, *without neglecting the others*" (Matt. 23:23).

Furthermore, whether addressing the law-covenant's repudiation or the law's replacement or reappropriation, the New Testament regularly speaks of the whole law as a unit. Paul says, "The commandments, 'You shall not commit adultery, You shall not murder, You shall not steal, You shall not covet,' and *any other commandment*, are summed up in this word: 'You shall love your neighbor as yourself'" (Rom. 13:9). The call to love neighbor most likely synthesizes not just a group of moral laws but every commandment, which would include *both* the proposed civil and ceremonial legislation.[10] Jesus, too, spoke broadly when he asserted, "Therefore whoever relaxes one of the least of these commandments and teaches others to do the same will be called least in the kingdom of heaven, but whoever does them and teaches them will be called great in the kingdom of heaven" (Matt. 5:19). There is no special categorizing of laws here. Paul stresses that the whole "law" brought curse to all (Gal. 3:10), that in Christ we are no longer under the law-covenant as a guardian (Gal. 3:24–25), and that "every man who accepts circumcision . . . is obligated to keep the whole law" (Gal. 5:3). James also notes, "Whoever keeps *the whole law* but fails in one point has become guilty of all of it" (James 2:10).

The New Testament repudiates *all* the Mosaic law-covenant, sees *all* Moses's law replaced with Christ's law, and reappropriates *all* Moses's law as revelation of God's character, as a pointer to Christ, and as a guide for Christian living. Scripture does not teach the threefold division of the law.

All Laws Are Moral, and Most Are Culturally Bound

Theonomists are correct to note that the so-called civil laws illustrate moral principles working their way out in Late Bronze- and Iron-Age culture.[11] To

---

10　So also Douglas Moo, *The Letter to the Romans*, 2nd ed., NICNT (Grand Rapids, MI: Eerdmans, 2018), 832.

11　See, e.g., the section titled "The Direction of the Law" in the introduction to Rushdoony, *The Institutes of Biblical Law*, vol. 1.

this we can add that the so-called ceremonial laws demonstrate ethical or moral elements through symbolism. For example, Israel's sacrificial system testified to Yahweh's holiness and mankind's depravity (e.g., Lev. 9:1–7), and when Israel distinguished themselves from their neighbors through dietary restrictions (e.g., Lev. 11:44–45; 20:25–26), they pointed to Yahweh's holiness, which was a loving act to pagan peoples.

Those holding to the threefold division of the law count the Ten Commandments as the premier example of "moral law," yet even they contain many culturally bound features:[12]

- The prologue identifies Israel as a people Yahweh redeemed from slavery in Egypt (Deut. 5:6), and this element also grounds the call to rest in the Sabbath command (5:14–15).
- The idolatry command assumes a religious system including carved images (Deut. 5:8).
- The Sabbath command presumes the context of ancient Near Eastern bond service, geographically limited animals, and cities with gates (Deut. 5:14); its use of "sojourner" (Hebrew *ger*) (5:14) implies the existence of the politically defined nation of Israel.
- The command to honor one's parents directly points to the existence of the nation of Israel in the land of Canaan (Deut. 5:16).
- The coveting commands assume a people acquainted with ancient Near Eastern bond service and with animals common in the Mediterranean world (Deut. 5:21).
- The commands principally address household-heads who enjoy wives, children, household servants, and property—all of which point to Israel's patricentric society.[13]

This list should caution those who want to distinguish "civil" or "ceremonial" laws from "moral" because of their temporal boundedness.

---

12 The initial five of these come from Dorsey, "The Law of Moses and the Christian," 330. The last is noted in Daniel I. Block, "'You Shall Not Covet Your Neighbor's Wife': A Study in Deuteronomic Domestic Ideology," *JETS* 53, no. 3 (2010): 457–58.

13 On the biblical vision of Israel's society being centered on the father as servant leader (i.e., patricentric) as opposed to dominated by a father as self-exalting dictator (i.e., patriarchal), see Daniel I. Block, "Marriage and Family in Ancient Israel," in *Marriage and Family in the Biblical World*, ed. Ken M. Campbell (Downers Grove, IL: InterVarsity Press, 2003), 33–102.

All Laws Have Devotional Benefit for Christians

Most theologians who hold to the threefold division of the law affirm the lasting value of *all* Scripture. However, the moral, civil, and ceremonial distinction has moved many laypeople to see Exodus's Book of the Covenant (Ex. 21–23) or Leviticus's instructions as having little lasting Christian relevance. Yet Jesus and Paul reaffirmed the prohibitions against reviling parents (Matt. 15:4; cf. Ex. 21:17) and leaders (Acts 23:5; cf. Ex. 22:28), Paul drew pastoral insight from the instructions on temple service (1 Cor. 9:13–14; cf. Lev. 6:16, 26; 7:6), and Peter called believers to holiness *because* God called for it in Leviticus (1 Pet. 1:15–17; cf. Lev. 19:2). "All Scripture is . . . profitable" for Christians (2 Tim. 3:16), and we align most closely with the Bible's testimony when we emphasize how loving our neighbor fulfills *every* commandment of the law and how all the law still matters for Christians, though not all in the same way. The old covenant law is not the Christian's legal code, but it was still written *for* us by portraying God's character and values, by directing our eyes to Jesus, and by clarifying how deeply and widely love for God and neighbor should consume our lives. Every commandment counts.

A Critique of Theonomy in Relation to the Tripartite View of the Law

The term *theonomy* ("God's law") commonly refers to one of two overlapping systems of thought related to the lasting value of Moses's law: Christian reconstructionist theonomy and general equity theonomy.[14] The difference between the two systems is more one of degree than kind, for both stress that God defines justice most clearly through Moses's law and that these principles of justice should guide both the church and society today. An additional category that overlaps with theonomy is Christian nationalism, which seeks to create "an earthly kingdom [that] is a Christian kingdom" in so far as "it orders the people to the kingdom of heaven."[15] I will introduce these three spheres and then offer critique of theonomy as a whole.

Associated with names like Rousas Rushdoony, Greg Bahnsen, and Gary North in the 1980s and 1990s, Christian reconstructionist theonomy confronts the world's increasing secularization by seeking to fulfill the "cultural mandate" of filling and subduing the earth and taking dominion (Gen. 1:28). It emphasizes that right order in this world will only be realized when all levels of society and government including nation-states surrender to Christ's authority by being governed by biblical law. In the words of Gary North and Gary DeMar, "The continuing validity and applicability of the whole law of God, including, but not limited to, the Mosaic case laws is the standard by which individuals, families, churches, and civil governments should conduct their affairs."[16] In Greg Bahnsen's words, Christian reconstructionist theonomy seeks "the transformation or reconstruction of every area of life, including the institutions and affairs of the socio-political realm, in accordance with the holy principles of God's revealed Word (theonomy)."[17]

The Christian church has strongly critiqued this movement,[18] yet it is on the rise again from two angles: (1) general equity theonomy through teachers like Douglas Wilson and Jeff Durbin[19] and (2) Christian nationalism through authors like Stephen Wolfe.[20] Those adopting the titles of reconstruction or Christian nationalism usually focus more on the society over

---

16 Gary North and Gary DeMar, *Christian Reconstruction: What It Is, What It Isn't* (Tyler, TX: Institute for Christian Economics, 1991), 81.

17 Bahnsen, "The Theonomic Reformed Approach to Law and Gospel," 118. Or, as Michael Gabbert summarizes, this form of theonomy seeks "to integrate every aspect of American life into a consistent world view based upon the abiding validity of the Old Testament law in exhaustive detail." Michael D. Gabbert, "An Historical Overview of Christian Reconstructionism," *CTR* 6, no. 2 (1993): 281. See also Merkle, *Discontinuity to Continuity*, 170–200.

18 See, e.g., Meredith G. Kline, "Comments on an Old-New Error: A Review Article," *WTJ* 41, no. 1 (1978): 172–89; William S. Barker and W. Robert Godfrey, eds., *Theonomy: A Reformed Critique* (Grand Rapids, MI: Zondervan, 1991); Poythress, *The Shadow of Christ in the Law of Moses*, 311–61; Gabbert, "An Historical Overview of Christian Reconstructionism," 281–301; T. David Gordon, "Critique of Theonomy: A Taxonomy," *WTJ* 56, no. 1 (1994): 23–43; Douglas J. Moo, "Response to Greg L. Bahnsen," in Strickland, *Five Views on Law and Gospel*, 165–73; Thomas R. Schreiner, *40 Questions about Christians and Biblical Law* (Grand Rapids, MI: Kregel, 2010), 223–26.

19 See, e.g., "General Equity Theonomy | Douglas Wilson (Reformed Basics #13)," YouTube video, February 25, 2022, https://www.youtube.com/; "Are You a Theonomist? | Doug Wilson," YouTube video, June 13, 2018, https://www.youtube.com/; "Jeff Durbin | Theonomy, Biblical Justice, and Church and State | Episode 2," YouTube video, June 17, 2021, https://www.youtube .com/. While the following was not yet published for my evaluation, see also Douglas Wilson, *Mere Christendom* (Moscow, ID: Canon, 2023).

20 Wolfe, *The Case for Christian Nationalism*. For two helpful critiques, see the four-part review by Neil Shenvi, "Of Gods and Men: A Long Review of Wolfe's *Case for Christian Nationalism*," Neil Shenvi—Apologetics, https://shenviapologetics.com/; Kevin DeYoung, "The Rise of Right-Wing Wokeism—Review: *The Case for Christian Nationalism* by Stephen Wolfe," The Gospel Coalition, November 28, 2022, https://www.thegospelcoalition.org/.

the church, whereas those employing the title of general equity commonly stress that the church must first be reconstructed according to God's law and then, through that, influence government.[21] Nevertheless, both approaches believe that the church and state are to operate as religious entities under Christ's authority.[22]

The language of "general equity" derives from the wording of the Westminster Confession of Faith 19.4. Speaking of Yahweh's relationship to old covenant Israel, it reads, "To them also, as a body politic, he gave sundry judicial laws, which expired together with the state of that people; not obliging any other now, further than the *general equity* thereof may require." From a theonomic perspective, the phrase "general equity" affirms that principles of love and justice stand behind every civil law and that these principles remain directly binding not only on the church but also on the society, even if the specific application of that law is passé due to the progression of salvation history.[23] Wilson and Durbin attempt to diminish the radical nature of their claims by saying that *all* Christians are "theonomists" of some sort because all Christians believe God's definition of justice informs all spheres of life.[24] Nevertheless, like the reconstructionists before them, they still seek to awaken a religiopolitical movement that unhelpfully employs the tripartite view of the Mosaic law, stresses too much continuity between the old and new covenants, and fails to distinguish laws and justice that Christ would approve (appropriate for nation-states) from a politic under Christ's leadership (something only realized in the church).

---

21 For this distinction, see timestamp 7:39–9:38 in "Are You a Theonomist? | Doug Wilson."

22 Rushdoony asserts, "Not only is every church a religious institution, but every state or societal order is a religious establishment. Every state is a law order, and every law order represents an enacted morality, with procedures for the enforcement of that morality. Every morality represents a form of theological order, i.e., is an aspect and expression of religion. The church thus is not the only religious institution; the state also is a religious institution. More often than the church, the state has been the central religious institution of most civilizations throughout the centuries." Rousas John Rushdoony, *Christianity and the State* (Vallecito, CA: Rose House, 1986), 7. For a similar view, see timestamp 14:15–18:33 in "Jeff Durbin | Theonomy, Biblical Justice, and Church and State | Episode 2."

23 Advocates of "general equity theonomy" believe they are simply carrying out the original expressed meaning of the Westminster Confession, but many others who affirm the confession strongly disagree with this application.

24 See timestamp 00:20–00:50 in "Are You a Theonomist? | Doug Wilson"; and timestamp 3:45–4:45 in "Jeff Durbin | Theonomy, Biblical Justice, and Church and State | Episode 2."

Christian nationalism seeks to counter secularism by urging people from the same place and culture to unite under the principles of God's law and to work for the common good.[25] This influential movement sees Moses's law as a "perfect application of [natural law]" that "remains relevant to all civil polities," but it differs from other forms of theonomy in that it stresses that Moses's law "*can* [rather than *must*] serve as a guide or source of law for all nations."[26] Speaking as a leading voice of Christian nationalism, Wolfe asserts,

> Theonomists were right about the direction of Reformed political theology. . . . I affirm a form of theonomy: civil law ought to be in accordance with God's law, and civil law ought to order man to both earthly and heavenly ends. I deny, however, that the civil laws in the Mosaic law are immutable and universally applicable.[27]

All forms of theonomy teach that God has only one law for all governments in all times. Christian reconstructionist theonomists and general equity theonomists affirm that Moses's moral and civil laws remain binding on all in the church *and* society, though with some necessary redemptive-historical or contextual progressions and/or adaptations. Christian nationalists do not require that Moses's law guide civil magistrates today, but they do see it as a perfect expression of God's natural law, which is binding on all nation-states everywhere. Because Greg Bahnsen sets forth the most biblically grounded arguments for a theonomic approach, my critiques will confront his claims most directly,[28] but my criticisms still apply more broadly to all those holding the forms of theonomy described above.

---

25 While lacking specificity regarding the actual makeup of a "nation," Wolfe states that "Christian nationalism is a totality of national action, consisting of civil laws and social customs, conducted by a Christian nation as a Christian nation, in order to procure for itself both earthly and heavenly good in Christ." Wolfe, *The Case for Christian Nationalism*, 9.

26 Wolfe, *The Case for Christian Nationalism*, 265–66 (emphasis in original).

27 Wolfe, *The Case for Christian Nationalism*, 270. On this point, Wolfe is not far from Bahnsen's own approach when discussing discontinuities in the application of old covenant civil law. See Bahnsen, "The Theonomic Reformed Approach to Law and Gospel," 100–108.

28 See especially Bahnsen, "The Theonomic Reformed Approach to Law and Gospel," 93–143; Greg L. Bahnsen, *Theonomy in Christian Ethics*, 3rd ed. (Nacogdoches, TX: Covenant Media, 2013).

CHRIST FULFILLS ALL MOSES'S LAW,
NOT JUST THE CEREMONIAL PARTS

First, Bahnsen says of Moses's ceremonial laws, "The ceremonial observations were stop-gap and anticipatory; Christ and the New Covenant are the *fulfilled reality*. Therefore, all Christians have had the ceremonial laws observed for them finally and completely *in Christ*."[29] Elsewhere he adds:

> [The] moral laws of the Old Testament, such as those that forbid adultery or oppressing the poor . . . do not foreshadow the redemptive work of Christ, show us justification by faith, or symbolically set apart the Jews from Gentiles. That the laws pertaining to the priesthood, temple, and sacrificial system do accomplish those ends, however, and are to be considered "put out of gear" by the coming of Christ is demonstrated by the author of Hebrews (esp. chaps. 7–10).[30]

These claims assume that the only discontinuities created in the coming of Christ relate to shadows and substance. Yet Christ does more than serve as the antitypical substitute sacrifice on behalf of a sinful world (Heb. 9:13–14, 23–28). He is able to "make many to be accounted righteous" and to "bear their iniquities" because he is the "righteous one" (Isa. 53:11; cf. 1 John 1:9–2:2). He perfectly obeyed his Father's will, even unto death (John 5:30; 6:38; 14:30–31; Phil. 2:8; Heb. 5:8), and this obedience included fulfilling Moses's broad teaching and not just his ceremonial instruction (Matt. 5:17; 23:2–3; Luke 24:44; John 8:46).

Speaking of Moses's "moral law," Bahnsen recognizes that "Christ came . . . to atone for our transgressions against those moral requirements (Rom. 4:25; 5:8–9; 8:1–3)."[31] Yet he then attempts to limit Paul's comments about the law's temporary imprisoning power and guardianship (Gal. 3:23–25) to the ceremonial legislation.[32] This will not do, however, for "the law, which came 430 years" after "the promises were made to Abraham and to his offspring" (Gal. 3:16–17) and "the law . . . [that] was added because of transgressions, until the offspring should come" was the whole Mosaic administration and

---

29 Bahnsen, *Theonomy in Christian Ethics*, 205 (emphasis in original).
30 Bahnsen, "The Theonomic Reformed Approach to Law and Gospel," 104.
31 Bahnsen, "The Theonomic Reformed Approach to Law and Gospel," 112–13.
32 Bahnsen, "The Theonomic Reformed Approach to Law and Gospel," 99.

not just the ceremonial aspects. "Christ is the end of the law for righteousness to everyone who believes" (Rom. 10:4). A proper Christian approach to Moses's law requires that we see Christ fulfilling *all* the law and not just the ceremonial portions (Matt. 5:17–18).

CHRIST'S KINGDOM IS NOT OF THIS WORLD

Second, Wolfe asserts that his ideal Christian nation and not Christ's church stands as the "analog of the heavenly city."[33] Somewhat similarly, Wilson longs to see America abandon secularism and reconstruct into his ideal "new covenant republic."[34] Bahnsen points to Isaiah's promise that the nations would gather to hear Yahweh's law in Zion (Isa. 2:2–3) in support for his claim that "the Gentiles were obligated to the same moral requirements as the Jews."[35]

Against these views, Isaiah was predicting the ingathering of God's multiethnic, transformed peoples (i.e., the church of Jesus Christ), who would heed Yahweh's word through his messianic servant (Isa. 42:4; 50:4, 10; 51:4; 54:13; 55:3; cf. Matt. 12:18–20; 17:5; John 6:44–46). Theonomists fail to appreciate that *the church* and not any modern state stands as the mixed, multiethnic "nation" the Old Testament prophets anticipate that God's kingdom people would become (e.g., Jer. 31:36; Ezek. 37:22; Mic. 4:7). Such is true because Jesus embodies this nation as God's servant "Israel" (Isa. 49:3)[36] and as Abraham's ultimate "offspring" (Gen. 22:17–18; Gal. 3:16). God counts all in Jesus as part of this single nation (Isa. 49:6; Jer. 12:16; Gal. 6:16), one people (Gal. 3:29; Eph. 2:15; cf. Zech. 2:11), treasured possession (Titus 2:14; cf. Ex. 19:6), and sacred dwelling (2 Cor. 6:16; cf. Lev. 26:11). Thus, Peter can declare the Christian community to be "a chosen race, a royal priesthood, a *holy nation*, a people for [God's] own possession, that you may proclaim the excellencies of him who called you out of darkness into his marvelous light" (1 Pet. 2:9).

Against any form of political Christian reconstructionism or nationalism, Jesus stresses, "My kingdom is *not* of this world" (John 18:36). He further

---

33 Wolfe, *The Case for Christian Nationalism*, 209; cf. 222.

34 See timestamps 4:15–20 and 5:50–6:45 in "Are You a Theonomist? | Doug Wilson."

35 Bahnsen, "The Theonomic Reformed Approach to Law and Gospel," 111.

36 See also Zech. 13:9, where Yahweh declares of his shepherd, "*He* is my people" (author's translation).

notes that his followers are to make disciples of "nations" not as political entities but as individuals that they can baptize and teach (Matt. 28:19–20).[37] Accordingly, Paul connects "the Jerusalem above" with those identified with Jesus by faith and not with any secular state (Gal. 4:26; cf. Heb. 12:22). He emphasizes that believers' "citizenship is in heaven" (Phil. 3:20) and that God has transferred Christians and not governments from "the domain of darkness . . . to the kingdom of his beloved Son" (Col. 1:13). Our allegiance, therefore, is to Christ's kingdom (Col. 3:1–4). We are resident aliens on earth (1 Pet. 2:11), *freely* subject to human systems but recognizing that our service is to God (2:16).[38]

God created humans in his image, which necessarily calls for love and justice to be part of every human society and governmental context. Furthermore, the principles of love and justice within Moses's law inform such activities in other salvation-historical periods. However, God's new covenant community is international and not associated with any geopolitical power or province. Indeed, it is made up of some from "every tribe and language and people and nation" (Rev. 5:9). Christ's kingdom is not yet of this world, but one day it will be when the present order is replaced at the final judgment (Matt. 6:10; Rom. 8:18–25; 2 Cor. 4:17–18; Rev. 5:10). Then—and only then—voices from heaven will ring forth, "The kingdom of the world has become the kingdom of our Lord and of his Christ, and he shall reign forever and ever" (Rev. 11:15).[39]

---

37 Jesus highlights this fact by unpacking his call to make disciples of "nations" (*neuter* plural *ethnē* in Greek) by calling for the church to baptize and teach peoples—"them" (*masculine* plural *autous* in Greek) (Matt. 28:19–20). Jesus never called his church to make nation-states into disciples.

38 For similar reflections, see John Piper, "Politics, Patriotism, and the Pulpit," Desiring God, July 4, 2022, https://www.desiringgod.org/.

39 At each stage in salvation history, God judges his people in accord with law associated with that covenantal era; those who are not his people will not be judged by his people's law (Rom. 2:12; 1 Cor. 9:21). In principle, therefore, God does not call non-theocratic nation-states to be ruled by his revealed word. While I affirm many of the claims Neil Shenvi makes regarding the benefits of "cultural Christianity," I find the title unbiblical and unhelpful, for it misrepresents Christ through improper association. I do agree with Shenvi that political states must limit religious freedom to spheres that do not violate the value of human life. Indeed, God creates the institutions of the family, church, and state, and all three are responsible on the basis of general revelation to care about human suffering and injustice against humans (whether physical, psychological, or developmental). Nevertheless, Christians and the church alone are qualified to show concern for eternal suffering and injustice against God, and this means that Christians alone can recognize and rightly judge spiritual harm and evaluate on the basis of

THROUGH CHRIST, MOSES'S LAW APPLIES
TO THE CHURCH, NOT THE STATE

Third, Bahnsen stresses that, according to Matthew 5:17–20, Jesus came "to confirm and restore the full measure, intent, and purpose of the Old Testament law."[40] Yet the theonomists' affirmation that Moses's law still bears lasting value fails to appreciate that when Jesus fulfills the Old Testament he not only maintains (e.g., never murder, muzzling an ox) and annuls (e.g., sin offering) various old covenant laws but also transforms others (e.g., Sabbath, capital punishment) *for the church*. Hence, Jesus notes that he, the "lord of the Sabbath," only gives rest to those who come to him (Matt. 11:28–30; 12:8); that is, rest is for the new covenant community and not the world in general. Similarly, Paul applies Moses's criminal legislation regarding the death penalty (Deut. 22:22) to the church's excommunication of professing members who refuse to repent from their sin (1 Cor. 5:13); he does not use it to ground the state's responsibility to bear the sword (Rom. 13:4).[41]

Through Amos, Yahweh declared punishments on Israel's neighbors based on their oppression of others (Amos 1:2–2:3), whereas he condemns Judah for rejecting "the law of the Lord" (2:3) and Israel for profaning his name and maligning his house (2:7–8). The "laws . . . statutes . . . everlasting covenant" that all the earth's inhabitants have violated, resulting in curse (Isa. 24:4–6), relate *not* to the Mosaic law but to principles of nature (i.e., image bearing and community justice) associated with the Adamic-Noahic covenant (cf. Gen. 6:11–12; Lev. 18:26; Zech. 11:10; Rom. 5:12–14). Hence, Paul speaks of the world's unrighteous people suppressing God's "truth" (Rom. 1:18), acting contrary to "nature" (1:26), and engaging in all forms

---

special revelation. In principle and not just in practice, these activities cannot be a role of the state, for the state is not governed by the special revelation of Scripture that alone provides the ultimate benchmark for truth and sanctifies people. Jesus prayed for his followers, "I do not ask that you take them out of the world, but that you keep them from the evil one. They are not of the world, just as I am not of the world. Sanctify them in the truth; your word is truth" (John 17:15–17). See Shenvi, "Of Gods and Men: A Long Review of Wolfe's *Case for Christian Nationalism*."

40 Bahnsen, *Theonomy in Christian Ethics*, 67; cf. 84.

41 Paul notes that God granted governments the responsibility to execute judgment, even unto death (Rom. 13:4). This fact is built into the fabric of being made in the image of God (Gen. 9:6) and clarifies why the old covenant called for Israel's government to ensure that the punishment fit the crime (e.g., Ex. 21:23–25; Lev. 24:19–20; Deut. 19:21). Nevertheless, that the government executes criminals today in no way *derives* from the lasting validity of the Mosaic law.

of wickedness despite their knowing "God's righteous decree that those who practice such things deserve to die" (1:32). Each of these standards points *not* to Moses's law but to every human's more fundamental awareness of right and wrong, apart from any special revelation.[42] Scripture distinguishes God's special revelation to Israel from his general revelation to mankind (Rom. 9:4–5). "All who have sinned without the law [i.e., the Gentiles] will also perish without the law, and all who have sinned under the law [i.e., the Jews] will be judged by the law" (Rom. 2:12). Yet because Israel was Yahweh's special covenant people, their failure to keep the revealed law proved that all without such a gift would also be under God's condemnation (Rom. 3:19). Thus, Israel's relationship to the law served as a paradigm for the world but not in the way theonomists argue.

The "law of Christ" and not the "law of Moses" stands as the direct authority over Christians today, and neither of these laws binds secular governments.[43] Secular government should enact laws that Jesus would approve, for the ruler of every nation-state is "God's servant for your good . . . an avenger who carries out God's wrath on the wrongdoer" (Rom. 13:4). Indeed, Christians should pray "for kings and all who are in high positions, that we may lead a peaceful and quiet life, godly and dignified in every way" (1 Tim. 2:2). It is through such settings that the gospel can advance unhindered (2 Tim. 2:3–6; cf. Col. 4:3). Nevertheless, while nation-states provide contexts for Christ's kingdom to advance on earth, they are themselves *not* the means or the agents of this advance. Local churches filled with redeemed saints alone perform this role as they serve God in complete freedom from every world power (1 Pet. 2:11–16).

Summary

The New Testament *repudiates* the Mosaic law-covenant, *replaces* it in its entirety with the law of Christ, and then *reappropriates* Moses's law

---

42 Frank Thielman, *Paul and the Law: A Contextual Approach* (Downers Grove, IL: InterVarsity Press, 1994), 169; Moo, *Epistle to the Romans*, 131–32; Thomas R. Schreiner, *Romans*, 2nd ed., BECNT (Grand Rapids, MI: Baker Academic, 2018), 108.

43 D. A. Carson proposes that the category of "moral law" is still helpful if one defines it as an *a posteriori* ("after the fact") reality that the New Testament discloses in relation to "those instructions and laws that change the least across time" and *not* as an *a priori* ("before the fact"), unchanging standard of God's love and justice that stands across all times and cultures and governs our understanding of continuity and discontinuity between the Testaments. D. A. Carson, "Matthew," in *Matthew–Mark*, 2nd ed., EBC 9 (Grand Rapids, MI: Zondervan, 2010), 177.

through Jesus by maintaining some laws (with or without extension) while transforming or annulling others. Jesus fulfills Moses's whole law, and all of Moses's law (and not just moral and/or moral-civil portions) bears lasting significance for Christians today.[44]

Alternative Dangerous Applications of Old Testament Law

Before explaining how to apply Moses's law through Jesus and supplying some extended case studies (chaps. 12–13), we must consider three troubling approaches to the Christian and the Old Testament law: (1) legalism, (2) antinomianism, and (3) the Old Testament is not Christian Scripture. For a warning related to the Hebrew Roots movement, see the end of the last case study in chapter 13.

Legalism

Legalism is operative when people trust in their own actions to enjoy right standing with God. Foundational to the very nature of the old covenant law was Yahweh's claim, "If a person does [my statutes and my rules], he shall live by them: I am the LORD" (Lev. 18:5). Because God gave the law to a mostly unregenerate people, their pursuit of righteousness by works and not by faith resulted in their ruin (Rom. 9:30–32; cf. Gal. 3:11–12).[45] As Paul claimed, "The very commandment that promised life proved to be death to me" (Rom. 7:10).

Legalism was the plague of the Pharisees, whom Jesus said "trusted in themselves that they were righteous, and treated others with contempt" (Luke 18:9). In the parable of the Pharisee and tax collector, Jesus associated self-righteousness with the one who declared, "God, *I thank you* that I am not like other men" (Luke 18:11), whereas it was a repentant tax collector who cried, "God, be merciful to me, a sinner," and "went down to his house justified" (18:13–14).

---

44 For further recent critiques of theonomy and Christian nationalism, see vol. 15 (April 2023) of *Church Matters: A Journal for Pastors* (formerly 9Marks Journal) devoted to the theme "A New Christian Authoritarianism? Christian Nationalism, Theonomy, and Magisterial Protestantism," https://www.9marks.org/.

45 See esp. Jason S. DeRouchie, "Question 34: How Does Galatians 3:12 Use Leviticus 18:5?," in Jason S. DeRouchie, Oren R. Martin, and Andrew David Naselli, *40 Questions about Biblical Theology* (Grand Rapids, MI: Kregel, 2020), 327–37; Jason S. DeRouchie, "The Use of Leviticus 18:5 in Galatians 3:12: A Redemptive-Historical Reassessment," *Them* 45, no. 2 (2020): 240–59.

Legalism was also the plague of the Judaizers in Galatia. Paul confronts them, declaring, "Are you so foolish? Having begun by the Spirit, are you now being perfected by the flesh?" (Gal. 3:3). Elsewhere, he also stresses, "We hold that one is justified by faith apart from works of the law" (Rom. 3:28). And again, "To the one who does not work but believes in him who justifies the ungodly, his faith is counted as righteousness" (Rom. 4:5).

Foundational to all Reformation doctrine is that justification before God (i.e., right standing) comes by grace *alone* through faith *alone* in Christ *alone*. We become legalists if we ever ground our justification in anything other than Christ's perfect obedience *alone*. "Therefore, as one trespass led to condemnation for all men, so one act of righteousness leads to justification and life for all men. For as by the one man's disobedience the many were made sinners, so by the one man's obedience the many will be made righteous" (Rom. 5:18–19).

Antinomianism

License refers to some professing Christians' sense of a right to live as they will. Such persons are *libertine* in the way they disregard moral principles, viewing themselves as "free" from all law or rule. Paul confronts the licentious and libertine when he declares, "What then? Are we to sin because we are not under law but under grace? By no means!" (Rom. 6:15; cf. 6:1–2). And again, "Do not use your freedom as an opportunity for the flesh, but through love serve one another" (Gal. 5:13). In the New Testament, *nomos* is the Greek term for "law," so *antinomian* means "against law." Antinomians are those who claim that God's rules need not influence Christians' daily ethics. In contrast, Paul stresses that he was not "outside the law of God but under the law of Christ" (1 Cor. 9:21) and that what counts is neither circumcision nor uncircumcision but "keeping the commandments of God" (1 Cor. 7:19).

While antinomians celebrate the beauty that Christ's obedience *alone* secures our justification (Rom. 5:18–19), they minimize the fact that once "you have been set free from sin and have become slaves of God, the fruit you get leads to sanctification and its end, eternal life" (Rom. 6:22). In doing so, they wound others' consciences (1 Cor. 8:12) and move them to desensitize their moral consciousness so that it no longer functions properly (1 Tim. 4:2; Titus 1:5). The supercharged consciousness of believers, due to

God's having written the law on our hearts (Jer. 31:33–34; cf. Rom. 2:15), is, therefore, set aside in the name of Christ.

Antinomians champion the glorious doctrine of justification by "faith alone" but fail to clarify that "faith by itself, if it does not have works, is dead" (James 2:17), and that there is a "holiness without which no one will see the Lord" (Heb. 12:14). They also fail to account for Jesus's claim, "Whoever has my commandments and keeps them, he it is who loves me" (John 14:21; cf. 14:23; 15:10).

Antinomians also stress that our salvation is unconditional. What they miss is that, while electing grace (Rom. 9:11; Eph. 1:4–5) and regenerating grace (Ezek. 36:26; John 3:3, 7–8; Eph. 2:8–9)[46] are *unconditional*, other graces are *conditional*, though never meritorious.[47] For example, faith in Christ stands as a condition for justification (John 3:16; Rom. 3:28; 5:1; Gal. 2:16; 3:24), sanctification (2 Thess. 2:13), and glorification (Col. 1:22–23). Furthermore, good works are conditions for various other blessings:

- Only those who forgive others will God keep forgiving (Matt. 6:14–15).
- Only those who have done good will enter eternal life (John 5:28–29; Gal. 5:21).
- Only those who love God will see all things work together for good (Rom. 8:28).
- Only those who persevere truly share in Christ (Heb. 4:14).
- Only those whose justifying faith has produced works will enjoy the final verdict of justification (James 2:24; cf. Rom. 2:13).[48]

Christ purchased *both* our justification and our sanctification. Thus, Paul praises, "Thanks be to God, that you who were once slaves of sin have become obedient from the heart to the standard of teaching to which you were

---

46 See also Acts 5:31; 11:18; 16:14; Rom. 8:30; 1 Cor. 1:23–24; 2 Cor. 4:4–6; Phil. 1:29.

47 See the section titled "VI. Unmerited, Conditional Future Grace" in John Piper, *Future Grace: The Purifying Power of the Promises of God*, 2nd ed. (Colorado Springs, CO: Multnomah, 2012), 229–72.

48 At the final judgment, God will act like an orchard owner who will assess the life of trees in accordance with whether they have fruit. The fruit (i.e., works/obedience) does not make the tree alive; it only proves the tree is alive. This is how final justification relates to past justification. Every truly justified person will produce works of righteousness. As John asserts, "Whoever practices righteousness is righteous, as he is righteous" (1 John 3:7).

committed" (Rom. 6:17). What the texts above reveal is that God's gracious love is not all the same; it's more complex than what antinomians suggest.[49]

Paul charges, "Work out your own salvation with fear and trembling, for it is God who works in you, both to will and to work for his good pleasure" (Phil. 2:12–13). Paul's point is that God is shaping the Christian's *will* and *work* through Jesus. The apostle gives no less than twenty-five imperatives in Philippians. In Philippians 1–2 alone we read, "*Let your manner of life be worthy of the gospel*" (Phil. 1:27); "*complete my joy by being of the same mind*" (2:2); "*have this mind among yourselves, which is yours in Christ Jesus*" (2:5); "*do all things without grumbling or disputing*" (2:14); "*be glad and rejoice with me*" (2:18); "*receive him in the Lord with all joy*" (2:29). Paul clearly has progressive sanctification in mind.

Growing in godliness by means of grace always should result in a higher sensitivity to our own sinfulness. Thus, Paul recognized himself as "the least of the apostles" (1 Cor. 15:9), "the very least of all the saints" (Eph. 3:8), and the "foremost" of "sinners" (1 Tim. 1:15). Growth in godliness should also result in a deeper treasuring of Christ (1 John 1:9–2:2) and in a heightened pursuit of holiness (Phil. 3:12). Jude warns of "ungodly people, who pervert the grace of our God into sensuality and deny our only Master and Lord, Jesus Christ" (Jude 4). Justifying grace is *never* a license for immorality. Thus, Peter urges, "Live as people who are free, not using your freedom as a cover-up for evil, but living as servants of God" (1 Pet. 2:16).

Long ago the Westminster theologians emphasized, "Faith, thus receiving and resting on Christ and his righteousness, is the alone instrument of justification: yet it is not alone in the person justified, but is ever accompanied with all other saving graces, is no dead faith, but worketh by love."[50] It is from this framework that, after forgiving the sin of the woman caught in adultery, Jesus commanded, "Go, and from now on sin no more" (John 8:11). Paul insists, "You also must consider yourselves dead to sin and alive to God in Jesus Christ. Let not sin therefore reign in your mortal body, to make you obey its passions" (Rom. 6:11–12). "Let the thief no longer steal" (Eph. 4:28). "This is the will of God, your sanctification: that you abstain from sexual immorality" (1 Thess. 4:3). "Let everyone who names

---

49 See D. A. Carson, "Love," *NDBT*, 646–50; D. A. Carson, *The Difficult Doctrine of the Love of God* (Wheaton, IL: Crossway, 2000).

50 Westminster Confession of Faith 11.2.

the name of the Lord depart from iniquity" (2 Tim. 2:19). Finally, Peter urges, "As obedient children, do not be conformed to the passions of your former ignorance, but as he who called you is holy, you also be holy in all your conduct, since it is written, 'You shall be holy, for I am holy'" (1 Pet. 1:14–16). Clearly, antinomianism is not an option for Christians.[51]

The Old Testament Is Not Christian Scripture

Throughout church history, some have denied that the Old Testament is Christian Scripture. Marcion of Sinope (ca. AD 85–160) ministered in Ephesus in the early second century. He did not equate the Creator God of the Old Testament with Jesus or the Father, and he elevated one gospel (the "Gospel of Marcion") and one apostle (the Marcionite Pauline corpus). The early church recognized both the Old and New Testaments as God's word with canonical authority, and they affirmed the biblical teaching that Jesus was God who came from his loving Father to save the elect from the Creator's just wrath. Nevertheless, Marcionism had a massive negative influence during the second century AD, especially after the early church excommunicated Marcion for his heretical teachings around AD 140. One positive effect of Marcion's false teaching was that it forced the church to become clear on its canon. But through the centuries, others have echoed some of Marcion's claims. Indeed, as John Clabeaux notes, "Since rejection of the OT was an essential feature of Marcionism, it is straining the point only a little to say that among Christians today there are many virtual Marcionites."[52]

In his book *Irresistible*, Andy Stanley rightly affirms that Christians are part of the new covenant and not the old, for by enacting the new covenant, God "makes the first one obsolete" (Heb. 8:6, 13). Stanley correctly observes how misapplications of the Old Testament have often produced dangerous results including the "prosperity gospel, the crusades, anti-Semitism, legalism, exclusivism, judgmentalism," and the like.[53] He also rightly recognizes that many Christians are confused regarding the lasting value of Moses's law, in how it relates to both personal ethics and politics.

---

51 For a more developed, helpful critique of antinomianism, see Mark Jones, *Antinomianism: Reformed Theology's Unwelcome Guest?* (Phillipsburg, NJ: P&R, 2013).

52 John J. Clabeaux, "Marcion," *ABD* 4:516.

53 Andy Stanley, *Irresistible: Reclaiming the New That Jesus Unleashed for the World* (Grand Rapids, MI: Zondervan, 2018), 158.

These true convictions, however, then lead him to make the unqualified request of church leaders to "consider unhitching your teaching of what it means to follow Jesus from all things old covenant."[54] Stanley is *not* a Marcionite. However, his book makes a number of false claims that run counter to Scripture and that dangerously diminish the vital place of the Old Testament in the Christian's life.

First, Stanley creates an unbiblical discontinuity between the Testaments when he asserts that in the Old Testament period Yahweh's ethics aligned with "the rules" of other nations' gods, all of whom were "human rights violators"[55] and that only in the New Testament does God reveal himself as a God of "love."[56] Yet Moses's hope—already at Sinai after Israel's sin with the golden calf—was that Yahweh was indeed "merciful and gracious, slow to anger, and abounding in steadfast love and faithfulness" (Ex. 34:6). Furthermore, the same God who spoke "by the prophets" now has spoken "by his Son" (Heb. 1:1–2), and his character has not changed. "Note then the kindness and the severity of God: severity toward those who have fallen, but God's kindness to you, provided you continue in his kindness. Otherwise, you too will be cut off" (Rom. 11:22).

Second, by calling the Old Testament the "Hebrew Bible" and the New Testament the "Christian Bible,"[57] Stanley blurs the distinction between the Mosaic old covenant (which Christians are *not* under) and the Old Testament as a whole, which Jesus came not "to abolish . . . but to fulfill" (Matt. 5:17) and which the apostles stress was written "for our instruction" (Rom. 15:4; 1 Cor. 10:11) and to "serve you" (1 Pet. 1:12). Stanley misses that the Old Testament writings supplied the only Bible Jesus and the apostle's had and that "all Scripture" is useful to Christians "for teaching, for reproof, for correction, and for training in righteousness" (2 Tim. 3:16).

Third, Stanley's proposal has no category for how the New Testament authors reappropriate Moses's law through and for Christ. After helpfully

---

54 Stanley, *Irresistible*, 315; cf. 158.
55 Stanley, *Irresistible*, 162–63.
56 Stanley, *Irresistible*, 223.
57 "What if, instead of Old and New Testaments, our texts were labeled *the Hebrew Bible* and *the Christian Bible*. That's clearer and more accurate. Whereas our New Testament (new covenant) contains a description of the new covenant initiated by Jesus, it too contains more than that. And whereas our Old Testament (old covenant) contains the contents of God's covenant with Israel, it contains more as well. . . . Combining the Hebrew Bible with the Christian Bible for convenience sake is a great idea. But why not call each by its actual name?" Stanley, *Irresistible*, 280–81.

noting how Christ stands as the substance and end of old covenant laws associated with worship (e.g., temple, animal sacrifices, earthly priests),[58] Stanley missteps in assuming that none of Moses's law matters today. He writes, "The Ten Commandments have no authority over you. None. To be clear: Thou shalt not obey the Ten Commandments."[59] He later adds, "Paul never leverages the old covenant as a basis for Christian behavior."[60] As I will show in the next two chapters, while we must affirm that the old covenant law has no *direct* and *immediate* authority in the Christian's life, through Jesus the whole law still matters. And, therefore, Paul *does leverage* the Ten Commandments when guiding believers in the life of Christian love and obedience (e.g., Rom. 13:9 with Ex. 20:13–17; Eph. 6:2–3 with Ex. 20:12).

Jesus's saving work abrogates or transforms some laws (e.g., dietary restrictions, temple worship, the Sabbath), but he maintains other laws, and Christians can receive helpful benefit from every portion of Scripture. The Bible of Jesus and Paul was what we call the Old Testament. Jesus saw it pointing to him and his work, and Paul agreed (e.g., Luke 24:44–47; John 5:39, 46; Acts 26:22–23). They also recognized that the whole Old Testament is Christian Scripture that God gave to instruct believers today (Rom. 15:4; 1 Cor. 10:11; 1 Pet. 1:12). We must affirm that Jesus came to "fulfill" the Old Testament Scriptures, not to "abolish" them (Matt. 5:17), and we should delight in the Law and the Prophets. Yet, as Christians, we must read them and apply them through Christ and for Christ.[61]

Conclusion

Many Christians distinguish Mosaic moral, civil, and ceremonial laws and then view only the moral—or only the moral and civil—as applying to Christians. Both approaches miss that no old covenant legislation directly binds believers today. All of Moses's law still serves Christians through Jesus but only in so far as he maintains (with or without extension), transforms,

---

58 Stanley, *Irresistible*, 17–65.
59 Stanley, *Irresistible*, 136.
60 Stanley, *Irresistible*, 209.
61 Three other books to help keep you properly connected to the Old Testament are Peter J. Gentry and Stephen J. Wellum, *God's Kingdom through God's Covenants: A Concise Biblical Theology* (Wheaton, IL: Crossway, 2015); Miles V. Van Pelt, ed., *A Biblical-Theological Introduction to the Old Testament: The Gospel Promised* (Wheaton, IL: Crossway, 2016); Dennis E. Johnson, *Journeys with Jesus: Every Path in the Bible Leads Us to Christ* (Phillipsburg, NJ: P&R, 2018).

or annuls the various laws. While principles of love and justice present in Moses's law also carry over into governments today, Christ's law binds the church and not the state. Finally, legalism, antinomianism, and the view that the Old Testament is not Christian Scripture are all dangerous, for they compromise Christ's saving work and the way the New Testament authors view and apply the law.

Review and Reflection

1. What are the three divisions of Moses's law as classically defined?
2. How do classic covenant theologians and theonomists differ on their approaches to the threefold division of the law?
3. Read through Leviticus 19 and note the different topics addressed by the laws. What about the arrangement and nature of the chapter speaks against the concept of the threefold division of the law?
4. Give some examples of how the New Testament regularly treats Moses's law as a whole and does not distinguish it as the threefold division advocates suggest.
5. Those affirming the threefold division of Moses's law point to the Ten Commandments as examples of Yahweh's moral law, which they define as timeless, culturally unbound principles relevant everywhere and always. Read through Deuteronomy 5:6–21 and highlight culturally bound features that indicate a weakness in this definition of the moral law in relation to the Ten Commandments.
6. What is the difference between Christian reconstructionist theonomy and general equity theonomy? What does the author view as unhelpful and/or misguided in both approaches?
7. Define *legalism* and clarify from Scripture why it is dangerous and destructive.
8. What is *antinomianism*, and how does this approach to biblical law minimize the need for progressive sanctification that Christ purchased with his own blood?
9. How would you respond to those who claim Christians must "unhitch" themselves from all things old covenant and not affirm that the Old Testament is Christian Scripture?
10. What was the greatest insight you gained in reading this chapter? What is your greatest takeaway?

12

When Jesus Maintains the Law

Keep all his commandments.

DEUTERONOMY 30:8

CHAPTER 10 EVALUATED how the Bible relates Old Testament law to Christians, and chapter 11 considered some of the errors and even dangers in alternative approaches. Chapters 12 and 13 focus on how Moses's law, when approached through Christ, supplies Christians a pattern for love and wise living today. The discussion below surveys a three-step process for applying Old Testament law today. It then offers two case studies on commands that Christ's new covenant law maintains with extension (house building, Deut. 22:8) and without extension (gender issues, Deut. 22:5). The next chapter will give examples of Moses's instruction that Jesus transforms (Sabbath, Deut. 5:12) and annuls (food laws, Lev. 20:25–26).

A Method for Applying Old Testament Law[1]

Moses anticipated that Yahweh's people would "keep all his commandments" once he empowered them to love him with all their heart and being (Deut. 30:6, 8). How should Christians, who enjoy Spirit-wrought

---

1 Some of this material builds on David A. Dorsey, "The Law of Moses and the Christian: A Compromise," *JETS* 34, no. 3 (1991): 332–33; Christopher J. H. Wright, *Old Testament Ethics for the People of God* (Downers Grove, IL: InterVarsity Press, 2004), 314–24.

circumcised hearts, keep the precepts of the law (Rom. 2:26–29)? The following three-step process will help believers faithfully assess, through Christ and for Christ, the lasting significance of Moses's law today.

1. Establish the Law's Original Revealed Meaning and Application

A. CATEGORIZE THE TYPE OF LAW

What type or kind of command are you assessing: criminal, civil, family, cultic/ceremonial, or compassion law? At stake here is the law's content, not form (e.g., apodictic vs. casuistic).[2] Table 12.1 distinguishes the types of old covenant laws by content (for an extended overview, see table 12.2).

Table 12.1   Types of old covenant laws by content (abridged)

Criminal Laws	Laws governing offenses that put the welfare of the whole community at risk (i.e., crimes). The offended party is the state or national community; therefore, the punishment is on behalf of the whole community in the name of the highest state authority, which in Israel meant Yahweh.
	Examples: Kidnapping, homicide, false prophecy, witchcraft, adultery, and rape.
Civil Laws	Laws governing private disputes between citizens or organizations in which the public authorities are appealed to for judgment or called upon to intervene. The offended party is not the state or national community.
	Examples: Accidental death and assault, theft, destruction of property, limited family issues like premarital unchastity, post-divorce situations, and the mistreatment of slaves.

2 Apodictic and casuistic are formal categories that speak to the grammatical shape and derivative purpose of the law. Apodictic laws are unconditional and imperative, usually beginning with a volitional verb in second person and often expressed negatively (e.g., "You shall have no other gods before me," Ex. 20:3). Casuistic laws are conditional and declarative, usually beginning with "if" or "when," in third person, and expressed positively (e.g., "When an ox gores a man or a woman to death, the ox shall be stoned, and its flesh shall not be eaten, but the owner of the ox shall not be liable," Ex. 21:28).

(Table 12.1 continued)

Family Laws	Non-civil, domestic laws governing the Israelite household.
	Examples: Marriage, inheritance, the redemption of land and persons, family discipleship, and the care of slaves.
Cultic/Ceremonial Laws	Laws governing the visible forms and rituals of Israel's religious life or ceremonies.
	Examples: The sacred sacrifice, the sacred calendar, and various sacred symbols like the tabernacle, priesthood, and ritual purity that distinguished Israel from the nations and provided parables of more fundamental truths about God and relating to him.
Compassion Laws	"Laws" dealing with charity, justice, and mercy toward others. These laws cannot be brought to court, but God knows the heart.
	Examples: Protection and justice for the weak, impartiality, generosity, and respect for persons and property.

B. ESTABLISH THE LAW'S ORIGINAL MEANING AND SIGNIFICANCE

Assess the makeup of the law in its original context. Clarify its social function and relative status. Is it central or peripheral to the dominant themes and social objectives we find in the rest of the material? Is it a primary expression of Yahweh's values and priorities, or is it secondary, reinforcing and supplying an example of a primary law? Resources like *The ESV Study Bible* or the *NIV Biblical Theology Study Bible* can serve as great resources when considering the law's original meaning and significance.[3]

---

3 *ESV Study Bible* (Wheaton, IL: Crossway, 2008); *NIV Biblical Theology Study Bible* (Grand Rapids, MI: Zondervan, 2018).

C. CONSIDER THE LAW'S ORIGINAL PURPOSE

What role did Yahweh intend the law to have in Israelite society? Ask the following: Who? What? When? Where? Why? How? How often? To what extent?

- What kind of situation was this law trying to promote or prevent?
- Whose interests was this law aiming to protect?
- Who would have benefited from this law and why?
- Whose power was this law trying to restrict, and how did it do so?
- What rights and responsibilities were embodied in this law?
- What kind of behavior did this law encourage or discourage?
- What vision of society motivated this law?
- What moral principles, values, or priorities did this law embody or initiate?
- What motivation did this law appeal to?
- What sanction or penalty (if any) was attached to this law, and what does that show regarding its relative seriousness or moral priority?

2. Determine the Law's Theological Importance

A. CLARIFY WHAT THE LAW TELLS US ABOUT GOD AND HIS WAYS

What does the law disclose to us about Yahweh's unchanging character, desires, values, concerns, or standards? We learn about God through his law, and meditating on Moses's law should move us to worship the Lord and to recognize and grieve over lawlessness as a direct affront to his person. It should also move us to celebrate his provision of Christ as the perfect law keeper and the righteousness supplier.

B. EVALUATE HOW CHRIST FULFILLS THE LAW AND CONSIDER ITS IMPACT ON APPLICATION

God's character remains unchanged, which means that every expression of his eternal law at different times in the progress of salvation history can instruct every other age and culture. This is true even if the specific legislation is no longer binding because of the changes in covenant and historical-cultural context. Christ's person, teaching, and work completely display the call to love God and neighbor, and Jesus fulfills the law not only in the way he perfectly met the law's demands but also in the way that he is the substance of all old covenant shadows (Col. 2:16–17). That is, he is the ultimate reality to which all the Old Testament types pointed, whether persons, events, or institutions. As we consider how Moses's law informs the law of Christ, some new covenant instructions look identical to Moses's teaching, that is, they are maintained without extension (e.g., covetousness), whereas others are maintained with extension (e.g., don't muzzle the ox), transformed (e.g., Sabbath), or annulled (e.g., animal sacrifices). Homosexuality is as wrong today as it was in the old covenant (Lev. 18:22; 20:13; Rom. 1:27; 1 Cor. 6:9), but unlike the Israelites (Lev. 11:7), Christians are free to eat bacon because Jesus's kingdom work rendered all foods clean (Mark 7:19; Acts 10:13–15; Rom. 14:14, 20; 1 Cor. 8:8). Because most often the various types of laws are mixed up in the Law, we must deal with each law on its own, considering how Christ's fulfillment impacts any given law.

Significantly, there are no laws from the old covenant that come to us directly; all must be mediated through Jesus. We do not obey the Ten Commandments, for example, simply because Yahweh commanded them through Moses. Rather, each of the commandments guides us only through the lens of Christ, and every one gets focused through him (see chap. 10). Even a command like "you shall not commit adultery" (Matt. 5:27) gains a new *pattern* in the life of Jesus (Phil. 2:5–7; Heb. 12:1–3; 1 Pet. 2:21; 1 John 2:6) and a new *power* through his work (Rom. 1:16; 1 Cor. 1:18). Jesus embodies for us a perfect example of what living out the law of Christ looks like in the way he treated women and controlled his own desires with the aid of the Spirit, and he secures power for our own pursuit of holiness through his blood-bought pardon (Rom. 6:6–7, 22; 8:10) and blood-bought promises (Rom. 8:32; 2 Cor. 1:20; 2 Pet. 1:4). Every law finds focus if not complete transformation in Christ—even those that his law fulfillment does not change in nature.

C. STATE IN A SINGLE SENTENCE THE LOVE PRINCIPLE BEHIND THE LAW

If indeed love is what God called the people to do and all the other commandments clarify how to do it at any given time in history (Matt. 7:12; 22:37–40; Rom. 13:8, 10; Gal. 5:14), we should be able to boil down every law

242   *How Jesus Makes Moses's Law Matter*

into a *principle of love*. Being as detailed as possible, complete the following statement for every law: God's call to love requires that _____.

Consider, for example, Moses's charge: "You shall not see your brother's donkey or his ox fallen down by the way and ignore them. You shall help him to lift them up again" (Deut. 22:4). This law of compassion seeks to build a service-focused community that helps others when they are in need. *God's call to love requires that I assist my brother when I come upon him in need* (cf. Luke 10:30–35).

3. Summarize the Law's Lasting Significance

Here we preserve both the portrait of God and the love principle behind the law but change the context, all in view of Christ's new covenant work. God's nature is unchanging, but his purposes progress over time. Furthermore, a proper approach to Old Testament law must account for the pattern Christ set for believers and the power he supplied through his victory and Spirit. As similar as the old and new covenants are in many respects, the internalization of grace in all members marks the new covenant as a massive progression within salvation history.

Table 12.2   Types of old covenant laws by content (extended)

Criminal Laws
Laws governing offenses that put the welfare of the whole community at risk (i.e., crimes). The offended party is the state or national community; therefore, the punishment is on behalf of the whole community in the name of the highest state authority, which in Israel meant Yahweh.

Kidnapping (Ex. 21:16; Deut. 24:7)
Sustained insubordination to parents (Ex. 21:15, 17; Deut. 21:18–21)
Homicide / premeditated or avoidable murder (Ex. 21:14; Num. 35:16–21, 30–31; Deut. 19:11–13)
Religious malpractice
  • Sabbath breaking (Ex. 31:14–15; 35:2; cf. Num. 15:32–36)
  • False prophecy (Deut. 13:1–5; 18:20)
  • Idolatry (Ex. 22:20; Lev 19:4; Deut. 13:1–18; 17:2–7)
  • Child sacrifice (Lev. 20:1–5)
  • Witchcraft (Ex. 22:18; Lev. 19:26, 31; 20:27)
  • Blasphemy (see Lev. 24:14–23)

(Table 12.2 continued)

Criminal Laws (*continued*)
Sexual offenses
- Adultery when married or engaged (Lev. 20:10; Deut. 22:22–24; cf. Gen. 38:24)
- Concealed premarital unchastity (Deut. 22:20–21)
- Rape of an engaged girl (Deut. 22:25)
- Prostitution of a priest's daughter (Lev. 21:9)
- Incest (Lev. 20:11–12, 14)
- Homosexuality (Lev. 20:13)
- Bestiality (Ex. 22:19; Lev. 20:15–16)

False witness in a capital case (Deut. 19:16–21)
Note: Nearly all the commands and prohibitions in the Ten Commandments are considered criminal offenses.

Civil Laws
Laws governing private disputes between citizens or organizations in which the public authorities are appealed to for judgment or called upon to intervene. The offended party is not the state or national community.

Non-premeditated killing
- Accidental death (Ex. 21:13; Num. 35:9–15; Deut. 19:1–13)
- Death due to self-defense (Ex. 22:2–3)

Assault
- Human against human (Ex. 21:18–19, 22)
- Animal against human (Ex. 21:28–32)
- Animal against animal (Ex. 21:33–36)

Breaches of trust
- Theft (Ex. 22:1–4, 7–9, 12; Lev. 19:11, 13)
- Destruction of property (Ex. 22:5, 6, 14)

Falsehood as a witness
- In non-capital case (Ex. 23:1–3)
- In commerce/trade (Lev. 19:35–36)

Limited family issues
- Premarital unchastity between consenting adults, whether real (Ex. 22:16–17; Lev. 19:20–22; Deut. 22:28–29) or potential (Deut. 22:13–21)
- Post-divorce situations (Deut. 24:1–4)
- The mistreatment of slaves (Ex. 21:20–21, 26–27)
- The handling of runaway slaves (Deut. 23:15–16)
- Failure to accept levirate marriage duties (Deut. 25:7–10)

(Table 12.2 continued)

Family Laws
Non-civil, domestic laws governing the Israelite household.

Levirate marriage (Deut. 25:5–6)
Inheritance (Deut. 21:15–16)
Jubilee and the redemption of land and persons (Lev. 25)
Family discipleship (Deut. 6:6–9, 20–25; 11:18–21)
Respect of and obedience to parents (Ex. 20:12; Lev. 19:3; Deut. 5:16)
Turning a daughter into a prostitute (Lev. 19:29)
Slavery including limits of service, inheritance, and protection (Ex. 21:2–11;
    Deut. 15:1–23)
Maintaining gender distinctions (Deut. 22:5)

Cultic/Ceremonial Laws
Laws governing the visible forms and rituals of Israel's religious life or ceremonies.

Sacrifice
- Altar and sacrifices (Ex. 20:24–26)
- Offering of firstfruits (Ex. 22:29–30; 23:19)
- Sacrifices
    - General guidelines (Ex. 23:18; 29:38–46; Lev. 1–7; 19:5–8)
    - Day of Atonement (Lev. 16)
    - Location (Lev. 17:1–9; Deut. 12)
Sacred Calendar
- Weekly Sabbaths (Ex. 20:8–11; 23:12; 31:12–17; 35:1–3; Lev. 19:3, 30;
    Deut. 5:12–15)
- Sabbatical year (Ex. 23:10–11; Lev. 25:3–7; Deut. 15:1–6)
- Feasts and sacred days (Ex. 23:14–19; 34:22–23; Lev. 23:9–22; Deut. 16:1–17)
- Jubilee (Lev. 25:8–55)
Sacred Symbolism and Distinction
- Tabernacle (Ex. 25–30)
- Priesthood
    - Garments (Ex. 28)
    - Consecration (Ex. 29:1–37; Lev. 8)
    - Administration of sacrifices (Ex. 29:38–46; Lev. 6–7)
- Ritual Purity (Clean/Unclean)
    - Food laws (Lev. 11:2–47; 20:24–26; Deut. 14:4–20) and the eating of
      blood (Lev. 17:10–16; 19:26)
    - Childbirth (Lev. 12)
    - Leprosy (Lev. 13–14)
    - Bodily discharges (Lev. 15)
- Distinction from the pagan nations
    - Interbreeding/mixing of cattle, seeds, garments (Lev. 19:19; Deut. 22:9–11)
    - Trimming of sideburns, cutting of body, tattoos (Lev. 19:27–28; Deut. 14:1)

(Table 12.2 continued)

Compassion Laws

"Laws" dealing with charity, justice, and mercy toward others. These laws cannot be brought to court, but God knows the heart.

Protection and care of others
- The sojourner (Ex. 22:21; 23:9; Lev. 19:9–10, 33–34; Deut. 14:28–29; 24:19–22)
- The widow and orphan (Ex. 22:22–24; Deut. 14:28–29; 24:19–22)
- The poor (Ex. 22:25–27; 23:6; Lev. 19:9–10; Deut. 15:7–11; 24:10–13, 19–22)
- One's neighbor (Lev. 19:13, 16–18)
- The disabled (Lev. 19:14; Deut. 27:18)
- The Levite (Deut. 14:28–29)
- The released slave (Deut. 15:12–15)
- The hired servant (Deut. 24:14–15)

Justice and impartiality (Ex. 23:7–8; Lev. 19:15; Deut. 24:17–18; 27:19, 25)

Honor of the elderly (Lev. 19:32)

Return of an enemy or brother's lost goods (Ex. 22:4; Deut. 22:1–3)

Help of an enemy or brother in need (Ex. 23:5; Deut. 22:4)

Excusal from war
- For a new homeowner (Deut. 20:5)
- For a new business owner (Deut. 20:6)
- For a newly married man (Deut. 20:7; 24:5)

Marriage to foreign widows of war (Deut. 20:10–14)

Preservation of means for food for future generations (Deut. 20:6–7; 25:4)

Building safe homes (Deut. 20:8)

Respect for others' means of sustenance (Deut. 23:24–25; 24:6)

Case Study 1: The Law Maintained with Extension— Housebuilding with Love in Deuteronomy 22:8

Our first example of applying Moses's law is simple and straightforward. It illustrates how some laws get extended into new spheres as times and culture change.

> When you build a new house, you shall make a parapet for your roof, that you may not bring the guilt of blood upon your house, if anyone should fall from it. (Deut. 22:8)

1. Establish the Original Revealed Meaning and Application of Deuteronomy 22:8

The law's conditional nature suggests that it stands as a secondary application of a more fundamental principle, one related to compassion. Yet the compassion law itself warns of something graver—failure to heed the command could result in tragedy at numerous levels.

Flat roofs are common throughout the Middle East, for the roof supplies an extra living space in the Mediterranean climate. A parapet is the low wall that surrounds the roof and protects people from falling off. Hence, a homeowner needs to build his house with a parapet to guard against another's accidental death. The law's main purpose was to minimize the number of domestic casualties brought about by avoidable mishaps or negligence. The mention of "blood guilt" suggests that God held a homeowner guilty of unintentional homicide if an accidental death occurred on his premises due to his own failure to shape a safe living environment. In Israel, unintentional homicide was still a criminal act that could be curbed only by the offending party fleeing to a city of refuge (Ex. 21:13; Num. 35:9–15; Deut. 19:1–10). And if innocent blood is shed and the manslayer does not take the prescribed actions, "the guilt of bloodshed" will remain on the people, thus incurring Yahweh's wrath (Deut. 19:10).

2. Determine the Theological Importance of Deuteronomy 22:8

God treasures when humans display his image, and he calls his people to value this display in others. If we take human life lightly, we are declaring that we take Yahweh lightly, and we will be judged. In Deuteronomy 22:8, Yahweh graciously warns against dangers that could ultimately result in injury to another and, by this, harm to his people.

Similarly, when Jesus used a coin to highlight the way God owns every person, he declared the lasting importance of God's image in others: "Jesus said to them, 'Whose likeness and inscription is this?' They said, 'Caesar's.' Then he said to them, 'Therefore render to Caesar the things that are Caesar's, and to God the things that are God's'" (Matt. 22:20–21). God's image is on us; therefore, we owe him our lives.

Building on his value of God's image, Christ called for the application of love of neighbor in all contexts. "So whatever you wish that others would do to you, do also to them, for this is the Law and the Prophets" (Matt. 7:12). This Golden Rule is evident in our passage, and it suggests that Christ's followers today must maintain the call to love others in the most practical of ways—including how we ready our living space for family members or guests. Such a principle is reinforced in how Jesus concluded the parable of the good Samaritan. Affirming the lawyer's answer that "the one who showed mercy" was indeed the one who "proved to be a neighbor to the man who fell among the robbers," our Lord declared, "You go, and do *likewise*" (Luke 10:36–37). Through Jesus, the principles found in compassion laws are maintained with extension to other contexts. The love principle of Deuteronomy 22:8 is as follows: *God's call to love requires that I make my living environment safe, removing potential dangers and respecting those made in God's image.*

3. Summarize the Lasting Significance of Deuteronomy 22:8

All homeowners bear the responsibility to watch out for the wellbeing of everyone who comes to their home. While many climates do not allow houses with parapets, the teaching of Deuteronomy 22:8 is naturally extended to include building a fence around a swimming pool or a raised deck, placing a protective gate above a stairwell where toddlers are present, or salting a sidewalk after an ice storm. Love for neighbor is to impact even the littlest details of daily life, as we live under the supremacy of God in Christ. We love our neighbors in these small particulars because of the way God first loved us in Christ (1 John 4:11, 19). We must ever care for others' welfare, valuing God's image in them. This means that we will make our homes places where others can thrive without undue safety risks.

Case Study 2: The Law Maintained without Extension— Not Confusing Genders in Deuteronomy 22:5

Much of the world is immersed in a gender identity crisis, causing tragic brokenness in various cultures. Some of you have yourselves wrestled with gender identity or have a loved one experiencing gender identity confusion. I ache for you, and I long for you to know the healing that only Jesus can bring.

When read through the lens of Jesus, Deuteronomy 22:5 speaks to the church on this issue. As will be seen, our alignment with this law should look today much like it looked for Moses and the Israelites.[4]

A woman shall not wear a man's garment, nor shall a man put on a woman's cloak, for whoever does these things is an abomination to the LORD your God. (Deut. 22:5)

1. Establish the Original Revealed Meaning and Application of Deuteronomy 22:5

While Moses's law bears lasting import for new covenant believers (Deut. 30:8; Rom. 15:4), Moses originally wrote it to Israel, and it is within this context that our assessment must begin. We note first that the prohibition in Deuteronomy 22:5 appears less a core principle than a secondary application of a more fundamental truth. On the surface, the verse relates to what could be tagged "gender expression." However, the law assumes a more fundamental rule—that there are two biological sexes (male and female) and that what is gender normative in Yahweh's world is that one's biological sex governs both one's gender identity *and* expression. Before God pours out his wrath, he seeks to correct gender confusion and transgender identity by this text.

Deuteronomy 22:5 stands independent within its context and comes to us as two prohibitions followed by a single motivation clause. Yahweh chose to frame these prohibitions with a Hebrew negative that expresses "never": "A woman shall *never* wear a man's garment, nor shall a man *ever* put on a woman's cloak."[5] From God's perspective, there is never a permissible time for the type of cross-dressing to which this passage refers.

Digging deeper into this prohibition, we should note that the term translated "man" is *geber* ("strong man") and not the more common *'ish* ("man, husband"). Some have suggested that *geber* means "warrior" here (cf. 2 Sam. 1:27; Ezek. 32:27),[6] but this meaning is more associated with the

---

4   What follows is abridged from Jason S. DeRouchie, "Confronting the Transgender Storm: New Covenant Reflections on Deuteronomy 22:5," *JBMW* 21, no. 1 (2016): 58–69. Used with permission.

5   In Hebrew, there are two types of negative commands—immediate (with *'al* meaning "don't!") and durative (with *lo'* meaning "never!")—and Deut. 22:5 includes the durative.

6   E.g., J. G. McConville, *Deuteronomy*, ApOTC 5 (Downers Grove, IL: InterVarsity Press, 2002), 336–37.

adjective *gibbor* ("mighty one," cf. Gen. 10:8–9; Deut. 10:17). Furthermore, within the Law all other instances of *geber* simply overlap in meaning with *'ish*, showing up in contexts that distinguish the men from the young (Ex. 10:7, 11) or from women and children (12:37).[7] The clear difference between *geber* and *'ish* is that, when paralleled with "woman" (*'isha*), *'ish* can often mean "husband," whereas *geber* never does in any of its twenty-four Old Testament uses. At the very least, then, this law concerning male-female relationships is not restricted to husbands and wives and thus family law but speaks to the broader society and community. *From God's perspective, maleness and femaleness bear implications beyond the home or gathered worshiping community. They also impact daily life in society.*

The term used here for the woman's "cloak" (*simlah*) is restrictive, pointing specifically to the outer wrapper or mantle that a female would wear.[8] In contrast, the term rendered "garment" (*keli*) in relation to a man is broader and suggests any object associated with men—whether clothing (1 Sam. 21:5), vessel (1 Kings 10:21), ornament (Gen. 24:53), or piece of equipment (Num. 19:18) that was specifically associated with men.[9] This could even include weapons of war (Gen. 49:5; Deut. 1:41; Judg. 9:54), but it was in no way limited here. Within Israelite culture, therefore, certain styles of dress, ornaments, or items distinguished men and women.

Thus, two principles are foundational in this law:

- Each person needs to let gender expression align with his or her biological sex.
- Each person needs to guard against gender confusion so that one's dress will not lead others to wrongly perceive a man to be a woman or a woman to be a man.

Whether due to pagan religious activity or to a desire to engage in roles restricted to the opposite sex, such practices opposed any form of godliness.[10]

---

7 "I גֶּבֶר," *HALOT* 1:175.
8 "שִׂמְלָה," *HALOT* 3:1337.
9 "כְּלִי," *HALOT* 2:478.
10 Harry Hoffner argues that the transgender practices evidenced here were potentially connected to the pagan religious rites or magical practices of Israel's neighbors. Harry A. Hoffner Jr., "Symbols of Masculinity and Femininity: Their Use in Ancient Near Eastern Sympathetic Magic Rituals," *JBL* 85, no. 3 (1966): 326–34. While possible, nothing in Deut. 22 explicitly links the text

The fact that this type of cross-dressing is called an "abomination to the LORD" highlights the gravity of the offense and associates it not only with the crimes of idolatry (Deut. 13:14; 17:4) and witchcraft (18:12) but also with the sin of dishonest gain, which could relate at the level of criminal, civil, or family law (25:16). What is it about idolatry, witchcraft, and dishonesty that makes them abominable to Yahweh? Idolatry gives glory to someone other than him; witchcraft looks to means other than God's word to discern the future or his will; dishonest gain diminishes the value of those made in God's image. We must conclude, therefore, that something about cross-dressing and gender confusion directly counters right order in God's world.

Indeed, what makes transgenderism abominable is that it maligns humanity's ability to reflect, resemble, and represent God rightly in this world. The possibility that it is also a criminal offense suggests that the sin endangers the welfare of the entire community. The clear distinctions between men and women laid out in Genesis 1–2 and maintained throughout the Law further suggest that this law bears a symbolic element. Those born boys are to live and thrive as boys, and those born girls are to live and thrive as girls. When corrupt desires lead us to alter from this course, we must choose with Yahweh's help the path that magnifies his majesty best, and that path is defined in Deuteronomy 22:5.

As for the purpose of the law, its objective appears to have been to maintain divinely created gender distinctions at all times and contexts. The goal of this pursuit was to nurture an environment that properly displays God's supremacy and the ever present head-glory distinction (cf. 1 Cor. 11:7; Eph. 5:22–23) between God and the people he is creating for himself.

2. Determine the Theological Importance of Deuteronomy 22:5

Deuteronomy 22:5 is the fruit of this truth: Yahweh is ever passionate to preserve and display right order in his world. This is the essence of his righteousness, and maintaining gender distinctions is an important part of

to cultic ritual. So, too, P. J. Harland, "Menswear and Womenswear: A Study of Deuteronomy 22:5," *ExpTim* 110, no. 3 (1998): 74–75. For further reflections on ancient Israel's problem of cross-dressing, see Nili Sacher Fox, "Gender Transformation and Transgression: Contextualizing the Prohibition of Cross-Dressing in Deuteronomy 22:5," in *Mishneh Todah: Studies in Deuteronomy and Its Cultural Environment in Honor of Jeffrey H. Tigay*, ed. Nili Sacher Fox, David A. Glatt-Gilad, and Michael J. Williams (Winona Lake, IN: Eisenbrauns, 2009), 49–71.

this order. The stress in Genesis 1–2 on the way males and females image God and the depiction in the Law of Yahweh's relationship with Israel as a marriage push readers to view our biological sex and gender identity and expression as primariliy about God. The rest of the Old Testament highlights this parabolic purpose of sex and gender distinctions in places like Hosea 1–3 (cf. Judg. 2:16–17; Isa. 1:21; 57:3; Jer. 2:2, 20; 3:1; 3:8–11; 31:31–32). Then the same is carried into the New Testament (see Matt. 9:15; 12:38–39; 16:1–4; Mark 2:19; 8:38; Luke 5:34), most clearly where Paul portrays the church as Christ's bride (Eph. 5:22–27; cf. Rev. 19:7–9; 21:9). To the level that we flatten the inborn distinctions between maleness and femaleness we flatten the distinctions between the sovereign Savior and the saved, between the exalted and the needy, between the blameless one and the sinner. We take glory away from God and his Christ when we act as though innate distinctions between men and women are nonexistent or a matter of preference. Furthermore, we hurt the community of faith and broader society both in the way we fail to point others to gospel righteousness and in the way we open them to God's just wrath.

How does Christ's law fulfillment impact this law? The New Testament suggests that it is maintained without extension to any new parties or contexts. First, Christ and his followers continued to distinguish men from women. Indeed, Jesus perfectly exemplified maleness in the way that he deeply respected women and stood as the ultimate provider, protector, and leader in servant-hearted love. Jesus . . .

- respected his parents (Luke 2:41–52; John 2:1–11),
- had female disciples (Luke 8:1–3),
- sought to protect women from male abuses (Matt. 5:27–30, 31–32; 19:3–12; Luke 7:36–50),
- portrayed women as models of faith (Matt. 25:1–13; Mark 7:24–30; Luke 4:24–26; 11:31; 18:1–8; 21:1–4),
- extended care and healing to marginalized female sufferers (Mark 1:30–31; 5:25–34, 35–43; 7:24–30; Luke 7:11–17; 13:10–17; John 4:1–42; 7:53–8:11; 11:1–44),
- received anointing from women (Luke 7:36–50; John 12:1–8), and
- disclosed himself first to women after his resurrection (Matt. 28:9; John 20:14–18).

Christ is the substance to which all biblical symbols point, but unlike some pictures such as the temple and clean/unclean food laws, which have reached their terminus in Christ's first appearing, the distinction between males and females will continue at least to the consummation (as is clear in texts like Eph. 5:22–33 and 1 Tim. 3:4–5). And even then, while earthly marriage will be no more (the picture being overcome by the reality, Matt. 22:30), there is no reason to think that the distinction between men and women, heads and their glory (1 Cor. 11:7), within the community of faith will alter in the new heavens and earth (cf. Rev. 21:24, where "kings" are distinguished). Maleness and femaleness will most likely provide an eternal reminder of God's order, wherein the Father and the Son operate supremely over all things.

Along with this, new covenant teaching maintains role distinctions between men and women, most explicitly in its instructions to husbands and wives (e.g., Eph. 5:22–32; 1 Pet. 3:1–7) and to local churches regarding their corporate worship, teaching, and leadership (1 Cor. 11:1–16; 14:33–35; 1 Tim. 2–3; Titus 1:5–16). It also calls for men to live as men, women to live as women, and for the young to be trained to live out the gender role related to their God-given sex (Titus 2:2–6). Paul exhorted Timothy to respect and encourage older men as fathers, younger men as brothers, older women as mothers, and younger women as sisters, in all purity (1 Tim. 5:1–2). All this instruction assumes that we can rightly identify those who are men and those who are women.

Building off the principle that every Old Testament commandment is summarized in the call to love our neighbor (Rom. 13:8, 10), in Deuteronomy 22:5, *God's call to love requires that people maintain a gender identity that aligns with their biological sex and express this in a way that never leads to gender confusion in the eyes of others.* We should always be able to distinguish boys as boys and girls as girls. When our biological sex aligns with our gender identity and our gender expression, we show our love for both God and our neighbor.

3. Summarize the Lasting Significance of Deuteronomy 22:5

Deuteronomy 22:5 was not originally given to the church, but it contains a portrait of God and a principle of love that can guide the church today when read through the finished work of Christ. In Jesus we have a perfect pattern for maleness in relation to femaleness. With this, in Jesus we are supplied unmatched power for our pursuit of rightly ordered living. The power comes through the pardon Jesus secured at the cross and the promises that he purchased at the cross. The gender identity crisis that we are facing today can only be confronted rightly in the context of past and future grace.

We have already noted that God's passion for right order has not changed in the new covenant, for it is part of his very being. With this, the physical and role distinctions between men and women have not changed this side of the cross. God's righteousness is unswerving, and we must ever be concerned to display the magnificence of Christ's love for his church in every situation of life.

This affirmed, Deuteronomy 22:5 becomes instructive for the church in helping us recognize the appropriate path for gender expression and the sinfulness of gender confusion, which includes cross-dressing and transgender practice. Stores in the West still distinguish men's and women's clothing, and there are certainly styles that are more masculine or more feminine.[11] As believers, we should be among those who celebrate men being masculine and women being feminine, even in the ways we dress. Having said that, cross-dressing is often culturally dependent. For example, in contemporary Western culture, women can wear slacks and collared shirts without the danger of anyone questioning their femaleness. What was at stake in Moses's law was gender confusion, and it is from this perspective that our outward apparel matters.[12]

---

11 As I finalize this material in 2022, the LGBTQ+ movement annually promotes a global "pride month," and a number of department stores sell what they term transgender clothing. "God opposes the proud" (1 Pet 5:5), and these abominations mock the common grace Yahweh bestows on creation through the Noahic covenant (Gen. 8:20–22; 9:12–17). These ungodly and unrighteous ones "suppress the truth" of "God's righteous decree that those who practice such things deserve to die" (Rom. 1:18, 32), and their present rebellion against the living God will result in their ruin (John 5:28–29; 1 Cor. 6:9–10; Gal. 5:19–21). May we remember the command of Christ: "Love your enemies and pray for those who persecute you, so that you may be sons of your Father who is in heaven. For he makes his sun rise on the evil and on the good, and sends rain on the just and on the unjust" (Matt. 5:44–45).

12 In the ancient Roman culture of the New Testament, women wore head coverings as a sign of marriage, whereas the only males who wore head coverings were the elite pagan priests who covered their heads with their togas when officiating in religious cults. See David W. J. Gill, "1 Corinthians," in *Romans to Philemon*, vol. 3 of *Zondervan Illustrated Bible Backgrounds Commentary: New Testament* (Grand Rapids, MI: Zondervan Academic, 2002), 155–58. Within this worldly context, a Christian man who covered his head in the church's public worship (thus signaling that he bore a socially elite status within the city) dishonored Christ as his authority, and a wife who uncovered her head dishonored her husband as her authority (1 Cor. 11:3–10).

Because the law in Deuteronomy 22:5 is focused on adults and because it addresses gender *confusion*, the law itself would not directly dissuade a young girl from dressing up with a mustache in a kids' play or a little boy putting on a girl's dress after ransacking the dress-up box. No one observing such child's play would be confused regarding the child's gender. Nevertheless, we must be cautious here, because we are always instilling into our children what is appropriate, and we are now living in a society that acts as though gender is a matter of choice rather than God's design through creation. This perspective is abominable, and Deuteronomy 22:5 speaks directly against it.

Furthermore, in arguing that there are some for whom "it is better not to marry" (Matt. 19:10), Jesus added, "There are eunuchs who have been so from birth, and there are eunuchs who have been made eunuchs by men, and there are eunuchs who have made themselves eunuchs for the sake of the kingdom of heaven" (Matt. 19:12). Our Lord speaks of three groups for whom celibacy is an acceptable alternative to marriage: (1) those with a birth defect, (2) those who have been castrated, and (3) those who "for the sake of the kingdom" have chosen a life of abstinence from sexual intercourse. In a world filled with gender dysphoria that includes many who have attempted to "transition" in ways that include "sex reassignment surgery,"[13] Christ's church must be ready to love those whose past has made them "eunuchs" and to guide them in living "for the sake of the kingdom" in alignment with the sexual identity God gave them at conception.

In closing, I call the church to be mindful of those broken in this gender identity crisis and to care deeply for the violators and the violated. One's self-identity will be forever maligned so long as we are only looking at a mirror and not also into the face of Jesus Christ. We need to help those struggling with transgender identity to find a new identity in Christ, and we need to help those who have been hurt by others to find the healing and relief that only Jesus brings. He alone is the Savior. He alone is the healer.[14]

While cultural perspectives may change, Paul affirms the lasting principle that men should look like men and women should look like women within any given culture (1 Cor. 11:14). The stated, biblical principles of modesty (1 Cor. 12:22–24; 1 Tim. 2:9) and human dignity (Prov. 31:25; Matt. 10:31; 12:12; Eph. 5:33) must trump any cultural bias.

13 Also called "gender confirmation surgery."

14 For more on this issue of maleness and femaleness in God's world, see John Piper and Wayne Grudem, eds., *Recovering Biblical Manhood and Womanhood: A Response to Evangelical Feminism* (Wheaton, IL: Crossway, 1991); John Piper, *What's the Difference? Manhood and Woman-*

Review and Reflection

1. How does one establish a given old covenant law's original revealed meaning and application?

2. Define the five types of Old Testament laws by content, giving at least one example of each.

3. What steps are necessary to determine an old covenant law's theological importance?

4. As a case study, consider the lasting significance of the law against tattoos in Leviticus 19:28. Why did Moses originally write it? What does it teach us about God, and what is the love principle behind it? Working through a salvation-historical lens that has Jesus at the center, how may a Christian rightly apply such a law in our present twenty-first century context?[15]

5. Using the same principles used in the case study on Deuteronomy 22:8, how may a Christian apply Deuteronomy 22:1–3 or 22:4 in a comparable way? Be sure to walk through each of the three steps for applying Old Testament law.

6. What more "fundamental rule" does the prohibition in Deuteronomy 22:5 appear to assume, and what two principles appear to be at stake in the law?

7. What was the original purpose of the law in Deuteronomy 22:5?

8. How would you summarize the theological importance of Deuteronomy 22:5, including its love principle?

9. Summarize the lasting significance of the prohibition of Deuteronomy 22:5 for today.

10. What was the greatest insight you gained in reading this chapter? What is your greatest takeaway?

---

hood Defined according to the Bible (Wheaton, IL Crossway, 2009); Owen Strachan and Gavin Peacock, *The Grand Design: Male and Female He Made Them* (Ross-shire, Scotland: Christian Focus, 2016). For more on the transgender issue itself and the modern notion of choosing gender identity, see Ryan T. Anderson, *When Harry Became Sally: Responding to the Transgender Moment* (New York: Encounter Books, 2018); Carl R. Trueman, *The Rise and Triumph of the Modern Self: Cultural Amnesia, Expressive Individualism, and the Road to Sexual Revolution* (Wheaton, IL: Crossway, 2020); Owen Strachan and Gavin Peacock, *What Does the Bible Teach about Transgenderism?* (Ross-shire, Scotland: Christian Focus, 2020).

15 For a brief but helpful wrestling with this question, see Andrew David Naselli and J. D. Crowley, *Conscience: What It Is, How to Train It, and Loving Those Who Differ* (Wheaton, IL: Crossway, 2016), 73–75. See also John Piper, "Tattoos in Biblical Perspective," Desiring God, December 20, 2013, https://www.desiringgod.org/; John Piper, "Six Reasons to Skip Tattoos," Desiring God, December 20, 2013, https://www.desiringgod.org/.

13

When Jesus Transforms
or Annuls the Law

Coastlands wait for his law.

ISAIAH 42:4

THE PREVIOUS CHAPTER provided two examples of how Moses's law can apply to new covenant members through Christ and for Christ. There we saw that Christ's fulfilling work can maintain the law with or without extension. This chapter considers how Christ's coming transforms (Sabbath) or annuls (food laws) old covenant instruction.

Case Study 3: The Law Transformed—
Sabbath Keeping in Deuteronomy 5:12–15

Our first example in this chapter of applying old covenant law this side of the cross relates to the Sabbath command and its relationship to Sunday worship. This is a disputable matter among Christians that we must not allow to separate us, even while we seek to become increasingly strong in faith with consciences that are calibrated to the truth of Scripture (Rom. 14:1–15:7, esp. 14:5).[1] Considering this old covenant law through Christ

---

1 Disputable matters are issues not directly related to the gospel that Scripture "neither required of Christians nor prohibited to them." Douglas Moo, *The Letter to the Romans*, 2nd ed., NICNT (Grand Rapids, MI: Eerdmans, 2018), 898. For a helpful discussion of how fellow Christians should relate when their consciences disagree about disputable matters, see Andrew David

and for Christ will show us how important it is to consider Christ's law fulfillment, which in this instance fully transforms the law and guides those strong in faith in the path of love:

> Observe the Sabbath day, to keep it holy, as the LORD your God commanded you. Six days you shall labor and do all your work, but the seventh day is a Sabbath to the LORD your God. On it you shall not do any work, you or your son or your daughter or your male servant or your female servant, or your ox or your donkey or any of your livestock, or the sojourner who is within your gates, that your male servant and your female servant may rest as well as you. You shall remember that you were a slave in the land of Egypt, and the LORD your God brought you out from there with a mighty hand and an outstretched arm. Therefore the LORD your God commanded you to keep the Sabbath day. (Deut. 5:12–15)

1. Establish the Original Revealed Meaning and Application of Deuteronomy 5:12–15

In Deuteronomy's version of the Ten Commandments, features in the text create five groupings of long and short commands that together highlight the centrality of the Sabbath within the old covenant (see table 13.1).[2]

Naselli and J. D. Crowley, *Conscience: What It Is, How to Train It, and Loving Those Who Differ* (Wheaton, IL: Crossway, 2016), 84–117.

2 Two features indicate that Deut. 5:6–10 form a unit: (1) Yahweh uses first-person speech in 5:6–10, whereas 5:11–21 portray him in third person. (2) The "gods" of 5:7 provides the most natural antecedent to the third-person masculine plural pronouns in 5:9 ("you shall not bow down to *them* or serve *them*"). Furthermore, unlike the version of the Ten Commandments in Ex. 20, Deuteronomy's final prohibitions (from murder through coveting) are all joined by the connector *waw* ("and"), creating a unit from 5:17–21. For an overview of the discourse features, see Jason S. DeRouchie, "Counting the Ten: An Investigation into the Numbering of the Decalogue," in *For Our Good Always: Studies on the Message and Influence of Deuteronomy in Honor of Daniel I. Block*, ed. Jason S. DeRouchie, Jason Gile, and Kenneth J. Turner (Winona Lake, IN: Eisenbrauns, 2013), 93–125. Norbert Lohfink recognizes the centrality of the Sabbath in Deuteronomy's Ten Commandments, but his approach to the Decalogue as a whole follows critical presuppositions that do not allow the biblical text's own witness to govern its interpretation. See Norbert Lohfink, "The Decalogue in Deuteronomy 5," in *Theology of the Pentateuch: Themes of the Priestly Narrative and Deuteronomy*, trans. Linda M. Maloney (Edinburgh: T&T Clark, 1994), 257.

Table 13.1   The centrality of the Sabbath in the Ten Commandments

Command 1	No other gods	Deut. 5:6–10	Command grouping 1: Long
Command 2	Bear Yahweh's name	Deut. 5:11	Command grouping 2: Short
Command 3	Observe the Sabbath	Deut. 5:12–15	Command grouping 3: Long
Command 4	Honor parents	Deut. 5:16	Command grouping 4: Short
Commands 5–10	Love neighbor	Deut. 5:17–21	Command grouping 5: Long

Everything that was to occur in Israel's relationship with Yahweh was to happen within the boundaries of their loving Yahweh ("no other gods") and valuing his image in others ("love neighbor"). And at the center of their identity was the Sabbath, which stood as the old covenant's "sign" (*'ot*) (Ex. 31:13, 17). Michael Fox notes how "signs" in the Old Testament functioned in one of three ways:

1. *Proof signs* demonstrated the truth of something (e.g., Isa. 38:7–8).
2. *Symbol signs* represented a future reality by virtue of resemblance or conventional association (e.g., Ezek. 4:1–3).
3. *Cognition signs* aroused knowledge of something by (a) identifying (e.g., Josh. 2:12–13) or (b) reminding (Ex. 13:9).[3]

---

3 Michael V. Fox, "The Sign of the Covenant: Circumcision in the Light of Priestly *'ōt* Etiologies," *RB* 81, no. 4 (1974): 562–63.

The Sabbath served first as a cognition sign and then as a symbol sign, and Christ's coming affects this dual role.

For Israel, Sabbath was an identity marker that distinguished them from the surrounding nations and reminded them of their purpose. There is no evidence that any other ancient peoples revered one day of the week more than others, so Sabbath keeping for Israel set them apart "to the LORD" (Deut. 5:14). More than is apparent in Exodus 20, the Sabbath law in Deuteronomy 5 called household heads to ensure that the same rest they enjoyed one day a week be extended to every household member (including slaves) (Deut. 5:14; cf. Ex. 23:12). As motivation for obedience, Yahweh urged them to "remember" their past hardship as slaves in Egypt (Deut. 5:15). The Sabbath, therefore, would serve as an outward symbol of a redeemed life by providing both rest and joy.

Hence, we see one way that Yahweh used the sign of the Sabbath to help Israel "know that I, the LORD, sanctify you" (Ex. 31:13; cf. 31:17). Sabbath keeping nurtured humility and empowered people to follow God in seeking the welfare of others. Furthermore, by not working one day a week, Israel would be forced to remember that Yahweh supplies their daily bread (Ex. 16:4–5, 23–26). As Israel observed the Sabbath "to the LORD" their God (Ex. 20:10; Deut. 5:14), they would increasingly become a "holy nation" and by this magnify Yahweh's majesty to their neighbors (Ex. 19:5–6).

Significantly, whereas Deuteronomy links the Sabbath law to the exodus (Deut. 5:15), the Exodus version explicitly says the reason for the Sabbath is because "in six days the LORD made heaven and earth, the sea, and all that is in them, and rested on the seventh day" (Ex. 20:11; cf. 31:17). The Sabbath is, therefore, explicitly connected with the two greatest Old Testament initiatory acts: God's creation of the world and his creation/redemption of a people for himself.

For Yahweh, the culmination of the creation week was not a rest of weariness but of refreshing sovereignty, wherein the great King, having established the sacred space of his kingdom, sat enthroned and enjoyed peace with all he had made (Gen. 2:1–3; Ex. 31:17; cf. Ps. 132:7–8, 13–14). While mankind's rebellion at the fall did not remove God's right and authority over all things, it did alter the universe's state of peace and rest. Thus, within the Law, the 6 + 1 pattern of creation days is used not simply as a portrait of what was but as a symbol of what should be. As the sign of the Mosaic covenant (Ex. 31:13, 17), Israel's weekly Sabbath was to remind them of their mission to see right order reestablished on a global scale. Their calling as a people was to honor God among the nations (Ex. 19:4–6; Deut. 4:5–8; 26:18–19) and to hope in their royal representative (Jesus Christ) who would operate as the instrument of curse reversal and global blessing (Gen. 22:17–18; 26:4; cf. Acts 3:25–26; Gal. 3:13–14, 16, 29).

Israel's pattern of Sabbath keeping was to symbolically identify them as and to remind them of their calling as the agent through whom God's sovereignty would be celebrated once again throughout the world (ultimately through their Messiah). It is in this context that Moses stressed in the Ten Commandments that "the seventh day is a Sabbath *to the Lord*" (Deut. 5:14); it was ultimately kept to see him exalted over all things. For Israel, then, the Sabbath symbolically portrayed a future reality in which both Israel and the world were to hope.

The entire makeup and purpose of the old covenant was eschatologically symbolized in the Sabbath, and its importance is highlighted by the fact that breaking it was a criminal offense deserving of death (Num. 15:32–36). The weekly, goal-oriented, 6 + 1 rhythm of life impacted the entire community for good, yet failure would negatively impact them and ultimately the world (cf. Rom. 3:19–20). While Sabbath was part of criminal law, its symbolism (like that of the dietary laws addressed in the next case study) suggests that it was also ceremonial law.

2. Determine the Theological Importance of Deuteronomy 5:12–15

The Sabbath command teaches us many things about God: (1) Yahweh is one who always watches out for the marginalized. He shows no partiality and emphasizes the need for regular rest for household heads in his covenant people and those under their care. (2) Yahweh is a God who sanctifies by providing means in his people's daily lives to test their trust and to develop their dependence. The weekly Sabbath did this for Israel. (3) Yahweh is passionate to restore and display right order in his world, wherein he is exalted as sovereign over all things. He created Israel for the sake of reconciling the world (cf. Gen. 12:3; 22:17–18), and Israel's weekly Sabbath was to ever remind them of their purpose of seeing the ultimate Sabbath restored on a global scale. This is what it means that the Sabbath was kept "to the Lord" (Deut. 5:14).

As we consider the implications of how Christ fulfills the Sabbath, we recall that Jesus saw himself as establishing God's kingdom and as the source of mankind's ultimate rest.

> All things have been handed over to me by my Father. . . . Come to me, all who labor and are heavy laden, and I will give you rest. Take my yoke upon you, and learn from me, for I am gentle and lowly in heart, and you will find rest for your souls. For my yoke is easy, and my burden is light. (Matt. 11:27–30)

Significantly, directly after this assertion, Matthew includes the story of Jesus allowing his disciples to pluck heads of grain on the Sabbath and then declaring himself both "greater than the temple" and "lord of the Sabbath" (Matt. 12:6, 8). Such a testimony was an overflow of the fact that not only was "the kingdom of heaven . . . at hand" (Matt. 10:7) but also "the kingdom of God has come upon you" (Matt. 12:28; cf. Luke 17:21).

Against the views of some, the divine Sabbath of the original creation week did not continue after the fall. As Jesus asserted directly after healing a lame man on the Sabbath, "My Father is working until now, and I am working" (John 5:17). Jesus's redeeming work brought Israel's global Sabbath mission to fulfillment. He is the one through whom the world is blessed (Gen. 22:17–18; Acts 3:25–26; Gal. 3:8, 14), and by his victorious resurrection he inaugurated the end-times Sabbath rest as a culmination of his new creational work. Jesus stands superior to Moses (Heb. 3:1–6), and those of us in him have already entered rest, even though we await its full consummation (Heb. 4:3–10).

As with all Moses's laws, a love principle stands behind the Sabbath command in Deuteronomy 5:12–15: *God's call to love required carrying out the 6 + 1 pattern of life as a witness to the kingdom hope of ultimate rest.* How this principle relates to Christians today will now be considered.

3. Summarize the Lasting Significance of Deuteronomy 5:12–15

Until the final judgment, God will maintain his commitment to his kingdom community, even those the world considers "the least." As believers look out for the marginalized among the people of God, we serve King Jesus (Matt. 25:31–40). This is a sustained application of the old covenant Sabbath command this side of the cross.

Furthermore, the old covenant command to keep the Sabbath teaches us of our own human need to rest, both to restore energy and to nurture increased dependence on God.

It is in vain that you rise up early
> and go late to rest,
eating the bread of anxious toil;
> for he gives to his beloved sleep. (Ps. 127:2)

Through our rest, God graciously counters human tendencies toward workaholism and nurtures deeper levels of trust in him, by which we can enjoy more grace (James 4:6; 1 Pet. 5:5). These general applications of the Sabbath command continue today.

Yet is there a place for the Sabbath itself in the church's life? As the sign of the old covenant, the Sabbath was by nature teleological, pointing toward a goal. It stood at the end of every Israelite's week and symbolized sovereign rest as life's aim. In contrast, for believers, Christ has already inaugurated the fulfillment of God's sovereign rest, as the "shadow" now finds its "substance" in Christ (Col. 2:16–17). As the royal representative Israelite, Jesus fulfills Israel's Sabbath-generating mission, and through him Yahweh's kingdom authority is once again realized on a global scale, moving out through the church from Jerusalem to Judea and Samaria to the ends of the earth (Acts 1:8).

Jesus declared, "All authority in heaven and on earth has been given to me" (Matt. 28:18). We must affirm that God has already put "everything in subjection to him," leaving "nothing outside his control," though "we do not yet see everything in subjection to him" (Heb. 2:8; cf. 1 Cor. 15:25–28). In this church age, believers are enjoying Sabbath rest under Christ's lordship seven days a week (Matt. 11:28–29; Heb. 4:8–11; cf. Acts 2:34–36; Rom. 15:5–6). Because we already "share in Christ" (Heb. 3:14), we have already entered the Sabbath rest he secures (Heb. 4:9–10). We are no longer striving to confirm our eternal destiny but are resting, certain that what Christ has already accomplished will be revealed fully at the future consummation.

In the new covenant there is not one specific day as opposed to others that marks the Sabbath (cf. Rom. 14:5–6; Gal. 4:9–10; Col. 2:16–17). Christ's resurrection initiates an eschatological shift from old creation to new (2 Cor. 5:17; Gal. 6:15), from Sabbath anticipation to Sabbath realization. Now, all week long, those in Christ enjoy Sabbath rest fully, though not finally.

Like the early church, our corporate worship follows a 1 + 6 rather than 6 + 1 pattern, gathering on the week's first day, not the last (Acts 20:7; 1 Cor. 16:2). Why? All the Gospel writers highlight that Jesus rose on Sunday (Matt. 28:1; Mark 16:2, 9; Luke 24:1; John 20:1), and by this they identify that Israel's hope of seeing the ultimate Sabbath restored was accomplished on that resurrection Lord's day (Rev. 1:10). On that first day of the week, light dawned into darkness, God initiated new creation, and God's kingdom in Christ was realized in a more substantive way than ever before. Sunday worship reflects that inaugurated nature of rest that we relish the remaining part of the week. It also nurtures within us hope for the day when our faith will become sight (2 Cor. 5:7) and when the rest we already taste will be completed through the removal of all evil, pain, and death at the glimpse of our Savior's face (Rev. 21:4; 22:3). As we presently delight in Sabbath rest every day of the week, we magnify Christ's curse-overcoming work, even as we continue to pray, "Your kingdom come . . . on earth as it is in heaven" (Matt. 6:10).

In the end, the old covenant call to keep the Sabbath establishes a sustained principle of rest for believers—resting so that we can run. We need to take breaks to refuel for our divine service, and sleep serves as a means of God's grace to nurture sustained surrender in our souls (Ps. 127:2). Nevertheless, in Christ there is no single day more important than another (Rom. 14:5–6; Col. 2:16–17; cf. Gal. 4:9–10), and God-dependent work on any day of the week is sanctified to the Lord. We must maintain a pattern of corporate worship (Heb. 10:25), and Sunday is a natural time for this (Acts 20:7; 1 Cor. 16:2) due to its end-times significance of being the day on which God ignited his new creation kingdom (Acts 26:23; Rom. 6:4; 1 Cor. 15:20, 23; 2 Cor. 5:17; 2 Thess. 2:13; Rev. 14:4). But corporate worship on another day of the week is not sin, nor is it necessarily wrong to paint your house, weed your garden, study for an exam, or engage in sports on a Sunday—so long as you work hard, as on every other day, in a way that never replaces grace (1 Cor. 15:10; Phil. 2:12–13; Col. 1:29; 3:17, 23). In all times and ways, we must live and labor by faith in the one from whom, through whom, and to whom are all things (Rom. 11:36) so that "in everything God may be glorified through Jesus Christ" (1 Pet. 4:11).[4]

Case Study 4: The Law Annulled—Restricting the Diet in Leviticus 20:25–26

This final illustration of applying Old Testament law to Christians addresses a command that Christ's coming annuls, yet in a way that we can still find significant Godward benefit from the law itself while celebrating the progressions in salvation history.

> You shall therefore separate the clean beast from the unclean, and the unclean bird from the clean. You shall not make yourselves detestable by beast or by bird or by anything with which the ground crawls, which I have set apart for you to hold unclean. You shall be holy to me, for I the LORD am holy and have separated you from the peoples, that you should be mine. (Lev. 20:25–26)

1. Establish the Original Revealed Meaning and Application of Leviticus 20:25–26

Distinguishing between "the holy and the common, and between the unclean and the clean" was vital within Israel's religious life (Lev. 10:10; cf. 11:46–47; 20:25–26). Yahweh's holiness is the reality and value of his divine fullness—as expressed in his self-sustainability, his non-dependence (or absoluteness) and uniqueness (or sole-ness), and his excellence and worth—and the beautiful harmony of all his acts with that fullness. Holiness is the very essence of what God is,[5] and Yahweh called his people to display the glories of his fullness to the world for his sake. "You shall be holy to me, for I the LORD am holy and have separated you from the peoples, that you should be mine" (Lev. 20:26).

---

4 For more on this approach to the Sabbath command, see Tom Wells and Fred G. Zaspel, *New Covenant Theology: Description, Definition, Defense* (Frederick, MD: New Covenant Media, 2002), 215–36; Thomas R. Schreiner, "Good-Bye and Hello: The Sabbath Command for New Covenant Believers," in *Progressive Covenantalism: Charting a Course between Dispensational and Covenant Theologies*, ed. Stephen J. Wellum and Brent E. Parker (Nashville: B&H Academic, 2016), 159–88.

5 See Jackie A. Naudé, "קדש," *NIDOTTE* 3:877–87; John E. Hartley, "Holy and Holiness, Clean and Unclean," *DOTP* 420.

THE HOLINESS CONTINUUM

Within the old covenant, holy and common related to the *state* or *status* of a person, object, space, or time in relation to Yahweh. Holiness is associated with the divine realm; everything not holy was common. Similarly, unclean and clean were distinct *conditions* associated with the ritual or moral standing of peoples, animals, and spaces. What was clean could be either holy or common, and what was common could be either clean or unclean. (In fig. 13.1, adjoining boxes represent these relationships.) However, what was holy was never to encounter what was unclean (i.e., contamination) or to be treated as if it were unclean (i.e, desecration). (In fig. 13.1, their boxes do not touch.)[6]

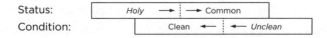

Figure 13.1   The holiness continuum

Holiness and uncleanness were also dynamic, in that each sought to influence and overcome its parallel state or condition. (Figure 13.1 highlights this by the dotted lines, directional arrows, and italic font.) However, the common and clean were static, unable to transfer their state or condition, and they were only understood in relation to their partner: cleanness was the absence of uncleanness, and commonness was the absence of holiness.

Uncleanness itself was a substandard condition acquired by bodily process or sin; it represented death or that which was abnormal or out of order.[7] Ritual (or tolerated) uncleanness resulted in exile from the community until purification (e.g., menstrual blood, bodily emissions, leprous or "dead looking" skin, contact with a corpse; see Lev. 11–15). Prohibited uncleanness (moral sin) resulted in exile and likely death; it could only

---

6   For this basic understanding of the holiness continuum in Leviticus, see Hartley, "Holy and Holiness, Clean and Unclean," *DOTP* 420–31; Jacob Milgrom, "Holy, Holiness, OT," *NIDB* 2:850–58; Richard E. Averbeck, "Leviticus," in *NIV Biblical Theology Study Bible*, ed. D. A. Carson (Grand Rapids, MI: Zondervan, 2018), 173–75. For a less convincing proposal, see Gordon J. Wenham, *The Book of Leviticus*, NICOT (Grand Rapids, MI: Eerdmans, 1979), 26.

7   Jacob Milgrom, *Leviticus 1–16: A New Translation with Introduction and Commentary*, AB (New Haven, CT: Yale University Press, 1991), 46–47; Milgrom, "Holy, Holiness, OT," 2:855–56.

potentially be remedied through repentance and substitutionary sacrifice (e.g., incest, adultery, idolatry, witchcraft; see Lev. 18, 20).

EATING ONLY WHAT IS CLEAN

With respect to Leviticus 20:25–26, what was it about certain animals that made their consumption unlawful? Scholars have offered different answers,[8] but the best response is that all unclean animals symbolically portray death through some association with the God-hostility or curse of the serpent in Genesis 3.[9]

The first explicit distinction between clean and unclean animals occurs in the narrative of Noah's flood, when Yahweh directed Noah to take "seven pairs of all clean animals, the male and his mate, and a pair of the animals that are not clean, the male and his mate, and seven pairs of the birds of the heavens also, male and female, to keep their offspring alive on the face of all the earth" (Gen. 7:2–3; cf. 7:8). Noah then used "some of every clean animal and some of every clean bird" when he offered burnt offerings to the Lord following the deluge (Gen. 8:20). Significantly, Yahweh gives no clear instruction in the account regarding the clean/unclean distinction. Noah appears to have already been aware of this dichotomy, and Moses assumes that readers of the Law will make the necessary connections. Prior to the flood story, the fall narrative of Genesis 3 is the only place where God forbids the eating of certain things (i.e., the tree of the knowledge pertaining to good and evil) and where the text associates an animal with evil (i.e., the serpent), so the reader is pushed back there to find answers.

When related to Genesis 3 and the Bible's broader portrait of evil, the division between clean and unclean animals is most naturally understood to be a result of the Adamic curse (see Gen. 3:14). The serpent was "more crafty than any other beast of the field" (Gen. 3:1), and by urging the woman

---

8 For a survey, see Hartley, "Holy and Holiness, Clean and Unclean," *DOTP* 428–29; cf. Walter Houston, *Purity and Monotheism: Clean and Unclean Animals in Biblical Law*, JSOTSup 140 (Sheffield: Sheffield Academic, 1993), 68–123.

9 Jacob Milgrom does not make this point, but he does suggest that the underlying principle between clean and unclean was the life-death nexus, wherein clean is connected to life, and unclean to death. Milgrom, *Leviticus 1–16*, 1001–3. Milgrom sees a level of randomness in the distinction between clean and unclean beasts, but he notes that Scripture promotes reverence for blood and life by limiting Israel's flesh intake to a minimal number of animals—herbivores from domesticated cattle and some wild game, fish, birds, and locusts.

to eat what God forbade, he deceived her into reversing right order and moving humanity from life to death (2:17; 3:1–7). As a result, God cursed him "above all livestock and above all beasts of the field" (Gen. 3:14). Most likely, the ancients growing up outside the garden considered animals to be unclean that most closely (1) resembled the serpent's murderous activity, (2) related to his attempt to move creation from order to chaos, or (3) recalled Yahweh's punishment against him. From this framework, Moses labeled the following groups of creatures "unclean":

1. those beasts that are predatory in nature—those with a will to kill and who, by this, image the serpent's "craftiness" (see John 8:44);
2. those animals ill-equipped to stand against the realm of chaos, death, and evil (i.e., the sea) (see Ps. 74:12–17; Isa. 51:9–10); and
3. those creatures most identified with the serpent's dust-eating, death-culminating curse that would be bottom-feeders (the realm of dust) and those linked in any way to the realms of death and waste (see Pss. 7:5; 22:29; 30:9; 72:9).

Additional help may be found in Leviticus. Leviticus 11 distinguishes the land, water, and air animals. Not all the associations with Genesis 3 are easy to assess, but a general pattern does emerge. Naturally, we must read between the lines, but this schema is more biblically grounded than alternative proposals that scholars have suggested.

Among the terrestrial creatures, the clean include those that are both split-hooved and cud-chewing (Lev. 11:2–8). Hooved animals are ungulates, animals that use the tip of their toe (or hoof) to support the weight of their bodies. They thus touch as little of the dust as possible, their weight resting on the hard or rubbery sole and a hard wall formed by a thick nail rolled around the tip of the toe (double protection from the cursed dust). Clean animals also had to be cud-chewing. That is, they were ruminants—herbivores who spend extra time "ruminating" (or meditating) on the food that God supplies. No clean land animal was a predator. The unclean land animals are those that do not share the above features. They were animals with paws (Lev. 11:27)—walking directly on the ground with no "protection" from the dust. They were also all the swarming creatures that surround and infest (Lev. 11:29–31) or that have multiple legs and crawl on their bellies in the dust (11:41–43).

We can best assess the water creatures when we recognize that Scripture often portrays the sea as the realm of chaos and death, evil and punishment.[10] Reflecting on creation, the psalmist notes how the waters "fled" at Yahweh's rebuke so that the mountains could rise (Ps. 104:7; cf. Gen. 1:9; 8:1, 5). The evil nations roar like the sea (Isa. 27:12–13; Jer. 6:23), and their beastly representatives rise from the sea (Dan. 7:3; Rev. 13:1). Yet as Yahweh did to the serpentine powers at the sea of the exodus (Ex. 15:9–10; Ps. 74:12–17; Isa. 51:9–10), so he will defeat both the serpent that is in the sea (Isa. 27:1) and the world's controlling system that is associated with it (Rev. 18:21). Scripture portrays the result symbolically both as a calm sea (Rev. 4:6; 15:2) and as if the sea were no more (Rev. 21:10). Growing out of such a perspective, the water creatures Moses designates as clean were those that were in some ways protected from this realm of death—those with fins that could control themselves by propelling or gaining balance against chaotic currents and waves, and those with scales that were shielded or guarded from attack or external influence (Lev. 11:9–12).[11] The unclean water creatures were those that lacked this type of stability or protection. These features were also missing from Adam's leadership in the garden, which likely provided the theological context for diserning which sea creatures were unclean.

Finally, Leviticus lists non-permitted birds and insects but gives no criteria for clean flying animals (Lev. 11:13–23). Like hooved creatures, bugs that hop have less contact with the dust and are clean; indeed, their action may even portray the crushing of Satan and the curse's end (Gen. 3:15; Rom. 16:20; cf. Gal. 3:13). In contrast, all birds of prey that thrive on consuming flesh are unclean, as are all winged insects that do not hop on the ground but rest there.

CONCLUSION

Before the fall, God prohibited the eating of a certain food (i.e., the tree of the knowledge of good and evil) to supply a context for mankind to mature in wisdom (Gen. 2:17; cf. 3:5). The first couple failed to obey, still gaining

---

10 See Tremper Longman III and Daniel G. Reid, *God Is a Warrior*, SOTBT (Grand Rapids, MI: Zondervan, 1995), 74–78, 84–88, 114–16; Michael A. Grisanti, "יָם (*yām*)," *NIDOTTE* 2:453–58.

11 I thank my doctoral fellow Brian Verrett for this insight.

knowledge of good and evil but by the wrong means (Gen. 3:22). The result was that God cursed the world and, with this, marked certain creatures as unclean (Gen. 7:2–3). Originally, the unclean/clean distinction appears to have only guided which animals could be sacrificed (Gen. 8:20; cf. 4:4), for after the flood Yahweh declared, "*Every* moving thing that lives shall be food for you," so long as they didn't eat the blood (Gen. 9:3–4; cf. 1:30; Lev. 17:11, 14). However, as part of distinguishing his old covenant people from the nations (Lev. 20:25–26), Yahweh forbade Israel from eating unclean animals (Lev. 11:1–47; Deut. 14:3–20).

Unclean creatures were those characterized by some commonality with the serpent's death-causing activities or curse. Because Israel's pagan neighbors were part of the serpent's offspring and represented the chaos, disorder, and death associated with him (see Gen. 3:15 and the discussion in chap. 6 above), Israel's perspective of unclean animals was to parallel God's perspective of the nations. Thus, Yahweh's prohibition of eating unclean animals symbolically distinguished Israel from their neighbors. It also set them up to point the world to Yahweh's uniqueness (Ex. 19:5–6; Deut. 4:5–8) as the only Savior who could overcome curse with blessing through his coming messianic deliverer (Gen. 12:3; 22:18).

2. Determine the Theological Importance of Leviticus 20:25–26

God is holy, and eveyone in the world should see and celebrate this. John Hartley notes that, within the old covenant, the rules dealing with clean and unclean animals "made the Israelites conscious at every meal that they were to order their lives to honor the holy God with whom they were in covenant."[12] Thus, for example, the ancient charge to not eat pork served to heighten awe of Yahweh's nature and worth and to distinguish God's people from those outside the covenant. We are told that pig's flesh was unclean because these animals do not chew their cud (Lev. 11:7–8). Some propose that not chewing the cud symbolized a failure to appreciate God's provision[13]—much like Adam and Eve failed to value God's provision in the

---

12 Hartley, "Holy and Holiness, Clean and Unclean," *DOTP* 429. The truth of this statement is emphasized by the fact that Scripture three times associates food regulations with the call to be holy because God is holy (Lev. 11:44–45; 20:25–26; Deut. 14:21; cf. Ex. 22:31).

13 Mary Douglas, *Purity and Danger: An Analysis of the Concepts of Pollution and Taboo* (New York: Praeger, 1966), 54.

garden. Pigs are indiscriminate with respect to their diet, not only in the way they will eat meat, vegetables, and even garbage but also in the way females at times attack and even consume their young. These features may further indicate why Yahweh considered them unclean.

With the progression of salvation history, however, Jesus has "declared all foods clean" (Mark 7:19), including those meals that only "unclean" pagans once ate. It is not what goes into a person's mouth but what comes out of a person's heart that defiles him, and Jesus's coming stresses this point (Mark 7:18–23). The Lord gave Peter a vision of unclean animals, commanded him, "Rise, Peter; kill and eat," and then asserted, "What God has made clean, do not call common" (Acts 10:10–15).[14] From this, Peter inferred that God would have believers in Christ no longer "call any person common or unclean" (Acts 10:28). This was the natural implication considering the way Yahweh's old covenant restriction from eating unclean animals separated Israel from the nations (Lev. 20:25–26). In Paul's words, Jesus "has broken down in his flesh the dividing wall of hostility [between Jews and Gentiles] by abolishing the law of commandments expressed in ordinances, that he might create in himself one new man in place of the two, so making peace" (Eph. 2:14–15). Sadly, Peter himself was inconsistent in his application of this change, and Paul had to confront him (Gal. 2:11–14).

Now, we must ask, "What exactly happened in salvation history to remove the dietary restrictions and to mark all creatures as clean?" Unclean animals represented the God-hostility and curse identified with the first creation and fall, and Israel's "regulations for the body" related to "food and drink and various washings" that were "imposed until the time of reformation" (Heb. 9:10). Yet with Christ's arrival, this reformation has dawned (cf. Mark 1:15; 1 Cor. 10:11; Gal. 4:4; 1 Tim. 2:6; Heb. 9:26), and "the great dragon was thrown down, that ancient serpent, who is called the devil and Satan" (Rev. 12:9).[15] Paul states that the change directly relates to what Jesus did "through the cross" (Eph. 2:16), by which God "disarmed the rulers and authorities and put them to open shame, by triumphing over them in

---

14 If God has pronounced animals once unclean as now "clean" and declared that they are not "common," he must now count all animals as "holy" (Acts 10:14–15).

15 This most likely is the exact eschatological reality spoken about in both Luke 10:18 ("I saw Satan fall like lightning from heaven") and Rev. 20:2 ("And he seized the dragon, that ancient serpent, who is the devil and Satan, and bound him for a thousand years").

[Christ]" (Col. 2:15). In Christ, "substance" has overcome all the "shadow" related to "food and drink . . . festival or a new moon or a Sabbath" (Col. 2:16–17). In Christ, God has inaugurated the new creation (2 Cor. 5:17; Gal. 6:15), has overcome the curse with blessing (Gal. 3:13–14), is saving some from once alienated nations (Eph. 2:11–16), and has declared *all* creatures good for food and symbolically clean (Mark 7:19; Acts 10:15).[16] In Paul's words, "I know and am persuaded in the Lord Jesus that nothing is unclean in itself. . . . Everything is indeed clean, but it is wrong for anyone to make another stumble by what he eats" (Rom. 14:14, 20; cf. 1 Cor. 8:7–13). And again, "Everything created by God is good, and nothing is to be rejected if it is received with thanksgiving" (1 Tim. 4:4).

What then was the love principle behind Leviticus 20:25–26? Within the original Old Testament context, *God's call to love required Israel to display God's holy animosity toward sin and the curse even in their diet.*

3. Summarize the Lasting Significance of Leviticus 20:25–26

God's holiness forever impacts his people's ethical obligations. "Be holy in all your conduct, since it is written, 'You shall be holy, for I am holy' " (1 Pet. 1:15–16). Peter echoes the truth of Leviticus 20:26 and then highlights that the church is now fulfilling what Yahweh commanded Israel: "But you are a chosen race, a royal priesthood, a holy nation, a people for his own possession, that you may proclaim the excellencies of him who called you out of darkness into his marvelous light" (1 Pet. 2:9).

From Genesis 3:15 forward, the reader of Scripture anticipates a male serpent-slayer who would triumph through tribulation, restoring order and

---

16 The United States prohibits alcohol consumption until the age of twenty-one. Similarly, ancient Israelites may have viewed the prohibition against eating unclean animals as a temporary reality that would be set aside when the anointed deliverer overcame the serpent (Gen. 3:15), thus allowing Yahweh's "son" Israel (Ex. 4:22–23) to gain freedom once they came of age—no longer "under a guardian" or "enslaved to the elementary principles of the world" (Gal. 3:23–4:7). This would parallel how God's goal for the first couple was that their nakedness (representing immaturity) would be temporary and that they would enjoy wisdom and kingship and be clothed with dignity and life (i.e, investiture) once they grew in the way God intended (i.e., by overcoming the test of the tree of the knowledge). For this reading, see William N. Wilder, "Illumination and Investiture: The Royal Significance of the Tree of Wisdom in Genesis 3," *WTJ* 68, no. 1 (2006): 51–69. This raises the possibility that the tree of the knowledge related to good and evil was a temporary prohibition and that the first couple would have had freedom to enjoy its fruit once they came of age. A challenge to this view is that Gen. 2:17 uses *lo' + yiqtol*, which usually expresses permanent prohibitions.

bringing life. Jesus fulfills the Old Testament's prohibitions against eating unclean animals in this way. Israel's dietary restrictions portrayed God's wrath against rebellion and his animosity against Satan's schemes. Clean animals certainly pointed to the cleanness that Christ would win for all in him (John 13:10; 15:3; Heb. 10:22), but the unclean creatures were also part of the shadow for which Christ is the substance (Col. 2:16–17; Heb. 10:1). The unclean symbolized what was evil and cursed; therefore, the unclean creatures were part of the sphere that Christ came to "reconcile to himself" (Col. 2:20; cf. 2 Cor. 5:18; Eph. 1:10). At the cross, Christ redeemed his elect from the curse (Gal. 3:13) and supplied the means for both common (Gen. 8:20–22) and saving grace (2 Cor. 5:21; 1 Pet. 2:24) to be operative. In Jesus, every promise is already "Yes" (2 Cor. 1:20), the new creation is already initiated (2 Cor. 5:17; Gal. 6:15), and the new covenant is already enacted (Heb. 8:6), rendering the old covenant already obsolete (Heb. 8:13; 10:9; cf. Gal. 3:23–26). Many who were once enemies have now been "reconciled to God by the death of his Son," and these same ones "shall . . . be saved by his life" (Rom. 5:10).

When considering how eating today relates to loving our neighbors, we must view it from two angles. First, love of neighbor means that those strong in faith who have freedom in their conscience to eat and drink anything must be careful not to despise or cause to stumble those believers who are weaker in faith and who choose to abstain from eating certain things.

> One person believes he may eat anything, while the weak person eats only vegetables. . . . Let us not pass judgment on one another any longer, but rather decide never to put a stumbling block or hindrance in the way of a brother. I know and am persuaded in the Lord Jesus that nothing is unclean in itself, but it is unclean for anyone who thinks it is unclean. For if your brother is grieved by what you eat, you are no longer walking in love. (Rom. 14:2, 13–15)

And again, "Food will not commend us to God. We are no worse off if we do not eat, and no better off if we do. But take care that this right of yours does not somehow become a stumbling block to the weak" (1 Cor. 8:8–9).

Second, love of neighbor means that we will *not* stop proclaiming that Christ has triumphed on our behalf, opening the door for all peoples to stand reconciled to him. One way we can do this is by eating creatures that

God once prohibited. Whereas old covenant believers *abstained* from these foods to proclaim and mirror God's holiness, today new covenant believers can *partake* of them for the same purpose—"So, whether you eat or drink, or whatever you do, do all to the glory of God" (1 Cor. 10:31). Within this framework, *bacon is victory food!*

Christians can now eat creatures once considered unclean as a testimony that Christ has defeated the serpent and, with that, the curse. We still await the consummation when "the God of peace will soon crush Satan under your feet" (Rom. 16:20). Nevertheless, Israel's dietary restrictions were "regulations for the body imposed until the time of reformation" (Heb. 9:10), and in Jesus this end-times shift from the old age of death to the new age of life has *already* begun. Indeed, the war against the serpent is decisively over. We can rest, confidently awaiting the day when the unclean will be fully cast out and the curse be no more (Rev. 21:27; 22:3).

A Final Note on Messianic Judaism and the Hebrew Roots Movement

Jesus was a Jew, meaning that he could trace his physical ancestry back to Abraham, Isaac, and Jacob. For centuries, many Jewish followers of Christ (i.e., messianic Jews) have chosen to follow Jewish customs like celebrating the biblical feasts (apart from sacrifice), worshiping on Saturday, welcoming the Sabbath with the traditional Friday evening ceremony and meal (*kabbalat Shabbat*), reciting the *shema* in their messianic congregations ("Hear, O Israel: The Lord our God, the Lord is one," Deut. 6:4), and eating *kosher* food (aligning with the cultural dietary restrictions). They recognize this as a free choice and not as an obligation either to Moses's law or Rabbinic tradition.[17] Paul would have blessed this practice, especially if part of their intent is to see more Jews saved: "To the Jews I became a Jew, in order to win Jews. To those under the law I became as one under the law (though not being myself under the law) that I might win those under the law" (1 Cor. 9:20).[18]

17 A solid example of this messianic Jewish approach is exemplified in Seth D. Postell, Eitan Bar, and Erez Soref, *Reading Moses, Seeing Jesus: How the Torah Fulfills Its Goal in Yeshua*, 2nd ed. (Bellingham, WA: Lexham, 2017), 120–23: "We do *not* celebrate the feasts or follow some of the traditions of our people out of a sense of obligation either to the Sinai covenant or to the rabbis. . . . [W]e live in close interaction with the Law and our traditions . . . to make the Messiah Yeshua real and understandable to our people."

18 Though Luke records Paul twice calling himself a Jew (Acts 21:39; 22:3), Paul only refers to himself as an "Israelite" in his letters (Rom. 9:3–4; 11:1; 2 Cor. 11:22; Phil. 3:5). In this way,

In contrast to this, devotees of a growing Hebrew Roots movement (who are primarily Gentile) identify with Yeshua (Jesus) the Messiah but claim his followers *need* to return to the roots of Jesus's faith by keeping as much of the Old Testament law as is possible without the existence of the temple. While most of these verbally affirm that justification before God is by grace alone through faith alone in Messiah Yeshua alone, they teach that all believers are still *bound* to keep Yahweh's unchanging (Mosaic) law by heeding the various Jewish feasts, treating circumcision as a religious rite, and adhering to the old covenant food laws. In short, from their perspective, Christians *must* adhere as much as possible to the old covenant cultic/ceremonial laws.[19]

Moses's law promised life based on perfect obedience (Lev. 18:5; Deut. 8:1; 28:1–14; 30:15–16) and treated righteousness as a goal and not the basis of relationship with Yahweh (Deut. 6:25). Yet Paul asserts, "The very commandment that promised life proved to be death to me" (Rom. 7:10). He further notes that most Israelites in the old covenant age who "pursued a law that would lead to righteousness did not succeed in reaching that law . . . because they did not pursue it by faith, but as if it were based on works" (Rom. 9:31–32). Paul, therefore, told the believers in Rome, "You also have died to the law through the body of Christ, so that you may belong to another, to him who has been raised from the dead, in order that we may bear fruit for God" (Rom. 7:4). Indeed, "Christ is the end of the law for righteousness to everyone who believes" (Rom. 10:4). For Paul, those who claim Moses's law-covenant is directly binding on Christians promote "a different gospel" that attempts to reverse salvation history and to "distort the gospel of Christ" (Gal. 1:6–7).

Paul may distinguish his cultural identity as an Israelite from his former obligation as a Jew under the Mosaic covenant. So Brian S. Rosner, *Paul and the Law: Keeping the Commandments of God*, NSBT 31 (Downers Grove, IL: IVP Academic, 2013), 49. Significantly, Paul does call a Christian "a Jew . . . inwardly" (Rom. 2:29; cf. Rev. 2:9; 3:9) and stresses that those "who worship by the Spirit of God and glory in Christ Jesus and put no confidence in the flesh" are the true "circumcision" (Phil. 3:3).

19 Hebrew Roots advocates are not of one stripe, but some of the expressions are captured at the following sites: https://www.hebrewroots.net/; https://new2torah.com/; https://www.119ministries .com/. Some Hebrew Roots advocates even reject Jesus's deity, but this is not a universal view. For a helpful evangelical introductory refutation of the movement, though with very little direct bibliographical engagement with those holding to Hebrew Roots, see R. L. Solberg, *Torahism: Are Christians Required to Keep the Law of Moses?* (Franklin, TN: Williamson College Press, 2019). For a useful synthesis of his critique, see R. L. Solberg, "The Dangers of the Hebrew Roots Movement," accessed March 6, 2023, https://rlsolberg.com/.

Paul and Barnabas went to Jerusalem to have the apostles and elders consider the question whether "it is necessary to circumcise [the Gentile converts] and to order them to keep the law of Moses" (Acts 15:5). In response, Peter stressed how salvation for both Jews and Gentiles comes by faith alone (15:9, 11) and queried the Jerusalem church leaders, "Why are you putting God to the test by placing a yoke on the neck of the disciples that neither our fathers nor we have been able to bear?" (15:10). Then, after citing "the words of the prophets" that anticipated how the transformed "tent of David" would include Gentiles (Acts 15:15–17), Jesus's brother James indicated how the Gentiles were free of the law but should still not give unnecessary offense to Jewish believers or unbelievers:

> My judgment is that we should not trouble those of the Gentiles who turn to God, but should write to them to abstain from the things polluted by idols, and from sexual immorality, and from what has been strangled, and from blood. For from ancient generations Moses has had in every city those who proclaim him, for he is read every Sabbath in the synagogues. (Acts 15:19–21)

At best, Hebrew Roots advocates are passing undue judgment on fellow believers (Rom. 14:3). At worst, those pursuing Hebrew Roots are reproducing the "bewitching" sins of the Galatian church, who saw "that Jesus Christ was publicly portrayed as crucified" yet failed to appreciate the changes he brought in salvation history (Gal. 3:1). "Having begun by the Spirit," their return to Moses's law shows that they are seeking to be "perfected by the flesh" (Gal. 3:2–3). They have become like the Pharisees who thanked God for not making them like other men and who, Jesus declared, "trusted in themselves that they were righteous" (Luke 18:9–14).

Those affirming Hebrew Roots theology need to hear Paul's warning:

> If you accept circumcision, Christ will be of no advantage to you. I testify again to every man who accepts circumcision [as a religious requirement] that he is obligated to keep the whole law. You are severed from Christ you who would be justified by the law; you have fallen away from grace. . . . In Christ Jesus neither circumcision nor uncircumcision counts for anything, but only faith working through love. (Gal. 5:2–4, 6)

By declaring, "You are severed from Christ," Paul indicates the seriousness of the offense. James elsewhere notes, "Whoever keeps the whole law but fails in one point has become guilty of all of it" (James 2:10). "Christ is the end of the law for righteousness to everyone who believes" (Rom. 10:4). Moses's law pointed to the need for Jesus, and to claim that any part of Moses's law is directly binding on Christians today is to act as though Christ had not come.

Part of the "offense of the cross" to the Jews (Gal. 5:11; cf. 1 Cor. 1:23) is that it makes circumcision unnecessary, treating Christ as having ended the administration of Moses's law as the direct authority for God's followers. "The law was our guardian until Christ came, in order that we might be justified by faith. But now that faith has come, we are no longer under a guardian" (Gal. 3:24–26; cf. Rom. 10:4). Those in Christ are no longer enslaved to the spirits of bondage associated with the law (Gal. 4:8–9), and the "freedom" in the Spirit that we now enjoy from the law actually empowers us to fulfill the law through "love" (Gal. 5:13–15). While Paul intentionally circumcised Timothy (who was both Jew and Greek) to assist the evangelistic mission among the Jews (Acts 16:3; cf. 1 Cor. 9:20), he did not force Titus as a Greek to be circumcised (Gal. 2:3).

Paul forewarned that "in later times" false teachers would arise who would "*require* abstinence from foods that God created to be received with thanksgiving" (1 Tim. 4:1, 3). He characterized these teachers as departing "from the faith by devoting themselves to deceitful spirits and teachings of demons" (1 Tim. 4:1). Indeed, "*everything* created by God is good, and nothing is to be rejected if it is received with thanksgiving" (1 Tim. 4:4). Whether dealing with food (Gal. 2:11–14), the observance of holy days (4:10), or circumcision (5:2), all who *require* following Moses's law as if Christ has not changed everything are seeking to "submit again to a yoke of slavery" (Gal. 5:1) and "are severed from Christ" and "fallen away from grace" (5:4). What matters today is faith in Christ working through love (Gal. 5:6). We cannot keep the whole law (Gal. 5:3; cf. Acts 15:10; James 2:10), so we must trust Christ who has fulfilled the law for his elect by his perfect obedience (Rom. 5:18; 8:4) and who fulfills the law (whether maintained, transformed, or annulled) through his elect by his Spirit as we live a life of love (Rom. 2:26–29; 13:8–10; Gal. 5:14).

Review and Reflection

1. What does the author mean by calling Sabbath keeping a "disputable matter"?

2. In what ways did the Sabbath serve as a sign of Yahweh's old covenant with Israel?

3. In what way did Israel's 6 + 1 pattern of life relate to the nation's mission of seeing Yahweh's reign realized again on a global scale?

4. In what way does Jesus's kingdom work fulfill the Sabbath command and realize the hopes to which it pointed?

5. Summarize the lasting significance of the Sabbath command for believers today.

6. Clarify the various relationships in the holiness continuum.

7. According to the author, what spiritual symbolism distinguished clean from unclean animals? What did Yahweh's restriction of Israel's diet to only clean animals symbolically say about the state and condition of Israel's neighbors?

8. What is the love principle behind the law in Leviticus 20:25–26, and how would you summarize the lasting significance of this law today?

9. If you know of someone engaged in the Hebrew Roots movement, pause now and pray that God will help them to celebrate the victory and freedom Christ has secured and to turn from Moses's law to the teaching of Jesus and the apostles in the New Testament as their decisive and direct authority.

10. What was the greatest insight you gained in reading this chapter? What is your greatest takeaway?

Conclusion

Tips for Delighting in the Old Testament

Sweeter . . . than honey.

PSALM 19:10

THIS BOOK HAS INVITED YOU to a feast of rich food, a fountain of living water, and a treasure of incomparable value. The Old Testament was Jesus's only Bible, and in it you can discover a perfect law that revives the soul, a sure testimony that makes wise the simple, right precepts that rejoice the heart, pure commandments that enlighten the eyes, a fear of Yahweh that is clean and endures forever, and true rules that are altogether righteous (Ps. 19:7–9).

> More to be desired are they than gold,
> > even much fine gold;
> sweeter also than honey
> > and drippings of the honeycomb.
> Moreover by them is your servant warned;
> > in keeping them there is great reward. (Ps. 19:10–11)

Through his perfect Son's life, death, and resurrection, the reigning God saves and satisfies sinners who believe, and he enables them to see and celebrate his Son's greatness through all of Scripture, including the Old

279

Testament. Jesus makes every promise "Yes" (2 Cor. 1:20) and fulfills every one of Moses's laws, supplying both the old law-covenant's goal and end (Matt. 5:17; Rom. 10:4).

> If you seek [the wisdom of God's Word] like silver
>   and search for it as for hidden treasures,
> then you will understand the fear of the LORD
>   and find the knowledge of God. (Prov. 2:4–5)

"The fear of the LORD is the beginning of knowledge" (Prov. 1:7), and "knowledge will be pleasant to your soul" (2:10). As a conclusion to this study, here are seven tips for those who aspire, as God intends, to enjoy the Old Testament through Christ and for Christ.

1. Remember That the Old Testament Is *Christian* Scripture That God Gave to Instruct Us

What we call the Old Testament was the only Scripture Jesus had, and the apostles stressed that the ancient prophets wrote God's word to instruct Christians. Why did Moses record events like God's guiding and protecting Israel through the wilderness and Red Sea? Paul says, "Now these things happened to them as an example, but they were written down for our instruction, on whom the end of the ages has come" (1 Cor. 10:11). Regarding the psalms and all the other prophetic writings of his Bible, Paul also stresses, "For whatever was written in former days was written for our instruction, that through endurance and through the encouragement of the Scriptures we might have hope" (Rom. 15:4; cf. 15:3). Similarly, Peter emphasizes, "It was revealed to [the Old Testament prophets] that they were serving not themselves but you"—the Christian church (1 Pet. 1:12).

When Moses wrote Deuteronomy, he was writing for Christians (Deut. 30:8). When Isaiah and Jeremiah wrote their prophecies, they were writing for Christians (Isa. 29:18; 30:8; Jer. 30:1–2, 24; 31:1, 33). When Daniel finalized his book, he knew that only those we now call Christians would fully grasp the import of all he penned (Dan. 12:5–10). The Old Testament is Christian Scripture that God wrote to instruct us. These "sacred writings . . . are able to make you wise for salvation through faith in Christ Jesus," and it is this "Scripture" that "is breathed out by God and profitable for teaching, for reproof, for correction, and for training in righteousness" (2 Tim. 3:15–17). *Old* in Old Testament does not mean unimportant, and we as Christians should approach the text accordingly.

2. Interpret the Old Testament with the Same Care You Would the New

Christians today must interpret the Old Testament with great care because it was Jesus's only Bible (Matt. 5:17), because in it we meet the same God (Heb. 1:1), and because Jesus said that it was about him and his mission (Luke 24:45–47).[1] Theologically, to give the same care to the Old Testament as to the New means that we treat the initial three-fourths of Christian Scripture as the very word of God for us (Mark 7:13; 12:36), which Jesus considered authoritative (Matt. 4:3–4, 7, 10; 23:1–3), believed could not be broken (John 10:35), and called people to know and trust so that they could guard against doctrinal error and hell (Mark 12:24; Luke 16:28–31; 24:25; John 5:46–47). Methodologically, caring for the Old Testament as we do the New means that with every passage we must establish the text, make careful observations, consider the context, determine the meaning, and make relevant applications. We consider genre, literary boundaries, grammar, translation, structure, argument flow, key words and concepts, historical and literary contexts, and theology (biblical, systematic, and practical).[2] God chose to disclose himself and his will by words in literature, so we must study in God-dependent ways each passage within its given book, within its place in salvation history, and in relationship to Christ.

So many Christians will give years to understanding Romans and only weeks to considering the Minor Prophets. They take great care in assessing the message and lasting relevance of Mark's Gospel but only dabble in Genesis, Psalms, or Isaiah, while rarely even touching the other books. When others take account of your life and ministry, may such realities not be said of you. We must consider how all of Scripture points to Christ (Luke 24:25–26, 45–47) and faithfully proclaim "the whole counsel of God" (Acts 20:27) as disclosed from Genesis to Revelation, ever doing so as one rightly handling "the word of truth" (2 Tim. 2:15).

1 Cf. Luke 24:26–27, 44; John 5:39, 46; Acts 3:18, 25; 26:22–23.
2 For each of these steps, see Jason S. DeRouchie, *How to Understand and Apply the Old Testament: Twelve Steps from Exegesis to Theology* (Phillipsburg, NJ: P&R, 2017).

3. Treat Properly the *Covenantal* Nature of the Old Testament

The early church fathers designated the two parts of the Christian Bible the Old and New Testaments because they rightly saw that each addressed principally the old and new covenants, respectively. We call Jesus's Bible a *testament* because of its covenantal quality (*testamentum* is Latin for "covenant"), which links it to a specific era in salvation history—an era before Christ. The Old Testament substantially addresses how God establishes and enforces his old Mosaic covenant. And unlike the New Testament that was written in the common language of Greek and initially targeted toward a multinational church, the Old Testament was written to Hebrews in Hebrew, and it contains peoples, places, and powers from a different period in salvation history.

The Old Testament bears a historical particularity that requires Christians to observe carefully, understand rightly, and evaluate fairly what is there before building a bridge to Christian application. For Christians to engage the Old Testament as a *testament* requires that they recognize the distinctive covenantal elements in the text and then consider how the coming of Christ influences the instructive or promisory nature of every passage.

4. Remember Why the Old Testament Is Called *Old*

Building off the previous point, the Old Testament addresses an era before Christ. It details a covenant of which Christians are not members and that has been superseded by the new. This fact requires that Christians carefully consider how Christ fulfills every Old Testament story, promise, and law before establishing its lasting relevance. The Old Testament ends with a demand for a sequel, a resolution. Jesus's Bible creates problems that he alone solves. The Old Testament provides the foundation on which Jesus and the New Testament build. We no longer live *directly* under the old covenant (Luke 16:16; Gal. 3:24–26), for "in speaking of a new covenant, he makes the first one obsolete" (Heb. 8:13; cf. 8:6). While Moses's instructions still have lasting value for Christians, they do so only through Christ, so we must consider how Jesus's saving work affects every law's lasting significance (Deut. 30:8; Matt. 5:17–19; 1 Cor. 9:20–21).

As Christians, we must interpret the Old Testament in the light of Jesus's coming. His life, death, and resurrection illuminate blind eyes and clarify the Old Testament's meaning. His person and work realize what the Old Testament anticipates (Matt. 5:17–18; Luke 24:44; Acts 3:18), and he stands as the substance of all Old Testament shadows (Col. 2:16–17). Every promise is "Yes" in Christ (2 Cor. 1:20), and he embodies every ethical ideal found in both the law and wisdom (Rom. 5:18–19). We need to read the Old Testament recognizing that one of its fundamental purposes is to help us celebrate Christ and all God would accomplish through the new covenant.

5. Read the Old Testament through the Light and Lens of Christ

Jesus supplies both the light and lens for reading the Old Testament rightly. Jesus as "light" indicates that interpreting the Old Testament properly is possible only for the regenerate who have seen "the light of the gospel of the glory of Christ" (2 Cor. 4:4). Jesus as "lens" stresses that his life, death, and resurrection disclose truths in the Old Testament that were always there but not yet clear (Rom. 16:25–26; 2 Cor. 3:14).

On the one hand, Christians must recognize significant continuities between the Testaments, such that many prophets, kings, and righteous people saw Christ from a distance and longed for him (e.g., Matt. 13:17; Luke 10:24; John 8:56; cf. Heb. 11:13). Thus, Peter could tell us,

> The prophets who prophesied about the grace that was to be yours searched and inquired carefully, inquiring what person or time the Spirit of Christ in them was indicating when he predicted the sufferings of Christ and the subsequent glories. It was revealed to them that they were serving not themselves but you. (1 Pet. 1:10–12)

On the other hand, there are significant discontinuities between the Testaments, in that the unbelieving rebel population was not given eyes to see and ears to hear the Old Testament message (Deut. 29:4; Isa. 6:9–10; 44:18; 29:10–11). Moreover, God did not fully disclose all of his meaning to the remnant until Christ came and revealed the mystery of the kingdom (Dan. 12:8–10; cf. Mark 4:11–12).

The New Testament authors note how, once seeing the risen Christ, they never read their Bible the same way again (cf. John 2:20–22; 12:13–16). They also highlight how the coming of Christ discloses the "mystery" of the Old Testament (Rom. 16:25–26) and removes the "veil" that allows us to read the full meaning of what the Old Testament discloses (2 Cor. 3:14).

The New Testament provides both the answer key and the algorithm for reading the Old Testament in its fullness. By elevating Christ's person and work, the New Testament signals the substance of all previous shadows, realizes the hopes of all previous anticipations, and clarifies how the various Old Testament patterns and trajectories relate and find their resolution. Through Jesus, God enables and empowers us to read the Old Testament as he intended. Jesus is both our light and lens.

6. Consider How to Faithfully See and Celebrate Christ in the Old Testament

Christians must seek to analyze and synthesize how the whole Bible progresses, integrates, and climaxes in Christ. Following the lead of the biblical text, we can see and celebrate Christ from the Old Testament in numerous ways.

1. Consider how *Christ stands as the goal and climax of the redemptive story*. Five major covenants (Adamic/Noahic, Abrahamic, Mosaic, Davidic, and new) guide the plotline of Scripture, and they all find their terminus in Christ.
2. Identify how *Christ fulfills direct messianic predictions*. Yahweh promises, "I will set up over them one shepherd, my servant David, and he shall feed them: he shall feed them and be their shepherd" (Ezek. 34:23), and Jesus directly claims to fulfill this prediction (John 10:11, 16).
3. Recognize how *Christ's coming creates numerous similarities and contrasts* between the old and new ages, creations, and covenants. For example, both covenants show a pattern of gracious redemption giving rise to gracious law giving. As for contrasts, whereas access to Yahweh's presence in the temple was restricted to the high priest on the Day of Atonement, Christ's priestly work opens the way for everyone in him to enjoy God's presence (Heb. 9:24–26; 10:19–22).
4. Determine how *Christ is the antitype to Old Testament types*. Old Testament characters (e.g., Adam, Melchizedek, Moses, David),

events (e.g., the flood, the exodus, the return from exile), and institutions or objects (e.g., the Passover lamb, the temple, the priesthood) clarify and anticipate Christ's person and work.

5. Reflect on how *Yahweh's person and work anticipate Christ.* Who Yahweh is and what he does reveals the identity and activity of the divine Son. When we hear Yahweh speaking and see him acting in the Old Testament, we are encountering the very one who became incarnate as Jesus of Nazareth.

6. Contemplate how *Christ embodies every ethical ideal* from Old Testament law or wisdom. When you do, revel in your justification, made possible through Christ's imputed righteousness by faith.

7. Instruct from the Old Testament *through Christ's mediation*— both through the pardon he supplies, which secures both promises and power, and the pattern of instruction and godliness that he sets.

7. Assess How the New Testament Authors Use the Old Testament

The early church devoted themselves to the apostles' teaching (Acts 2:42), and the whole church is built on the foundation of the apostles and prophets, with Jesus as the cornerstone (Eph. 2:20). Yet what Bible were Jesus and the apostles using? They were preaching from the Old Testament, and they were making much of Christ from it. "From morning till evening [Paul] expounded to [those in Rome], testifying to the kingdom of God and trying to convince them about Jesus both from the Law of Moses and from the Prophets" (Acts 28:23). The New Testament is loaded with quotations, allusions, and echoes of the Old Testament, and we need to note the significance of these citations.

When Paul asserted to the Corinthians, "I decided to know nothing among you except Jesus Christ and him crucified" (1 Cor. 2:2), he did so as an Old Testament preacher. And when he claimed that "all Scripture is . . . profitable" (2 Tim. 3:16) and commanded Timothy to "preach the word" (4:2), Paul principally had in mind the Old Testament. If you are a herald of God's word, you will help yourself and your people to cherish the whole counsel of God (Acts 20:27) and to appreciate that the whole Bible is Christian Scripture when you take time to wrestle with how the New Testament uses the Old.

Conclusion

The Old Testament is Christian Scripture, and we can enjoy it best when we approach it *through* Christ and *for* Christ. The Old Testament magnifies Jesus in numerous ways, and his person and work clarify how to rightly discern the continuities and discontinuities in the progress of salvation history. Through the light and lens that Christ supplies, Christians can delight in the same God and the same good news in both Testaments. We can also embrace all God's promises and rightly apply Moses's law as revelation, prophecy, and wisdom. Start delighting in the Old Testament through Christ and for Christ!

Glossary

Already-but-not-yet: See *overlap of the ages.*

Antinomianism: An approach to life claiming that God's rules need not influence daily Christian ethics and that Christians have a license to live as they will.

Antitype: See *typology.*

Apodictic laws: A formal category associated with laws that are unconditional and imperative, usually beginning with a volitional verb in the second person, and often expressed negatively (e.g., "You shall have no other gods before me," Ex. 20:3). See *casuistic laws.*

Appropriate/reappropriate: To take for one's own use; to claim Old Testament promises as lastingly relevant or to use Old Testament laws for teaching, reproof, correction, or training in righteousness. See also *repudiate.*

Atonement: See *penal substitutionary atonement.*

Blessing-commission: The commission couched as a blessing in Genesis 1:28 that God gave to humanity in the beginning and that relates to progeny (offspring), property (land), and power (sovereignty).

Blessings/curses: The covenant promises related to provision and protection that were conditioned on the obedience or loyalty of the vassal (see esp. Lev. 26; Deut. 28, 30). The old covenant included original blessings/

curses and restoration blessings/curses (for the period related to the new covenant).

Canon: A term meaning "rule, authority" that refers to the church's authoritative collection of holy books; the scriptural canon guides Christian faith and practice because the church recognizes the Bible as the covenant Lord's only revealed word. The canon relates to both rule (which books) and list (what arrangement). See also *Christian Scripture.*

Casuistic laws: A formal category associated with laws that are conditional and declarative, usually beginning with "if" or "when," in third person, and expressed positively (e.g., "When an ox gores a man or a woman to death, the ox shall be stoned, and its flesh shall not be eaten, but the owner of the ox shall not be liable," Ex. 21:28). See also *apodictic laws.*

Ceremonial laws (as part of the threefold division): Those symbolic requirements related to Israel's religious rituals and cult worship that find their typological end in Christ. See also *civil laws* and *moral laws.*

Christian nationalism: A theonomic approach to society that seeks to create an earthly kingdom that is "Christian" in so far as it orders people to the kingdom of heaven; it embraces the threefold division of the law but, unlike most theonomic approaches, views Moses's civil laws only as exemplary and not universally applicable. See also *Christian reconstructionism* and *theonomy.*

Christian reconstructionism: A type of Reformed, postmillennial theology that embraces the threefold division of the law and teaches that the law, as Scripture reveals it (especially Moses's old covenant law), should be used to *reconstruct* all societies in every time. See also *theonomy.*

Christian reconstructionist theonomy: See *theonomy.*

Christian Scripture: A perspective on the church's collection of holy books that affirms that both the Old and New Testaments bear lasting revelatory and pedagogical value for Christians. See also *canon.*

Christocentric interpretation: A characteristic of biblical interpretation that approaches all Scripture through Christ and for Christ, seeing Christ Jesus as the center of all God's purposes in creation, redemption, and revelation. Jesus's person and work give unity to Scripture, for he is the one to whom all the Old Testament points and the one who fulfills all that the Old Testament anticipates. See also *salvation history.*

Civil laws (as a category of content): Laws governing private disputes between citizens or organizations in which the public authorities are appealed to for judgment or called upon to intervene; the offended party is not the state or national community. E.g., accidental death and assault, theft, destruction of property, limited family issues like premarital unchastity, post-divorce situations, and the mistreatment of slaves. See also *compassion laws, criminal laws, cultic/ceremonial laws,* and *family laws.*

Civil laws (as part of the threefold division): Directives that related to Israel's political and social structures and supplied case-specific applications of the moral law in Israel's context. See also *ceremonial laws* and *moral laws.*

Clean: See *unclean/clean.*

Close context: A passage's immediate literary setting within the whole biblical book. Here we observe carefully what and how the text communicates, accounting for both the words and the theology that shapes those words. See also *complete context* and *continuing context.*

Common: See *holy/common.*

Compassion laws: Laws dealing with charity, justice, and mercy toward others; these cannot be brought to court, but God knows the heart. Examples include protection and justice for the weak, impartiality, generosity, and respect for persons and property. See also *civil laws, criminal laws, cultic/ceremonial laws,* and *family laws.*

Complete context: A passage's placement and use within the broader biblical canon. We consider whether and how later Scripture uses or builds on this passage. We also keep in mind revelation's progressive nature, the way Christ's work influences all history, and how the divine authorship of Scripture allows later passages to clarify, enhance, or deepen the meaning of earlier texts. See also *close context* and *continuing context*.

Completes/annuls: Jesus fulfills some old covenant promises or laws by uniquely realizing them in a way that terminates them. See also *maintains (with or without extension)* and *transforms*.

Consummate: To complete or make perfect, often associated with the period of the new heavens and the new earth.

Continuing context: A passage's place within God's story of salvation. We examine how an Old Testament text is informed by antecedent Scripture (e.g., the Old Testament use of the Old Testament) and contributes to God's unfolding kingdom drama, whether by progressing the covenants or developing a biblical theme or typological pattern that culminates in Christ. See also *close context* and *complete context*.

Corporate solidarity: Treating a group as a unified whole, often with one representing many.

Counsel of God: See *whole counsel of God*.

Covenant mediator: The human agent whom God chose as head or representative of a covenant. The main covenant mediators in Scripture are Adam/Noah, Abraham, Moses, David, and Jesus. See also *covenant*.

Covenant: A chosen (as opposed to natural or biological) relationship in which two parties make promises to each other with God as witness. Five main divine-human covenants mark major turning points in Scripture's storyline: Adamic-Noahic, Abrahamic, Mosaic, Davidic, and new. The initial four are titled after the covenant head or mediator, whereas the new covenant contrasts with the old Mosaic administration. See also *covenant mediator*.

Criminal laws (as a category of content): Laws governing offenses that put the welfare of the whole community at risk (i.e., crimes). The offended party is the state or national community; therefore, the punishment is on behalf of the whole community in the name of the highest state authority, which in Israel meant Yahweh. Examples include kidnapping, homicide, false prophecy, witchcraft, adultery, and rape. See also *civil laws, compassion laws, cultic/ceremonial laws,* and *family laws.*

Cultic/ceremonial laws (as a category of content): Laws governing the visible forms and rituals of Israel's religious life or ceremonies. Examples include the sacred sacrifices, the sacred calendar, and various sacred symbols like the tabernacle, the priesthood, and ritual purity that distinguished Israel from the nations and provided parables of more fundamental truths about God and relating to him. See also *civil laws, compassion laws, criminal laws,* and *family laws.*

Curses: See *blessings/curses.*

Direct messianic predictions: Statements that explicitly foretell of Christ's person and/or time. See also *typology.*

Disputable matters: Issues not directly related to the gospel that Scripture neither requires nor prohibits for Christians; these are matters of conscience.

Double narratives: An account of connected events that tells two stories at once: the story on the surface and the deeper story unveiled at the end of the narrative. Once the end of the story is known, the interpreter cannot go back to the first narrative, for the second overshadows it. See also *mystery* and *progressive revelation.*

End times: See *eschatology* and *last days.*

Eschatology: The study of the end times or last days. See also *last days.*

Ethical ideals: God's moral standards as captured in his laws and wisdom.

Family laws (as a category of content): Non-civil, domestic laws governing the Israelite household. Examples include marriage, inheritance, the redemption of land and persons, family discipleship, and the care of slaves. See also *civil laws, compassion laws, criminal laws, cultic/ceremonial laws.*

Fulfill: To complete, actualize, or realize in space and time something God promised or foretold regarding the last days. Jesus fulfills the Old Testament. See also *last days.*

General equity theonomy: See *theonomy.*

Good news: See *gospel of the kingdom.*

Gospel of the kingdom: The good news that the reigning God saves and satisfies sinners who believe through Christ's life, death, and resurrection.

Health and wealth gospel: See *prosperity theology.*

Heavenly council: Yahweh and his host of angelic and prophetic messengers and agents. See also *pantheon.*

Hebrew Roots movement: A group of primarily Gentile devotees who identify with Yeshua (Jesus) the Messiah but claim his followers *must* return to the roots of Jesus's faith by keeping as much of the Old Testament law as is possible without the existence of the temple (e.g., Jewish feasts, circumcision, food laws).

Holiness continuum: See *holy/common* and *unclean/clean.*

Holy/common: Holy and common relate to the state or status of a person, object, space, or time in relation to Yahweh; everything not holy was common. Holiness is the reality and value of Yahweh's divine fullness—as expressed in his self-sustainability, his non-dependence (or absoluteness) and uniqueness (or sole-ness), and his excellence and worth—and the beautiful harmony of all his acts with that fullness. Holiness is a state associated with the very essence of what God is. Other persons, objects, spaces, or times bear holy status when they are devoted to God. To pursue holiness is to seek a clean condition that accords with a holy status that requires displaying the glories of God's fullness to the world for his sake. See also *unclean/clean*.

Jesus as light and lens: Jesus is "light" in the way he alone gives rebirth and awakens spiritual senses to see and celebrate biblical truth in ways otherwise impossible. Jesus is "lens" in the way his person and work alone disclose the mysteries of the Old Testament.

Jesus's Bible: The Old Testament arranged as the Law, Prophets, and Writings.

Justification: The action of declaring a person righteous in God's sight; because of humanity's depravity, the only way to enjoy right standing with God is by grace alone through faith alone in Christ alone. See also *righteousness*.

KINGDOM: An acronym to help recall Scripture's storyline: Kickoff and Rebellion (creation, fall, flood), Instrument of Blessing (patriarchs), Nation Redeemed and Commissioned (exodus, Sinai, wilderness), Government in the Land (conquest and kingdoms), Dispersion and Return (exile and initial restoration), Overlap of the Ages (Christ's return and the church age), Mission Accomplished (Christ's return and kingdom consummation). See also *gospel of the kingdom* and *salvation history*.

Last days (*or* latter days): The period of the church age that Christ's first coming inaugurated and that will continue until his second coming. See *eschatology* and *fulfill*.

Law of Christ: The instructions coming from Christ and his apostles that God gave to guide Christians and the church in this world; the law of Christ is synthesized in the call to love God and neighbor and is also called the perfect law, the law of liberty, and the royal law. See also *law of Moses*.

Law of liberty: See *law of Christ*.

Law of Moses: The stipulations or instructions that God gave through Moses to guide Israel's religion and society during the old covenant. See also *law of Christ* and *Torah*.

Law/Pentateuch: The Bible's first five books that Moses substantially authored (i.e., Genesis, Exodus, Leviticus, Numbers, Deuteronomy). See also *Prophets*, *Torah*, and *Writings*.

Legalism: An approach to life in which someone trusts in his own actions in order to enjoy right standing with God.

Lens: See *Jesus as light and lens*.

License: See *antinomianism*.

Light: See *Jesus as light and lens*.

Love principle: The fundamental truth or proposition related to love that stands behind any given old covenant law. Because "love is the fulfilling of the law" (Rom. 13:10), we should be able to synthesize every legal requirement in a statement related to love.

Maintains (with and without extension): Jesus fulfills some old covenant promises and laws by retaining their form, though at times by relating them to a broader audience. See also *transforms* and *completes/ annuls*.

Meaning: A full sense of the message that an author intends to communicate through his words, both explicitly and implicitly, including all potential referents.

Mediator: See *covenant mediator*.

Messianic Jew: A biological descendant of Abraham who follows Jesus and who views following Jewish customs as a free choice and not an obligation either to Moses's law or rabbinic tradition.

Moral laws (as part of the threefold division): Fundamental ethical principles that are eternally applicable, regardless of the time or covenant. See also *civil laws* and *ceremonial laws*.

Mystery: An end-times reality that was largely (though not entirely) hidden in the Old Testament but that God now discloses more fully through Christ. See also *double narratives* and *progressive revelation*.

Obsolescence: To become obsolete or out of date—a reality associated with the old covenant.

Organic connections and unity: Scripture's quality that allows later parts to comment on earlier parts in ways that align with the original context and author's intended meaning. The Old Testament relates to the New like an acorn relates to a mighty oak tree.

Overlap of the ages: The period between Christ's first and second comings in which the new age, creation, and covenant have intruded on the old age, creation, and covenant. Christ has already fulfilled all that God promised, but the full enjoyment is not yet realized. Truly fulfilled now; fully enjoyed later.

Pantheon: The court of gods over a people; in ancient Israel Yahweh claimed the sole status of causer, King, Judge, and Savior in heaven's pantheon. See also *heavenly council*.

Penal substitutionary atonement: The truth that Christ Jesus died on the cross as a substitute for sinners who believe. God imputed or counted the sins of the elect to Christ and counted his perfect righteousness to us. God punished Christ in our place and by this satisfied the demands of justice so that God would justly forgive sinners without compromising his holy standard.

Pentateuch: See *Law/Pentateuch*.

Perfect law: See *law of Christ*.

Progressive revelation: The idea that God discloses himself and his purposes in increasing and developing ways through history, both with respect to general revelation (creation) and special revelation (Scripture). See *double narratives* and *mystery.*

Progressive sanctification: A Christian's developing growth in holiness.

Promise: A statement assuring that one will do a particular thing or that a certain thing will happen. Scripture's main promises relate to offspring, land, blessing or curse, and divine presence.

Prosperity theology: The type of teaching (1) that disregards a new covenant expectation of suffering, (2) that prioritizes present-day health and wealth and the exploitation of others, and (3) that denigrates a true relationship with Christ that counts all else as loss in relation to knowing him. See also *gospel of the kingdom.*

Prophets: Either Yahweh's covenant messengers (e.g., Moses, David, Isaiah) or a specific canonical division following the Law in Jesus's Bible. As a canonical division, it refers either to all the Old Testament books outside the Law (e.g., Matt 5:17) or specifically to the second of three Old Testament divisions containing the Former Prophets (Joshua, Judges, Samuel, Kings) and Latter Prophets (Jeremiah, Ezekiel, Isaiah, the Twelve) (e.g., Luke 24:44). See also *Law/Pentateuch,* and *Writings.*

Realize: See *Fulfillment.*

Reappropriate: See *appropriate/reappropriate.*

Rebels: The unbelieving majority who resist Yahweh's authority and covenant and oppose his remnant. See also *remnant.*

Redemptive history: See *salvation history.*

Remnant: Usually of the small minority of people who remain faithful to Yahweh. See also *rebels.*

Repudiate: To refuse to accept; what the New Testament authors do when asserting that the old covenant law is no longer directly authoritative for followers of God. See also *appropriate/reappropriate.*

Retribution principle: The idea that "what you sow, you will reap"; it shapes the structure of God's covenants and wisdom tradition.

Righteousness: Either the quality of moral uprightness based on God's measure or the standard of right order in the world and in ethics wherein God is always at the top. See also *justification.*

Royal law: See *law of Christ.*

Salvation history (*or* redemptive history): The story of God's glory in Christ that develops through Scripture from Genesis to Revelation and that includes creation, the fall, redemption, and consummation. All salvation history culminates in Christ. See also *Christocentric interpretation, gospel of the kingdom,* and *KINGDOM.*

Servant of the LORD: One of the main titles Isaiah gives to the coming King and anointed conqueror, whom we know as Jesus.

Syncretism: The blending of different religions or worldviews that sought to maintain some association with Yahweh while paying homage to other so-called gods.

Theocracy: A term meaning "rule of God." It was the nature of old covenant Israel's government under Yahweh, wherein he was the supreme King.

Theonomy: A term meaning "God's law" that relates to approaches embracing the threefold division of the law. *Christian reconstructionist theonomy* teaches that God has only one law for all governments in all times and that Moses's moral and civil laws remain directly binding for all in the church and in the world's societies. *General equity theonomy* stresses that the expression of God's justice in Moses's law testifies to lasting principles that apply in all contexts and times, beginning with the church and extending to all levels of society. See *Christian nationalism* and *Christian reconstructionism*.

Threefold division of the law: The distinction between moral, civil, and ceremonial laws. See also *ceremonial laws*, *civil laws*, and *moral laws*.

Torah: The anglicized form of the transliterated Hebrew noun *torah*, which is routinely if inadequately translated "law." Moses's "law" or torah contains a blending of religious and societal instructions captured under terms like "testimonies," "rituals/statutes" and "rules/judgments," "commandment(s)," and "charge/restriction." The term is also applied to the initial major division of the Old Testament, also called the Pentateuch. See also *law of Moses*, *Law/Pentateuch*.

Transforms: Jesus fulfills some old covenant promises and laws by altering their form while maintaining their substance. See also *completes/annuls* and *maintains (with or without extension)*.

Type: See *typology*.

Typology: The study of how Old Testament characters (e.g., Adam, Melchizedek, Moses, David), events (e.g., the flood, the exodus, the return to the land), and institutions or objects (e.g., the Passover lamb, the temple, the priesthood) serve as God-intended patterns or types for other characters, events, or institutions that serve as antitypes. The antitypes repeat the previous typological situations but in an escalated, climactic way within salvation history. Types operate as indirect prophecy, bearing meanings that clarify, color, and predictively anticipate the Messiah's life and work. See also *direct messianic prediction*.

Unclean/Clean: Distinct conditions associated with the ritual and moral standing of peoples, animals, and spaces. What was clean could be either holy or common, and what was common could be either clean or unclean. However, what was holy was never to encounter what was unclean (i.e, contamination) or to be treated as if it were unclean (i.e., desecration). Uncleanness was a substandard condition acquired by bodily process or sin; it represented death or that which was abnormal or out of order. See also *holy/common*.

Whole counsel of God: The entirety of God's purposes in salvation history as Scripture reveals them.

Writings: The third division of Jesus's Bible containing the Former Writings (Ruth–Psalms, Job, Proverbs, Ecclesiastes, Song of Songs, Lamentations) and Latter Writings (Daniel, Esther, Ezra-Nehemiah, Chronicles). See also *Law/Pentateuch*, *Prophets*, and *Torah*.

Yahweh: The personal name of the living, trinitarian God. The spelling is related to the verb "to be" and means "he causes to be" all things. Most English translations render the personal name as LORD.

Illustration Credits

Figures

3.1. Image originally appeared in Jason S. DeRouchie, "The Mystery Revealed: A Biblical Case for Christ-Centered Old Testament Interpretation," *Them* 44, no. 2 (2019): 246. Used with permission.

3.2. I thank my student Benjamin Holvey who initially inspired this lens illustration. Image originally appeared in Jason S. DeRouchie, "The Mystery Revealed: A Biblical Case for Christ-Centered Old Testament Interpretation," *Them* 44, no. 2 (2019): 247. Used with permission.

4.1. Image originally appeared in Jason S. DeRouchie, *What the Old Testament Authors Really Cared About: A Survey of Jesus' Bible* (Grand Rapids, MI: Kregel, 2013), 32. Published by Kregel, Inc. Used with permission.

4.2. Image originally appeared in Jason S. DeRouchie, *What the Old Testament Authors Really Cared About: A Survey of Jesus' Bible* (Grand Rapids, MI: Kregel, 2013), 31. Published by Kregel, Inc. Used with permission.

4.3. Image originally appeared in Jason S. DeRouchie, *What the Old Testament Authors Really Cared About: A Survey of Jesus' Bible* (Grand Rapids, MI: Kregel, 2013), 39. Published by Kregel, Inc. Used with permission.

8.1. Image originally appeared in Jason S. DeRouchie, "Is *Every* Promise 'Yes'? Old Testament Promises and the Christian," *Them* 42, no. 1 (2017): 22. Used with permission.

9.1. Image originally appeared in Jason S. DeRouchie, "Is *Every* Promise 'Yes'? Old Testament Promises and the Christian," *Them* 42, no. 1 (2017): 35. Used with permission.

9.2. Image originally appeared in Jason S. DeRouchie, "Is *Every* Promise 'Yes'? Old Testament Promises and the Christian," *Them* 42, no. 1 (2017): 38. Used with permission.

9.3. Image originally appeared in Jason S. DeRouchie, "Is *Every* Promise 'Yes'? Old Testament Promises and the Christian," *Them* 42, no. 1 (2017): 38. Used with permission.

9.4. Image originally appeared in Jason S. DeRouchie, "Is *Every* Promise 'Yes'? Old Testament Promises and the Christian," *Them* 42, no. 1 (2017): 39. Used with permission.

9.5. Image originally appeared in Jason S. DeRouchie, "Is *Every* Promise 'Yes'? Old Testament Promises and the Christian," *Them* 42, no. 1 (2017): 42. Used with permission.

10.1. Image has been adapted from Jason S. DeRouchie, *How to Understand and Apply the Old Testament: Twelve Steps from Exegesis to Theology* (Phillipsburg, NJ: P&R, 2017), 431. Used with permission.

10.2. Image originally appeared in Jason S. DeRouchie, *How to Understand and Apply the Old Testament: Twelve Steps from Exegesis to Theology* (Phillipsburg, NJ: P&R, 2017), 432. Used with permission.

13.1. Image originally appeared in Jason S. DeRouchie, *What the Old Testament Authors Really Cared About: A Survey of Jesus' Bible* (Grand Rapids, MI: Kregel, 2013), 110. Published by Kregel, Inc. Used with permission.

Tables

4.1. Table originally appeared in Jason S. DeRouchie, *What the Old Testament Authors Really Cared About: A Survey of Jesus' Bible* (Grand Rapids, MI: Kregel, 2013), 30. Published by Kregel, Inc. Used with permission.

8.1. The lists of "Curses" and "Restoration Blessings" are excerpted from Douglas Stuart, "Malachi," in vol. 3 of *The Minor Prophets: An Exegetical and Expository Commentary*, ed. Thomas Edward McComiskey, copyright © 1998 (pp. 1259–60). Used by permission of Baker Academic, a division of Baker Publishing Group. The table originally appeared in Jason S. De-Rouchie, *What the Old Testament Authors Really Cared About: A Survey of Jesus' Bible* (Grand Rapids, MI: Kregel, 2013), 272. Published by Kregel, Inc. Used with permission.

8.2 Table adapted from Jason S. DeRouchie, "Is *Every* Promise 'Yes'? Old Testament Promises and the Christian," *Them* 42, no. 1 (2017): 25. Used with permission.

12.1 Table originally appeared in Jason S. DeRouchie, *What the Old Testament Authors Really Cared About: A Survey of Jesus' Bible* (Grand Rapids, MI: Kregel, 2013), 466–67. Published by Kregel, Inc. Used with permission.

12.2. Table originally appeared in Jason S. DeRouchie, *What the Old Testament Authors Really Cared About: A Survey of Jesus' Bible* (Grand Rapids, MI: Kregel, 2013), 466–67. Published by Kregel, Inc. Used with permission.

General Index

Scripture Index